The Discovery of South America

The Discovery
of South America

J. H. Parry
Gardiner Professor of Oceanic History and Affairs,
Harvard University

Taplinger Publishing Company
New York

First published in the United States in *1979*
by TAPLINGER PUBLISHING CO., INC.
New York, New York

Frontispiece *La Virgen del Buen Aire*, the 'Virgin of the Navigators', by Alejo Fernández, *c.* 1543. This famous picture was painted for the chapel of the *Casa de la Contratación*, the Indies House, at Seville, and now hangs in the Alcázar.

Library of Congress Catalog Card Number: 78-57599
ISBN 0-8008-2233-1

Contents

Acknowledgements

The author and publishers are indebted to the following individuals, libraries, museums, archives and organizations for permission to reproduce maps, engravings, paintings, drawings and photographs: Trustees of the British Museum: Jacket illustration 3, 4, 5, 6, 7, 8, 9, 12, 14, 15, 16, 17, 18, 19, 20, 21, 22, 23, 24, 25, 26, 27, 28, 30, 31, 32, 34, 35, 36, 37, 39, 40, 41, 42, 43, 44, 45, 46, 47, 49, 50, 51, 54, 55, 56, 57, 58, 61, 62, 63, 70, 71, 72, 73, 74, 76, 77, 78, 80, 82, 83, 87, 88, 89, 90, 91, 94, 95, 97, 98, 99, 100, 101, 102, 103, 104, 105, 106, 107, 108, 109, 110, 112, 115, 116, 117, 118, 119; Phillips Academy, Andover, Mass.: 11; Biblioteca Estense, Modena: 33; Bibliothèque Nationale, Paris: 92; Bristol City Museum: 59; John Carter Brown Library, Providence, R.I.: 38, 52, 60, 64, 93, 111, 113, 114; Germanisches Nationalmuseum, Nürnberg: 65, 66; Hispanic Society of America: 81; Interpublishing, Sweden: 13; MAS, Barcelona: frontispiece; Museo del Oro, Bogotá: 85, 86, 96; National Maritime Museum, Greenwich: 29, 48; Peabody Museum, Harvard: 53, 75; Science Museum, South Kensington: 10, 84; Staatliche Museen zu Berlin: 69; University of Utah Press: 67, 68. Many of the photographs of originals at the British Museum were taken by John R. Freeman & Co. Ltd.

Acknowledgement of author and title for all extracts quoted from published works is given in the text. However, the publishers would like to acknowledge permission in particular for the following: extracts from the Hakluyt Society publications are used by permission of the Society and the publishers, Cambridge University Press; extracts from *Conquest and Colonization of Yucatán* by R. S. Chamberlain and *European Treaties* by F. G. Davenport from the Carnegie Institution; *De Orbe Novo*, trans. and ed. by F. A. McNutt from G. P. Putnam's Sons; *Life of Columbus by his son* trans. and annotated by Benjamin Keen from Rutgers University Press; *Cortés, Letters from Mexico* trans. and ed. A. R. Pagden from Grossman Inc. and Oxford University Press Ltd; *The Conquest of the Incas* by John Hemming from Macmillan Publishers Ltd and Harcourt, Brace Jovanovich Inc.; *The Broken Spears* ed. by M. León-Portilla from Beacon Press; *Discovery of the Amazon* by J. T. Medina, trans. B. T. Lee, ed. H. C. Heaton from the American Geographical Society; *Columbus, Journals and other Documents* by S. E. Morison from The Heritage Press; *Magellan's Voyage* by A. Pigafetta trans. and ed. by J. A. Robertson from A. H. Clark Co; *El Nuevo Mundo* by Vespucci trans. and ed. by Robert Levillier from Editorial Nova; *Discovery of the Yucatán* by Cordoba trans. and ed. by H. R. Wagner from The Cortes Society.

List of illustrations

Prefatory note:

A book consisting largely, as this book does, of eye-witness accounts of discovery, should be illustrated, as far as possible, by contemporary, eye-witness drawings. For the early discoveries in South America, however, few such drawings exist. No competent artist accompanied the early expeditions; the arts of book illustration and engraving were then in their infancy; and the Iberian discoverers seem, on the whole, to have been conspicuously insensitive to their visual surroundings. One thinks of Hernando Pizarro—most articulate of the Pizarro brothers and the only literate one—on his way to the spoil of Pachacamac, riding along the eastern rim of the tremendous chasm known today as the Callejón de Huaylas, with the towering spires of Huascarán on his left and the Santa River in its gorge far below him on his right; all he could find to say about it was that the snow made the going hard for the horses.

The New World Spaniards were more interested in the works of man than in the works of nature; more interested in cultivated fields than in forests; more interested in domestic animals than in wild ones; and more interested in the uses of things, than in what they looked like. Oviedo, comprehensive and conscientious, has excellent accounts of the principal Amerindian food crops, with crude but recognizable woodcuts; on wild plants and wild animals he is much less convincing, even perfunctory. Presumably in many instances he relied on descriptions given by Indians rather than observing for himself. He rarely succeeds in conveying a clear impression of the plant or animal he is describing. Nor have we, from Spanish writings, still less from Spanish drawings, clear visual impressions of the people of the New World. The ethnologist friars—Sahagún, Durán and—most distinguished of all in this respect—Juan de Tovar, all found it necessary to employ Indian painter-scribes, *tlacuilos*, to illustrate their manuscripts. It is odd that the only really lively drawings of Mexican Indians made by a European at the time of the conquest were done by a German. Cortés, when he visited Spain in 1528, took with him several Mexican notables and a troop of acrobats and jugglers. The appearance of these people aroused great interest, and water-colour drawings were made of them by Christoph Weiditz, medal engraver of Augsburg, who happened to be about the court on business unconnected with America. They are preserved in 'Das Trachtenbuch des Christoph Weiditz', in Nürnberg; odd, again, that so valuable a record should be tucked away in a collection of drawings of costumes.

We have, on the whole, a clearer visual record of the primitive peoples of America, and of the areas where they lived, than we have of the more sophisticated peoples and the cities that they built; better drawings of North America, when first settled by Europeans, than of South. No artist of any distinction visited South America in the sixteenth century. Those who did try to draw or paint what they saw there, were almost all north Europeans, not Iberians. The German mercenary Hans Staden did his amateur best to record the 'wild, naked man-eating people' by whom he was captured in Brazil. Jean de Léry's account of coastal Brazil has, in its second (1580) edition, good illustrations. They do not compare, however, with the work of John White in Virginia and Labrador, or of Jacques le Moyne in Florida. In a later generation, it is true, both the wild people and the wild animals of Brazil were to receive distinguished attention, again from northern Europeans, from the artists and naturalists employed and encouraged by Prince Johan Maurits of Nassau, as governor during the Dutch occupation of Pernambuco. Piso and Margraf, Post and Eckhout, provided the first full scientific visual record of any part of America; but they came late, to an America already losing its maidenhead.

The finest, the most splendid visual record of early America is provided by the illustrations in the noble folios of de Bry's *Grands Voyages*. The art of engraving made immense strides between Oviedo's day and de Bry's, especially in the Netherlands. De Bry's engravings are consistently magnificent; as eye-witness records, however, they range from cool fidelity to wild imagination. When Theodor de Bry was planning the work, he searched all over Europe for material on which to base his illustrations, and the ubiquitous Hakluyt brought the drawings of White and le Moyne to his attention. So it came about that, in that vast and justly celebrated monument to European enterprise in the New World, the pictures of North American natives—some of them at least—are after the work of artists who were familiar with their subject at first hand, who observed with a clear eye; those of Mexican or Peruvian natives are based on written descriptions or hearsay. De Bry's Mexicans—where they are not enduring servile torment at the hands of armoured Spaniards—present the features and attitudes of ancient Rome. This is natural enough. The ancient Mexicans and Peruvians, like the ancient Romans, built cities; this was the feature of their societies which most astonished and impressed Europeans. The Spanish invaders wrote breathless descriptions of these cities; yet they never drew them. We have a crude early map or plan of Tenochtitlan-Mexico, which Ramusio later reproduced, but—except for archaeologists' reconstructions—no picture of the island city that put Bernal Díaz in mind of Amadis de Gaul. The earliest picture of Cuzco—a fine engraving from the 1574 *Civitates Orbis Terrarum*—was clearly drawn by a man who had never seen the place. It shows the capital of the Incas with the quadrangular walls of a Roman *castra*. By the time the engraving was made, Cuzco and Mexico alike had been reduced to ruins, and built over as completely as the Roman cities of Europe.

Epigraph

It would seem to have been especially ordered by Providence that the discovery of the two great divisions of the American hemisphere should fall to the two races best fitted to conquer and colonise them. Thus, the northern section was consigned to the Anglo-Saxon race, whose orderly, industrious habits found an ample field for development under its colder skies and on its more rugged soil; while the southern portion, with its rich tropical products and treasures of material wealth, held out the most attractive bait to invite the enterprise of the Spaniard.

W. H. Prescott, *Conquest of Peru*
Book II, cap.1

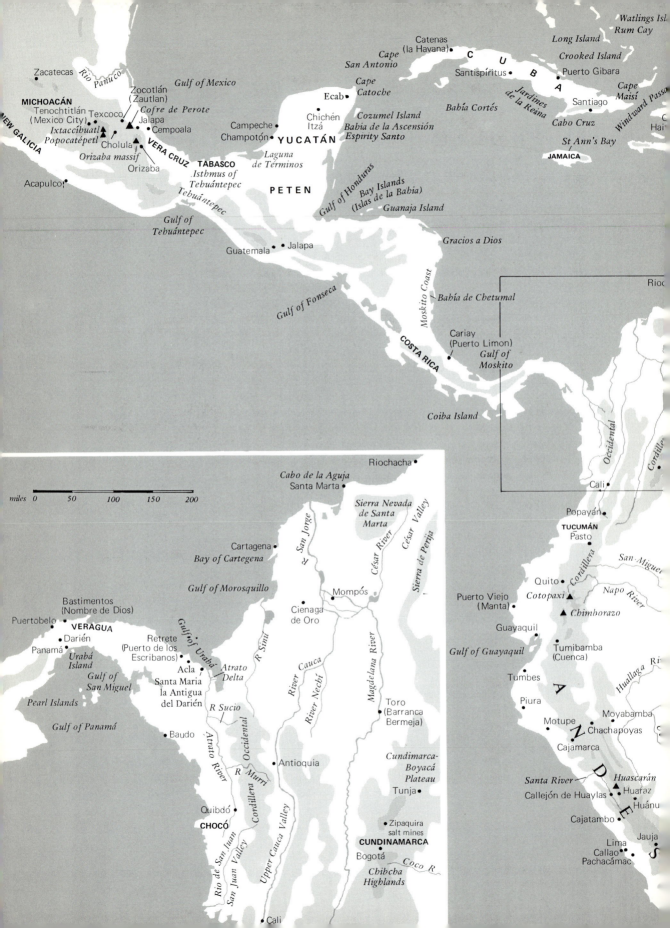

uga Channel
ul Bay
bo Isabela
Samana Bay
Las
Flechas
NIOLA

Mona Passage

St Thomas

**PUERTO
RICO**

nto
mingo
Catalina Island

Nevis
Redonda
Montserrat
The Saintes

Antigua

Guadeloupe
Marie Galante
Dominica

Martinique

St Lucia
St Vincent

Barbados

ve de la Vela
Aruba
Curacao

Grenada

Tobago

Boca del Dragón

ajira
insular
Coro
Gulf of
Maracaibo

Cordillera de Merida

mplona

Meta River

Paría Peninsular
Margarita
Cape Codera
Cumana
Gulf of Paría

Galeota Point
Trinidad
Boca de la Sierpe

Orinoco River

River Caroní

G U I A N A

Serra Parima
Orinoco River

River Amazon

• Belém

River Amazon

• **Acla** archaic sites

miles   0   50   100   200   300   400   500

Belém

Cape Consolation
(Cape Sao Roque)

Cape São Agostinho
Pernambuco (Recife)

Bahia de Todos os Santos

Monte Pascoal ▲
Porto Seguro

Guanabara Bay
Rio de Janeiro

São Vincente (Santos)

Catarina Island

Port St Julian
San Julian

Magellan's Straits

Cape Pillar
Desolation
Island
Cape Froward

Punta Arenas

TIERRA
DEL FUEGO

Le Maire Strait

Staten Island

Beagle Channel

Cape Horn

Diego Ramírez Islands

Preface

The area covered by this book is more extensive than the title suggests. It includes not only the continent of South America, but also Central America, Mexico and the Antillean islands: the whole great extent from the Rio Grande to Cape Horn. Most of the area has been inhabited by man for many millennia, and little is known certainly about the circumstances of its original settlement; in this book, discovery is defined arbitrarily to mean discovery by Europeans.

Explorers from southern Europe first reached the fringes of the area in the late fifteenth century, sailing west across the Atlantic in the zone of the northern Tropics. In the sixteenth century they identified it as a distinct continuous land-mass, and traced roughly the outline of its coasts. In many places adventurers, mostly Iberian, penetrated inland. Their explorations were neither systematic nor complete, and some parts of the area are still almost unexplored; but many Iberians established themselves permanently, chiefly in regions which already had large native populations. Almost everywhere they settled they became a dominant group, and the area as a whole is known as Latin America today.

The purpose of this book is to relate the story of European discovery and penetration, largely in the discoverers' own words. The extracts quoted are from explorers' narratives and descriptions; from comments by informed contemporaries; and from accounts left by the 'discovered' – the native Americans who described or drew their early impressions of the invaders. The illustrations are nearly all taken from contemporary maps or pictures, mostly European, some Amerindian. In a few instances only, modern pictures or photographs have been used to illustrate landscapes or natural features which have changed little since the sixteenth century.

The author of such a book necessarily incurs many debts of gratitude, and the friends and colleagues whose ideas, informed comment, and suggestions for illustrations contributed to the preparation of this book, are too numerous to be listed in full. My thanks are due in particular to Tom Adams, Jeanette Black, and the staff of the John Carter Brown Library; to Maria Grossmann and Martha-Eliza Shaw of the Harvard College Library; to Frank Trout and the staff of the Map Room in the Harvard Library; to Helen Wallis and the staff of the Map Room in the British Library; and especially to my assistant Phoebe Wilson, without whose skilled help and insistent urging the book would never have been finished.

JHP

Introduction

The common phrases of history, the labels conventionally attached to major series of events, reflect the summarised judgements of historians; they do not necessarily reflect the experience of the men who took part in the events described. Contemporaries may have used the same words, but often with different meanings. So with discovery: in modern usage, to discover is to find something new, the existence of which had formerly been unknown. We do not say that the astronauts 'discovered' the moon; people had always known it was there. An astronomer, on the other hand, using a powerful telescope, may 'discover' a galaxy whose existence had never been suspected. In mediaeval Europe, the word was sometimes used in this same sense – a navigator might discover a wholly unknown island; but more often 'discover' meant simply to uncover, to reveal, to find something which had formerly been unfamiliar or inaccessible, but which – whether from hearsay, rumour, or written authority – was known to exist.

The idea of major *new* discovery was difficult of acceptance in a society which believed in a divinely ordered universe and which tended to assume that essential knowledge was contained in a limited number of writings: the Scriptures, the Fathers, the Ancients. The way to enlarged understanding seemed to lie in more intensive study of revered authorities rather than in extensive search. This conservative deference, this limiting of horizons, applied as well to geography as to other branches of knowledge, as well to active exploration as to cosmographical theory. Fifteenth-century explorers did not quarter the seas in generalised curiosity to see what they could find; their objects were specific. For the most part they sought not new lands, but new routes to old lands, lands long known at least by name and reputation. In the process, it is true, they made some wholly new discoveries; but until the last quarter of the century, these were of islands, attractive, perhaps, to settlers, and potentially productive, but insignificant in relation to the land-mass from which the explorers had set out.

The great discoverers, like the rulers and investors who sent them out, were practical men, and their purposes were practical: to connect particular places in Europe, by safe sea routes, with other places known to exist and believed to be of political and commercial importance. The men who discovered America had particular destinations in mind, destinations whose approximate position they thought they knew. There are differences of opinion about what those destinations were. Intervening islands probably formed part of the plan, but however interesting and attractive these might be, and however useful as ports of call, they were incidental. The main and ultimate object of the discoverers was to reach inhabited places on the far coasts of the *orbis terrarum*, the tripartite land-mass of Europe, Africa and Asia which, for most mediaeval cosmographers, was all the world that existed. The last thing they expected to find – until the Americas loomed from the sea – was an intervening continent.

They blundered upon the islands and mainlands of what is now called America, then, in the course of a search for something else. To say this is not to deny the authenticity of the eleventh-century Norse expeditions which landed and attempted to settle at some point, or points, in North America. Records of those events survived, and may even have been known outside Scandinavia; but there is no evidence of any connection between the Norse voyages and the fifteenth-century discovery of America, no surviving record which suggests that southern European explorers were influenced by knowledge of the sagas. Whatever the discoverers of America were looking for, it was not Vinland.

'Discovery of America' is an ambiguous phrase. The America of modern history and geography is largely a European creation. Most of its inhabitants are the descendants of old-world immigrants. Many of its major crop plants, its agricultural weeds and pests, nearly all its domestic animals and even some of its wild plants and animals are of old-world origin. The very name America is European, coined to commemorate a Florentine explorer who coasted much of South America and drew attention to its vast continuous extent. Columbus and his successors, one might say, did not discover America; they discovered the land-mass upon which America was to be constructed.

The discoverers, as might be expected, were initially very reluctant to accept the full implications of what they found; to understand that a new, separate land-mass of vast and unknown extent must be added to the map of the world. Such a land-mass, if it existed, would be a contradiction of accepted geographical authority. It would be a severe commercial disappointment, an obstacle to cherished hopes. It would be, moreover, a challenge to faith. The new lands were inhabited. Were Christian Europeans to believe that a whole branch of the human race had lived, perhaps since the Creation, separated from the rest of mankind, cut off from the possibility of redemption, not, as Muslims were, by contumacy and diabolical misdirection, but cut off by hard physical fact? The implications were profoundly disturbing; it is not surprising that many informed Europeans were slow to accept them. A whole generation of explorers and geographers tried, by any arguments they could find, to fit America-to-be into the accepted pattern of the world; to suggest a connection between the new lands and distant parts of the *orbis terrarum* which they had not seen but which they had heard of or read about. There is an ambiguity in many contemporary narratives, descriptions and maps which makes it difficult to define in precise modern terms what the explorers were looking for and what they thought they had found. In common phrases such as 'new land', 'new country', even 'new world' (which occurs fairly frequently in late fifteenth-century discussion), 'new' certainly meant new to Europeans, but it did not necessarily mean unheard-of. It was not until Magellan had revealed the daunting size of the Pacific, and Cortés had discovered the wealth and complexity of Mexican society, that the informed in Europe accepted America unequivocally as a wholly new continent, of wide interest and promise in its own right.

The process of discovery was, in the main, a southern European achievement, a combination of Italian knowledge and judgement with Iberian determination and skill. The leading centres of cosmographical erudition in the fifteenth century were in Italy; the commercial cities of northern Italy harboured also the principal schools of practical chart-makers; and Rome itself, though not a place of much commercial importance, was a great clearing-house of geographical gossip, because of the international comings and goings of ecclesiastics. Italian scholars appraised the nature and significance of discoveries and Italian printers published the results. Italians also played a prominent practical part in discovery, mostly as mercenaries in the employ of foreign governments. The Italian governments showed little direct interest in the process, and the great Italian merchant houses concerned themselves only as investors; but the Castillian government often employed Italians, and so did the crowns of northern Europe. Even the Portuguese government, though it very rarely entrusted ships to foreign command, consulted Italian experts and sometimes employed them at sea. Columbus was a Genoese, Vespucci a Florentine, John Cabot a Genoese naturalised in Venice. Of the second generation of American explorers, Sebastian Cabot was a cosmopolitan personage of Italian parentage, Verrazzano a Florentine. The list of these famous Italians' names is almost a list of the major voyages of American discovery.

Most of the early expeditions, however – nearly all those to the southern parts of the Americas – sailed from Iberian harbours, in Iberian ships manned by Iberian officers and seamen. Portuguese interest in oversea enterprise, and the special skills developed by Portuguese navigators and ship-builders in the course of the fifteenth century, are well known. Towards the end of the century, however, Portuguese activity was directed mainly to West Africa, and a little later to the Indian Ocean. Despite modest successes in settling some of the Atlantic islands, Portuguese interest in western exploration was relatively marginal, and remained so even after the great extent of the Americas had been revealed. The most significant discoveries of early Portuguese expeditions in the Americas were in the old area of Norse adventure, in the north-western Atlantic from Greenland to Newfoundland; and on the east coast of Brazil. In the first of these areas, the sea itself, with its teeming cod-banks, was of more interest and promise than the forested, rocky and fog-bound coasts. Brazil at first sight had nothing to offer except wild dye-wood and the convenience of an occasional port of call, and until well into the sixteenth century the Portuguese paid it little attention. The most populous, the most obviously interesting and productive areas of America lay in its central and south-western parts, and these areas were explored, seized and settled almost entirely by Spaniards.

The Spaniards were a generation or two behind the Portuguese in developing a serious interest in oversea adventure; but this relative tardiness could be attributed to the political preoccupations of the Spanish kingdoms rather than to lack of aptitude or motive. Throughout the first three quarters of the fifteenth century Castille, the biggest, most populous and most powerful kingdom, had been torn by intermittent civil war, paralysed by aristocratic disaffection and lack of effective royal leadership. Isabella, confirmed on the throne by a savage succession war against Portugal in the 1470s, had set about a vigorous restoration of discipline; her marriage with Ferdinand of Aragon safeguarded Castille on its eastern flank and ensured a co-ordination of policy between the two kingdoms. From 1482 to 1492 the attention of both sovereigns was concentrated upon the reduction of Granada, the last Muslim enclave in Spain. The capture of the capital city in 1492 released, still only partially satisfied, the great store of energy and enthusiasm fostered by successful war. This energy was inspired both by territorial acquisitiveness and by proselytising zeal, and initially it spilled over in projects of conquest in North Africa and the western Canaries. The appearances of Columbus about the court, his persuasiveness and persistent importunity, provided an occasion for employing some of this energy in more distant enterprises, far out in the Atlantic.

In the Spain of Columbus' day the store of knowledge and experience

1 Sketch map of the Iberian peninsula in the sixteenth century

26

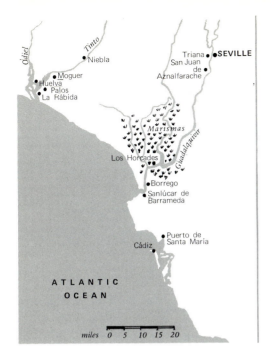

2 Sketch map of Seville and its outports in the sixteenth century

relating specifically to long ocean voyages was much smaller than that in Portugal; but Spain – or at least some parts of Spain – had many skilled sailors, and the basic nautical equipment of the two countries was comparable. That of Spain, indeed, by reason of the great length and diversity of its coasts, was the more varied. Portugal possessed relatively few large and safe harbours; the Spanish Kingdoms had many. Aragon-Catalonia had long been an area of sophisticated maritime commerce, with a string of ports stretching from Barcelona south to Alicante. It is true that the commercial interests of the King of Aragon's subjects were chiefly in the Mediterranean; few Aragonese, Catalans or even Valencians concerned themselves directly with Atlantic discovery and trade. Nevertheless, after the union of the crowns, Aragon-Catalonia represented a pool of business and maritime experience upon which Castille could draw. Luis de Santángel, who did more than anyone to persuade Queen Isabella to back Columbus, and who raised a large part of the necessary money, was an Aragonese official.

A different and more directly relevant type of nautical experience was available in the north, in the ports of the Biscay coast and the Atlantic coast of Galicia: San Sebastian, Laredo, Santander, Coruña, Vigo. The commercial fortunes of these places were built chiefly upon the export of Castillian wool to northern Europe, a trade which had expanded rapidly in the later Middle Ages; but they were also fishing and whaling ports, whose ships went far out into the Atlantic, and ports moreover with a long tradition of ship-building. The Cantabrian hinterland was one of the few regions in Spain where big trees were both abundant and accessible. Cantabrian ships were solidly built, bluff and broad in design, and square-rigged in the northern European manner. Columbus' *Santa María* was built in Galicia. In later years the region was to supply many of the seamen and many of the ships – most of the big ships – employed in trans-Atlantic trade.

27

In the thirteenth century Ferdinand III had conquered the Berber Kingdom of Seville. The conquest was annexed to Castille which thereby acquired a second Atlantic seaboard, in western Andalusia. This was an event of great importance for the future development of Spain. Seville itself, it is true, was not then the splendid, opulent city it later became. In the sixteenth century it was to be the capital of the Indies, the biggest and richest city in all Spain; but when Columbus arrived there, it was still a cramped and crowded mediaeval town confined within massive walls, communicating with an industrial suburb, Triana, across the river by a

pontoon bridge. It was, however, a city of importance, with perhaps forty thousand people, prosperous, industrious, the political and economic capital of a productive agricultural region, and a considerable seaport. It was not then, in a physical sense, the principal port of the area. In order to reach it, ships had to cross a treacherous sand-bar and travel sixty miles up a winding, muddy river. Cadiz, with its rocky headland sheltering a spacious bay, was a far better harbour, and despite its relative isolation on the landward side, handled considerably more shipping in the fifteenth century than Seville itself. The principal merchant houses of Seville

3 Cadiz and Seville; engravings from Georg Braun and Franz Hogenberg, *Civitates Orbis Terrarum* (6 vols.; Antwerp, 1574), vol. I, fo 2.

29

managed much of their oversea business through agents resident at Cadiz. There were many smaller ports: Puerto de Santa María on Cadiz bay; San Lúcar de Barrameda at the mouth of the Guadalquivir; and the cluster of small towns – Huelva, Palos, Moguer – on the Odiel-Río Tinto estuary. Each of these small places had its own local community of ship-owners, ship-builders and seafarers, its own specialised commercial interests; yet the coastal area as a whole, even before the discovery of America and the development of the Indies trade, derived a degree of unity and cohesion from the commercial and financial predominance of Seville. In the sixteenth century the port of the Indies was to be not Seville alone, but the whole riverine and coastal complex of Seville and its outports.

The commercial and seafaring population of western Andalusia was by Spanish standards remarkably diverse. After the conquest the region had drawn immigrants from all over Spain, attracted by good land, by an easy climate, by the luxurious and sophisticated life of the southern cities, and by the prospect of lording it over a Muslim population reduced by conquest to an inferior status. Castillian noblemen acquired great fiefs and built themselves great town houses in Seville; but many humbler people also immigrated, including seamen from Biscay, from Galicia and Portugal, who settled in Seville or in the outports. For more than two hundred years this steady drift to the south continued. In Andalusia, Castillians in all ranks of society acquired a more flexible, more enterprising attitude towards trade than was usual in Castille itself. It was conventionally assumed, in Andalusia as in the rest of Spain, that *hidalgos* did not buy and sell: that a gentleman should live off his patrimony, that rents were the safest and socially most acceptable form of income; but in practice, noblemen in Andalusia regularly invested in all manner of commercial enterprises. Some of the greatest territorial magnates – the dukes of Medinaceli and Medina Sidonia, for example – were also mercantile ship-owners on a large scale in the late fifteenth century. Nowhere in Spain was capital more readily available for oversea trade than in Seville.

Seville was a magnet that also attracted foreigners. The German Hanse was represented there, as it was in most of the major commercial centres of Europe. There was a small but respected English colony, engaged in importing cloth and shipping Andalusian wine and fruit to England. Much the biggest and most influential foreign group, however, was Genoese. Genoese traders had done business in Seville while the kingdom was still in Muslim hands. After the conquest a few had settled there. The use of Cadiz, and occasionally Seville itself, as ports of call for Genoese shipping on passage to Bruges and Southampton, created a need for resident factors. In the second half of the fifteenth century the Genoese colony grew rapidly in numbers and in wealth. Its members were assiduous in business, adventurous but shrewd in investment, orthodox and conventional in conduct. In that busy money-making city, they were socially accepted; many, in the second or third generation of residence, became thoroughly hispanicised. Some married into the nobility, some entered public office, but most stuck to trade. They were clannish, putting business in one another's way and helping new arrivals to become established. The Seville Genoese were kind to their compatriot Columbus, as the Lisbon Genoese had been. One of them, Francisco Pinelo, put money into Columbus' first two voyages, and set a fashion for investment in the Indies trade which many other Genoese were to follow. In 1503 Pinelo became one of the first officials of the new *Casa de la Contratación*, but contrived at the same time to maintain his own private business. In general, the Andalusian Genoese provided an essential channel through which Italian capital, Italian commercial and financial acumen, Italian maritime experience and skill, were transmitted to Spain.

The commercial interests of the Andalusian ports were as diverse as their population. At the time of the conquest the maritime trade of the region had been directed chiefly to Morocco. Two hundred years later, Morocco was still an important market for Andalusian goods, paid for partly in trans-Saharan gold, but many other commercial contacts had been developed: with northern Spain, dependent on Andalusian grain in years of bad harvest; with the Biscay ports of France; with England, then as now, an eager market for Andalusian fruit and wine. More adventurous Andalusian ships followed in the wake of the Portuguese to Guinea. The Portuguese claimed exclusive rights of trade and navigation on the whole West African coast. Isabella, at the end of the succession war, recognised the claim and formally ordered her subjects to respect it; but to judge from repeated Portuguese complaints, illicit trade persisted, and formed part of the Andalusian apprenticeship to ocean voyaging. The Portuguese themselves, in their long African voyages, acquired basic techniques of ocean navigation which, though crude, went considerably beyond pilotage and simple dead-reckoning: how to calculate, from a traverse table, the distance required on a particular course to make good a given difference of latitude; how to ascertain latitude from the altitude of the Pole Star or, towards the end of the century, from the meridian altitude of the sun; how to observe these altitudes with some approach to precision, by means of quadrant or astrolabe. It may be presumed that Andalusian skippers, making similar voyages in similar ships, also learned some of the appropriate navigating skill.

The Treaty of Alcáçovas of 1479, which recognised the Portuguese monopoly in West Africa, confirmed Castille in its claim to the Canary Islands. The pursuit of this claim also formed part of the Spanish apprenticeship in oversea adventure. Western Andalusia, and Seville in particular, provided the base for the private expeditions, operating under Crown contracts, which conquered and settled the islands; Andalusian investors, Genoese prominent among them, supplied the capital for agricultural development, and Andalusian ships handled the resulting trade.

Many of the ships which participated in these trades were built in Andalusia. Most of them were small; big oaks were scarce, and the local pine too light and fragile to provide timber for big ships. The ship-wrights of western Andalusia, like those of the neighbouring Portuguese coast, specialised in the small coasting vessels generally known as caravels, widely admired for their seaworthiness and handling qualities. The term caravel may have covered a considerable variety of types – no precise dimensions or details survive – but certain characteristics seem to have

31

been common to them all. They were singled-decked vessels, probably rarely exceeding sixty or seventy feet in overall length, with relatively fine lines by the standards of the time, with little or no raised superstructure forward and only a modest poop. Most fifteenth-century caravels were lateen-rigged in the Mediterranean manner; but increasing contact with northern Spain and northern Europe in general, brought home to southern builders the advantages, in simplicity and economy, of square rig also. In the last decades of the century the practice spread among Andalusian builders, of crossing the yards on one or two masts to improve performance when running and to increase the total sail area, while retaining the lateen mizen or mizens for the sake of manoeuvrability. Caravels under this hybrid rig – *caravelas redondas*, square-rigged caravels – were favoured for relatively long ocean passages, such as the run to the Canaries. They were to prove big enough and seaworthy enough to cross the Atlantic safely, yet well suited by their manoeuvrability for the exploration of unknown coasts. Because of their small size, moreover, they were relatively expendable; they could be employed in ventures of uncertain outcome, where governments and investors would hesitate to risk expensive armadas. In the discovery of America, caravels were to pioneer the passages which bigger ships were later to exploit.

The Iberian kingdoms in the later fifteenth century stood poised on the brink of a great leap into the new world of the Ocean Sea. For this leap they were, by the standards of the time, not only technically well equipped, but psychologically prepared. They were accustomed to the idea of territorial expansion both by land and by sea, and to the responsibilities and difficulties which it entailed. In Andalusia, Castillians had developed their own domestic imperialism and formed habits of conquest and settlement which they would later seek to exercise beyond the boundaries of Spain. In Granada they faced the problems not only of subduing, but of governing, a population of sophisticated culture and alien religion. What was to be done, for example, with the native nobles? Were they to be placated by official employment, or would it be safer to send them away to join their friends in North Africa? Both policies were tried in Granada. The duty of religious conversion, to which many highly-placed Castillians were passionately committed, and to which everybody paid at least lip service, presented even more difficult dilemmas. Was it to be achieved by force or by persuasion? If by persuasion, how were men to be recruited and trained for the task? The policy of gentle assimilation achieved little; the campaign of stern compulsion conducted, with the Queen's approval, by Cisneros, provoked bloody revolt; both policies conflicted with the interests of Castillian noblemen who received fiefs in the region and wished only to exploit fertile land and a skilled and docile labour force.

The conquered Canaries provided experience more directly relevant to the problems initially to be encountered in the New World. In the Canaries Spaniards found a primitive, pagan population and much uncultivated land. A labour force had to be recruited from the one in order to exploit the other; and religious conversion presented difficulties different from those in Granada. In dealing with the native Guanches, Spaniards tested a range of administrative and social devices which were to be applied, on a wider scale, in the West Indies.

Nothing could be more misleading than to picture Columbus presenting a new world to a society of feudal bravos who, apart from plunder, had no idea of what to do with it. Bravos certainly went to the New World, in large numbers; had Spain not possessed a reserve of under-employed fighting men, the Indies could not have been so rapidly explored and conquered; but the ideas and methods applied in the process of discovery and development were not merely those of an irregular soldiery. Many groups had their contributions to make: scholarly geographers, curious and dedicated explorers, serious investors and developers, merchants, missionaries and lawyer-administrators. Competent representatives of all these types were present in Spain in the late fifteenth century. Many concerned themselves with the Indies, directly or indirectly. Some went there, and soon found themselves in conflict – often violent conflict – with the bravos. All could draw, in their dealings with the New World, upon appropriate or seemingly appropriate precedents derived from experience in the Old.

All regions of the Iberian peninsula were to make their contribution, directly or indirectly, to the discovery and conquest of America; but western Andalusia was the starting point. It could supply the appropriate equipment, the appropriate skill and even, in limited degree, the appropriate experience. Of all the regions of Europe, except only Portugal, it was geographically the best placed for the purpose. Seville and Lisbon were Europe's principal observation posts on the broad expanses of the Atlantic. It was no mere chance that took Columbus, disappointed in Portugal, to Andalusia. There he had no difficulty, once his proposals were accepted, in finding ships and men well suited to his needs. His greatest difficulty was initial acceptance. The backing of the Castillian Crown cost him eight years of stubborn argument and strenuous persuasion.

I

The Unexpected Continent

1 The Ocean Sea

Responsible rulers and sceptical investors, in Spain or anywhere else, did not send ships out deliberately on long and possibly dangerous voyages away from the known routes of commerce, merely in the hope of making chance discoveries, or in order to investigate vague and implausible reports of discoveries made in the past. Such decisions were taken as the result of a process of geographical reasoning. Experts were consulted, both experienced seamen and scholarly students of cosmography. The proposals of would-be discoverers were discussed and tested with reference to an accepted body of geographical information or informed conjecture, concerning the shape and size of the world and the disposition of oceans and land-masses, lakes and islands, upon its surface. Some of this information was based on familiar knowledge or attested eyewitness report, some on hearsay or tradition, some on academic theory derived from the Scriptures, patristic writings and the writings of the ancient world. Much of it, by the early fifteenth century, was set out in books and maps.

Late mediaeval cosmographers thought of the known and inhabited land area of the world as a huge continuous mass, *orbis terrarum*, with many peripheral islands, the whole set in a continuous encircling ocean. To European makers of *mappae-mundi* – scholars' maps as distinct from marine charts – the land area was of interest, the ocean was not; they normally depicted the *orbis terrarum* schematically in circular form, usually with Jerusalem at the centre, and with the ocean shown as a conventional border round the circumference. The *orbis terrarum*, though continuous, was deeply cut and indented by arms of the sea and by great rivers. Three of these waterways – the Mediterranean and the rivers Nile and Don – were treated as principal boundaries, dividing the earth into its three major regions, Europe, Asia and Africa. These were not considered as continents in the modern sense. The idea of continents – separate insular or near-insular land-masses of very large size – as recognised geographical units, is relatively modern. It was brought into general use largely in order to accommodate and define the Americas; it defies precise definition to this day. In the Middle Ages, and into the sixteenth century, geographers more commonly spoke of 'parts' or 'regions'. When they used the word *continens*, they might mean any large, compact, continuous area of inland territory. Martin Waldseemüller, in the famous passage of *Cosmographiae Introductio* praising Vespucci's achievements, says that the world is divided into four parts, of which three are continents, the fourth—America—is an island.[1] There was no fixed rule. Petrus Apianus, in his later work of the same name, cites Saxony and Bohemia as examples of continents.[2]

The phrase *terra firma*, mainland, occurs frequently in fifteenth-century geographical descriptions and maps, including marine charts, and

4 The so-called 'Psalter' world map. A thirteenth-century conventional monastic *mappa-mundi*, centred upon Jerusalem, with schematic distribution of land-masses. *British Museum, Add. MS 28681 fo 9.*

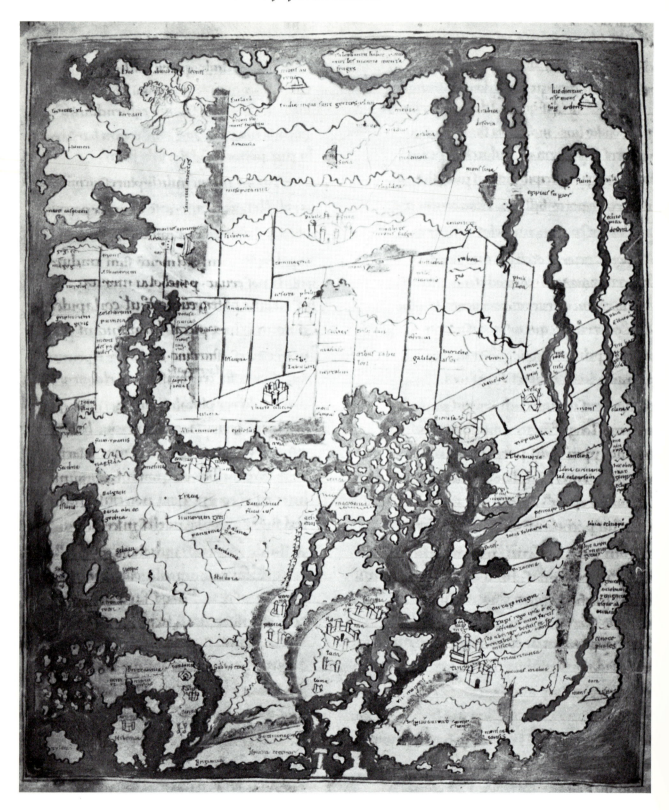

in modern translations is often rendered 'continent'; but again, it did not usually mean continent in the modern sense. It was more commonly used at the time to describe some particular coast of the *orbis terrarum*, to distinguish it from adjacent islands. It might also mean a large island, such as the legendary Antilia, the land of the Seven Cities. It could be used in the plural, presumably meaning different stretches of mainland coast. Columbus, in his capitulations with Ferdinand and Isabella in April 1492, was granted hereditary rights in 'all those islands and mainlands' which he might find and acquire in the Ocean Sea.[3]

Mediaeval opinions differed greatly on the proportion between land and sea on the surface of the globe. Some, basing their theories on Scriptural texts and on the apocryphal—but popular—Books of Esdras, believed that the land area greatly exceeded the sea, and indeed surrounded it; others, citing other texts, that the land area, extensive though it was, stood in an even vaster expanse of encircling ocean. The latter was, perhaps, the more orthodox view, though both were theologically respectable; on the shape and extent of the known and habitable world, there was similar disagreement. Some theorists considered the *orbis terrarum* to be confined to the northern hemisphere; others, including Roger Bacon—who inclined to favour the big-earth, small-sea school—thought that the peninsulas of Africa and Asia extended south of the equator.

An important shift in scholarly thought on the subject resulted from the re-discovery of Ptolemy's *Geography* at the beginning of the fifteenth century, from its translation into Latin and its diffusion in manuscript through the learned centres of Europe. Ptolemy re-introduced, to a Europe which had largely forgotten it, the ancient notion of antipodes. Fifteenth-century maps drawn to his specifications depict a great land mass, *Terra Australis*, stretching across the southern hemisphere, connecting Africa with Asia by a massive land bridge and making *Mare Prasodum*, the Indian Ocean, a land-locked sea.

These were new and disturbing suggestions; but Ptolemy, despite the immense respect which he commanded among the European learned, was not everywhere wholly accepted. Some geographers were bold enough to point out that he could have had no first-hand knowledge of the southern hemisphere; they were sceptical of the land-locked Indian Ocean. Practical explorers, mostly unlearned men, suspicious of book-geography, pursued their search for the extremities of Africa. Some academic geographers—the Florentine Lorenzo Buonincontri, for example, in 1476—were led by their reading of Ptolemy and Strabo to speculate on the nature of a possible fourth continent,[4] but no-one felt impelled to go looking for it, as an object of interest in its own right. *Terra Australis* was widely supposed, if it existed, to be uninhabited. Some literal-minded writers ridiculed the notion that people could walk, presumably upside-down, on antipodean soil. Many believed—until the explorers proved them wrong—that whatever land existed in the southern hemisphere was cut off from the inhabited world by an impassable belt, whether of land or of sea, in the torrid zone. The inhabited world was what chiefly interested geographers and explorers alike. Ptolemy's *Terra Australis* was of

5 The so-called 'Cottonian' or 'Anglo-Saxon' world map. An eleventh-century monastic *mappa-mundi*, possibly Irish, showing somewhat more detail and attempt at realism than most of its kind. Jerusalem is not at the centre, but near it. East is at the top. *British Museum, Cotton MS Tiberius B. v. fo 56v.*

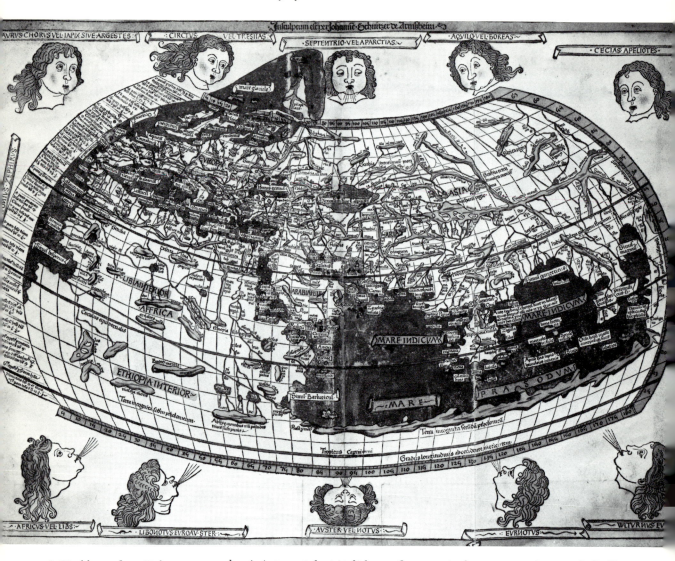

6 World map from Ptolemy, *Geographia* (Ulm, 1482)

academic interest, but it did not, for practical purposes, destroy belief in a continuous *orbis terrarum*, nor challenge the assumption of a continuous ocean between its western and eastern shores.

Most late mediaeval academic geographers, whether European or Arab, like most of their predecessors and mentors among the ancients, concentrated their attention first on the world they knew best, the world of the Mediterranean and the lands surrounding it, and then upon little-known but immensely attractive lands further east: a vaguely defined 'India', and from the thirteenth century onwards an even vaguer 'Cathay'. The encircling ocean was marginal in their thought, as it was marginal in their maps: vast, remote, little known, perhaps even unknowable or scarcely worth knowing. Though remote, it was alarming in its immensity and its frequent violence. Some of the names attached to it—*mare tenebrosum*, green sea of darkness—suggest the awe which it inspired. For seafaring peoples on the Atlantic coasts of Europe, on the other hand, the

40

Ocean Sea, or that part of it which beat upon their shores, had long been a sea of opportunity, a rich source of food and a highway for plunder, trade or migration. Western European seamen treated the Atlantic with a proper respect, naturally, but they were not afraid of it. They knew it to be navigable, at least locally, and they knew that it was not an unbroken expanse; it contained many islands. Some of these were fertile, attractive, inhabited; others, barren in themselves, were still of use to fishermen. Some of the places discovered by early Irish or Norse wanderers, it is true, had been abandoned and forgotten; but Iceland, Shetland, the Faeroes remained continuously within the area of European knowledge, and intermittently of European trade. In the fourteenth and fifteenth centuries whole new groups of Atlantic islands further south were added to the list.

The Canaries, the 'Fortunate Isles' of antiquity, had been known intermittently to Europeans for many centuries. Pliny had described them. The easternmost islands lie only a hundred miles or so off the African coast, and wind and current made them easily accessible. The first attempts at settlement were made in the middle of the fourteenth century; the first successful attempts, under Castillian auspices, early in the fifteenth. The archipelago is extensive—more than three hundred miles from east to west—and individual islands are large and mountainous. The inhabitants, the Guanches, though primitive, were vigorous and warlike. The process of conquest and settlement was slow and long; in the western islands it was still incomplete when Columbus sailed in 1492. In the Canaries, navigators found themselves on the northern fringe of the great belt of prevailing north-easterly winds, the trade winds which, as Columbus was to discover, could in a good season carry a ship clear across to the West Indies with scarcely a hand to sheets or braces. All Columbus' trans-Atlantic voyages took their departure from the Canaries. In later years, hundreds of ships bound for America paused at one or other of the islands for wood, water and provisions, and for thousands of emigrants the last sight of Europe was to be the towering cone of Tenerife.

The prevailing winds off the Canaries posed a problem to Iberian seamen: the problem of return. The weatherly qualities of their caravels enabled them to find a solution, in a long board to seaward, north or north-west, until they could find a westerly wind to take them home. It was probably in the course of this *volta do mar* that Portuguese or Genoese seamen first sighted the islands of the Madeira group. Settlement there began in the 1420s by Portuguese, with the help of Genoese capital and under princely patronage. The islands soon attained a modest agricultural prosperity: both sugar and wine were being exported by the 1450s. Madeira made its own modest contribution to the discovery of America. One of the early settlers was Bartolomeo Perestrelo, an Italian naturalised in Portugal, an efficient and energetic pioneer who became a leading figure in the life of the islands and whose daughter, years later, married Christopher Columbus.

The remote Azores, the Hawks' Islands, form an archipelago even more extensive than the Canaries—the length of the whole chain, south-east to north-west, is about four hundred miles—but the islands are individually smaller and the sea distances between them correspondingly greater. The westernmost islands, Flores and Corvo, are a hundred miles from Fayal their nearest neighbour. A ship can pass between the islands without sighting any of them; though in the daytime cloud formations, birds and marine life would indicate their presence to an observant navigator. Some of the islands of the eastern group were discovered, or rediscovered, in the 1420s; the western islands not until the 1450s. The Azores are less obviously inviting than Madeira, windswept and treeless; Portuguese settlement and development accordingly was slower, a modest progression from livestock to grain and eventually to sugar. In the Azores the Portuguese were a third of the way across the Atlantic. The easternmost point is eight hundred miles from Portugal; the furthest extremity of the Old World is not the Fortunate Isles, but the wind-carved cliffs of Corvo. Prevailing westerly winds prevented the use of the Azores as a point of departure for exploration further west; but they were to become very important indeed as a port of call for ships returning from the Americas.

7 Sixteenth-century ships: a sea fight off the Azores. Detail from a *portolano* by Diogo Homem, 1558. *British Museum, Add. MS 5415 A, fo 20.*

The Cape Verde Islands lie much further south, five hundred miles off what is now the coast of Senegal. They were first sighted in 1455, from ships trading to Guinea, and though arid and uninviting, were settled because of their convenience in that trade. Like all the other groups, these islands had a contribution to make to the discovery of America. Ships heading out into the south Atlantic could get water and provisions there. Pero Alvarez Cabral, who in 1500 first sighted the east coast of Brazil, took his trans-Atlantic departure from the Cape Verde Islands.

All these island enterprises helped in varying degrees to prepare the way for the 'enterprise of the Indies': the discovery of America. That is not to say, of course, that they formed part of a conscious ocean strategy, or that the men who settled the islands thought of them as stepping-stones to some greater prize. The islands were valued for their own sake. Some of them, it is true, had a place in commercial strategy. The Portuguese were always sensitive about islands on the route to Guinea; hence Prince Henry's encouragement of settlement in the Cape Verde Islands, and the repeated but unsuccessful Portuguese attempts to secure a foothold in the Canaries. Most of the islands, however, were valued chiefly as agricultural settlements, and as such most of them proved successful and profitable. Free land was the main attraction. Inflation at home bore hard upon the knightly class. It raised prices, enriched tenants who paid fixed money rents, and brought many landlords to penury. Small land-owners, as well as landless *hidalgos*, had a strong incentive to move out, either to restore their fortunes by piracy off the Barbary coast, or to acquire new estates on new terms; estates which might be made to produce saleable goods instead of derisory money rents.

There was no great difficulty in obtaining labour for such settlements. The Guanches of the Canaries, it is true, did not take kindly to wage-earning work, and all the other island groups were uninhabited; but emigrants could be recruited from among landless labourers, or among peasants whose holdings were arid and infertile, or whose tenures were on unfavourable or irksome terms. Capital was a more difficult problem; but a new and vigorous industry was to help in solving it. Throughout the thirteenth and fourteenth centuries the cultivation of sugar cane and the

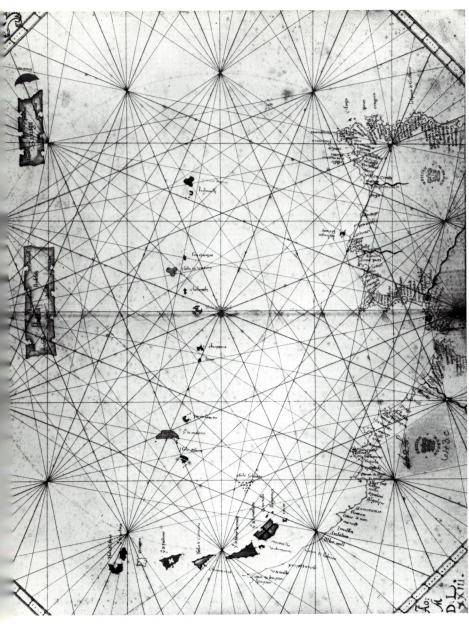

8 Atlantic Islands, from a chart by Grazioso Benincasa, dated 1473. Antilia and Satanazes are at the extreme left. *British Museum, Add. MS 18454.*

manufacture of sugar had been spreading from Syria and Egypt westward through the Mediterranean countries to south-eastern Spain and southern Portugal. Sugar was a scarce and costly 'spice', a valuable article of commerce. By the fifteenth century there existed in Andalusia and southern Portugal vigorous groups of sugar producers interested in extending their operations. For this purpose the Atlantic islands proved very suitable. Sugar interests provided much of the capital needed for island development. Here was yet another unwitting preparation for America. Sugar was one of the first Old-World crops to be introduced in the West Indies.

The island settlements prefigured the discovery of America not only in particular ways, as administrative or economic rehearsals, as points of departure or ports of call on return, but also in a more general sense. They helped to form an attitude of mind, a mental 'climate', in which trans-Atlantic discovery became not only possible but probable; one might almost say inevitable. Obviously regular trade between Andalusia and the Canaries, between Portugal and the Azores, accustomed sailors to longer stretches out of sight of land than had been usual in earlier centuries, and increased their confidence in their ability to navigate safely on long voyages. Perhaps even more significant, the settlements set a fashion for island-finding. Throughout the fifteenth century adventurers were discovering, seizing and settling attractive islands in the Atlantic. The supply of islands seemed inexhaustible, and there was no apparent reason why the process should not go on indefinitely.

Tradition, legend and hearsay report added imaginary islands to the real islands which were actually being settled. Some of these legends and the lovely nostalgic names associated with them—St Brandan's Isle, Brasil (from Braes-ail, the blessed), Yma the holy, Perdita the lost—originated in centuries-old tales of the wanderings of Irish saints. Others—Antilia, Satanazes, Lovo, Capraria—were of southern European origin. When Roderic, the last Visigothic King of Spain, lost his kingdom to the invading Moors—so the story went—seven bishops had fled out to sea with their flocks and had established themselves on an Atlantic island, where their descendants might still be living. In the fifteenth century this Isle of Seven Cities was commonly described as Antilia, the island opposite. Antilia was the most attractive, the most evocative, of all the imaginary lands in the Ocean Sea. Many attempts were made to find it, all, needless to say, unsuccessful.

The dream islands received not only literary, but also cartographic recognition; not in scholarly *mappae-mundi*, which gave only marginal and perfunctory attention to the Ocean Sea and its islands, nor in the later Ptolemaic world maps, but in marine charts. Many fifteenth-century charts of Italian origin show a long string of islands, some real, some imaginary, running north and south from the Azores to the Canaries. The arrangement varies to some extent from chart to chart. Antilia is usually placed out in the ocean, west of the Azores, a rectangular island about the size of Ireland. In a marine chart of 1424[5] it is drawn in considerable, though conventional detail, with its seven cities marked and named. North of it in the same chart, of the same conventional shape but a little smaller, is Satanazes, with five towns. Each has a smaller satellite island. In all, the 1424 chart shows twenty-three oceanic islands. Later charts were to retain all or most of them, and to add the recently-settled Azores to their number. To men who used such charts the Ocean Sea, or at least that part of it within navigable reach of Europe, must have seemed full of islands, known or awaiting discovery.

The Atlantic islands had a counterpart in late mediaeval maps, in an extensive archipelago off the other extremity of the *orbis terrarum*. The celebrated Catalan Atlas of 1375—a world map which shows, in many of its sections, an attempt to adapt the style of the marine cartographers—has dozens of islands, scattered arbitrarily in the sea off the south-east coasts of Asia. Makers of decorated presentation maps were naturally tempted to fill empty spaces of ocean with islands, sometimes, one suspects, with no other purpose than to cover unsightly blanks; but for the existence of these Spice Islands there was the testimony of an eye-witness report. Marco Polo on his return from Cathay—Kublai Khan's China—had travelled by sea and had called at a number of ports in Indo-China and the Malay archipelago. Marco Polo, it is true, was not generally received as an authority, with the deference accorded to, say, Pliny or Ptolemy. Some people thought him an impostor. The *Description of the World* was read by many as a traveller's tale for entertainment rather than serious information; but its acute observation and careful descriptions stood the test of time, and for many years it was almost all that European cartographers, in delineating the shape of eastern Asia, had to go on. In particular, it was the only available book that mentioned the island of Cipangu (Japan). Marco never went to Japan himself, but heard about it when he was in China. According to him, Cipangu was a powerful and prosperous island kingdom lying in the Ocean Sea some 1500 miles off the coast, east of the harbour city of Quinsay (Hangchow). Just as the island groups lying off the west coast of Europe and North Africa had their counterpart in the archipelago off the east coast of Asia, so, further out to sea, Antilia found a symmetrical analogue in Cipangu. Both were large, inhabited, rich; conveniently and appropriately they lay, according to report, in the same latitude. Fifteenth-century geographers could not know that Japan was real, Antilia a figment of the imagination; they inclined, if anything, to find Antilia more plausible than Cipangu; but some of them accepted both, and drew appropriate conclusions.

If the earth was round and the Ocean Sea continuous, a ship might sail round the world. As early as the first century AD, Strabo had proclaimed the theoretical possibility. However wildly impossible in practice, the notion of circumnavigation appealed to amateurs of the strange and marvellous. The author of that justly popular book of traveller's tales, *The Travels of Sir John Mandeville*—a gifted romancer widely versed in the travel literature of his day—had exploited the idea in characteristic fashion.

And therefore I say sickerly that a man might go all the world about, both above and beneath, and come again to his own country, so that he had his health, good shipping and good company, as I said before. And always he should find men, lands, isles and cities and towns, as are in their countries. . . . nevertheless of a thousand peradventure one should not do it in all his life, for to take the right way all about the earth till he come til his own country again that he came from. For there are so many ways and countries that a man should lightly fail, but if it were by special grace of God. For the earth is right great and large.[6]

Mandeville had his circumnavigator pass by 'India'. India at that time was a loose and compendious term which might be applied to almost any territory east of the Nile. South-east of it they placed the peninsula of the Golden Chersonese and the myriad islands of Marco Polo's story. North-east was Cathay, the China of Kublai Khan, land of silk, known chiefly from Marco Polo's description. During the hundred years or so of the Tartar Peace, from the mid-thirteenth century to the mid-fourteenth, both India and Cathay had been accessible to adventurous Europeans; ambassadors, missionaries and merchants had travelled to the East, whether by overland caravan or by sea from the ports of the Persian Gulf. This coming and going had been stopped by the Black Death, and subsequent political upheavals throughout Asia prevented its resumption. In terms of contact with the East, Europe was back where it had been before Chinghis Khan.

Fifteenth-century Europeans, therefore, knew nothing directly of India. A fairly extensive literature, from Pliny to Poggio Bracciolini, informed them vaguely that it contained rich and powerful kingdoms; that it produced spices and other commodities which were scarce and valuable in Europe; and that some of its inhabitants, including one of its rulers, the Prester John of legend, were said to be Christians. None of this literature stated precisely where India was. Cathay could be fixed geographically with slightly more precision, since it was known to lie at the extreme eastern end of the *orbis terrarum*; but after the middle of the fourteenth century, no news came from there, and Chinese silk, which had reached Europe mostly by overland routes, became almost unobtainable; the introduction of sericulture and silk manufacture from Byzantium to Italy provided inadequate quantities of an inferior substitute. With spices, the situation was different. Europe, because of its winter climate and its meat-eating habits, was a major market, consuming a significant proportion of the total south Asian production. Import substitution was impossible; most spices could not be grown in Europe. The trade continued, therefore, with only occasional and brief interruptions; but in the fifteenth century it was almost confined to a single route, from the Malabar ports by sea to Aden and thence up the Red Sea. In the Cairo bazaars an established group of Arab middlemen sold spices by wholesale to an established group of Venetian middlemen; the Sultan took his duties, and the costs were passed on intact to the European consumer.

All major commercial groups in Europe, except the Venetians, thus had strong motives for desiring more direct and more varied contacts with Asia. Nor was commerce the only consideration. For a variety of political, religious and intellectual reasons, the resumption of direct contact with India and Cathay was for many Europeans a cherished nostalgic dream. The steady expansion of Islam in the near East and the growing military and naval power of the Ottoman Turks prevented such contact by any of the traditional routes, except by means of hazardous subterfuge such as the adventurous Venetian Nicolò de'Conti had employed. The capture of Constantinople in 1453, and the feeble reaction in western Europe, showed how complete Muslim domination in the eastern Mediterranean had become. The land barriers between Mediterranean and Indian Ocean could not be forced. No crusade could be mounted in that region with any serious hope of success. The only hope of establishing direct contact with India and Cathay lay in finding a completely new route.

The practical possibility of sailing from Europe to India or Cathay must have seemed, in the first half of the fifteenth century, as remote as

Mandeville's circumnavigation. There is no evidence that Prince Henry of Portugal, for example, ever seriously contemplated it. In the second half of the century, however, seamen grew more and more accustomed to long voyages, and from about 1470 governments began to take the possibility seriously. It was obvious to anyone who knew the world was round that there might be a choice of routes, eastward or westward. An eastward route would involve sailing round or through the continent of Africa. The westward route would take ships directly to Cathay; not to a source of spices, but to a source of silk and, it was believed, gold. From Cathay, it should be possible to reach the Spice Islands and eventually mainland India. The voyage to Cathay would cross a notoriously stormy ocean, but it would be a direct voyage, in the latitudes of Europe, with no dangerous detour in the torrid zone, and (probably) with large inhabited islands along the way. Some thirteenth-century theorists had declared the Ocean Sea in these latitudes to be relatively narrow, and had cited weighty authority to support their belief. According to Roger Bacon:

Aristotle says that the sea is small between the end of Spain on the west and the beginning of India on the east. Seneca in the fifth book of Natural History [i.e. *Quaestiones naturales*] says that this sea is navigable in a few days if the wind is favourable.[7]

This judgement was repeated almost verbatim in the early fifteenth century by Cardinal Pierre d'Ailly, whose *Imago Mundi* was Columbus' most favoured geographical authority.

The most distinguished scholarly proponent of the western route in the fifteenth century was Paolo dal Pozzo Toscanelli, member of a well-known Florentine merchant-banking family, eminent physician and learned amateur of travel. Toscanelli was one of the few scholars of that time who appreciated the value of Marco Polo's *Description of the World*. He was also familiar with Conti's claims to have visited the Spice Islands, which had been the subject of considerable gossip among participants in the Church Council that met at Florence between 1438 and 1445; he may have interrogated Conti personally. Toscanelli's reputation was known in Portugal. In 1459 he supplied information about the East, probably in return for news of West Africa, to members of a Portuguese mission then visiting Florence. In 1474 he was consulted, through a Canon Martins as intermediary, by the Portuguese King. The date is significant; Portuguese explorers had just suffered a severe disappointment in the discovery of the southerly trend of the African coast south of the Cameroons. Africa was proving more of an obstacle than had been expected, and the King wanted to know what Toscanelli had to say about alternative routes. Toscanelli's answer was clear and confident:

. . . On another occasion I spoke with you about a shorter sea route to the lands of spices than that which you take for Guinea. And now the Most Serene King requests of me some statement, or preferably a graphic sketch, whereby that route might become understandable and comprehensible, even to men of slight education.

Although I know that this can be shown in a spherical form like that of the earth, I have nevertheless decided, in order to gain clarity and save trouble, to

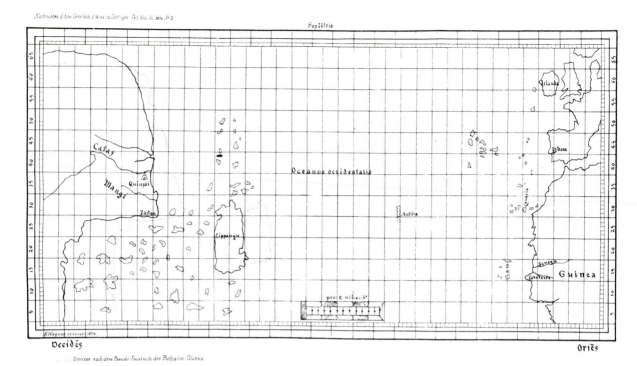

9 Reconstruction of the chart drawn for the King of Portugal by Paolo dal Pozzo Toscanelli, showing Antilia and Cipangu on the route to Mangi and Cathay; from Hermann Wagner, 'Die Rekonstruktion der Toskanelli-Karte vom J. 1474 . . .' *Nachrichten von der Königl. Gesellschaft der Wissenschaften zu Göttingen, Philologisch-historische Klasse*, 1894, no. 3.

represent [that route] in the manner that charts of navigation do.

Accordingly I am sending His Majesty a chart done with my own hands in which are designated your shores and islands from which you should begin to sail ever westwards, and the lands you should touch at and how much you should deviate from the pole or from the equator and after what distance, that is, after how many miles, you should reach the most fertile lands of all spices and gems, and you must not be surprised that I call the regions in which spices are found 'western,' although they are usually called 'eastern,' for those who sail in the other hemisphere always find these regions in the west. But if we should go overland and by the higher routes we should come upon these places in the east.

The straight lines, therefore, drawn vertically in the chart, indicate distance from east to west; but those drawn horizontally indicate the spaces from south to north. . . .

From the city of Lisbon westward in a straight line to the very noble and splendid city of Quinsay 26 spaces are indicated on the chart, each of which covers 250 miles. [The city] is 100 miles in circumference and has 10 bridges. Its name means City of Heaven; and many marvellous tales are told of it and of the multitude of its handicrafts and treasures. It [China] has an area of approximately one third of the entire globe. This city is in the province of *Mangi*, evidently in the vicinity of the province of Katay, in which is the royal residence of the country.

But from the island of Antilia, known to you, to the far-famed island of *Cippangu* [Japan], there are 10 spaces. That island is very rich in gold, pearls, and gems; they roof the temples and royal houses with solid gold. So there is not a great space to be traversed over unknown waters.[8]

Columbus, during his residence in Portugal, probably in 1480 or 1481, corresponded with Toscanelli and procured copies of the 1474 letter and its accompanying chart. The chart is lost, and the only surviving version of the letter is a copy in Columbus' hand on the flyleaf of one of his own books. Toscanelli's notes to Columbus himself are brief and condescending.

> . . . I received your letters together with the things you sent me; I was greatly benefited by them, and I esteem your noble and grand desire to navigate from the East to the West, as is shown by the chart which I am sending you; which would have better been shown in the form of a round sphere. I am greatly pleased that it is well understood. For the said voyage is not only possible, but it is sure and certain and will bring honor, inestimable gain and the widest renown among all Christians.
>
> But you will not be able to understand it perfectly except by experience or practice, as I have had most abundantly, and good and true information from illustrious men of great learning who have come from the said regions to this court of Rome, and from merchants, also, who have trafficked for a long time in those regions, persons of great authority.
>
> . . . I am not surprised that you, a man of great courage, and all the nation of the Portuguese, who have always been men of courage in all great enterprises, should be seen with heart aflame with great zeal to carry out the said voyage.[9]

Doubts have been cast on the authenticity of this correspondence, though it is difficult to see what interest anyone could have had in forging it. Assuming it to be genuine, it suggests that Columbus had already, before writing to Toscanelli, conceived the idea of a western voyage to some part of Asia, and that he sought from the Florentine no more than learned support. His own handling of orthodox cosmography, indeed, was more Procrustean than Toscanelli's. Columbus was not concerned with theory for its own sake, but with promoting a practical proposal. He had to show that the westward distance from Europe to Asia was within the operating range of the available ships. From the authorities which he selected for quotation, from marginal annotations—the earliest dated 1481—in his surviving books, from his own later writings, and from the biography written by his son Fernando, we can trace how he set about it.

First Ptolemy, in an important respect, had to be rejected. According to Ptolemy, the land area of the world covered about 180° of longitude, measured eastward from the meridian of Cape St Vincent to that of 'Catigara' at the extremity of Asia. For Columbus, the remaining 180° of water were too much. He found a more acceptable figure in the *Cosmographiae Tractatus* of Pierre d'Ailly, the author of the *Imago Mundi*, who in this second treatise, following Marinus of Tyre in preference to Ptolemy, allotted 225° of longitude to the land and only 135° to the water. Cardinal d'Ailly, however, had known nothing of Marco Polo, who had revealed to Europeans the enormous east-west length of Asia. Columbus, therefore, added 28° of land for Marco Polo's discoveries, and a further 30° to allow for the reported distance from the Cathay coast to the island of Cipangu. This left only 77° of longitude between western Europe and Cipangu, from which a further 9° could be subtracted, since Columbus proposed to embark on his ocean passage from the western Canary Islands, leaving 68°. By a final arbitrary correction, almost breath-taking in its illogic, on the assumption that Marinus had over-estimated the length of a degree, Columbus succeeded, to his own satisfaction, in reducing this 68° to 60°.

The next problem was to translate longitude into linear distance. There had been many estimates, from which Columbus could choose, of the length of a degree of longitude at the equator. For a modern navigator the figure is sixty nautical miles; the nautical mile as a unit of arc being 1′, as a unit of distance approximately 6000 feet. Eratosthenes in the third century BC had come near that figure; translated into nautical miles, as units of distance, for convenience of comparison, his estimate was 59·5. Ptolemy, following Marinus, made it about 50. Casting about for a smaller figure, Columbus found one, or thought he found one, in the *Imago Mundi*: the estimate of Alfragan, the mediaeval Arab cosmographer. This was 56⅔ Arabic miles, which would be 66·2 nautical miles; but Columbus assumed, wrongly, that Alfragan's mile had been the shorter Roman mile. On that basis, Alfragan's degree would have been only 45 nautical miles at the equator, or 40 nautical miles in latitude 28°N, where Columbus proposed to make his crossing—probably the shortest estimate of a degree ever made. Columbus' world, in other words, had a circumference 10 % smaller than Ptolemy's and 25 % smaller than the real world. The airline distance westward from the Canaries to Japan is 10,600 nautical miles. Toscanelli estimated it as the equivalent of 3000. Columbus' calculations would have made it 2400: a long voyage, but feasible, especially if a stop could be made at Antilia.

Such was the basis, in rough summary, of the case Columbus had to present, to secure the backing of a government or a private investor. Little is known of the form in which he presented it in Portugal. According to Barros, the best of the sixteenth-century Portuguese chroniclers:

... he read a great deal in Marco Polo, who spoke persuasively of oriental matters, of the Kingdom of Cathay and of the great island Cypango, and formed the idea that one could sail over the western Ocean Sea to this island Cypango and to other unknown lands. For, since in the time of the Prince Dom Henrique the Azores were discovered, so there should be other islands and lands to the west; for nature could not have designed the globe so inappropriately as to give the water preponderance over the land destined for life and the creation of souls. With these fancies ... he came to ask the King Dom João to give him ships to discover the island of Cypango across the western ocean. .... The King, seeing that this Christavão Colom was full of words, boastful of his achievements, and that he spoke of the island Cypango out of imagination and fancy rather than from certain knowledge, gave him little credit. Because of his importunity, however, he was told to confer with Dom Diogo Ortiz, Bishop of Ceuta, Master Rodrigo and Master José [Vizinho], to whom the King had entrusted these problems of cosmography and discovery. They all decided that the arguments of Christavão Colom were worthless, based on imagination or on rumours like that of Marco Polo's island of Cypango.[10]

Barros, writing long after the event, with the advantage of hindsight, naturally emphasized the absurdity of Columbus' proposition, and probably exaggerated the contempt which it provoked. The King's committee—occupied at that time with the very practical problem of determining latitude by means of sun sights—may well have had their doubts about Cipangu; when Columbus descended to detail, they would certainly have questioned his assumptions, and challenged the process of reasoning by which he applied a series of selected corrections all in his own favour; but in the state of geographical knowledge at the time, they could not be sure that Columbus' theories were wildly wrong. His proposal was refused, but not laughed out of court, and the possibility of future negotiation was not ruled out. In 1484, however, the time was inopportune. The King was interested in the undoubted spice trade with India, rather than in the reputed gold of Cipangu and Cathay. He was already exploiting a lucrative source of gold in West Africa. Diogo Cão had just returned with deceptive reports of a passage to the Indian Ocean. There was no inducement to divert royal ships and money to expeditions in the opposite direction. If the King's subjects cared to go searching for Antilia or Cipangu or some such place, well and good, but not at the King's expense. In the very next year, the Fleming Dulmo or van Olmen of Terceira contracted with the King, in return for future privileges, 'to seek and find a great island or islands or mainland by its coast, which is presumed to be the Isle of the Seven Cities'—a plan not wholly dissimilar from Columbus'; but 'all this at his own proper charge and cost.'[11] Nothing came of it; and meanwhile Columbus had turned to Castille.

The story of Columbus' early years in Spain has been told many times: the journeys, the weary importuning, scraping acquaintance with men of modest influence in order to obtain introduction to others more influential, until he penetrated to the royal presence. Of his detailed negotiation with the Crown, very little is known. Possibly Columbus had learned from his rebuff in Portugal to avoid excessive detail, to stick as far as possible to generalities and to dark hints of secret information, in his dealings with men more highly placed and better educated than he was. He had great persistence, and on generalities could be extraordinarily persuasive; on detail he could be challenged. He seems, quite early on, to have convinced some people of the value of his proposal. Eventually, after several refusals and after powerful intervention on his behalf, he secured the royal support. The expedition was a modest affair: a small *nao* chartered for the purpose and two still smaller caravels commandeered. The cost to the Crown was relatively small; much of the capital was advanced from private sources. The extensive privileges promised to Columbus were contingent on success; if he failed, he would get nothing. We do not know whether Columbus undertook explicitly to sail to destinations in Asia, or, if he did, whether the Queen and her advisers believed him; his final capitulation with the Crown simply refers in formal terms to 'those islands and mainlands which by his labour and industry shall be discovered or acquired in the said Ocean Sea.'

Of Columbus' own intention of reaching Asia there is little doubt; at least, none of the chroniclers of the voyage—Peter Martyr, Las Casas, Fernando Colón—who knew him personally, expressed any doubt. None of them, writing after the event, can have had any interest in associating him with an exploded geographical theory; but they all did. What he proposed to do if he actually reached Cipangu or Cathay, can only be guessed. With three small unarmed ships there could obviously be no question of conquest. Columbus carried letters of credence to present to the rulers of any inhabited territory he might find; but he had none of the

10 Woodcut of a Spanish ship of 1496. *Science Museum, South Kensington, London.*

panoply of an ambassador, and no diplomatic presents. The only goods the fleet carried were small truck—beads, hawks' bells, scarlet cloth—such as the Portuguese used for barter in West Africa. Probably Columbus' purpose, on reaching an Asian destination, was to get permission to establish a trading post, a *fondaco*, perhaps on an offshore island; there were plenty of precedents, both Genoese and Portuguese, for such an arrangement. These considerations, however, were probably secondary in his mind. Proceedings on arrival could be left to divine guidance or the inspiration of the moment. The immediate problem was to get there, and for that the plan was straightforward, the same plan that Toscanelli had recommended: due west from the Canary Islands—Antilia—Cipangu—Quinsay.

2 Islands and Mainland

The first major Spanish voyage of exploration, in contrast with the calculated, stage-by-stage proceedings of the Portuguese in the same generation, was an amateurish affair. Vasco da Gama was selected to command an expedition long under royal consideration; Columbus' proposals were his own. Da Gama sailed for India in 1497 with instructions as precise as the available intelligence could make them, guided by the experience of many earlier attempts, in ships built specially for the service. Columbus in 1492 was sent off to an undefined destination in the ships that happened to be available. Da Gama's officers, selected by him from a wide range of experienced men, were appointed by the Crown. Columbus' people were recruited informally, by personal contacts in the smaller harbours of western Andalusia.

This is not to suggest that Columbus' ships were unsuited to their task, or that his ships' companies were incompetent; their achievements prove the contrary. The *nao Santa María*, it is true, was somewhat unhandy for inshore work, as Columbus complained; on the initial run down to the Canaries the *Pinta's* steering gear gave trouble; and the little lateen-rigged *Niña* had difficulty in keeping up with the others when before the wind. At the Canaries, however, *Pinta's* rudder was re-shipped and *Niña* was re-rigged as a *caravela redonda* like *Pinta*. Thereafter the ships performed well. It is remarkable evidence of the development of ship design in fifteenth-century Spain and Portugal, that this very long and uncertain voyage could be made with confidence in ships built for ordinary coasting trade.

The officers in the caravels were mostly members of leading seafaring and ship-owning families in Palos and Moguer: the Pinzón, the Niño and others. Probably these respected citizens recruited their own crews. Some of them were less than wholly loyal to Columbus. Probably his secretiveness about his exact intentions, and his vague muddled exuberance, irritated them; and Martín Alonso Pinzón of the *Pinta* showed a recurrent tendency to assert his own independence. They were experienced chiefly in coasting, in sailing to the islands, and perhaps in clandestine voyages to the Guinea coast. No one doubted their competence as seamen. The *Santa María's* company was more mixed; some were seamen from the north of Spain, some not even seamen. Her master and owner, the Biscayan Juan de la Cosa, was to display negligence or cowardice, perhaps worse (according to Columbus) when his ship grounded. It was in this ship that mutterings of mutiny and complaints about the length of the voyage were to be raised, and that Columbus was to deliver resolute speeches, 'holding out to them bright hopes of the gains which they could make' and adding 'that it was vain for them to complain, since he was going to the Indies and must pursue his course until, with the help of Our Lord, he found them'.

11 Model of the Santa María,
made by R. C. Anderson.
One of several conjectural
reconstructions of this
famous ship, and probably
the most plausible. None of
the original ship's
dimensions is known.
Gallery of American Art,
Phillips Academy, Andover,
Mass.

Columbus as commanding officer suffered from three serious disadvantages: foreign birth, humble origin and lack of experience in command. He had made several longish voyages, whether as seaman or as supercargo, but had never, so far as is known, commanded a ship, much less a fleet. Many captains of discovery had one or other of these disadvantages, but few had all three. Columbus overcame them, to a great extent, by self-confident imagination, strength of will and tenacity of purpose; and he had one major natural advantage. He was a born navigator. In 1492 he did his own navigating from the start, and did not rely on Peralonso Niño to tell him where he was. His skill was not derived from formal training; he was not ahead, nor even abreast, of the development of celestial navigation in Portugal in his day; but he had a flair for dead-reckoning which, shaky at first, improved voyage by voyage. His accurate landfalls were too frequent to be attributable to luck. He carried a compass rose in his head.

Columbus' choice of Gomera in the Canaries as his point of departure for the ocean passage showed sound judgement. If he had sailed under Portuguese orders this choice might not have been open to him, and the voyage might have had a different outcome, or no outcome at all. As it was, the fleet had a prosperous passage from Gomera to the West Indies, thirty-three days, with favouring winds nearly all the way, clear weather, and calm to moderate sea. The health of the ships' companies was good throughout—another sharp contrast with da Gama's experience five years later. The course of the voyage has been described many times; but all accounts derive directly or indirectly chiefly from a single source, Columbus' own journal. In its original form this was a very full record, containing descriptions of places and people, and Columbus' own reflections upon them, in addition to navigational data. Columbus made entries almost daily through most of the voyage, and on arrival at court presented the whole document, apparently unedited, as it stood, to the sovereigns. The original disappeared into the archives, and is lost. One or two copies were made, one being retained for a time, apparently, by the Columbus family, but these too are lost. Our knowledge of the journal today comes from summaries or abstracts, and of these, three are important.

The earliest was made by Columbus himself, at sea, in the last few weeks of the voyage, and despatched overland to the Spanish court, probably from Lisbon, or perhaps from Palos. Copies of this communication were sent—whether from the court, or directly by Columbus himself, we cannot be sure—to a number of people who had helped in setting out the expedition, particularly to Columbus' friend and sponsor Santángel. One or more of the recipients quickly exploited this early information, and the text got into the printers' hands in a matter of weeks.

The second summary, in point of time, was that of Columbus' son Fernando Colón, the bibliophile, whose *Life* of his father was written in the late 1530s and published, at Venice in Italian translation, in 1571. The journal forms the basis of twenty-five of the hundred and eight chapters of this work.

The third and most valuable summary was made, about the middle of the sixteenth century, by the Dominican missionary and historian Bartolomé de las Casas, probably from a copy in Fernando Colón's library, to which las Casas had access after the owner's death. This summary was to be used in the preparation of las Casas' *History of the Indies*. Though a passionate polemist, he was a conscientious historian, and all the evidence suggests that he summarised faithfully and well. His abstract is consistent in essentials with the other two, but is much fuller and more detailed, and contains long *verbatim* extracts from the original. It is by far the most important source of information about the 1492 voyage. It records day by

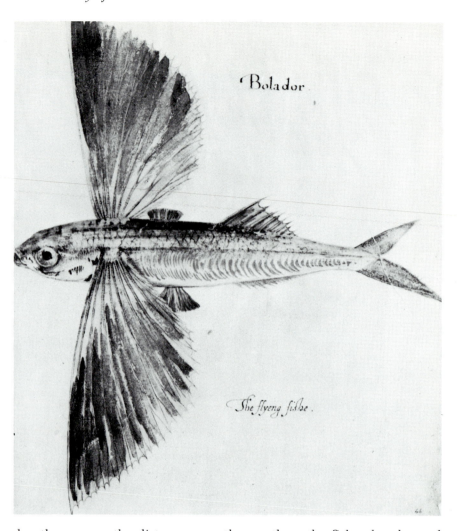

'Bolador'

The flyeng fishe.

12 Flying fish; drawing by John White. 1585. *British Museum, 81 C.*

day the course; the distance run; the weather; the fish—dorados and flying fish chiefly—caught on calm days; the sheets of floating gulf weed, which initially alarmed the sailors; and the birds sighted. These last were considered valuable indicators: the navigators were good enough naturalists to disregard petrels and other pelagic species, but to be excited by terns, frigate-birds and boobies, which were known to roost ashore. They were unfamiliar, apparently, with the habits of tropic-birds—a pelagic species common in the Sargasso area—and regarded them, wrongly, as evidence of nearby land.

Between the seventh day out and the eleventh, these sightings of birds were so numerous as to suggest islands in the neighbourhood—Antilia, perhaps—but in the steady trade wind the fleet held on to the west, and the birds thinned out. On the sixteenth day rumours of land again ran round the fleet, apparently because Columbus' chart marked islands—this time possibly Cipangu or its neighbours—roughly in that position; but again no land. On the twenty-ninth day Columbus, convinced by flocks of land birds migrating south-west that he had passed, or was passing, to the north of his destination, altered course west-south-west in the wake of the birds. This was an important decision, as it turned out; it ensured that the fleet would find land in the middle of the Bahamas rather than further north, perhaps on the coast of Florida; that the West Indies, not North America, should be the first part of the New World to be explored by Spaniards. Four days later, during the night, land was sighted: a low-lying island, almost certainly Watlings Island. It has low coral cliffs on its eastern shore, which were visible, even at night, from a distance of six or seven miles. The fleet prudently shortened sail and stood

off and on until dawn, then sailed round to the western, the lee side of the island, where a break in the girdle of reefs allowed them to enter the lagoon and send boats ashore. At once the local people, the naked Arawaks, came crowding down to the shore in excited curiosity.

Two great branches of the human race, separated for many millennia, met on that day. It was not quite the first meeting; the Norsemen had encountered both Eskimo and Beothuk Indians, and almost certainly there had been other contacts from time to time across the Pacific, even possibly across the Atlantic; but Columbus' landing on the sunlit beach of Guanahaní was the beginning of regular, permanent, irreversible association, with all that it implied in enrichment and destruction. No one could have been more keenly aware of this than las Casas. He was characteristically much more interested in relations between people than in navigational detail or descriptions of the natural scene. With simple but powerful dramatic effect—at this point in his narrative he dropped his detached third-person summary—he transcribed in full Columbus' description of the simple people of Guanahaní.

13 Columbus' fleet becalmed; conjectural painting in Björn Landström, *Columbus* (Stockholm, 1966), pp. 56–57. The fleet is shown before its departure from the Canaries, *Niña* still with her lateen rig.

. . . it seemed to me that they were a people very deficient in everything. They all go naked as their mothers bore them, and the women also, although I saw only one very young girl. And all those whom I did see were youths, so that I did not see one who was over thirty years of age; they were very well built, with very handsome bodies and very good faces. Their hair is coarse almost like the hairs of a horse's tail and short; they wear their hair down over their eyebrows, except for a few strands behind, which they wear long and never cut. Some of them are painted black, and they are the colour of the people of the Canaries, neither black nor white, and some of them are painted white and some red and some in any colour that they find. Some of them paint their faces, some their whole bodies, some only the eyes, and some only the nose. They do not bear arms or know them, for I showed to them swords and they took them by the blade and cut themselves through ignorance. They have no iron. Their spears are certain reeds, without iron, and some of these have a fish tooth at the end, while others are pointed in various ways. They are all generally fairly tall, good looking and well proportioned. I saw some who bore marks of wounds on their bodies, and I made signs to them to ask how this came about, and they indicated to me that people came from other islands, which are near, and wished to capture them, and they defended themselves. And I believed and still believe that they come here from the mainland to take them for slaves. They should be good servants and quick of intelligence, since I see that they very soon say all that is said to them, and I believe that they would easily be made Christians, for it appeared to me that they had no creed. Our Lord willing, at the time of my departure I will bring back six of them to Your Highnesses, that they may learn to talk. I saw no beast of any kind in this island, except parrots. . . .

They came to the ship in boats, which are made of a treetrunk like a long boat and all of one piece. They are very wonderfully carved, considering the country, and large, so that in some forty or forty-five men came. Others are smaller, so that in some only a solitary man came. They row them with a paddle, like a baker's peel, and they travel wonderfully fast. If one capsizes, all at once begin to swim and right it, baling it out with gourds which they carry with them. They brought balls of spun cotton and parrots and spears and other trifles, which it would be tedious to write down, and they gave all for anything that was given to them. And I was attentive and laboured to know if they had gold, and I saw that some of them wore a small piece hanging from a hole which they have in the nose, and from signs I was able to understand that, going to the south or going round the island to the south, there was a king who had large vessels of it and possessed much gold. I endeavoured to make them go there, and afterwards saw that they were not inclined for the journey. I resolved to wait until the afternoon of the following day, and after that to leave for the south-west, for, as many of them indicated to me, they said that there was land to the south and to the south-west and to the north-west, and that those of the north-west often came to attack them. So I resolved to go to the south-west, to seek the gold and precious stones. This island is fairly large and very flat; the trees are very green and there is much water. In the centre of it, there is a very large lake; there is no mountain, and all is so green that it is a pleasure to gaze upon it. The people also are very gentle and, since they long to possess something of ours and fear that nothing will be given to them unless they give something, when they have nothing, they take what they can and immediately throw themselves into the water and swim. But all that they do possess, they give for anything which is given to them, so that they exchange things even for pieces of broken dishes and bits of broken glass cups. I even saw one give sixteen balls of cotton for three *ceotis* of Portugal, which are a Castilian *blanca*, and in these balls there was more than an *arroba* of spun cotton. I should forbid this and should not allow anything to be taken, unless it be that I command all, if there be a quantity, to be taken for Your Highnesses. It grows here in this island, but owing to lack of time, I can give no definite account; and here is also produced that gold which they wear hanging from the nose. But, in order not to lose time, I wish to go and see if I can make the island of Cipangu.

So on to the south-west, by Rum Cay, Long Island, Crooked Island, Fortune Island and the Islas de Arena, the Sand Islands. Off Fortune Island:

All the other things and lands of these islands are so lovely that I do not know where to go first, and my eyes never weary of looking at such lovely verdure so different from that of our own land. I believe, moreover, that here there are many herbs and many trees which will be of great value in Spain for dyes and as medicinal spices, but I do not recognise them and this causes me much sorrow. When I arrived here at this cape, there came from the land the scent of flowers or trees, so delicious and sweet, that it was the most delightful thing in the world. In the morning, before I go from here, I will land to see what there is here at this point. There is no village, except further inland, where these men, whom I have with me, say that there is a king and that he wears much gold. Tomorrow I wish to go so far inland to find the village and to see or have speech with this king, who, according to the signs which these men make, rules all these neighbouring islands and is clothed and wears on his person much gold, although I do not put much trust in what they say, both because I do not understand them well and because they are so poor in gold that any small amount which this king may wear would seem to be much to them. This point here I call Cape Hermoso. I believe that it is an island separated from that of Samoet, and even that there is another small island between them. I make no attempt to examine so much in detail, since I could not do that in fifty years, because I wish to see and discover as much as I can, in order to return to Your Highnesses in April, if it please Our Lord. It is true that if I arrive anywhere where there is gold or spices in quantity, I shall wait until I have collected as much as I am able. Accordingly I do nothing but go forward in the hope of finding these.

Again off Crooked Island:

The singing of little birds is such that it seems that a man could never wish to leave this place; the flocks of parrots darken the sun, and there are large and small birds of so many different kinds and so unlike ours, that it is a marvel. There are, moreover, trees of a thousand types, all with their various fruits and all scented, so that it is a wonder. I am the saddest man in the world because I do not recognise them, for I am very sure that all are of some value, and I am bringing specimens of them and also of the herbs. As I was thus going round one of these lagoons, I saw a snake, which we killed, and I am bringing its skin to Your Highnesses . . . Here I recognised the aloe [wrongly; it was not the valuable *lignum aloes*, but a common agave] and tomorrow I am resolved to have ten quintals brought to the ship, since they tell me that it is very valuable. . . . I shall presently set out to go round the island, until I have had speech with this king and have seen whether I can obtain from him the gold which I hear that he wears. After that I wish to leave for another very large island, which I believe must be Cipangu, according to the signs which these Indians whom I have with me make; they call it 'Colba.' They say that there are ships and many very good sailors there. Beyond this island, there is another which they call 'Bofio,' which they say is also very large. The others, which lie between them, we shall see in passing, and according to whether I shall find a quantity of gold or spices, I shall decide what is to be done. But I am still

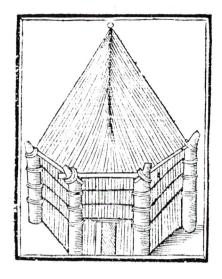

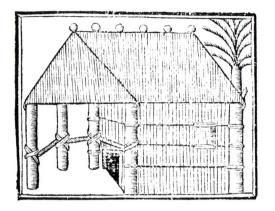

14 Woodcuts from Gonzalo Fernández de Oviedo y Valdés, *Historia General de las Indias* (Seville, 1547): *Above and above right* Native houses in Hispaniola, fos lviii v and lix. *Right* Native hammock, fo xlvii v. *Below* Y-shaped pipe, smoked through the nostrils, fo xlviii

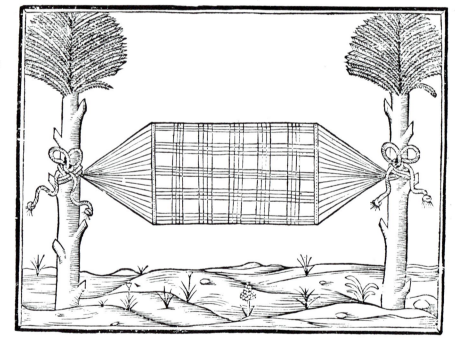

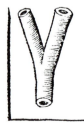

determined to proceed to the mainland and to the city of Quisay and to give the letters of Your Highnesses to the Grand Khan, and to request a reply and return with it.[1]

'Bofio' or *bohío* is the Arawak word for house or hut; Columbus mistook it for the name of the large island which, a little later, he called Española, Hispaniola. 'Colba' was Cuba, which Columbus named Juana, though he thought it might be Cipangu. The fleet reached the north-east coast of Cuba at Bahía Bariay in late October.

Columbus never explained why, with his ships initially provisioned for a year, he wished to be back in Spain by April; and his wanderings among the islands suggest an ambiguity of purpose in sharp contrast with the steady determination of his westward course across the ocean. He was not single-minded about the quest for Cathay, and seemed willing to abandon it for any destination—Cipangu or any other—which offered more immediate promise of gold. Gold obsessed Columbus. He wrote eagerly of it again and again. It was always the principal object of his searchings among the islands. Here and there natives were seen wearing small scraps of gold as ornaments, and were questioned, by signs, about the source of the gold. Even if they understood the questions, their vague answering gestures were difficult to interpret; but there were two familiar general principles which could be applied: that gold came chiefly from hot countries, and that hot countries lay south, not north. Other things being equal, Columbus always preferred a southerly over a northerly course of exploration; and most often, as it happened, informants indicating the source of gold pointed south, towards 'Bohío'—Hispaniola.

The route to Cathay, however, lay west, and the coast of Cuba, though

TABACOLOGIA. 9

15 Tobacco plant; engraving from John Neander, *Tabacologia* (Leyden, 1622), p. 9.

with many indentations, trended west-north-west, heavily forested, thinly inhabited by primitive people. Clearly this was not Cipangu, and Columbus, noting the mouths of several fair-sized rivers, began to think that Cuba was not an island at all; that it might itself be part of the mainland of Cathay. If so, it must be a remote and outlying part; nothing suggested cities, harbours and busy shipping nearby. Columbus did not persevere for long. After only three days' sailing, geography and weather combined to give him reason to reverse his course. At a point where the coast turned north for a short distance he encountered the beginnings of a 'norther', with a sharp drop in temperature. Prudently, he put his ships about and ran back along the coast to the nearest safe harbour, 'Río de mares', which Morison identifies as Puerto Gibara.

The explorers spent eleven days in this agreeable place. They sampled a variety of native food crops—maize, beans, sweet potatoes—saw tobacco smoked, and acquired hammocks—precious gifts of America to the seamen of the world—in barter for beads. They found a variety of spurious spices, but still no gold. The *converso* Luis de Torres, who understood Hebrew and a little Arabic, was sent inland to seek out the local ruler, to establish friendly relations, and to get information on the distance and direction of Quinsay and Zayton. He found the chief in a village of fifty or so tent-shaped huts, was received with courteous, if primitive, hospitality, but learned of no cities. That was the end, for this voyage at least, of the search for Cathay; there is no further mention of it in the *Journal*. When Columbus left Puerto Gibara he sailed not north-west, but south-east, beating against the trade wind, to Cape Maisí at the eastern extremity of Cuba and across the Windward Passage to the north-east coast of Hispaniola. The rest of his time in the West Indies was devoted to the search for gold.

Columbus' reversal of direction off Cuba, like his alteration of course before reaching the Bahamas, had important consequences. It ensured that for a whole generation most Spanish exploring in the West Indies would be done, not north of Cuba towards Florida, Yucatan and the Gulf of Mexico, but south to the Main coast and the Isthmus of Panama; that Hispaniola, not Cuba, would be the initial centre of Spanish activity in the area.

Cuba had been a disappointment; in Hispaniola prospects brightened. The population was denser, the local economy more developed and varied, and hammered gold ornaments more plentiful. The country was fertile and pleasant—the northern plain of Haiti, which in French hands two centuries later was to become the most productive colony in all the Americas. The ships sailed on east along the coast, beat through the Tortuga Channel, and in Acul Bay made contact, through messengers, with Guacanagarí, the first chief they had encountered of more than local influence. Natives in great numbers came on board to trade, with food, including wood ducks—the first European mention of that beautiful and all-too-edible creature—skeins of cotton and scraps of gold. From Guacanagarí's people the Spaniards got their first firm information about the source of gold. It came from streams in the mountainous area known to the Arawaks as Cibao. Two weeks later Martín Alonso Pinzón, who from

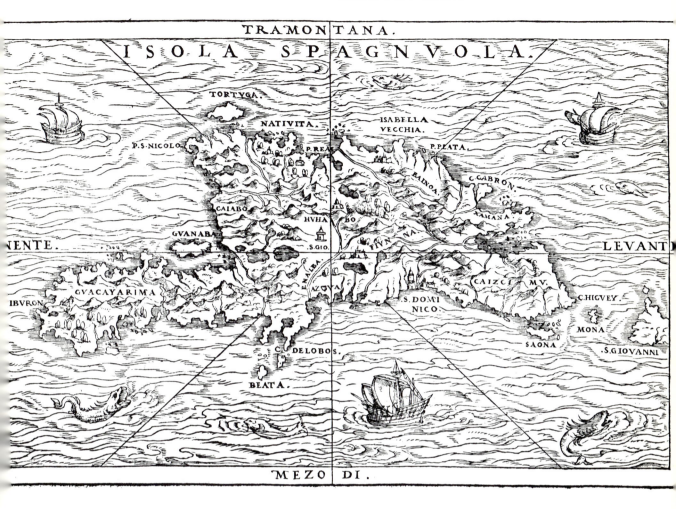

TRAMONTANA.

ISOLA SPAGNVOLA.

PONENTE.

LEVANTE

MEZO DI.

Cuba had gone off on an unauthorised gold hunt of his own, confirmed this; he reported on rejoining that he had explored forty or fifty miles inland from somewhere on the coast near Monte Christi, and had actually reached the gold-bearing region of Cibao. Columbus, presumably from the similarity of the names, drew the conclusion that the great island he was coasting was indeed Cipangu.

A few miles east of Cap Haitien, on Christmas Eve, the *Santa María* went on a reef, broke up, and had to be abandoned. Guacanagarí's people in their canoes throughout the next day helped to transfer her stores and gear to a dump ashore. Guacanagarí himself proved friendly and helpful, and his hospitality encouraged Columbus to establish the first—and until then unintended—European settlement in the West Indies. Probably he had no choice; the *Pinta* had not yet rejoined, and the forty-odd men from the *Santa María* could not have been crowded into the *Niña* for a trans-Atlantic passage. A rude blockhouse was built from the *Santa María's* planking on the open bay which Columbus named Navidad, and about forty people were left behind to man the place, to plant crops and search for gold. None of them was to survive the year.

16 Map of Hispaniola; from G. B. Ramusio, *Delle Navigationi e Viaggi* (Venice, 1556), III, 44.

It is curious, perhaps, that after the reunion with the *Pinta*, Columbus did not investigate more thoroughly the clues to the Cibao gold; but the expedition was in poor condition for further exploring, with the flagship lost, forty men left behind and the senior officers at loggerheads. The caravels were riddled with ship-worm, and some time had to be spent at Monte Christi in scraping, caulking and plugging holes. Everyone, including Columbus, apparently wanted to get home. They ran out the north coast as far east as Samaná Bay, where they had another unpleasant experience, their first serious brush with natives. These Ciguayos, according to las Casas, were all too familiar with Carib raiders. The place is called Las Flechas, The Arrows, to this day. From Samaná Bay the fleet set sail for Spain, standing to the north, close-hauled on the trade wind, until in the 30s of north latitude they found a west wind for home. This was to become standard practice. During the passage the caravels became separated in bad weather, and Columbus in the *Niña* had twice to put into harbour for shelter, first in the Azores (which also became standard practice) and then, most unwillingly, at Lisbon.

17 A late fifteenth-century ship, from a woodcut illustrating a printed version of Columbus' letter on his first voyage, 1493.

The summary of his adventures which Columbus despatched from Lisbon, and which survives—the so-called *Letter* to Sánchez or to Santángel—is skilfully composed and brief.[2] It omits all navigational data, doubtless for reasons of security. It lacks the exuberance and day-to-day candour of the *Journal*. It is disingenuous on the reversal of course off Cuba, still more so on the loss of the flagship. It does not explicitly identify Hispaniola with Cipangu, and though it refers confidently to 'Indies' and 'Indians' and to possibilities of trade with the 'Great Khan's' dominions, it does not particularise about Asian geography; possibly security considerations affected this reticence also. It makes no very sensational claims, but dwells heavily on the Hispaniola gold. Clearly, in writing this (for him) relatively sober report, Columbus kept himself carefully in hand, and confined himself, on the one hand, to what he thought his backers would like to hear, and on the other, to what they might be expected to believe.

Columbus' actual report to the sovereigns, in which this 'letter to Sánchez' was enclosed, is lost, but presumably it contained much the same information. Whatever its precise wording, it served its purpose. The sovereigns at once confirmed the titles and rewards they had promised to Columbus. With or without their consent, the 'letter to Sánchez' was printed; at least seventeen editions, in Spanish, Latin, French, German or Italian, appeared before 1500. All of them are now very rare, some known only from unique copies, but at the time they must have been widely read. Thanks to this early distribution, literate people in Europe first read of Columbus' exploit in Columbus' own words.

European reactions to the news were very diverse. The Portuguese, by chance, were the first to receive it. When Columbus, driven by stress of weather, put into Lisbon, he had to give some account of himself, if only to convince his hosts that he had not been trespassing in their Guinea preserve. According to Rui de Pina, he may have been in some personal danger; but after questioning, the King and his advisers accepted the story of the westward voyage into the Ocean Sea. They made no attempt to detain Columbus or to intercept his correspondence; they supplied his needs and courteously sent him on his way. John II may well have regretted not having paid more attention to Columbus in 1484—as Pina suggests—but he was not seriously put out. The naked Arawaks did not suggest the silken East; and in any event, neither Cathay nor (if such a place existed) Cipangu was a major concern of the Portuguese; they were interested in India. They concluded that Columbus had found yet another group of Atlantic islands; Hispaniola was probably Antilia. The West Indies soon became known in Portuguese circles as the 'Antilles of the King of Castile', and are so marked in the Cantino map.

In northern Europe the news travelled slowly and was received at first with comparative indifference. Latin editions of the *Letter* were printed in Basel and Antwerp in 1494, but no German translation appeared until 1497. The *Nürnberg Chronicle*, published four months after Columbus' return, makes no mention of him. In Italy, on the other hand, the news spread very quickly, not only through printings of Columbus' *Letter* but also through private letters written by Italian diplomats and business men

18 One of the species of birds described by Columbus in the journal of the first voyage: the yellow-billed tropic-bird, *phaethon lepturus*; from J. J. Audubon, 'Elephant Folio' of *Birds* (London, 1827–1838), vol. III, plate 262.

in Spain to correspondents at home. The interest revealed in these letters, and subsequent comment on them, was chiefly literary and scientific. The gold of Hispaniola, and the river beds in which it was said to be found, recalled for the well-read the legend of King Midas and the river Pactolus. Another favourite topic was the prelapsarian innocence of the natives of Columbus' islands, their peaceable disposition, their lack of weapons, above all their nakedness; and in dramatic contrast, the ferocity of their neighbours and enemies, the Caribs, whose cannibal habits provided gruesome material for illustrators and sent pleasurable shivers of horror down the spines of readers all over Europe. Animals and plants, particularly crocodiles (presumably iguanas), parrots and, naturally, spice-bearing trees, provoked some comment. As for the geographical position of the new discoveries, phrases such as 'islands in the Indian Ocean', 'islands of India', 'islands toward the Orient', occur in most of the surviving letters; but Asia, as everyone who had read Marco Polo knew, covered an immense area. Its peoples were extremely diverse, and even included cannibals, if Conti were to be believed. Informed Italian opinion seems to have accepted, at first, that Columbus' islands lay in or near some region of Asia, but a remote and primitive region, far from any of the places in which Europeans were commercially interested.

Official reactions in Spain, as might be expected, were less academic, more practical. Columbus had found fertile, inhabited, gold-bearing

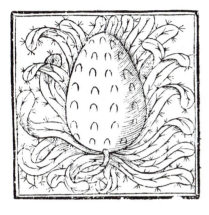

19 Woodcuts from Gonzalo Fernández de Oviedo y Valdes, *Historia General dé las Indias* (Seville, 1547): *Above* A manatee, 'manateo', the 'mermaid' of Columbus' journal, fo cvi. *Left* A tuna, fruit of the prickly pear, fo lxvi, v *Below* A pineapple, a fruit native to the West Indies, fo lxvi, v.

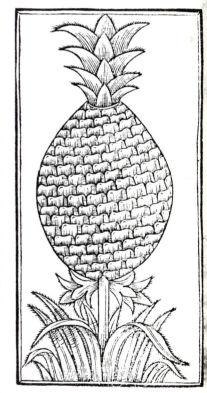

territories. These territories might well, as Columbus alleged, form parts of Asia; but precise geographical definition could be left for further exploration to determine. The immediate objects of royal policy were to establish a Spanish presence in the area, to organise a regular system for procuring gold by barter, and to get Spanish title to trade and settle, to the exclusion of other Europeans, internationally recognised. This last, in view of the information which had already reached Portugal, was a matter of urgency. The Spanish sovereigns at once set about the task of establishing their legal monopoly, addressing themselves initially to the Papacy. The Pope—unquestionably, for Catholic Christians—had the right and the duty to provide for the instruction and conversion of pagan peoples. By extension, so some canonists maintained, he might grant corresponding temporal sovereignty in territory not claimed by Christian princes. This was dubious doctrine, even for the orthodox; but the Portuguese Crown had invoked it in West Africa, and now it was the turn of Castille. The Pope of the time, Alexander VI, was a Spaniard, conscious of favours received from Ferdinand and Isabella, and looking for favours to come in support of his Italian political ambitions. The bulls which he issued in 1493 were to constitute, for Spanish officialdom in the next three hundred years, the legal and moral basis of Spanish rule in the Americas. They were drafted in answer to successive Spanish demands, framed on Columbus' advice.

The first two bulls simply granted sovereignty over Columbus' discoveries to Castille; but that was not enough. The Portuguese already claimed, under the bull *Aeterni Regis* of 1481, a monopoly of navigation south of the Canary Islands, and in order to authorise Columbus' Atlantic crossings in more southerly latitudes it was necessary to restrict the monopoly. Accordingly, the third bull, the famous *Inter Caetera*, drew an imaginary boundary line from north to south a hundred leagues west of the Azores and Cape Verde Islands, and provided that the land and sea beyond the line, in any latitude, should be reserved for Spanish exploration. The fourth, *Dudum Siquidem*, went further:

> But since it may happen that your envoys and captains, or vassals, while voyaging towards the west and south, might bring their ships to land in eastern regions and there discover islands and mainlands that belonged or belong to India . . . we . . . extend our aforesaid gift . . . to all islands and mainlands whatsoever, found and to be found, discovered and to be discovered, that are or may be or may seem to be in the route of navigation or travel toward the west or south, whether they be in western parts, or in regions of the south and east and of India. . . .[3]

The exact purport of these enactments has been the subject of much controversy, then and since, and their legal force was disputable; but they were sufficiently sweeping and sufficiently explicit to alarm the King of Portugal, who used all the resources of diplomacy to limit their effect. Unable to move the Pope, he opened direct negotiations with Ferdinand and Isabella. Dropping any possible claim to Columbus' islands for himself, he accepted the bull of demarcation, *Inter Caetera*, as a basis for discussion, but asked that the boundary line be moved 270 leagues further west, to protect his African interests. The Spanish monarchs, relying on Columbus' geographical reasoning, agreed. Both sides must have known that so vague a boundary could not be accurately fixed. The longitudes of the Azores and the Cape Verde Islands are in fact different; neither was accurately known; distances could be measured only approximately; and no one could mark the sea. Both sides, however, were anxious to avoid an open quarrel, and since their immediate objects did not conflict, a rough formula sufficed. The Treaty of Tordesillas was duly signed in 1494. It established the starting line, so to speak, in a race for the markets of southern and eastern Asia, in which the Portuguese were to sail east, the Spaniards west. It could not bind third parties; in countering French and English encroachments later, the Spaniards had to fall back on the papal donation, and force of arms.

Both parties to the treaty had negotiated in geographical ignorance. Even the Portuguese probably did not grasp, at the time, the magnitude of their diplomatic success. They gained, so far as Spain was concerned, the exclusive use of the only practical sea route to India, and the right to

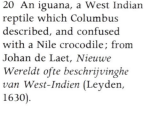

20 An iguana, a West Indian reptile which Columbus described, and confused with a Nile crocodile; from Johan de Laet, *Nieuwe Wereldt ofte beschrijvinghe van West-Indien* (Leyden, 1630).

exclude Spaniards from a vast territory in eastern South America. In return, they accepted their own exclusion from the rest of an undiscovered New World.

Columbus was back in the West Indies long before these negotiations were concluded. His instructions[4] were based on his own recommendations, which in turn derived from his knowledge of what the Portuguese had been doing over the past few decades in West Africa. The gold trade was to be a royal monopoly. The consent of local rulers to the establishment of Spanish posts was assumed—not unreasonably, in view of Columbus' dealings with Guacanagarí. In the intervals of establishing and administering the settlements—a task for which he was both temperamentally and socially ill-equipped—Columbus was to pursue his exploration and find more islands and mainland. Asia was not explicitly mentioned, but was undoubtedly implied. Columbus sailed in September 1493 with seventeen ships and 1200 eager adventurers to the land of gold.

No log or journal of this voyage has survived. Our knowledge of it comes chiefly from letters or summary narratives written either by participants, or by people who had opportunities for questioning participants shortly after their return to Spain. Dr Chanca, surgeon of the fleet, wrote a detailed account of the outward passage in a letter dated 1494, addressed to the city council of Seville. Michele de Cuneo, a Genoese gentleman volunteer, after his return in 1495 wrote a letter to a friend describing the outward passage, the Hispaniola settlement, and the exploration of the south coast of Cuba. Nicolò Syllacio, lecturer in philosophy at Pavia, received letters from a friend who participated in the voyage, and compiled from them a twenty-page pamphlet in Latin, which was printed at Pavia in 1494 or 1495. This tract, dedicated to the reigning Duke of Milan, is the earliest known printed work on the New World except for Columbus' 1493 *Letter*. Andrés Bernáldez, *cura* at Los Palacios, with whom Columbus stayed after his return in 1496, included an account, derived from conversation, in his chronicle, *Historia de los Reyes Católicos*, which was written some time before 1500. The crude world map of Juan de la Cosa, or its surviving copy, which bears the date 1500, incorporates information derived from this voyage, in which la Cosa was a participant. Of the eye-witness accounts, Cuneo's is the most vivid and most comprehensive, and much the most entertaining.

Columbus on this voyage followed the best possible route across the Atlantic, somewhat to the south of his course in 1492. The fleet made a prosperous passage, with the trade wind all the way, and a good landfall at Dominica, the wild Carib island whose sharp volcanic spires were to be, for thousands of later travellers, their first glimpse of the New World. In contrast with the Greater Antilles and the Bahamas, where Columbus' original names were soon disused, many islands in what are now the Windward and Leeward groups still bear the names Columbus gave them on this second voyage: Dominica itself, Marie-Galante, the Saintes, Guadeloupe, Montserrat, Redonda, Antigua, Nevis. Many of these names commemorate famous shrines of the Virgin in Castille, Catalonia and Italy. They appear, though in muddled and inaccurate fashion, on Juan de la Cosa's map.[5] The fleet sailed through this beautiful arc of islands, through

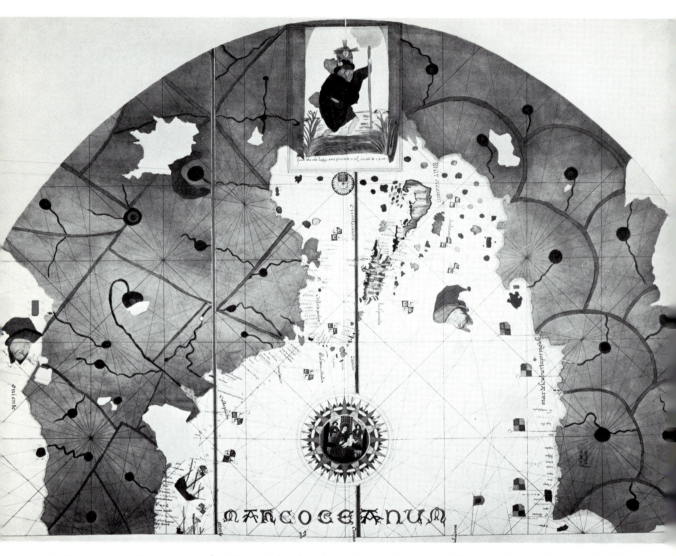

MARCOGEANUM

21 The New-World section of the manuscript world map attributed to Juan de la Cosa, dated 1500, and thus (if the date is correct) the earliest surviving world map to show the newly discovered Indies. *Museo Naval, Madrid.*

the Virgin Islands, along the south coast of Puerto Rico and so, guided by their returning 'Indian' passengers, across the Mona Passage to the north coast of Hispaniola. Here they found the fort of Navidad destroyed and all its garrison dead. The work of settlement had to be started afresh.

One of the chief causes of the failure of early settlements in the Americas was over-optimism about the extent to which expeditions could live off the country. Columbus' fleet carried tools, seed and domestic animals, but not enough European food to supply so large a company for the months which must elapse before animals multiplied and crops came to harvest. During that interval they were dependent upon the Indians; indeed they could not escape from dependence, since much of the seed they brought— wheat, for example—was unsuited to the climate, and they themselves lacked the discipline and the willingness to work steadily at manual tasks, which successful pioneering required. The Indians were initially hospitable, but the food they had to offer was unattractive to Europeans.

70

Their domestic animals were few and small. There were no wild animals of consequence; they ate instead fish, shellfish and lizards. Their principal crops—cassava, sweet potatoes, maize—were all strange to the settlers; and they were not in the habit of storing a large surplus of anything. When they became unable or unwilling to supply food to the settlements the Spaniards had no recourse but to grind their seed corn and slaughter their brood animals, or else forage by force.

The settlers suffered great hardship, from exposure—not to cold but to frequent rain—and from lack of accustomed food; probably also from ignorance in preparing such food as was available. Cuneo, for example, writes of

roots like turnips, very big and in many shapes, absolutely white, of which they make bread in the following way: they shred those turnips on certain stones which look like cheese graters as we do with cheese; then they put on the fire a very large stone on top of which they place that grated root and they shape it in the form of a cake and use it as bread and it keeps good for fifteen or twenty days, which bread several times was very handy for us. This root is their main food, they eat it raw and cooked.[6]

This, presumably, is a description of cassava, the most important Arawak food crop; but cassava tubers do not in the least resemble turnips; did Cuneo confuse them with sweet potatoes? Cassava, also, before it can be used for food, must be not only shredded, but soaked, pressed and dried, to get rid of the bitter juice. If any settlers tried to eat cassava 'raw or cooked', without these precautions, they would have been poisoned. Whatever the causes, many fell sick, some died, many more left the colony and returned home at the first opportunity. That occurred in February 1494, when Columbus sent twelve of his seventeen ships back to Spain under Antonio de Torres, with his first report from Hispaniola. The main features of this report were explanations of the small amount of gold so far collected, promises of better things to come, and urgent requests for supplies.

22 Sweet and bitter cassava (yucca) distinguished by their leaves; woodcuts from Oviedo, *Historia General*, fo lxiii. Bitter cassava was the principal native bread-stuff of the West Indies and of large areas in northern South America.

That which you, Antonio de Torres . . . are to say and ask on my behalf of the King and Queen. . . . There have been found so many rivers, so filled with gold, that all of those who saw it and collected it, merely with their hands as specimens, came back so delighted . . . that I feel diffidence in repeating what they say . . . I was very desirous to be able to send [Their Highnesses] by this fleet a greater quantity of the gold which it is hoped may be collected here, if only the majority of our people had not fallen suddenly ill . . . the preservation of health depends upon this people being provided with the food to which they are accustomed . . . and this provision should continue until a supply can be secured from that which is here sown and planted. . . . You shall say that on account of . . . the bad work which the coopers did in Seville, the greatest need which we now have . . . is of wine. And though we have enough biscuit, as well as corn, for some while, yet it is necessary that some reasonable amount be sent, for the voyage is long and provision cannot be made every day, and likewise some salt meat, I mean bacon and other salt flesh, which should be better than that which we have brought on this voyage. . . . It would be well to give orders that in the ships which come there be brought in addition to the other things, which are for the maintenance of the community, and to medicine, shoes and skins from which they can be ordered to be made, coarse shirts, and for other things, doublets, linen, sacking, breeches, cloth for making clothes, at a reasonable price; and other things, such as conserves, which are outside the rations and which are for the preservation of health. . . . You shall say to Their Highnesses that, although the rivers contain the amount of gold which is reported by those who have seen them, yet it is certain that the gold is produced not in the rivers, but on land, and that the water, penetrating the mines, carries it away mingled with sand.[7]

This—except for the over-optimism in the matter of gold—was a sober and business-like report, and to judge from the annotations, was well received. Most of Columbus' requests and suggestions were approved, at least on paper, and the supplies he requested were promptly despatched. His position, nevertheless, was precarious. Many of his companions, including some better born and better educated than he, had joined the expedition as volunteers, were not on its payroll and not expressly subject to Columbus' authority, which they often resented. Even the paid men sometimes resented being told to perform tasks which in Spain would have been beneath their dignity. Columbus himself complained of the Hermandad troopers, who would do no work that could not be done on horseback. More serious still, Columbus was bound by instructions which set him incompatible tasks. He could not in practice establish a self-supporting Spanish colony, 'treat the Indians very well and lovingly and abstain from doing them any injury,' as his instructions bade him, and at the same time produce revenue. He could not attend to the day-to-day government of disorderly, comfortless settlements, first at Isabela on the north shore, subsequently at Santo Domingo on the south, and at the same time pursue the search for Cathay. Dilemmas such as these were to plague many young settlements in the New World, and the success or failure of pioneer governors was often to depend on their skill in deciding which parts of their instructions they would ignore; but Columbus was the first; he had no experience or precedent to guide him. He had no personal following of any consequence in the colony, no body of backers in Spain committed to his support. Utterly dependent upon the Crown, he was haunted by the fear that his employers, if dissatisfied with his diligence or disappointed of the revenue he had promised, might abandon the enterprise. Cuneo, indeed, on his return seems to have heard waterfront gossip of this possibility. Disgruntled tale-bearers, gaunt with hunger and yellow with fever, were trooping back to Spain. Columbus could not afford—or thought he could not afford—to disregard any part of his instructions. He set about the many tasks confronting him with dizzying energy, but his actual performance of some of them was unavoidably perfunctory or incomplete.

At the beginning of 1494, only a few days after landing at Isabela, Columbus had sent Alonso de Ojeda inland with a small party to explore the Cibao—the northern flank of the central Cordillera—and its gold-bearing streams. Ojeda had returned after two weeks with an over-optimistic report based on Indian tales. Two months later—huts erected and seeds sown at Isabela, and the Torres fleet despatched—Columbus himself set out with a much larger party for the same destination. Cuneo accompanied this expedition, and described it.

In the month of February, after the 12 caravels sent by the Lord Admiral had departed for Spain, 500 of our men went together with the said Lord Admiral to that place of Cibao, not too well fitted out with clothes; and on that trip, between going, staying and returning, we spent 29 days with terrible weather, bad food and worse drink; nevertheless, out of covetousness of that gold, we all kept strong and lusty. We crossed going and coming two very rapid rivers [the Yaque and the Amina?] swimming; and those who did not know how to swim had two Indians who carried them swimming; the same, out of friendship and for a few trifles that we gave them, carried across on top of their heads our clothes, arms and everything else there was to be carried. We went to that place called Cibao and shortly we built a fort of wood in the name of St Thomas, unconquerable by those Indians. This fort is distant from our settlement 27 leagues or thereabouts. Several times we fished in these rivers, but never was found by anyone a single grain of gold. . . . While we were staying in our fort many Indians came to see us from as far as ten leagues as if we were marvels, bringing to us some of the gold they had, and they exchanged it with us so that we collected gold to the value of about 2000 *castellanos*.[8]

Columbus stationed large bodies of men at St Thomas and in other makeshift stockade forts on the route to the Cibao, with instructions to continue the search for gold and send it down to Isabela. They had little success. The accumulated store of easily-found nuggets had already been collected. No one in the island, Spaniard or Indian, knew anything about placer mining. Effective gold mining—as distinct from collecting—did not begin in Hispaniola until the royal monopoly had been abandoned and private prospecting permitted on payment of royalty; and this did not happen until after Columbus' disgrace and recall in 1500. The men whom Columbus sent inland in 1494 wandered about in small parties, living on the natives. Their depredations provoked resistance and reprisal, which in turn led to punitive expeditions and slave hunts. The caravels which took Cuneo back to Spain in 1495 carried five hundred Arawak slaves. Half of them died in passage; as Cuneo sadly remarked, 'they are not working people and they very much fear cold, nor have they long life.' The survivors were released by the Queen's order and sent back, so that even the slave trade brought no revenue.

Meanwhile the problems of exploration by sea claimed Columbus' attention. Where was the mainland of Asia? In April 1494, only four weeks after his return from the Cibao, Columbus set out with three caravels—the well-tried *Niña* and two smaller vessels—to explore to the west. Cuneo went with him; he and Bernáldez are our chief sources of information about this voyage. The fleet sailed through the Windward Passage, along the south coast of Cuba to Cabo Cruz, and then south to Jamaica. Columbus remarked on the natural beauty of Jamaica, and on the size and good workmanship of the canoes in use there. Returning to Cabo Cruz, the caravels sailed on west, now following the coast with its harsh xerophytic vegetation, its shoals and its mangroves, now navigating offshore through the maze of low cays which Columbus called the Jardines de la Reina. It was a long and intricate navigation, with little rest for pilots and look-outs. The furthest point reached (according to Morison) was Bahía Cortés, about fifty miles short of the western extremity of Cuba. Here the coast trends south for a short distance. Columbus persuaded himself that this south-trending shore was the beginning of the Golden Chersonese and that the coast they had been following was a peninsula of the Chinese mainland. He had found no civilised people, no cities, no gold; even the oysters, of which the explorers consumed a great many, contained no pearls; but he was convinced, as he had been on the first voyage, that the cities of China were nearby. As before, however, he did not test his belief further. He contented himself with collecting documentary evidence that he had carried out his instructions. He required all his company to attest under oath that the coast of Cuba was so extensive that it could not be an island; it was '*tierra firme*, in particular the province of Mangi'.[9] How many of Columbus' companions really accepted his geographical reasoning, is impossible to guess. Cuneo did not, to judge from his flippant allusions to it. Probably most of them had no thought but of returning to civilisation (or to Hispaniola, the nearest available substitute) and did not care what they signed.

The first recorded sighting of an undoubtable mainland coast in the region of Columbus' 'Indies' was made four years later, in 1498. Columbus had returned to Spain in 1496 to explain as best he could the slow progress in producing gold. He had been received, if not with enthusiasm, at least with courtesy and patience, and after some delay was allowed six caravels for his return to the Indies. He had difficulty over manning; jails were opened and pardons offered for the purpose, an expedient which Columbus subsequently regretted. Three of the six ships were sent directly to Santo Domingo with supplies; their navigators lost their bearings somewhere in the Caribbean and fetched up, after several months, at the western end of Hispaniola. With the other three caravels Columbus embarked on a new voyage of discovery, on a course much further south than on either of the previous voyages.

According to Las Casas, who made an abstract of the journal of this voyage as he had done of the first, Columbus had heard in conversation with the King of Portugal (presumably in 1493) of an extensive mainland in the Atlantic west of Guinea. There is no good ground for identifying this with any particular land—Brazil, for example—discovered or to be discovered; it may equally well have been a hypothetical antipodean continent suggested by one or other of the academic geographers; Vincent of Beauvais, perhaps. Apparently Columbus proposed to look for this continent, among other objectives. He had always had a predilection for exploring to the south; south was the direction for 'gold and things of value'. He proposed to cross the Atlantic in the latitude of Sierra Leone as far as the meridian of Hispaniola and then, if no land had been found, turn south.

With these intentions Columbus sailed by way of Madeira and Gomera to the Cape Verde Islands and thence south-west for a week, until the Doldrum calms brought the fleet to a standstill. They drifted for eight days. Eventually they caught the northern edge of the south-east trade wind, approximately in the latitude of Sierra Leone; steered west, and made their landfall at Galeota Point, the south-eastern corner of Trinidad. Columbus made no doubt that Trinidad was an island, for he sailed through the dangerous channel which he named Boca de la Sierpe, the

Serpent's Mouth, along the south and west coasts, and out to the open sea through the Boca del Dragón; Columbian names which, with the name Trinidad itself, survive to this day. He seems to have thought initially that the Paría peninsula was also an island, and sailed along its south coast in search of an opening to the sea; but finding himself in shoal water, he turned first south, then east, then north again, returned to the Boca del Dragón, and battled his way through. He then followed the north coast of the Paría peninsula far enough to convince himself that it was part of *Tierra Firme*. During his cruise in the Gulf of Paría he noted the great volume of fresh muddy water, which flows from the western mouths of the Orinoco. The Orinoco, like many of the world's biggest rivers, is unimpressive from the sea. The muddy delta stretches flat and low for hundreds of miles, with many mouths; and Columbus—who had never seen a river bigger than the Tagus or the Guadalquivir—naturally took the mouths his people discovered for separate streams. He grasped, however, that such rivers must drain an immense expanse of land. So vast a mainland, extending so far east, obviously posed problems for the cosmographers. Columbus, with his peculiar views on the longitude of eastern Asia, might have been expected to identify the new coast with Marco Polo's Locac—Indo-China; but instead, he declared it to be the Garden of Eden, described in Genesis as the source of the four great rivers of the world. According to Isidore of Seville and many other writers, this terrestrial paradise lay at the furthest extremity of the East.

In the long and rambling letter which Columbus sent to the sovereigns,[10] he cited a list of mediaeval authorites for the location of the earthly paradise, and propounded his celebrated theory of a pear-shaped earth, with paradise perched on the protuberance at the stalk end of the pear. This letter may well have been taken by its recipients as evidence of failing mental powers. Columbus, it is true, also mentioned specific products of value in Paría: gold (which turned out to be heavily alloyed with copper) and pearls, worn by the native women. Failing, however, as he so often did, to follow up an important discovery, he missed the source of the pearls—the extensive oyster beds of Margarita Island, off the Venezuelan coast. By the time he reached Margarita, Columbus was reminded, by the deterioration of the supplies he carried, of his duties in Hispaniola. He sailed there directly from Margarita, by a remarkable feat of navigation. He arrived to find half the settlers in armed rebellion against his brother's government, and the natives harried by both factions. Columbus bought off the rebellion—having no real choice—by concessions at the expense of the natives, who were formally organised for forced labour. The decline in their numbers from that time—whether from ill-treatment, starvation or disease—was rapid and continuous.

Ferdinand and Isabella not unreasonably decided in 1499 that Columbus must be superseded as governor of Hispaniola. At the same time, they also decided—or Juan Rodríguez de Fonseca decided for them—that the new mainland coast, with its gold and its pearls, need not be considered within the terms of Columbus' original grant. It could be opened to other more practical, less imaginative explorers.

3 A New World?

'Colonus ille novi orbis repertor'; so Columbus was described in November 1493 by the cultivated humanist and court ecclesiastic, Pietro Martire d'Anghiera, who wrote the earliest detailed chronicle of New World discovery. Peter Martyr, one might suppose, had perceived, so early, the true significance of Columbus' discovery. Yet too much should not be made of a conventional phrase. Columbus' islands might be new to Europeans; they were not necessarily new to geography. Peter Martyr did not reject out of hand Columbus' own interpretation of what he had found; for some years he preserved an open mind, and inclined, like many of his contemporaries in Spain and Italy (but not in Portugal), to give Columbus the benefit of the doubt.

Columbus was directly responsible for the colossal error of identification which made the western shore of the Atlantic the eastern shore of Asia. Probably the error was essential, not only to the initial enterprise, but also to the further progress of discovery. It is unlikely, for example, that the eastern Caribbean and the Isthmus would have been so promptly explored, the existence and size of the Pacific so quickly revealed, had the explorers not been given reason to hope for a short cut to Cathay and the Spicery. Shrewd geographers to be sure, soon decided that Hispaniola was not Japan, that Cuba was a long way from China and further still from India; but for many years many of them continued to believe that the new discoveries were connected with Asia in some way. Traces of their belief lingered in language long after the geographical facts became known. For three hundred years after Columbus' landfall, the lands he discovered were known as the Indies of the Crown of Castile; their native inhabitants—those who survive—are known as Indians to this day.

The ambiguities, both of geographical interpretation and of policy, implied in the use of these names, appeared immediately on Columbus' return in 1493, and can be traced in detail in Peter Martyr's correspondence. Peter Martyr was an Italian by birth and upbringing but a Spaniard by choice, resident for most of his adult life at the Castillian court. His official duties, as chaplain to Isabella and as apostolic protonotary, kept him about the court and gave him opportunities to question returned explorers, but also left him plenty of time for writing. He was a prodigious letter-writer, supplying news and gossip to many eminent correspondents in Spain and Italy. From 1493 onwards his correspondence concentrated more and more upon the progress of western discovery. He compiled from his letters and conversations a connected history which was printed in instalments, some of them pirated. The whole series of eight 'Decades' finally appeared at Alcalá in 1530 under the title *De Orbe Novo*: the earliest connected account of the exploration of the New World, and of the intellectual reactions to discovery in informed circles in Europe. Peter Martyr never went to the

New World, but he became titular bishop of Jamaica and ended his life as a respected Councillor of the Indies.

Peter Martyr was with the court at Barcelona when Columbus arrived there in April 1493, and remarked casually to a correspondent a few weeks later that a certain Christophorus Colonus had returned from the western antipodes with samples of gold. He had doubts initially about the identification of these 'antipodes' with Asia. In October he wrote: 'A certain Colonus has sailed to the western antipodes, even to the Indian coast, as he believes. He has discovered many islands which are thought to be those of which mention is made by cosmographers, beyond the eastern ocean and adjacent to India. I do now wholly deny this, although the size of the globe seems to suggest otherwise, for there are not wanting those who think the Indian coast to be a short distance from the end of Spain.' Again in November: 'He [Columbus] says that he has discovered the isle of Ophir, but if we take into account the teaching of the cosmographers, these islands are the Antillas and other adjacent ones.' Yet Peter Martyr clearly wanted to believe Columbus, like most people in Spain who thought of the matter, and marshalled all the arguments he could find in his support. 'The Spaniards brought back with them some forty parrots, some green, others yellow, and some having vermilion collars like the parrakeets of India, as described by Pliny; and all of them have the most brilliant plumage. Their wings are green or yellow, but mixed with bluish or purple feathers, presenting a variety which enchants the eye. I have wished, most illustrious Prince, to give you these details about the parrots; and although the opinion of Columbus seems to be contradictory to the theories of the ancients concerning the size of the globe and its circumnavigation, the birds and many other objects brought thence seem to indicate that these islands do belong, be it by proximity or by their products, to India.'[1] Some West Indian plants suggested the same conclusion: 'Mastic, aloes, cotton . . . and twigs cut from the trees, which in their form resemble cinnamon, but in taste, odour and the outer bark resemble ginger.' So did the iguanas which the 'Indians' hunted for food, 'in no wise different from the crocodiles of the Nile, except in point of size.'

Yet the geographical doubts remained. Columbus' second voyage did nothing to remove them. His claim that he had found Cathay, and that Cuba was part of it, impressed nobody, even among his friends. Cuneo said that most of the subscribers to the oath at Bahía Cortés really thought that Cuba was just another big island. Juan de la Cosa the navigator, even if he believed at the time the statement he swore to, changed his mind later; his world map shows Cuba as an island. The earliest flat rejection of the Cathay-Cuba thesis came from Bernáldez, Columbus' host in 1496: 'It is my belief that in the direction in which the admiral sought for Cathay, traversing that firmament of sea and land for a further thousand two hundred leagues he would not arrive there, and so I told him.' This was the reaction of an unlearned but literate man-in-the-street, in contrast with the sophisticated, fence-sitting comment of Peter Martyr and the erudite ingenuity of the cosmographers. The author whom the good *cura* cited as his authority for contradicting Columbus was not Pliny, nor

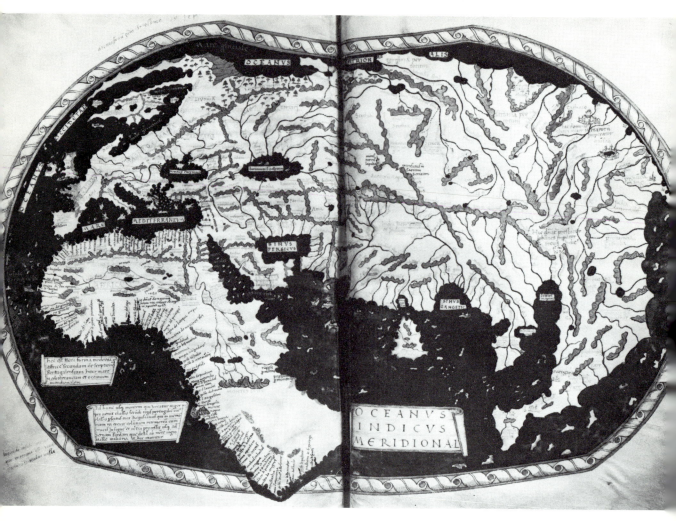

23 World map by Henricus Martellus, *c.* 1490. The world of Ptolemy modified by the discoveries of Dias. *British Museum, Add. MS 15.760, ff. 689–690.*

Ptolemy, but Sir John Mandeville.

The discoveries of 1498 were more promising, but also more puzzling. There seemed to be no doubt about the continental character of the land Columbus had found, but much doubt about its identity. The point at which Columbus first sighted its coast was well to the east of the easternmost meridian of Hispaniola; and according to his Indian informants it stretched far to the west and south. These first reports were amply confirmed by other explorers over the next three years. To fit such a continent into a Ptolemaic or quasi-Ptolemaic pattern of the world, required considerable ingenuity; but some late fifteenth-century world maps, influenced by Ptolemy, suggested a way of doing it. These maps— the Martellus map of about 1490 is a good example—show four great peninsulas jutting from the south coast of Asia. The westernmost is the Arabian peninsula, the second a truncated peninsular India, the third the Golden Chersonese, the Malay peninsula. East of the Golden Chersonese is a great arm of the sea, the Great Gulf; and east of that, almost enclosing it, the fourth peninsula. This is much larger than any of the others. It extends from 'Mangi' on the southern confines of China, across the equator, south to the Tropic of Capricorn. On the Tropic, much attenuated, it bends west, to end in the cape of Catigara, so-called from a city of that name on the south-east shore of the Great Gulf. This imaginative construction—with a remote origin, possibly, in garbled reports of Indo-China—appearing on the most up-to-date maps, offered an easy explanation of Columbus' discovery: the new-found mainland was the great peninsula of Asia. Follow the coast north-west and north, and one could eventually reach Cathay. Follow it south-east, south, and west, and one could eventually reach the cape of Catigara and cross the Great Gulf to the Golden Chersonese and India.

That Columbus himself shared this opinion may be doubted. The muddled exuberance of his writings, and his refusal ever to admit himself mistaken, make it difficult to be sure what, in his more sober moments, he really believed; but if one ignores his more extravagant flights, and if one compares his reported observations on the third voyage with his actual proceedings on the fourth, a reasonably consistent pattern emerges. The land he had found, Columbus believed, was of vast extent; it was wholly new to cosmography, *otro mundo*, 'another world'; it belonged to Asia, to the extent that it was adjacent, 'at the end of the East', and that its products—gold, pearls and spices—appeared to be Asiatic; but it was insular, separated from the Asia long known to cosmographers by a channel of the sea. The existence of this channel had to be inferred, since Columbus—so he believed—had on his second voyage coasted part of southern China and reached almost to the Golden Chersonese; and since Marco Polo, long before, had sailed by a direct sea passage from China to India. Columbus' fourth voyage in 1502 was a logical application of these ideas, an attempt to follow in Marco Polo's track.

It was characteristic of Columbus to stumble, from time to time, on sound and original ideas, but then to support them with reasoning so bizarre as to render them implausible. His own interpretation of his 1498 discovery convinced no one; yet it was an important step towards the truth. Columbus had indeed found 'another world', or at least another continent. He never took the further step of perceiving that it had nothing to do with Asia, was nowhere near Asia; that would have been too bold, too radical a notion for so conservative a man, besides being a most unwelcome suggestion. Asia was a long-sought goal, not only for Columbus, but for most explorers of that generation and the next. It was intellectually difficult, moreover, for anyone who revered the Scriptures, the Fathers and the Ancients, to accept the idea of a major land mass, especially an inhabited land mass, totally unknown to any of them. The suggestion was made, and made in print, early in the sixteenth century, and soon attracted a following; but the more orthodox idea, that South America was the great peninsula of Asia, continued to confuse explorers and interpreters of discovery for many years. The concept of a New World did not come fully into its own until a generation after Columbus first sighted París.

The extent and nature of the new mainland could be established only by further exploration. The Spanish rulers had received little or no return on their investment in Columbus' expeditions and were reluctant to incur further expense; but reports of gold and pearls suggested that other adventurers might be willing to make voyages at their own expense, paying the Crown a royalty on any precious objects they obtained. The 1492 agreement with Columbus stood in the way; but Columbus could hardly be allowed to pre-empt a whole continent. The stretch of mainland coast he had actually explored was relatively short, and even there he had been confined to his ship by illness and had not gone ashore to 'take possession' formally. The disorders in Hispaniola, therefore, were made the occasion not only for removing Columbus from his government there, but also for limiting his prerogatives elsewhere.

In 1499 the Crown, or Fonseca on the Crown's behalf, began to grant licences for voyages to the main coast, with only a perfunctory stipulation that the licensees should avoid places actually discovered by Columbus. Voyages under these instruments were made by Vicente Yáñez Pinzón; by Diego de Lepe; by Peralonso Niño in partnership with Cristóbal Guerra (one of three brothers, bakers of ships' biscuit in Triana); by Alonso de Ojeda with Juan de la Cosa (who was a man of means as well as a navigator) and with Amerigo Vespucci, the Medici representative at Seville. Some of these men were Columbus' former officers exploiting their knowledge of the Caribbean, others entrepreneurs who contributed financial backing or commercial experience.

All the 1499 voyages combined trade with exploration, and one at least was highly profitable. The Guerra-Niño expedition coasted from París to Cape Codera, bartering, and collected about a hundredweight of pearls. Pinzón was less fortunate. He reached the coast a long way east of París, at a cape which he called Cape Consolation, and which is usually identified as Cape São Roque. He coasted west, entered an area where the sea water was fresh and muddy, and discovered the mouth of a huge river, presumably one of the principal mouths of the Amazon. Further west, he noted the eastern mouths of the Orinoco, which he called Río Dulce; entered the Gulf of París; and cut a cargo of brazil-wood on the París peninsula before clearing for home. He encountered bad weather in the Windward Islands and lost two of his four ships. Despite the brazil-wood which the surviving ships brought back, the voyage was a commercial failure. So was Lepe's, in the same general area. The Ojeda-Vespucci expedition made land on the coast of what became French Guiana. At some point—either on the coast or in the open Atlantic, we do not know—Ojeda and Vespucci parted company. Ojeda and la Cosa took the main body north-west, through the Gulf of París and thence on west, presumably in search of pearls. Vespucci with two caravels headed south-east on an extended coastal reconnaissance, with the intention—as he wrote after his return—'to see whether I could sail round a point of land which Ptolemy calls the Cape of Catigara, which is near the Great Gulf'. Vespucci found the delta of the Amazon, wrote the first recognisable description of it, and like Yáñez Pinzón, noted the great volume of fresh muddy water pouring through its mouths and far out to sea. He spent some days in boats exploring one of the principal mouths, but in the wall of jungle lining the river could find no place to land. Then on south-east along the coast of what is now

Brazil, to Cape São Roque or a little beyond, at the extremity of the 'bulge'. Here, like many other ships in later years, the caravels were driven back by a combination of the south-east trade wind and the northern branch of the equatorial current; they put about and returned north-west up the coast.

24 Chart of the coast of Brazil from Trinidad to Cape São Roque (approximately), probably drawn in Naples, *c.* 1508. East is at the top. *British Museum, Egerton MS 2803, fo 9r.*

The second leg of Vespucci's voyage was in Ojeda's wake. His description of the Guiana coast, with its mud and its mangroves, is recognisably accurate. He visited two of the islands off the Venezuela coast: Curaçao—where he was so impressed by the stature of the people that the place was known for years as Isla de los Gigantes—and Aruba. The name Venezuela, Little Venice, was first given to Aruba, because the inhabitants, according to Vespucci, built their houses on piles over the water. Finally the caravels coasted the inhospitable shores of the Gulf of Venezuela and the Goajira peninsula. Somewhere off the Venezuelan coast, probably near Cape Codera, Vespucci overtook Ojeda. The combined fleet sailed west as far as Cape de la Vela, and thence made for Hispaniola. The pace of exploration had been too fast to allow much time for trading or even looting; but in western Hispaniola Ojeda stole a cargo of brazil-wood which had been cut and was awaiting shipment. After a much-needed refit and provisioning, Vespucci's caravels made a rapid slaving cruise in the Bahamas, to complete their lading, and returned to Cadiz early in 1500. Between them, Ojeda, Vespucci and Yáñez Pinzón had established that a continuous coast stretched from Cape São Roque to Cape de la Vela.

Vespucci summarised the achievements of his voyage in a letter which he wrote from Seville to his patron Lorenzo di Pier Francesco de' Medici, in 1500.

We were absent thirteen months on this voyage, exposing ourselves to terrible dangers, and discovering a very large part of Asia, and a great many islands, most of them inhabited. According to the calculations I have several times made with the compass, we sailed about five thousand leagues. ... We passed the equinoctial line six and a half degrees to the south, and afterwards turned to the north, which we penetrated so far that the north star was at an elevation of thirty-five degrees and a half above our horizon. To the west we sailed eighty-four degrees distant from the meridian of ... Cadiz. We discovered immense regions, saw a vast number of people, all naked, and speaking various languages. On the land we saw many wild animals, various kinds of birds, and an infinite number of trees, all aromatic. We brought home pearls in their growing state, and gold in the grain. We brought two stones, one of emerald colour, the other of amethyst, which was very hard, at least half a span long and three fingers thick. The sovereigns esteem them most highly, and have preserved them among their jewels. ... We brought many other stones which appeared beautiful to us, but of all these we did not bring a large quantity, as we were continually busy in our navigation, and did not stay long in any one place.

When we arrived in Cadiz, we sold many slaves, finding two hundred remaining to us ... thirty-two having died at sea. After deducting the cost of transport, we made only about five hundred ducats, which, having to be divided into fifty-five parts, made the share of each very small. However, we are satisfied with having saved our lives, and thank God that during the whole voyage, out of fifty-seven Christian men, which was our number, only two had died, having been killed by the Indians. ...

They are fitting out three ships for me here, for a new voyage of discovery, and I think they will be ready by the middle of September. May it please Our Lord to give me health and a good voyage, as I hope again to bring great news and to discover the island of Taprobana, which is between the Indian Ocean and the Sea of Ganges.[2]

The modest success of the Ojeda-Vespucci venture, and the striking success of the Guerra-Niño, ensured the continuance of Caribbean voyages. The Guerra brothers had no interest in further discovery and no further need of Peralonso Niño, but they made four more voyages to the Pearl Coast, which for some years was tacitly recognised as their preserve. When the stock of pearls available for barter became exhausted the Guerras turned to pillage and slaving further west. Cristóbal Guerra was killed by Indians in one of these forays in 1504. The direct exploitation of the Cubagua pearl beds, by Spaniards employing slaves brought in from the Bahamas, was a later development and owed nothing to the Guerras. Ojeda also returned to the Venezuela coast in 1501 on a trading and raiding expedition which discovered nothing and which failed to cover expenses. Ojeda was a man of great physical courage and endurance, a superficially attractive leader, but irresponsible and incompetent as an organiser. Having quarrelled violently with his companions, he ended his voyage in prison at Santo Domingo.

Neither of Ojeda's former partners accompanied him on this 1501 voyage. Vespucci, in his search for Taprobana, transferred his attention from the Caribbean to the Atlantic. La Cosa returned to the Caribbean early in 1501, this time in partnership with Rodrigo de Bastidas. The partners refrained from raiding and slaving, and successfully combined exploration and trade. Las Casas, then newly arrived in Hispaniola, met them there on their way back to Spain in 1502, and wrote, years after, a brief account of their voyage.[3]

This was the first European expedition west of Cape de la Vela. Las Casas never visited this coast himself, and his summary account, though it tells us roughly where the explorers went, says nothing about what they saw. The Goajira peninsula is rocky semi-desert; but from near the cliffs west of modern Riohacha they caught their first glimpse of snow-covered mountains, the isolated massif of the Sierra Nevada de Santa Marta, which rises steeply to 18,000 feet. It is curious that this magnificent range received so little notice, so far as we know, from the early explorers.[4] It is usually visible from the northern coast, except in the few weeks of thick weather in November and December. Sixteenth-century Spaniards were little impressed by mountains, except as obstacles to be surmounted. More to the point, west of Riohacha the explorers entered a region rich in gold. Hundreds of streams in what is now Colombia contained alluvial gold, and many of the peoples of the region were skilled in working it. The gold artefacts of the northern Andes were far removed from the crude nuggets or cold-hammered plates of the island Arawaks. Gold-workers understood many techniques: beating, forging, soldering, and moulding by lost-wax and other methods. They produced a profusion of articles for use, ornament or ceremony, including burial and grave goods. Most of the gold-working peoples lived inland in the mountain valleys and highland savannahs and were not discovered by Spaniards until the 1530s; but some had territories reaching to the coast: Tairona, on the north slope of the Sierra Nevada, Sinú in the country drained by the San Jorge, Nechí and Sinú rivers. These rivers rise in the highlands of what is now Antiquia. The first two flow into the Cauca, but the Sinú empties directly into the Gulf of Morosquillo, and the great swamp through which it flows in its lower reaches is known as the Ciénaga de Oro to this day. Coastal peoples who had no direct access to gold could easily obtain gold trinkets by trade. Such a people were the Cuna, on the shores of the Gulf of Urabá, who to this day wear the beautifully fashioned gold ear-rings and nose-rings which attracted the attention of Spanish explorers. None of these people, apparently, thought of gold as precious in itself. They valued gold artefacts for their workmanship, their beauty or their use, but for many purposes they preferred an alloy of gold with copper, known locally as *guanín*, which was harder than pure gold yet had a lower melting point. Even fish hooks were made of it. To the Spaniards, naturally, this practice of adulterating gold with copper was both incomprehensible and infuriating; but finding people who possessed gold of any kind in significant quantity, and were willing to part with it in trade, was a powerful incitement to explore, perhaps to settle.

La Cosa and Bastidas, in their leisurely voyage along the coast, probably encountered Tairona, Sinú and Cuna, was well as various Carib groups. Their success in bartering for gold was enough in itself to attract attention to the Gulf of Urabá and the Isthmus coast. The voyage had another important consequence: the navigators, la Cosa and Andrés de Morales, made sketch charts as they went along. In Santo Domingo, while Bastidas' people, with their treasure, were awaiting passage back to Spain, there arrived no less a personage than the old admiral, Columbus himself, on his fourth and last trans-Atlantic voyage. In calling there, Columbus had disregarded his instructions, and Ovando refused him permission to land; but according to las Casas there was some communication between the navigators of the two expeditions. Presumably charts were passed round and discussed. As a result, when Columbus eventually found himself off the coast which Bastidas and la Cosa had explored, his navigators were able to recognise where they were.

Columbus' fourth voyage was a final throw, a last desperate attempt to re-establish privileges and reputation. The Sovereigns once again provided him with ships, more perhaps from desire to be rid of importunity than from any great confidence in Columbus' proposals. Once again the purposes of the voyage were left vague, but they certainly had to do with Asia. Columbus, at his own request, was furnished with a letter to 'the Captain of the King of Portugal'—presumably Vasco da Gama, who had just left on his second voyage to India –'since by good fortune you may meet at sea'. Almost certainly Columbus hoped to find a sea passage between the Asian coast of which he thought Cuba was a part and the 'otro mundo' which he had discovered in 1498. He sailed from Seville in April 1502, departed from Hispaniola—after surviving a hurricane which destroyed most of a fleet leaving for Spain—in July, and finally left the known for the unknown somewhere in the Jardines de la Reina off southern Cuba.

Columbus' fourth voyage is much better recorded than the Bastidas venture which preceded it. Columbus' own account—the so-called *Lettera rarissima*, addressed to the Sovereigns—is too incoherent to be of much use as a narrative of the voyage, but there are several other eye-witness

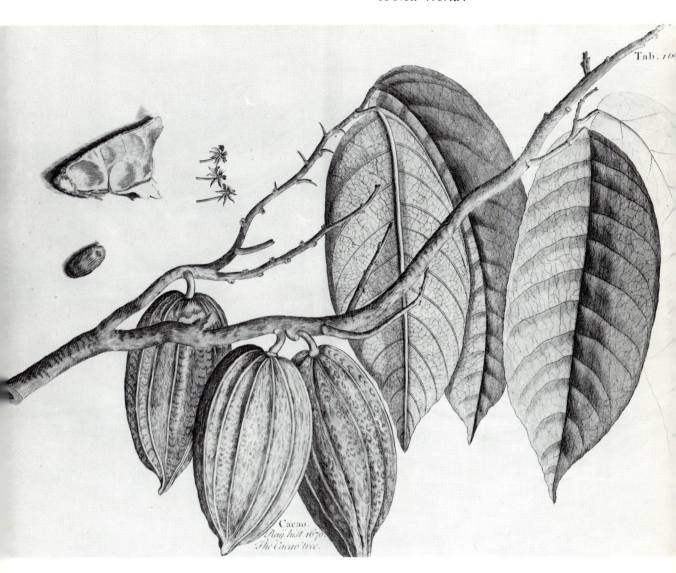

Tab. 10

Cacao.
Ray, hist. 1670.
The Cacao tree.

accounts, all of which have been printed. The terse narrative of the notary Diego de Porras is reliable, though markedly hostile to Columbus and critical of his command. The brave and resourceful Diego Méndez, a loyal personal adherent of Columbus, many years later included in his will a vivid account of the later part of the voyage, especially of his own exploits. These included a voyage from Jamaica to Hispaniola in a native canoe in order to get help, after the last two surviving ships of the expedition had been beached in St Ann's Bay. Columbus was in the habit of describing his fourth voyage as *el alto viaje*, the high enterprise, and to some, at least, of his companions also it seemed, in retrospect, the great adventure of their lives; certainly to Diego Méndez, who directed that a canoe be carved on his tombstone; and certainly to Columbus' son Fernando, who accompanied his father on the voyage. He was only thirteen when the expedition sailed, fifteen when he got back to Spain. He

25 Leaves and bean-pods of cacao; engraving from Hans Sloane, *A Voyage to the Islands Madera, Barbados, Nieves, S. Christopher and Jamaica* (2 vols.; London, 1707), vol. II, fig. 2.

85

was to spend the rest of his life in bookish comfort at Seville; but many years later, in the late 1530s, he included in his *Life* of his father the most extensive of all the accounts of the voyage, all its details recalled with the freshness of boyhood memory.

The first unknown land they sighted was Guanaja, one of the Bay Islands in the Gulf of Honduras; and there they were encouraged by a sea encounter which Fernando describes:

. . . there arrived at that time a canoe as long as a galley and eight feet wide, made of a single tree trunk like other Indian canoes; it was freighted with merchandise from the western regions around New Spain. [This was written in the 1530s.] Amidships it had a palm-leaf awning like that which the Venetian gondolas carry; this gave complete protection against the rain and waves. Under this awning were the children and women and all the baggage and merchandise. There were twenty-five paddlers on board, but they offered no resistance when our boats drew up to them. Our men brought the canoe alongside the flagship, where the Admiral gave thanks to God for revealing to him in a single moment, without any toil or danger to our people, all the products of that country. He took on board the costliest and handsomest things of that cargo: cotton mantles and sleeveless shirts embroidered and painted in different designs and colours; breechclouts of the same design and cloth as the shawls worn by the women in the canoe, being like the shawls worn by the Moorish women of Granada; long wooden swords with a groove on each side where the edge should be, in which were fastened with cord and pitch flint knives that cut like steel [this was the earliest European encounter with the *maquauhuitl*, the obsidian-edged battle-axe]; hatchets resembling the stone hatchets used by the other Indians, but made of good copper; and hawks' bells of copper, and crucibles to melt it. For provisions they had such roots and grains as the Indians of Española eat, also a wine made of maize which tasted like English beer. They had as well many of the almonds which the Indians of New Spain use as currency [cacao beans]. . . . The Admiral . . . ordered his people to treat them well, and gave them some trading truck in exchange for what our men had taken from them. He detained only one, an ancient named Yumbé, who seemed to be the wisest among them and of greatest authority, to inform him about the secrets of that land and to persuade the others to talk to the Christians; he served us very willingly and loyally all the time we were in the region where his speech was understood.[5]

The people in the canoe—whether Maya, or of a coastal tribe influenced by the Maya—represented a culture far more sophisticated than any the Spaniards had so far encountered. Fresh evidence of this appeared on the mainland coast which, with high hills a short distance inland, is visible from Guanaja. When Columbus landed to take formal 'possession', he found people dressed in dyed and woven cotton fabrics, who brought presents—so Fernando recalled—of 'fowls of the country which are better than ours, geese, dried fish, and red and white beans like frijoles'. The geese were Muscovy ducks, the fowls domestic turkeys; this was the first European encounter with either.

The Honduras coast runs east and west; which direction should Columbus take? The canoe had come from the west; evidence, though Columbus did not recognise it, of an extensive native commerce. The wind blowing steadily from the east with frequent drenching rain, also pressed the ships in that direction. Columbus' plan, however, required him to make southing. Believing Cuba to be a mainland peninsula, he probably suspected that if he turned west he would find himself sailing along a continuous coast, which would eventually lead him back to Cuba. There might also be danger in getting too far to leeward and possibly becoming embayed. So the fleet beat painfully to the east, taking a month to make less than two hundred miles, until they could round the cape which Columbus named Gracias a Dios. From there they sailed rapidly down the Moskito Coast of what is now Nicaragua—flat, covered in dense bush, harbourless and almost uninhabited—and the Costa Rica coast, where mountains, cultivations and settled villages reappeared. At Cariay (now Puerto Limón), an agreeable *pueblo* set among fruit trees, Columbus was told of nearby sources of gold. In his own words, 'I . . . learned of the gold mines of the province of Ciamba, which I was seeking . . . they named me many places on the coast where the said gold and mines were to be found. The last was Veragua, which was about 25 leagues away.' Ciamba was Marco Polo's name for part of Indo-China; an indication of where Columbus thought he was.

Veragua was to be for many years the Spanish name for the northern coast of the Isthmus. It was an exposed, wave-beaten coast. Ranges of cliffs alternated with river mouths, blocked at times by bars thrown up by the waves, then re-opened by freshets. These rivers rose in the cloud-capped, rain-drenched *serranía* of the interior. In the sand and silt they brought down in their short and turbulent courses was some alluvial gold. The rivers gave access, by canoe, to settled villages. The natives, initially civil, were much more formidable than the island Arawaks. They soon became resentful and hostile, attempts to establish a settlement failed, men were killed in shore-side fighting when they tried to take in water or buy or steal food. Most of this coast today is unbroken rain forest, but Fernando described much of it as inhabited and cultivated. The best harbours, and the densest settled population, were on the eastern portion of the coast, east of the area where alluvial gold occurred. Columbus entered and named several important harbours: Puertobelo, so called—according to Fernando—'because it is very large, beautiful and populous, and has about it much cultivated land'; Bastimentos (later Nombre de Dios) 'because all the surroundings and small islands were full of maize fields'; Retrete, 'a secluded place in which there was no room for more than five or six ships'. Retrete (today usually identified with the little harbour known as Puerto de los Escribanos) was the end of Columbus' discovery; it had probably been the end, a year or two earlier, of Bastidas'. 'On some sailing charts of some of the mariners', wrote Porras, 'this land joined that which Ojeda and Bastidas had discovered.'

The Bastidas-la Cosa voyage and Columbus' fourth voyage, taken together, had important geographical consequences. The reports they produced of wrought gold, abundant food and relatively sophisticated people ensured that the Darién-Veragua coast would receive concentrated Spanish attention for the next decade or so. The area would be explored and exploited, however, for its own sake, not because it lay on the route to India and the Golden Chersonese. Well-informed Spaniards now knew that there was no outlet from the southern Caribbean; instead, a continuous coast all the way from the Gulf of Honduras to the 'bulge' of what is now Brazil. Columbus' newly discovered land, whatever its attractions, was not Indo-China.

While the southern Caribbean coasts were thus being revealed for Spain, still more extensive discoveries were being made in the Portuguese Atlantic. Two expeditions—one Spanish and one Portuguese, each unknown to the other—sighted the east coast of what is now Brazil in 1500. The Spanish expedition, of two caravels, though originally planned for four, was mounted by Alonso Vélez de Mendoza in partnership with the Guerra brothers, Luis Guerra commanding one of the ships.[6] Very little is known of this voyage, and that little comes from statements made years later by witnesses in the *Pleitos de Colón*. It was a trading voyage, probably intended for the Caribbean, via the Cape Verde Islands; but through navigational error or stress of weather the actual landfall was apparently made south of Cape São Roque. The caravels then coasted south instead of north-west, to a point south of Cape São Agostinho, whence they returned to Spain with a cargo of Indian slaves. One of the witnesses specifically stated that the Indians on this stretch of the coast had never seen Europeans before. No attempt was made to follow up the discovery.

The Portuguese expedition was a more serious affair, and somewhat better recorded. After Vasco da Gama's triumphant return from India, a second and larger India fleet was despatched from Lisbon under the command of Pedro Alvares Cabral. Like da Gama, Cabral made his first stop at the Cape Verde Islands; but on departing thence in the usual southerly light airs of summer, he sailed directly south-west, instead of making (as da Gama had done) an initial board to the south-east. He thus made his passage through the central Atlantic further west than da Gama had done, and though he missed Capes São Roque and São Agostinho, he sighted the Brazilian coast further south: the commanding height of Monte Pascoal, in about 17°S, some two hundred miles south of modern Bahía. So far as we know, the sighting was unexpected. Cabral may have been instructed to look for a coast whose existence was already known or suspected, but there is no record of such instruction; on the other hand, there is no record of storm or navigational error forcing him off his course. The south-east trade wind—which, within a general pattern, is capable of wide variation—could have put him over to the Brazil coast, and probably that is what happened.

Cabral spent only a few days at anchor, in the harbour he called Porto Seguro, before sailing on to the Cape and India. Geographical features of the coast were noted only in very general terms. Contacts with the local Tupinambá Indians, though amiable, were necessarily superficial. The only detailed account which survives—the letter of Pedro Vaz de Caminha addressed to the King—describes nakedness; body paint; feather ornaments; the use of long bows; trumpets made of wood, hollow bones or conch shells; log rafts; stilt-built houses. It makes no mention of tattooing, of cannibalism, or of the use of tobacco, characteristics which greatly impressed later visitors; most notably Hans Staden, Hessian gunner in Portuguese service. Staden published in 1557 a naïve account of

Arrop

26 Staden in captivity; from
Hans Staden, *Warhaftig
Historia . . . in Neuen
Welt* (Marburg, 1557), fo
g iv, v.

his adventures among the Tupinambá, by whom he had been captured
while out hunting, and almost (so he said) cooked and eaten.

According to Vaz de Caminha, there was some discussion—very
characteristic of the conduct of voyages at the time—about how the new
discovery should be reported:

. . . he [Cabral] asked all of us whether it seemed well to us to send news of the
finding of this land to Your Highness by the supply ship, so that you might order it
to be better reconnoitred, and learn more about it than we could now learn,
because we were now going on our way. And among the many speeches which
were made regarding the matter, it was said by all or by the greater number, that
it would be very well to do so; and to this they agreed. And as soon as the decision
was made, he asked further whether it would be well to take here by force two of
these men to send to Your Highness and to leave here in their place two convicts.
In this matter they agreed that it was not necessary to take men by force, since it
was the general custom that those taken away by force to another place said that
everything about which they were asked was there; and that these two convicts
whom we should leave would give far better information about the land than
would be given by those carried away by us, because they are people whom no
one understands, nor would they learn [Portuguese] quickly enough to be able to
tell it as well as those others when Your Highness sends here, and that
consequently we should not attempt to take anyone away from here by force, but

in order to tame and pacify them the more, we should simply leave here the two convicts when we departed. And thus it was determined . . .,[7]

very sensibly, except from the point of view of the weeping convicts; though even they might have been more cheerful had they known what lay in store for the fleet.

Gaspar de Lemos got back to Lisbon with his supply ship some time in the summer of 1500, and no doubt the news he carried soon spread; for though the navigational details would be kept confidential, there would be no way of preventing sailors' gossip about the general fact of discovery. The news caused no great stir; Cabral had found nothing of commercial valuc, not even brazil-wood, and though macaws and naked savages were always interesting, the attention of the informed public was on the passage to India and the prospect of pepper. The King, however, naturally wanted a more thorough examination of the new coast. 'Santa Cruz'—that is Monte Pascoal and its surroundings—was assumed, correctly, to be on the Portuguese side of the Tordesillas line, but there was some doubt as to whether it was part of a mainland coast or merely a large island. If mainland, was it continuous with the coast which the Spaniards had been exploring further north? The Portuguese government was aware, no

27 Staden protests against cannibal practices; from Hans Staden, *Warhaftig Histora . . . in Neuen Welt* (Marburg, 1557), fo k iv, r.

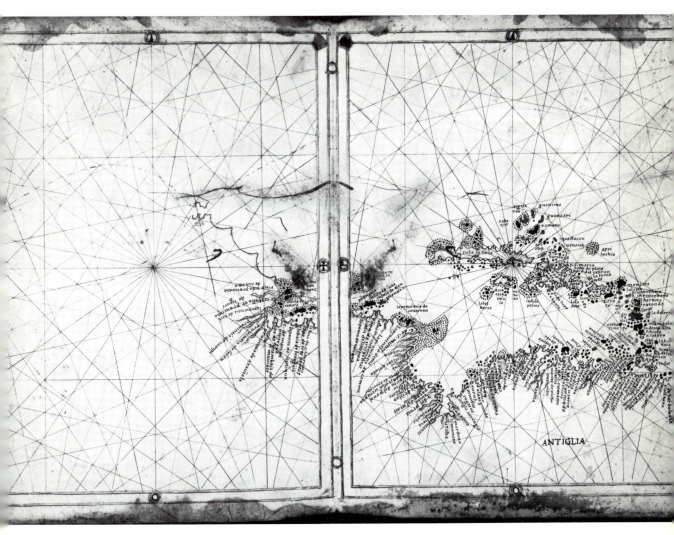

doubt, of these Spanish activities, but cannot have been informed in detail of their extent: Ojeda, Vespucci and Pinzón had only fairly recently returned to Spain and Vélez de Mendoza was still at sea. It was likely but not, in Lisbon, as yet certain, that they had all trespassed across the line. If they had, and if the coast they had explored proved to be continuous with Cabral's Santa Cruz, the Portuguese would be in a very strong position: a strict interpretation of the Treaty of Tordesillas might reserve the whole south Atlantic to Portugal. The King, therefore, took the advice of Cabral's council and in the spring of 1501 sent off three caravels to investigate. The recruitment of officers for this expedition may have presented problems, since most of the leading navigators of the kingdom had gone off to India with Cabral. The command was entrusted, almost certainly, to Gonsalvo Coelho, about whom little else is known; but with him sailed the Florentine Amerigo Vespucci.

Vespucci, it will be remembered, had expected to sail in another Spanish expedition; possibly in that of Vélez de Mendoza.[8] Vélez,

28 Chart of the West Indian Islands and the Main coast, *c.* 1508. This chart incorporates the results of several early sixteenth-century expeditions into the Gulf of Urabá and shows a continuous coast in that region. *British Museum, Egerton MS 2803, fos 7 v. and 8 r.*

however, was forbidden, shortly before he sailed, to ship foreigners in his company. This ruled out Vespucci—it may, indeed, have been aimed at him; perhaps his habit of sending detailed accounts of voyages to Florentine notables had aroused suspicion. It is also probable, however, that at this juncture Vespucci actually preferred Portuguese employment. In 1499 he had been defeated in his search for Catigara and Taprobana by the wind and current off the extremity of the Brazilian 'bulge'. If he wished to pursue the search he would have to cross the Atlantic in a more southerly latitude and begin his coasting from a point south of Cape São Roque. In common with others—Pinzón, for one—who had ventured along the north coast of Brazil, Vespucci probably guessed that the 'bulge' extended to the east of the Tordesillas line, and that Spanish ships could not, without risk of international trouble, make the voyage he proposed. As a Florentine business man and as a professional explorer and consultant, so to speak, on cosmographical matters, Vespucci had no particular obligations or loyalty to Spain. Portuguese backing would do equally well; and the Portuguese government had strong reasons to seek his services. He came to them recommended by his compatriots in Lisbon as a clever man with a rising reputation as an expert on discovery, and as having up-to-date knowledge of Spanish voyages. So Vespucci—in what precise capacity we do not know—sailed with Coelho. He wrote the only surviving eye-witness account of the voyage; to judge from this account, it was very much Vespucci's voyage.

The fleet wooded and watered on the way out near Cape Verde in West Africa, where by one of the extraordinary coincidences of ocean discovery they fell in with two of Cabral's ships returning from India. The letter[9] which Vespucci sent to his Medici patron describing this encounter is an important piece of evidence on Cabral's proceedings. Vespucci had some difficulty in reconciling what Cabral's people told him about Indian Ocean geography with what he had read in the authorities; he inclined to think that the Portuguese navigators, through ignorance of Ptolemy and lack of astronomical skill, had mistaken the positions of many of the places they had visited.

From Cape Verde the ships made a slow and difficult passage across the Atlantic, and sighted land somewhere in the neighbourhood of Cape São Agostinho or a little further south. They then coasted south or south-south-west; how far, can only be guessed. Vespucci's own account, on first sight, seems clear enough:

[From Cape Verde] we sailed south-south-west, close-hauled, until after sixty-four days we came to a new land which, for many reasons to be given later, we judged to be mainland. We coasted this land for about eight hundred leagues, always sailing south-west a quarter west. . . . We sailed so far in those seas that we entered the Torrid Zone and passed south of the Equator and the Tropic of Capricorn, until the South Pole was fifty degrees above the horizon, and this was my latitude from the Equator. We navigated four months and twenty-seven days without seeing the Arctic Pole nor the Great nor Little Bear; but I discovered opposite them in those southern skies many beautiful constellations invisible in the north, noted their wonderful movements and their splendour and measured their positions. . . . I collected the most remarkable things that happened to me in this voyage in a little work which I hope to complete when I have leisure, and which will ensure me some fame after my death. I was going to send you a summary, but at present the King has it; when he returns it, I will pass it along to you. . . . The land is very pleasant, heavily forested with tall trees which never lose their leaves; all year they give off an aromatic fragrance, and bear great quantities of fruits, many of them good to eat and wholesome. In the open country there are grasses, many flowers, and sweet and wholesome roots. Sometimes . . . I fancied myself near the earthly Paradise.[10]

50°S and 800 leagues from the first landfall would be roughly the position of San Julián, the bleak Patagonian inlet where Magellan and his people, eighteen years later, were to spend a mutinous and miserable winter. Magellan's chroniclers referred to San Julián by name with a casual familiarity which suggested that someone had been there before: Vespucci? Yet Vespucci's descriptions are all of tropical regions; none suggests Patagonia. Distances travelled at sea could not then be measured; they could only be estimated. Columbus habitually over-estimated his distance made good; Vespucci may have done the same. Latitude could be measured, roughly; but 50°S might be a copyist's error; the only Portuguese chronicler to mention this voyage, Galvão, made it 35°S. We cannot even be sure whether the expedition reached the Río de la Plata. The left bank of the Plata estuary is in 35°S. Vespucci, if he reached that latitude, could not have overlooked a river which drives muddy water eighty miles out to sea; unless, indeed, he passed far out of sight of land. The Canerio or Caverio map, of 1502–04, shows a Río Giordan in approximately the right latitude. So far as we know, this information could only have come from the Vespucci expedition; but the evidence of maps, unsupported by documents is rarely conclusive, and no surviving writing of Vespucci's mentions the river.

Possibly answers to some of these questions could have been found in the 'little work' which Vespucci lent to the King, and which is lost. In any event, the precise point reached by the expedition is not a matter of great importance. The main, the certain result of Vespucci's voyages and reports was the knowledge of a huge land-mass with a continuous coastline running thousands of miles from the western end of the Caribbean to a point, still to be found, far south of the Tropic of Capricorn. Whether Vespucci himself in 1502 believed this land-mass to be a separate continent is uncertain. In the letter just quoted he spoke, to be sure, of a 'new country'; but many other explorers, including Columbus, used such phrases without attaching much importance to them. Vespucci may still have supposed that in coasting South America he was coasting the great peninsula of Asia. There is good reason to think that Magellan, who followed Vespucci's exploration to its conclusion, also set out with some such belief.

The tenacity with which intelligent people in Europe clung to the notion of Asia-in-the-west, in the face of mounting evidence against it, is one of the most remarkable aspects of the discovery story. John Cabot claimed that Newfoundland was an outlying province of Cathay, and many believed him. The Portuguese, though extremely sceptical of Columbus' claims and prompt to label the West Indies *As Antilhas*, were

29 Oval planisphere by Francesco Rosselli, *c.* 1508. Signed. Folio 2 of a two-folio book. Copper engraving on vellum. North America is shown as a peninsula of north-east Asia. *National Maritime Museum, Greenwich.*

themselves credulous where their own people were involved. So well-informed a person as Valentim Fernandes—historian of travel and friend of explorers—in his *Livro de Marco Paulo* of 1502 could congratulate King Manoel because his subjects, the brothers Corte-Real, had reached the north-eastern extremity of the Great Khan's dominions. The Contarini-Rosselli map of 1506—the earliest printed map to show the New World—admirably illustrates this concept. Asia-in-the-west was not simply a personal idiosyncracy of Columbus', nor a peculiarly Spanish delusion. Spaniards, however, had the strongest possible motives for accepting it. All the more curious, therefore, that the earliest printed book to dismiss the whole idea as nonsense was written and published not in Portugal nor in Italy, but in Spain.

Rodrigo de Santaella's *Libro del famoso Marco Paulo veneciano*, first

published in Seville in 1503, resembles Fernandes' book in general plan, and borrows from it. It contains Spanish texts of Marco Polo's *Travels* and of Poggio Bracciolini's *India recognita*, with Poggio's account of Conti's travels; and a *Cosmographia breve introductoria* by Santaella himself. The book was influential in its own day as the first Spanish translation of Marco Polo was likely to be; it went through several editions, and later received gratuitous publicity from the attack which Fernando Colón made upon it in his *Life* of his father. Fernando accused Santaella of ridiculing Columbus' geographical theories and pointed out, correctly, that those theories, though eventually disproved, had been reasonable when Columbus propounded them. What Santaella actually wrote about the West Indies, as Englished by John Frampton, is as follows:

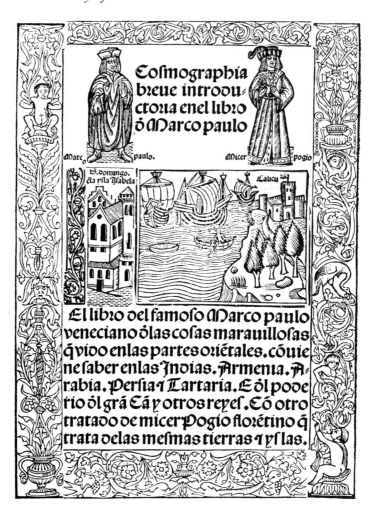

30 Title page, Rodrigo Fernandez de Santaella, *El libro del famoso Marco Paulo Veneciano . . .* (Seville, 1503).

And whereas the vulgar people, and men for the most part, do thinke that *Antilla*, or those Islandes lately found out by commandemente of the Catholike King Don Fernando, and Lady Isabell Queene, be in the *Indias*, they be deceyved therein, to call it by the name of the *Indias*. And for bycause that in *Spaniola*, or newe Spayne, they do find gold, some doe not let to say it is *Tharsis*, and *Ophir*, and *Sethin*, from whence in the time of Salomon, they brought gold to *Hierusalem*. And thus augmenting erroures upon erroures, let not to saye that the name of oure Lorde God should be pronounced to people that have not hearde of it, and in places and Countreys very farre off, and aparted, which is sayd to be understanded by the places mentioned in the holy Scripture, and the Catholike doctors, and that this secret God hath kept hidden all this time, and by finding out these Islands did reveale it. I seeing how they are deceyved in their vayne inventions, and great simplicities, for zeale and good will of the truth, and to kill this canker, that it creepe no more nor ingender greater erroures, answering to the said muttering talkers, according as to every of them doth require.

And later, after describing the subdivisions of India in the East:

Besides these three *Indias*, whiche lye towards the rising of the Sunne, there can not be found neyther Author nor Man that hathe travelled the firme land,

nayther the Seas adioyning thereunto, that can say, there is anye other Province
or Islande named *India*, sauing that if anye woulde give to understand, that going
towarde the West, he wente towardes the East, and that although he came unto
the terrenall Paradise, and that these Islands shoulde lye in the greate Weast
Ocean Seas, it appeareth, playnely, for that those that sayle thither, steame [i.e.,
stem] their Shippe towards the Occident, and his direct wind which he sayleth
withall, is out of the Orient or the East. So it appeareth, that they sayle not unto
the *India*, but that they flye and depart from the *India*. And thus it appeareth that
he would say, that the firste name that euer it hadde, or was sette, naming it
Antillya, seeming that by the corruption of the vulgar, naming it *Ante India*, as to
say against *India*, euen as Antechrist is contrary or against Christ, or Antenorth
against the north. And thus it appeareth, that it can not be named *India*, but to
understande it as an antephrase, clean contrary.[11]

These are the views of literal-minded common sense; we need not
suspect, as Rinaldo Caddeo and others have done, that Santaella was a flat-
earth fundamentalist. It is curious, however, that an educated man,
interested in travel literature, living and writing in (of all places) Seville in
the early sixteenth century, should have been so ill-informed, or so
indifferent, about the actual progress of trans-Atlantic exploration.
Santaella wrote only of islands in the Ocean; he ignores completely the
mainland discoveries of 1498 onwards. His book helped to discredit Asia-
in-the-west, but it made no positive suggestion about the identity of the
land-mass of Santa Cruz.

The lack was supplied, to some extent, by two printed pamphlets
which appeared shortly after Santaella's book, both bearing Vespucci's
name: *Mundus Novus*, and *Lettera di Amerigo Vespucci delle isole
nuovamente trovate in quattri suoi viaggi*. *Mundus Novus* is in form a letter
from Vespucci to Lorenzo di Pier Francesco de' Medici, describing
Vespucci's 1501 voyage. Its first dated edition was printed at Augsburg in
1504. This pamphlet has been the subject of heated controversy for years.
Many, perhaps most, Vespucci scholars now think it was written not by
Vespucci himself but by an enterprising publisher or editor who, having
access to genuine correspondence of Vespucci's, expanded and altered it
to suit a wide reading public. It is longer than the manuscript letter about
the same voyage, which has already been quoted; it dwells more heavily
upon such topics as nakedness, sexual promiscuity and cannibalism; and
it is much more confident, much less cautious about the separate identity
of the new-found mainland.

On a former occasion I wrote to you at some length concerning my return from
those new regions which we found and explored with the fleet, at the cost, and by
the command of this Most Serene King of Portugal. And these we may rightly call
a new world, because our ancestors had no knowledge of them, and it will be a
matter wholly new to those who hear about them. For this transcends the view
held by our ancients, inasmuch as most of them hold that there is no continent to
the south beyond the equator, but only the sea which they named the Atlantic;
and if some of them did aver that a continent there was, they denied with abundant
argument that it was habitable land. But that this their opinion is false and utterly
opposed to the truth, this my last voyage has made manifest; for in those
southern parts I have found a continent more densely peopled and abounding in
animals than our Europe or Asia or Africa.[12]

Das sind die new gefundÿ menschÿ oÿ volcker Ju form vñ gestalt Als sie hie stend durch dÿ Cristenlichen Künig von Portugall gar wunderbarlich erfunden.

ff Albericus vespucius Laurencio petri Francisci vil grues mit glücklicher furt/am vierzehenden tag des monats may thausent fünffhundert ein jar schieden wir von Ulissipo nach gebot des obgenanten künigs mit drey schyffen zuersuche Newe lande vñ Jnsell gegenmittentyon sind also hin vñ her geschiffe mit grosser vñ gestürmigkeyt des meers bisz auff den sibenÿtag des monats Augusto des obgemelet jars gesunde ein grosses Lande vñ Reygiorÿ so grosse volcker scharen vñ leüt/dÿ die nyemant erzelt mocht als man lißt in Apocalipsis Ein volck sich ich ein milde gütig vñ hantweysig vñ gend all nackent beyde weyß vñ man vnnd ganz on bedeckung irer leibe an alle enden/wie sie auß mutter leib kume/also gend sie biß sie sterbÿ dan sie sind groß vñ leib vierschrötig wol geschickt guter schön er glidm ist vñ geferbe der etlicher inaÿ gegÿ roten/das ich mein dise so ÿ vinÿ ich kume das sie nacket gond vñ von der süne beschein also geferbt werdÿ sie haben weit vñ groß harlockÿ vñ schwarz sie sind in irem gang vñ mit spil treibÿ thetig vñ gering vñ gütiger vñ schöner anding die sie doch inÿ selbs beschÿ machÿ vñ vngestalt dan sie poÿ in iren selbs löcher in die packÿ die mundleffzÿ vñ die nasen vñ die orenÿ Du siht auch mit gedenckÿ dz solche löcher klein sein oÿ sie sein alein baß lanÿ ich etlich geseheÿ hab die in irem antlyg alein sibel löcher/der yegliches so groß was das ein kriech oÿ haselnus wol in eins gon möcht/sie vßstossen inÿ selbs solche löcher mit plaÿ steinen/Cristallÿ/Marmor vñ Alabaster gar hübsch vñ schön/vnnd mit weyssen geben vñ mit andern dingÿ/so mit künste gemachet werdÿ/nach irer gewonheit/Und so du also sihest ein so fremd vngewont dingÿ du würdest mit on grosse verwundÿ sein Dan ich hab dick wargenumÿ vñ vber scheyt dz sibÿ solch er steÿt am gewicht habÿ.rvj.lot vber/vñ on das sie in dÿ orenÿ die inÿ lochÿren durch stochÿ sind sie noch ander stein tragÿ die in ringen bange vñ die weiß vñ sitÿ ist allein der manÿ dan die frawen zerstechÿ inen selbs ir antlyg mit also mit löcherung dan allein ir orenÿ Ein ander sitÿ vñ weiß ist auch vñd vñ bey inÿ ge meÿg abweysig vñ wider alle menschliche glaubung Das ir frawÿ der eben gelüstig vñ gayl sind vñ in imanÿ machen das inen ire menndliche glit geschwellen in solcher vbÿ dick das sie vngestalt vñ schmelich erscheinÿ vñ das thon sie mit etliche giffstige thierlaÿ vñ vÿ solcher stich geschicht dz inen vil ir gemecht vÿderbÿ die in von mangels wegÿ der argenen saule/vnd belassen on gemecht. Sie habÿ kein thuech noch deckÿ/weder leines noch baumwolles/dan sie es nit bedürffen vñ haben kein aygÿ gut. Sunder alle ding seind vnder inen gemein/sie habÿ auch kein künig oder regierer. Sunder ein yeder ist im selbs ein herr/soul welcher nimÿ sie so vil sie wöllÿ/vñ der sun mit der mutter/vñ der bruder mit d schwester/vñ der erst mit d ersten/vñ der begegner mit der begegnerin Vnd verinigen sich als dick als sie wöllÿ/scheidÿ sie die es wöll halte ganz kein ordenung/darumb haben sie auch keinen tempel vñ haltÿ kein gesaÿ/vñ sund nit abgöttÿ. Was soll ich mer sagÿ sie lebÿ nach der natur dz sie wol Epicurÿ Rauchfüller genant werdÿ miltgÿ dan Senica. Bey inen send kein kaufleÿt noch kauffmans guet Die scharÿ des volcks haben auch krieg vñ an kunst vñ ordnung/ire eltern mit irÿ rethÿ vñ geboten vnder biegen die junge zuthon was sie wöllÿ vñ rüstÿ sich zustreytÿ Jn solchem sie einanÿ grausamlich zu tod schlahen/vñ welche sie also in krieg vñ streit fahÿ die füren sie hin domit sie die bey lebÿ lassÿ/vñ sie behaltÿ das sie dar vÿ mestig en vñ sie essen dan einer den andern der do obligt vñ vnder andern fleysch ist yr mensché fleysch ein speyß/Es hat der vater sein sun vñ sein weyß gessen ich hab eink gesehen von dem sagÿ man er het wol vber drey hundert mensche leyben gessen/ich bin gewesen an einem end da hab ich gesehen gesalzen mensché fleysch vñ auff gehenktÿ zu derrÿ/wie bey vns das schwaink fleysch/ich wil in von solcher pöser weyß zulassen/vñ sie thieten vns dar von zulassen/vñ ob die frawÿ schön ploß vñ nacket gond/so habÿ sie doch ir leib hübsch vñ vol sauber vñ send nit so schentlich als einer gedenckÿ möchÿ wan sie gnug leibig seind/so wirt ir scham hindert gesehen vns nagÿ weinÿ das vnder inen keine gesehen ward die do lampÿ prust het oder die gebinder heten dz der selben bauch anderst gestalt werde dan dz junckfraÿ vil die nie gebindet/vñ on andern glidern vñ enden des leybs der gleiche vmerckt ward/das ich alles von erzamkeit weyter vngerdÿ laÿ/dan wan sie sich möchten su den Cristen mensche gefliegen als sie auf der massen gayl sind/so legtÿ sie alle scham vÿ in zu volbringÿ böse werck. Sie lebÿ hundert vñ fünfftzig jar vñ werdÿ selt krank/vñ ob sie etwan krank werdÿ so heylen sie sich selber mit wurtzlen vñ mit gutÿ kreütern vñ vil ich von in dÿsem vil erkennen mochÿ/so ist in irem land nymÿ kein kürtzelÿ oder annicherley siechtagÿ die ein bösen lufft kumendÿ vñ sie nit mit freud on einander tode schlÿbeg so möchÿ sie so lange zeÿt lebÿ/ich mein das in dem land alle zeÿt die mittegige wind wehen vñ voralt allermeÿt dañ wir nem etwan der inen also ist wie wir der michenig wind genant Aquilo sie send kunstreych mit Jischsahen dañ auch das selbig meer Jysch reych ist vñ wen ich wolt alle vñ yegliche ding erzellen die in dÿsen land send/von selrame so gÿn vñ thieren von edlen gestein das wer ein ding gar zulang vñ on maÿ/vñ ob glanß das vnser Plinius dem th.ausent theyl nit zu kumen sey. Des volckes der seekuste vñ der andern vogl vñ thieren in disen land mit so mancherley vnderscheyd der ante lyÿ von frawen das der volkumneste leüt maller kunst beriembt meister Polliclerus die aÿ zemalen erügt müsten vñ on zweyffel halt ich oÿ das in dÿsch paradeis auf Ferdrich das dz nie verr von dÿser lanÿschafft sey. So ist kürlich vñ offenbar dz wir den vierde theyl der welt durch schyffÿ habÿ. Vnd dÿse Episteln auß Italischer sprach in Latein vñ verÿ gedeüscht. Der hübsch tholmetsch gezogÿ hat. Vmb das alle latener vñ deüsche vÿstanden wie vil grosser vñ wunderlicher dingÿ von tag zu tag gesunden vñ offenbar werden. Disditÿ missive in deüsch gezogÿ Auß dem exemplar das von Pariÿ kam ym Mayen monat. Nach Cristi gebürt Fünffzehenhundert vñ fünff Jare.

Whether or not Vespucci wrote this, and whether or not it accurately represents his views, there can be no doubt of the importance of *Mundus Novus* as a factor in the formation of geographical opinion. It was sold and read all over Europe. It was included in the collection of narratives of voyages published by Francanzano de Montalboddo at Vicenza in 1507, under the title *Paesi novamente retrovati*. This was a very influential book, the first great source book of the discoveries. It went through six Italian editions, six French and two German. Through *Mundus Novus* in its many appearances, the notion gained ground, in some quarters at least, that a new world had been found and that Amerigo Vespucci—though not indeed its discoverer—was the first to identify and describe it.

The *Lettera* is a longer and more ambitious work, in form a letter addressed to the Florentine *Gonfaloniere*, Piero Soderini; a personage for whom neither the Medici nor Vespucci had any friendly feelings. It purports to have been written in 1504, but was first printed in 1505 or 1506, in Italy. The language of the earliest edition is a Hispanic-Italian jargon not easily attributable to Vespucci, who habitually wrote either in good Castillian or in the Italian of Tuscany. Whoever wrote it, however, knew his business as a narrator. It is eminently readable, full of detailed, sometimes bizarre descriptions and of dramatic incidents. One example, from the coast of Brazil:

Almost every day many people came to the beach, but never would they converse with us. And the seventh day we landed, and found that they had brought their women with them. And when we jumped ashore, the men of the land sent many of their women to talk with us. And seeing that they did not take courage, we decided to send them one of our men who was a very agile and energetic youth; and we, to give them greater confidence, entered the boats. And he went among the women, and when he approached them they made a great circle around him; and touching him and gazing at him, they displayed their wonder. Meanwhile we saw a woman approaching from the hill, and she carried a big club in her hand. And when she reached the place where our Christian stood, she came up behind him, and raising her club, struck him such a hard blow that she stretched him out dead on the ground. In a moment the other women seized him by the feet and dragged him toward the hill; and the men sprang toward the beach and began to shoot at us with their bows. Our people, sitting in the boats which were made fast by anchors to the shore, were so demoralised by the shower of arrows that nobody thought of laying hand on his weapons. We fired four Lombard shots, but without hitting anyone. When the reports were heard, they all fled toward the hill, where the women were already cutting up the Christian. And by a great fire which they had built they were roasting him before our eyes, displaying the pieces to us, and eating them.[13]

This passage in the *Lettera* made a considerable impression on its readers, and several contemporary maps carry vignettes illustrating the incident.

The *Lettera* attributes four voyages to Vespucci, suggesting a deliberate analogy with Columbus. Of the four voyage-narratives, the second and third, respectively, are of the 1499 and 1501 voyages, well attested from other sources. The first, though geographically vague, appears to describe a voyage in 1497–98 along the coasts of Venezuela, Central America, Yucatán and the Gulf of Mexico. No surviving documentary evidence

31 'Das sind die new gefunden menschen . . .' Broadside introducing an early edition of Vespucci, *Mundus Novus* (Leipzig, ?Stöckel, 1505). Probably unique. *Herzog August Bibliothek Wolfenbüttel.*

32 Four woodcuts illustrating an early German edition of Vespucci's *Lettera*, or *Quatuor Navigationes* (Strassburg, durch Joh. Grüninger, 1509). Pictures such as these, of the savage habits of some of the natives of the New World, enjoyed a great vogue, especially in Germany.

corroborates this account. The Canerio map of 1502–04, it is true, marks a large island-studded bay which appears to represent the Gulf of Mexico; but there is no ground for associating this discovery with Vespucci or for ascribing to it a date at least five years earlier than that of the map. The story in the *Lettera* may equally well be merely a confused account of the last leg of the 1499 voyage, from Cape de la Vela to Hispaniola and the Bahamas. The fourth narrative concerns a Portuguese voyage in 1503–04 with six ships into the south Atlantic with an ultimate destination, 'Melaccha', in the Indian Ocean. An expedition did in fact leave Lisbon in 1503 with six ships, under Fernão de Noronha, for the south Atlantic. It was a disaster; four ships were lost and the only discovery was the island which bears the commander's name. No firm record connects Vespucci with this adventure. Possibly the compiler of the *Lettera* made up his story by combining garbled reports of the Noronha voyage with opinions expressed by Vespucci, on an earlier occasion, about Catigara and Taprobana. The 'first' and 'fourth' voyages described in the *Lettera* are unsupported by any other documentary evidence. Probably they are apocryphal.

This is not to say, of course, that they were impossible. We have no certain knowledge of Vespucci's activities, or even of his whereabouts, at the times in question. He might have been at sea. In that period of busy exploration, voyages were made—perhaps many voyages—of which no record now remains. Unofficial explorers did not necessarily keep written records. Commanders of official expeditions did, but their reports—especially in Portugal—were treated as confidential. They had a very

33 *Left* Western hemisphere, from the Cantino world map or chart, 1502. The Portuguese interpretation of the New World discoveries, splendidly displayed. The large land mass N.E. of the Antilles may represent Florida, or possibly Yucatán, though no record survives of the discovery of either at so early a date. Cantino was not the maker of the map, but the agent who procured it for the Duke of Ferrara. *Modena, Biblioteca Estense.*

101

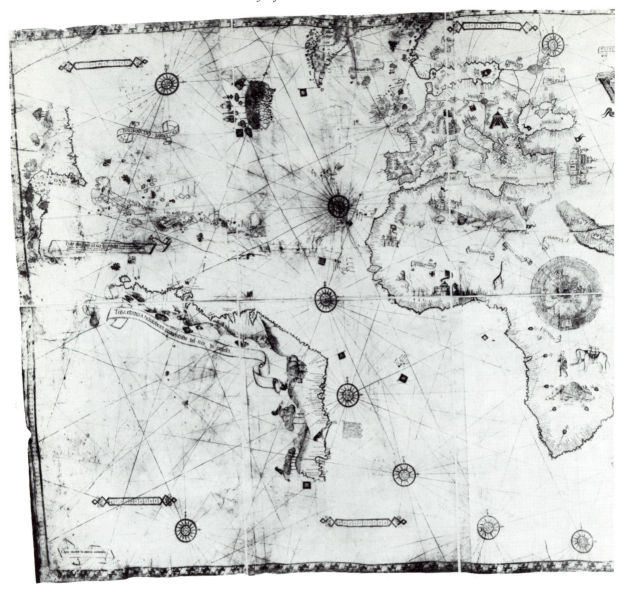

34 World chart by Nicoló
Caneri or Caveri, *c.*
1502–1506, signed 'Opus
Nicolay de Canerio [or
Caverio] Jannensis.' The
earliest surviving world
chart to indicate (apparently)
Florida, Yucatán and the
Gulf of Mexico, at a date
considerably earlier than the
earliest recorded discoveries;
and the earliest to give the
New World a (doubtless
imaginary) western coast
line. *MS Bibliothèque
Nationale, Paris.*

limited circulation, and often, apparently, were not even copied. The originals, each unique, have run the gauntlet through the centuries of fire, earthquake, natural decay and the negligence of archivists. Many have disappeared, and the voyages they recorded can only be traced, uncertainly, in private correspondence such as Vespucci's, or in popular accounts such as the pamphlets attributed to him, or in contemporary maps. Maps of Vespucci's time show many coastal features which bear a recognisable resemblance to reality, but whose discovery cannot be associated with particular voyages. The Gulf of Mexico in the Canerio map is one example; Florida (if it is Florida) in Cantino and Canerio, another.

Old maps are slippery evidence. They are difficult to date precisely, and even when they bear a date—as the la Cosa world map does, for example—the possibility of subsequent emendations and additions cannot easily be

Previous page
35a The New World, in the world map by Martin Waldseemüller, *Universalis Cosmographia secundum Ptolomei Traditionem et Americi Vespucci aliorum lustrationes* (St Dié, 1507). The name America appears on the southern New World continent. Only one print of this woodcut has survived. *The private library of Prince von Waldburg zu Wolfegg-Waldsee, Wolfegg Castle, Würtemburg.*

Above
35b Inset from the world map by Martin Waldseemüller, with a portrait of Vespucci.

excluded. Nevertheless, the best maps of Vespucci's day fall into a plausible and fairly consistent pattern. They show the New World growing more solid and detailed year by year; the possibility of a sea-way between its land-masses correspondingly more limited. Tentatively at first, but with increasing confidence, they show it separated alike from Europe, Africa and Asia. In the Cantino map, the east coast of Asia borders on open water, but the New World land-masses (except Newfoundland) have no west coast; they are bounded only by the edge of the map. The map, however, covers only 257° of longitude, leaving 103° unaccounted for. Obviously the compiler thought that some of this unknown area was open sea. The Canerio map, a little later, is more explicit: it gives the central land-mass a western coastline, and a long isthmus or peninsula stretching towards the southern land-mass *Terra Crucis*. Between the central land-mass and an insular Newfoundland-Labrador, is open sea. None of the land-masses has any connection with Asia.

The tentative suggestions of the Cantino and Canerio maps, and many reports of voyages, were combined in a splendid synthesis: the huge twelve-sheet woodcut 'Map of the World according to the traditions of

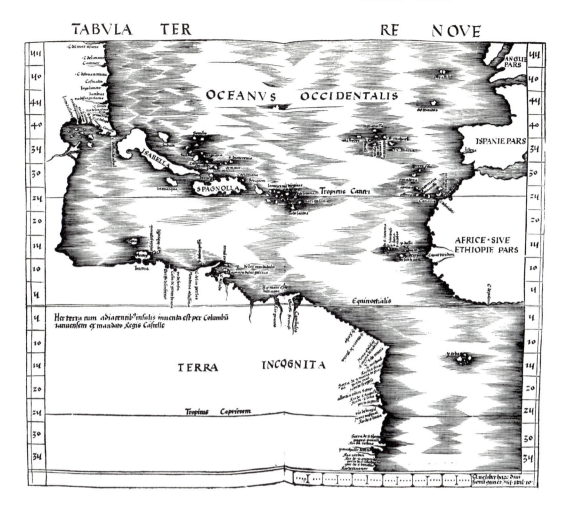

TABVLA TER   RE NOVE

OCEANVS OCCIDENTALIS

ISPANIE PARS

AFRICE·SIVE
ETHIOPIE PARS

Tropicus Cancri

Equinoctialis

Hec terra cum adiacentib⁹ insulis inuenta est per Columbū
ianuensem ex mandato Regis Castelle

TERRA   INCOGNITA

Tropicus Capricorni

Ptolemy and the voyages of Americus Vespucius', produced by Martin
Waldseemüller at Saint-Dié in Lorraine in 1507. Only one copy of this map
now survives; but according to its maker, a thousand copies of the
original edition were printed, and its influence on geographical thought
was great and lasting. It shows the New World as northern and southern
continents, of which the southern is much the larger. In the main map the
two continents are separated by a narrow strait, but in an accompanying
inset they are connected by a continuous isthmus. East of the continent or
continents is the Atlantic; to the west is another great sea, with the island
'Zipangri' in the middle, and its western shore marked 'Chatay'. The west
coast of the New World is conventional, *terra ultra incognita*; but though
its configuration is vague, it is undoubtedly a coastline. There is open-
water access between the two oceans at both ends of the continent, north-
about and south-about, as well as through the problematical strait.

Waldseemüller not only made the new world unequivocally a separate
continent; he also attached a name to it. The great map was accompanied,
in the same year, by a slim treatise, *Cosmographiae Introductio*, which in
popularity (though not in merit) rivalled *Paesi novamente retrovati*. Like

36 'Tabula Terre Nove': the
New World by Martin
Waldseemüller, from
Ptolemy, *Geographia*
(Strasburg, 1513). The name
America has been discarded.

37 The only surviving print of the Contarini-Rosselli world map, 1506: the earliest printed map to show any part of the New World. North America is shown as a promontory of Asia. *British Museum, c.2.cc 4.*

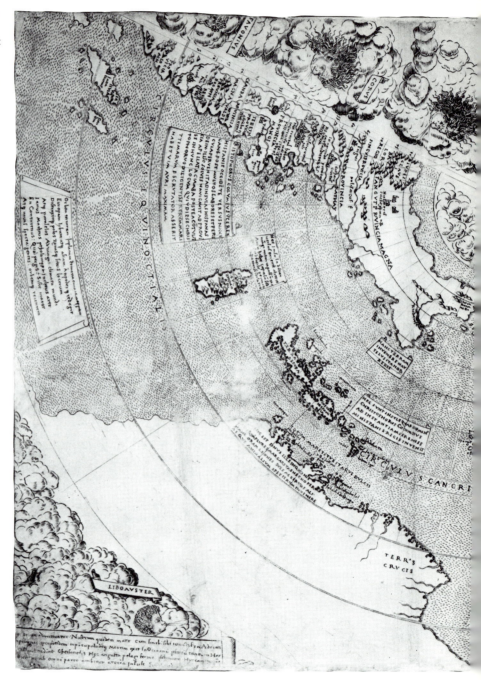

the *Paesi*, it made much of Vespucci's exploits, but it went further; it included a Latin version of the *Lettera*, under the title *Quattuor navigationes*; and it contained, in a preface, the statement that 'another or fourth part [of the world] has been discovered by Americus Vespucius; in virtue of which I believe it very just that it should be named Amerige, after its discoverer Americus, a man of sagacious mind; or let it be named America, since both Europe and Asia bear the names of feminine form'. The southern part of the New World in the map, accordingly, is labelled America. The name caught the popular fancy in northern Europe, though not initially in southern. It was confined to South America for half a century or so, until Mercator extended its use to include North America also. Waldseemüller himself soon discarded it; in the map of the world which he drew for the Strasburg Ptolemy in 1513, south America is labelled simply *Terra incognita*; but the name America stuck.

Waldseemüller's 1507 map, and even more its New World inset, provided so neat a solution, and in general conception came so near to the truth, that it might have been expected, with its derivatives, to dominate geographical thought thereafter. Rival geographical theories, however, were still very much alive. The printed Contarini-Rosselli map has open water north and west of the Antilles; to the south, the continent *Terra Crucis*; to the west, out in the ocean, Cipangu; far to the north, a great

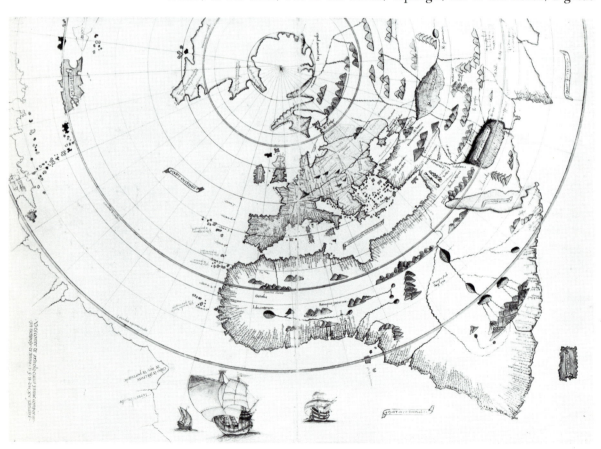

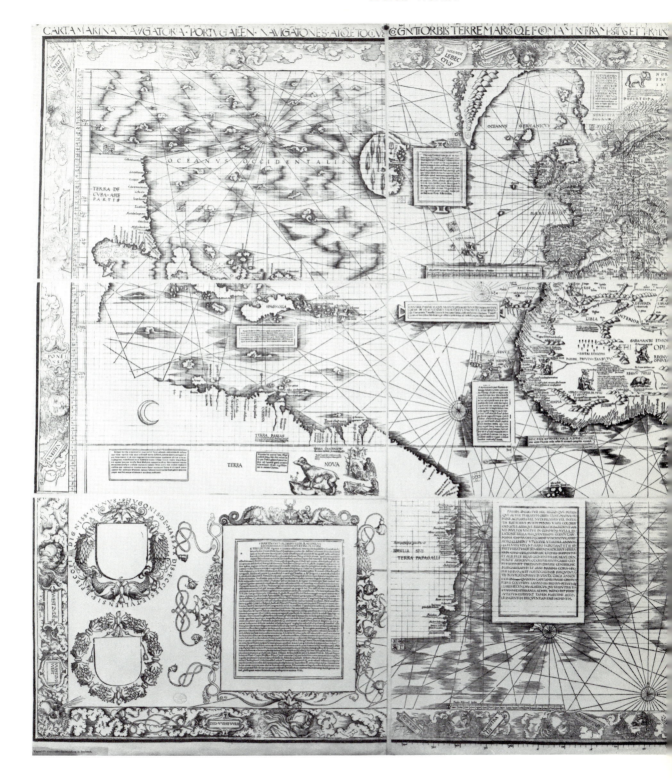

peninsula of Asia, *Tanguti provincia magna*, stretches across the map from west to east, terminating in 'land found by the King of Portugal's ships', presumably compounded of Greenland, Labrador and Newfoundland. The Ruysch map of 1508 and the manuscript Maggiolo map of 1511 follow, with variants, roughly the same tradition. These 'open-water' maps were already out of date when they were drawn, but they were not without influence.

A more serious obstacle to the general acceptance of Waldseemüller's ideas was the persistence of Ptolemy. It was still difficult for academic cosmographers trained in the tradition of deference to the Ancients and familiar with a world-picture based on Ptolemy, to accept a totally new, totally separate continent. They accepted, perforce, the existence of continental land north, west and south of the Antilles, as more and more such land was revealed by exploration; but they felt—rather than reasoned—that this land could, and must, somehow be fitted into the Ptolemaic pattern; must at some point be connected with the continent of Asia. Waldseemüller himself was not immune to doubts, and in 1516 he retreated significantly from his 1507 position. His *Carta marina* of that year shows the central American land-mass abutting on the western edge of the map and labelled *Terra de Cuba Asiae partis*.

The America of 1507, then, was an inspired guess. It was deservedly influential—Waldseemüller had many imitators—but it was not immediately and universally accepted. It contradicted a great body of accepted theory, and was inadequately supported by eye-witness knowledge. No European explorer had actually seen the west coast of continental America. No one could be *sure* whether or not America was separated from Asia; whether or not another ocean lay to the west; whether or not the other ocean, if it existed, was accessible to Atlantic ships.

4 Gold or Spices?

The mainland discoveries of the early sixteenth century presented a dilemma to those Spaniards interested in oversea adventure, and of course to the Spanish Crown. Should they concentrate energy and resources on exploring and exploiting the New World they had found? or should they pursue, in competition with Portugal, the search for the Spicery? The New World offered the prospect of territorial dominion, free land and docile (though inefficient) labour. It was known to produce commodities of value, gold and pearls particularly, though so far in relatively small amounts. It seemed to promise quick, if modest, profit to traders and settlers, and indirectly to the Crown. Its exploitation would cost the Crown—in theory at least—very little. Settlers and prospectors, traders and slavers, would finance their own undertakings.

The search for the Spicery, on the other hand, would involve a long period of arduous and possibly fruitless reconnaissance. The Crown would have to provide ships, pay the crews, find the navigators. Competent navigators were few in Spain, and there were risks in employing foreigners. Those who might, a little anachronistically, be called professional explorers, were much sought after; they could make their own terms, and their loyalties, like those of any *condottiere*, were mercenary and temporary. They might sell to other governments the information they gathered for Spain. If reconnaissance were successful, moreover, if a Spanish route to the Spicery were found, it could be exploited only by well-armed, disciplined fleets, equipped with the paraphernalia of ceremony, provided with money for purchases, or loaded with saleable goods. This, certainly, had been the Portuguese experience. Heavy capital investment would be needed. Risk capital was hard to come by in Spain, and foreign investors might be expected to prefer the demonstrated success of Portuguese voyages to the doubtful prospect of Spanish. But if the difficulties were great, so were the possible rewards. Few doubted that access to the spice and silk markets of the East would prove more valuable, in the long run, than all the pearls and gold trinkets of Urabá.

The obvious ideal was to combine the two projects. Since Spanish expeditions to eastern Asia were confined by treaty to a western route, their hope of success depended on more thorough exploration of the New World which lay across that route. The planners needed to know the geographical relation of the New World to Asia, the relation of its various land-masses, one to another, and the position of navigable passages between them or round them. In theory, American exploration could still subserve the search for Asia. In the course of discovery, settlements would be established in the New World, which might serve as ports of call, as sources of provisions and even perhaps of bullion, for expeditions to the Spicery. In practice, however, Asian and American voyages could

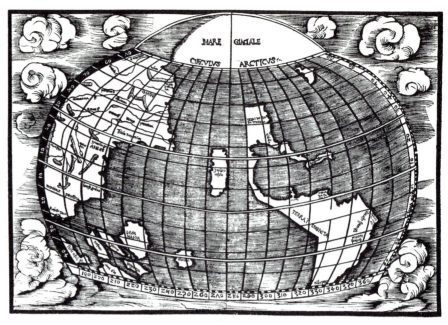

40 The western hemisphere, from the world map by Johannes de Stobnicza, in *Introductio in Ptholomei Cosmographia* (Cracow, 1512). Clearly derived from the Waldseemüller map of 1507.

not easily be combined. Not only did they require different types of men, different kinds of equipment and skill, and offer different rewards; they would probably have to use different routes. By 1505 it seemed clear to informed Spaniards that those parts of the New World which were most worth settling, which yielded the most profitable trade or plunder—the Pearl Coast, Urabá, Veragua—were navigationally dead ends. The sea passages to Asia, if they existed, were either further north, north of Hispaniola and Cuba, or much further south, south of the southernmost point Vespucci had reached in 1501.

In the event, there were to be two separate series of developments. The Spanish Crown, in the first quarter of the sixteenth century, sent out a number of expeditions to search for a sea passage via the New World to eastern Asia. Some of these were commanded or navigated by foreigners specially commissioned for the task. The cost was borne chiefly by the Crown, though some private investment was permitted. The New World itself, on the other hand, was explored and settled chiefly by private enterprise. The Crown sometimes invested in projects of discovery and settlement, and often provided arms and supplies; but in general its role was that of a regulating agency. It issued (or withheld) licences for voyages. It granted contracts to individual applicants, for *entradas* of discovery, conquest or settlement in particular areas, in order to avoid duplication of effort and possible conflict. It supported leaders whom it approved, by delegating to them authority to govern settlers and natives; authority without which, in those bands of fortune-hunting individualists, a governor's orders could be challenged by any malcontent or sea-lawyer in his company. There was no delegation of sovereignty. The West Indies were the Indies of the Crown of Castile, and the Crown shared in the proceeds of every *entrada*.

In 1503 the *Casa de la Contratación de las Indias* was established at

Seville, to execute Crown policy concerning the Indies and to collect the accruing revenue. One of the first duties of its officials, prescribed in their inaugural instructions,[1] was to arrange for a follow-up expedition to 'the land discovered by Bastidas'. Bastidas himself—now resident in Hispaniola, a rich man, becoming richer by shrewd investment—made an unsuccessful bid. The contract went to Juan de la Cosa, and included permission—though not an instruction—to found a settlement in Urabá. Shortly after, the Queen issued a decree authorising the capture, and sale as slaves, of 'a certain people called cannibals' who—so the Queen was informed—regularly made war on peaceful traders and missionaries.[2] The decree—though obviously, in practice, capable of application to the whole Main—specified certain places as open for punitive slave-catching, including the Bay of Cartagena, where the city of that name was later to be built. So far as is known, the only expedition which had ever visited that stretch of coast was the Bastidas-Cosa venture, which had been received peacefully. The Queen had been misinformed, probably deliberately; and it seems likely—though there is no evidence of it—that la Cosa was the source of the misinformation. He certainly took full advantage of the decree. His voyage of 1504–06 was devoted to slaving and looting, all the way from Cumaná to Cartagena and from Cartagena to Urabá.

In Urabá la Cosa lost his ships, probably through ship-worm damage, and spent more than a year in a temporary fortified camp, living off the country, while his company built boats in which to try to sail via Jamaica to Hispaniola. Less than fifty tattered survivors, out of more than two hundred, eventually reached there, and so returned to Spain. They had made no new discoveries. 'Their purpose', said Oviedo, 'was not so much to serve God and King as to rob. . . . This assault and robbery Juan de la Cosa was later to pay for'. The people of the whole coast, initially, on the whole, amiable to strangers, became fiercely hostile, using their poisoned arrows which they normally employed in hunting, to resist the dreaded invaders. A secondary consequence of the expedition was anthropological confusion. The ethnic and cultural pattern of the coastal population was complex; Carib groups lived alongside peoples of more sophisticated culture, speaking Chibcha languages. The Spaniards, by using the terms 'Carib', 'cannibal' and 'hostile native' interchangeably, made it impossible, from that day to this, to be sure who all these people were. On the other hand, la Cosa and his surviving companions, though they had lost their ships and their slaves, clung grimly to their loot in pearls and gold ornaments; from that aspect the expedition was a success and was sure to be repeated.

While la Cosa was away, the Crown's advisers turned their attention to the problem of Asia. In 1505 a conference convened at Toro, to discuss, among other matters, prospects in the Indies, recommended that Vespucci and Vicente Yáñez Pinzón should take out a fleet to search for the Spice Islands; but the disturbed political situation following Isabella's death prevented its despatch.[3] In 1508, with King Ferdinand again in effective control, a second conference met at Burgos. The expert consultants on this occasion were Vespucci (who at the same meeting was nominated pilot-major in the *Casa*); la Cosa; Pinzón; and Juan Díaz de Solís of Lepe, who, though of Spanish descent, was Portuguese born and had seen service in Portuguese ships in eastern waters. The *junta* of Burgos produced comprehensive plans for pursuing maritime discovery and territorial conquest and settlement, simultaneously. A royally commissioned fleet was to search for the strait; authorised private adventurers were to settle the most promising parts of *Tierra Firme*. Pinzón and Solís were sent off in the same year, with instructions not to linger in the West Indies but to 'follow the navigation for the discovery of that channel or open sea which you are sent to discover'.[4] No report of this voyage has survived; our knowledge of it comes from las Casas, from Fernando Colón, and from witnesses in the *pleitos de Colón*. The explorers called at Santo Domingo, then made for Guanaja island, where Columbus had been in 1502, and thence steered 'north and west'. Las Casas says that they coasted much of Yucatán, but does not say how far they went. One witness in the *pleitos* said that they reached $23\frac{1}{2}°$N. A mention of high mountains, by another witness, suggests that they entered the Gulf of Mexico. So far as is known, they made no landings. The unbroken wall of mountains behind the Vera Cruz coast would have put an end to any hope of a strait in that region.

The settlement plan took longer to implement, since the contractors, when selected, had to raise their own capital, the Crown providing only arms. Two contracts were issued in 1508, for the areas then roughly known, respectively, as Urabá and Veragua. Urabá included the east shore of the gulf of that name and the Main coast as far east as Cape Codera, and the contract to exploit it went to Columbus' troublesome companion and Fonseca's favourite, Alonso de Ojeda, with two partners, both men of means (which Ojeda was not). One partner was the experienced Juan de la Cosa, the other a prosperous Hispaniola lawyer, Martín Fernández de Enciso, who was given the office of *alcade mayor*. Veragua, however—the north-east coast of the Isthmus, enthusiastically described by Columbus—was thought the greater prize, and this went to Diego de Nicuesa, a rich settler in Hispaniola, apparently because he made the highest bid. Both leaders recruited men in Hispaniola, Ojeda about three hundred, Nicuesa twice that number—too many for safety, since they all had to be fed. Both had permission to procure provisions in Jamaica.

Both expeditions were disastrous failures. La Cosa was the only one among the leaders who had any organising experience or any common sense, and he was killed at the outset by a poisoned arrow, in a slave raid at Cartagena Bay. Ojeda's party eventually landed at Urabá, attracted, no doubt, by la Cosa's accounts of the gold found there on previous visits. They were short of food, and constantly assailed by the arrows which their raiding and foraging provoked. They built a makeshift fort which they called, with grim irony, San Sebastián; but Ojeda, himself, pricked by a poisoned arrow, returned to Hispaniola, and the sixty or so starving survivors were also in process of leaving when Enciso arrived, with supplies and reinforcements, to take charge. Among the reinforcements was a stowaway, Vasco Núñez de Balboa, who had been on the coast before, with la Cosa and Bastidas. It was Balboa who suggested that they should seek food and refuge from the arrows of Urabá among more peaceable people—people, at least, who had not been rendered hostile by slaving razzias—on the west, the Darién coast of the Gulf. They seized and occupied the Indian town of Darién, built on a good site several miles up a minor river, the Tanela.[5] The course of the Tanela has since been diverted by the build-up of the Atrato delta; then it emptied into the Gulf north of the delta and offered access from the sea. So was founded Santa María la Antigua del Darién, the first Spanish settlement on the American mainland which was more than a makeshift camp.

Nicuesa's party, though better supplied and equipped than Ojeda's, had fared worse. Nicuesa allowed his ships and people, in an eager search for gold, to scatter along several hundred miles of the Veragua coast, where they starved, were killed by arrows, or died of illness. After nine months, a disorganised handful of survivors, huddled in a makeshift fort which they built at Nombre de Dios, were rescued by ships from Darién. According to the rescuer, Rodrigo de Colmenares, 'the cause of his [Nicuesa's] failure was that this land was discovered by the Lord Admiral [Columbus] who gave information that it was the richest in the world, whereas in fact it has little gold and its coast, the most dangerous stretch in more than a hundred leagues, is an impossible place for settling and for planting necessary provisions, and therefore its Indians are for the most part fishermen'.[6] Colmenares was charitable to Nicuesa, and underrated Veragua. The expedition failed because Nicuesa was a fool. He held the King's contract, however, and foolishly insisted that Darién was within his grant. Balboa, rather than hand over, decided, with the support of the settlers, to get rid of him. This he did by packing him off, with some of his friends, to Hispaniola, in a leaky boat which was never heard of again. The other competitor for command, the judge Enciso, was similarly expelled shortly afterwards, in a somewhat better boat; he reached Hispaniola, and eventually Spain, where he busied himself—understandably—in a vendetta against Balboa. Enciso had poor judgement in practical matters and lacked power of command, but he was no fool. His book on geography is an important source of information about the Indies, the work of an intelligent and observant man. He was a dangerous enemy, both in Spain and in the Indies, to which he returned in 1514 in the train of Pedrarias Dávila.

Meanwhile, however, Balboa was left in effective command, an unenviable responsibility. Life in Darién, in the midst of a numerous and prosperous Indian population, involved difficult adjustments, even to men who came from Hispaniola and were familiar with native society there. Food habits, in particular, were different, as Enciso noted: 'The bread and wine is made of the meal of maize, as it is in Cartagena. There are also the roots from which the bread is made in the islands . . . but here they are of another quality, for those of the islands are dangerous, and if one eats of one of them one dies as one would by eating realgar, but those of this land of Sinú and the land beyond to the west can be eaten raw or cooked. . . .'[7] Enciso meant that the staple food of the islands was bitter cassava, which is poisonous when raw, but when properly prepared can be made into a filling and reasonably palatable bread. Cassava bread will keep for months; it was excellent for victualling ships or for carrying on

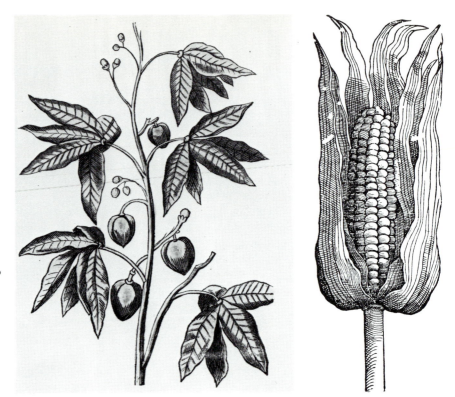

Left
41 Cassava plant; from
Georg Margraf, *Historia
Plantarum* (bound in W. Piso
and G. Margraf, *Historia
Naturalis Brasiliae*; Leyden
and Amsterdam, 1648),
p. 55.

Right
42 Ear of maize; from G. B.
Ramusio, *Navigationi e
Viaggi* (Venice, 1556), III, 55.

entradas; and the Spaniards, although they did not much like it at first, had grown used to it. West of (approximately) the Gulf of Maracaibo, however, bitter cassava was, and is, unknown. The staple roots were sweet cassava—an insipid tuber, useless for bread—and various kinds of sweet potatoes. The staple bread-stuff there was maize. Spaniards had encountered maize in the islands, but only as a vegetable, eaten green; its use in bread was new to them. Oviedo wrote the first reliable description:

Its ears are about a span in length and bear grains the size of chick-peas. Ground is prepared for planting by clearing the scrub and weeds and burning them. The burning breaks up the soil and the ash makes good manure. The Indians then make holes with a long pointed stick and drop seven or eight grains into each hole, repeating the process at each step as they advance in a line across the cleared ground. The grain is ready for harvest in three or four months. They build shelters for the boys who mind the fields and scare off parrots, monkeys, pigs [peccaries] and deer. . . . The grain is ground by women, on a large and concave stone, with another, smaller, round stone held in the hands. . . . They mix water with the meal as they grind and make a paste like dough, which they wrap in leaves or corn husks and bake in the embers. It comes out something like white bread, crusty on the outside, soft and crumbly in the middle. It is best eaten hot. . . . This bread keeps only a few days. After four or five days it goes mouldy.[8]

Maize bread, then, could not be stored or carried on exploring expeditions. Maize in the grain or on the cob, when dry, keeps well; it could be carried on the march or procured from native corn-cribs on the way; but fresh bread had to be made almost daily. The Darién Spaniards not only depended on native farmers to supply them with grain; both in their permanent settlements and in their *entradas*, they needed the regular service of large numbers of native women to provide their daily bread, to say nothing of their daily wine, whether it were made from maize, mamey apples or peach palm fruits. True, the mainland forests were full of game, unlike the islands; but to kill game in significant quantity the Spaniards needed Indian help. They depended on the Indians at every turn; and the Cuna Indians, though amiable on the whole, were better organised, better armed, more difficult to cow and coerce than the naked Arawaks of the islands.

Balboa was the first *caudillo* in the New World who made himself a leader by his ability to win and hold followers. He had a way with Indians too. He was capable of savagery—what *conquistador* was not? On occasion he used dogs for hunting Indians—his own Leoncillo was a famous fighter—but his displays of ferocity were economical and calculated. In dealing with recalcitrant chiefs, he would scare them initially by a show of force, then promise friendship and protection. He kept his promises and made his companions do the same. He respected the structure of native society and government. Warned, we may suppose, by experience in Hispaniola, he worked through the *caciques*, who in that region were hereditary chiefs, and through them was able to obtain food and services more or less as he required. The native town at Santa María was soon re-occupied. The Indians there, and many others further west, came to accept the Spaniards as tolerable parasites, even in some instances as useful allies. He granted no *repartimientos*, exacted no fixed tribute, allowed no individual pillaging; yet his government produced revenue, largely from the gold washings which he or his people found and exploited in the Serranía del Darién, a dozen miles west of Santa María. This was the first effective discovery by Spaniards of placers on the mainland. Before that, all collection of gold had been by *rescate*, and Balboa, first of the *conquistadores*, had the wit to see that the accumulation of gold artefacts available for loot or barter was not inexhaustible.

The most striking tribute to Balboa's administrative and diplomatic skill was written after his supersession, by a man usually sharply critical of Spanish settlers: the licentiate Alonso Zuazo, inspector general of the Indies at the time of the Jeronymite administration in Hispaniola. Zuazo wrote, in 1518, that

Vasco Núñez had laboured with very good skill to make peace with many caciques and principal lords of the Indians, by which he kept in peace about thirty caciques with all their Indians, and did so by not taking from them more than they were willing to give, helping them to resolve their quarrels one with another, and thereby Vasco Núñez became so well liked that he could go in security through a hundred leagues of Tierra Firme. In all parts the Indians willingly gave him much gold and also their sisters and daughters to take with him to be married or used as he wished. By these means peace was spread and the revenue of Your Highnesses greatly increased.[9]

Balboa's chief fame, however, was as an explorer. From Santa María he organised and commanded a series of expeditions, both on the Isthmus and in what is now Colombia. In 1511 he explored north-west a hundred miles or so along the Caribbean coast of the Isthmus, then inland into the inhabited mountain country west of the Serranía. The following year he took a force south into the low, wide basin between the western Cordillera and the Pacific coast hills, drained by the Atrato and its confluents, of which the Gulf of Urabá forms the seaward end. On this expedition we have a letter which Balboa himself—usually no great writer—sent to the King, a more coherent account by Oviedo, and one by Peter Martyr, who got his information from a participant, Nicuesa's friend Colmenares. The Atrato is immense and widely flooding, a huge moving sea of muddy water, often distinguishable only by its current from the lakes and swamps through which it flows. Rainfall is heavy and the forest dense. 'The manner in which this river must be navigated', wrote Balboa, 'is by canoes of the Indians, for there are many small and narrow arms, some closed by trees, and one cannot enter except in canoes three or four palms wide. After this river has been explored, boats eight palms wide may be made to employ twenty oars, as in *fustas*, for it is a river of great current and not easy to navigate even in Indian canoes.'[10] The expedition threaded this maze of water and trees for several hundred miles, as far probably as the neighbourhood of Quibdó, the modern capital—if so grand a title can be applied to so miserable a place—of the Chocó. The object was to find the source of the gold artefacts which were traded down the Atrato in exchange for salt fish from the Gulf. Balboa noted the important confluences of the Sucio and Murrí rivers, coming down from the mountains to the east, and learned (correctly) that the gold originated in the highlands of what is now Antioquia, between the western and the central Cordilleras. 'These mines are in a country that appears to have the highest mountains in the world . . . so high as to be covered with clouds. In the time we have been here the crest has only been seen twice, for the sky is continuously covered. From this highest part it drops away. To that point [to the north] it is covered with great forests, and beyond [to the south] there are mountain ridges without trees . . .'—a fair description of the Cordillera Occidental. Balboa was not equipped for exploring high mountains, and wisely did not attempt it. The region he penetrated is still one of the least known parts of the Americas. Oviedo considered this Atrato expedition one of the most important and distinguished achievements of Spaniards oversea, and said that Balboa had no equal in foresight or in care for his men. Certainly no penetration into an unknown interior equalled this, until Cortés' march into Mexico.

Balboa's third exploring enterprise was shorter and less arduous, but more dramatic and more fruitful in results. This was the famous expedition across the Isthmus to the coast of the Pacific, in 1513. In the course of his first reconnaissance in 1511 he had heard from Indian informants of the proximity of the 'other sea' and of gold and pearls in the possession of coastal chiefs. This information may have been proffered in the hope of encouraging unwelcome guests to move on; but it was geographically accurate, and Balboa had taken it seriously. Early in 1513, after his return from the Atrato, he wrote to the King outlining his plan for an expedition. He described the method of washing gold from streams in the Serranía already known to him, and went on, 'they say that gold is

found in quantity in all the rivers of the other coast and in large nuggets.
. . . They tell me that the other sea is very good to navigate in canoes, being
always pacific, and does not become wild as it does on this coast. . . . I
believe that in that sea are many islands and pearls in quantity and large
ones, and that the *caciques* have chests full of them. . . .'[11] He made
detailed proposals for a chain of forts across the Isthmus and asked for five
hundred or a thousand men, with arms and supplies. Curious *naïveté*, in a
bold leader and successful man of action! Balboa was an obscure
adventurer—'an egregious ruffian', according to Peter Martyr. He had
evicted the King's representatives and seized command by force and—
worse—through acclamation. His best hope of retaining that command lay
in making himself inconspicuous and avoiding the royal notice, until he
could confront the King with a *fait accompli* in the form of a dramatic
success. Instead, he called attention to the modest but growing
profitability of his government, held out glittering prospects for the
future, and asked for expensive reinforcements. The King's immediate
reaction was to appoint a trusted man of standing, to take charge of what
was clearly becoming an important enterprise; to supersede Balboa and to
investigate Enciso's complaints against him. Pedrarias Dávila—'Our
Captain General and Governor of Golden Castille in Darién'—was a man of
good family, one of the circle about Fonseca, an old man already, with a
respectable military record and a reputation for skill in jousting. His
government was to include both the Ojeda and Nicuesa grants, but not
Veragua, which was claimed by the Columbus family and was the subject
of litigation. He was to come with a fleet and following appropriate to his
rank and office. When Balboa received this news in the summer of 1513,
he saw that his only hope of protecting himself against so formidable a
personage lay in achieving his dramatic success quickly, and getting news
of it back to Spain, if possible before Pedrarias sailed. Hence the feverish
haste with which the expedition to the Other Sea was mounted, in the
rainy season, the autumn of 1513.

The best account is Oviedo's; he was not present, but he knew Balboa
later, and took charge of his papers after his death. The party—about
eight hundred people, mostly Indians—left Santa María on 1 September
by sea, in a string of canoes towed by a sailing ship, and landed at Acla
about eighty miles up the Caribbean coast. From the point of landing they
struck inland on foot, for a two-day march over the Serranía to the
headwaters of the Mortí or the Subcutí, and thence through the flooded
lowlands of the Balsas. The exact route can only be guessed; towns and
regions were identified by the names of the ruling chiefs, and much of the
area through which the explorers passed is now an uninhabited jungle.
They travelled by Indian trails and relied on Indian settlements for guides
and for supplies. In one friendly settlement, that of Ponca, they rested for
two weeks. Amicable relations were maintained, on the whole; but the
urgency and strain of the expedition showed itself in occasional outbursts
of ill-tempered impatience, as Oviedo—who admired Balboa—regretfully
records. From time to time the dogs were loosed: in the curious and
unexplained episode of the 'transvestites' of Quareca, for instance—
Balboa, like most Spaniards of his type and time, was moved to ferocity by

the suggestion of unnatural vice—and then against the chiefs of Pacra who would not, probably could not, guide Balboa to a source of gold. On 27 September, from the crest of a savanna ridge, they saw the Other Sea: in fact, the Gulf of San Miguel, a cluster of drowned valleys reaching far inland. Oviedo, obviously impressed—as was Balboa—by the importance of the occasion, records the sonorous detail of the proceedings:

On Tuesday the twenty-fifth of September* of that year 1513, at ten o'clock in the morning, Captain Vasco Núñez, having gone ahead of his company, climbed a hill with a bare summit, and from the top of this hill saw the South Sea. Of all the Christians in his company, he was the first to see it. He turned back toward his people, full of joy, lifting his hands and his eyes to Heaven, praising Jesus Christ and His glorious Mother the Virgin, Our Lady. Then he fell upon his knees on the ground and gave great thanks to God for the mercy He had shown him, in allowing him to discover the sea, and thereby to render so great a service to God and to the most serene Catholic Kings of Castille, our sovereigns. . . .

And he told all the people with him to kneel also, to give the same thanks to God, and to beg Him fervently to allow them to see and discover the secrets and great riches of that sea and coast, for the greater glory and increase of the Christian faith, for the conversion of the Indians, natives of those southern regions, and for the fame and prosperity of the royal throne of Castille and of its sovereigns present and to come. All the people cheerfully and willingly did as they were bidden; and the Captain made them fell a big tree and make from it a tall cross, which they erected in that same place, at the top of the hill from which the South Sea had first been seen. And because the part of the coast which they first discovered was a gulf or inlet, Vasco Núñez gave it the name Gulf of Saint Michael; for the feast of the Archangel fell four days later. And he ordered that the names of all the men who were with him should be written down, so that a record should be kept of him and of them, being the first Christians who ever saw that sea. And they all sang together the hymn of the glorious holy fathers of the Church, Ambrose and Augustine, led by a devout priest Andrés de Vera, who was with them, saying with tears of joyful devotion *Te Deum laudamus, Te Dominum confitemur.*

. . .

And on the twenty-ninth of the month, St Michael's Day, Vasco Núñez named twenty-six men, those who seemed to him best fitted, to accompany him with their arms, and left the rest of his force encamped at the village of Chape. He marched with this party down to the shore of the South Sea, to the bay which they had named Saint Michael, which was about half a league from their camp. They found a large inlet, lined with forest, and emerged on the beach about the hour of vespers. The water was low, and great areas of mud exposed; so they sat by the shore waiting for the tide to rise, which presently it did, rushing into the bay with great speed and force. Then Captain Vasco Núñez held up a banner with a picture of the Blessed Virgin, Our Lady, with her precious Son Our Lord Jesus Christ in her arms, and below, the royal arms of Castille and León; and with his drawn sword in his hand and his shield on his arm, he waded into the salt sea up to his knees, and paced back and forth, reciting 'Long live the most high and most mighty monarchs, Don Fernando and Doña Juana, sovereigns of Castille and Aragon and Navarre, etc., in whose names, and for the royal crown of Castille, I now take possession, in fact and in law, of these southern seas, lands, coasts, harbours and islands, with all territories, kingdoms and provinces which belong to them or may be acquired, in whatever manner, for whatever reason, by whatever title, ancient or modern, past, present or future, without let or hindrance. And if any other prince, Christian or infidel, of whatever allegiance,

* Presumably an error for 27 September. 25 September 1513 was a Sunday.

standing or belief, should claim any right to these lands or seas, I am ready and armed to defy him and defend them in the name of the Kings of Castille, present and future, who hold authority and dominion over these Indies, both islands and mainland, from Arctic to Antarctic, on both sides of the Equinoctial Line, within and without the Tropics of Cancer and of Capricorn, as most fully and lawfully belongs to Their Majesties, their heirs and successors for ever, as I declare more at length by writ setting forth their title to this their royal patrimony, now and for all time, so long as the world shall endure, until the last day of judgement.' And so he performed the ceremony of taking possession, without let or hindrance, in due form of law. . . . And having done these acts and made these proclamations, binding himself to defend the royal title with sword in hand, by land and by sea against all comers, he called for witnesses. And all who were with him replied to the Captain Vasco Núñez de Balboa that they also were servants and natural vassals of the Kings of Castille and León, and were ready and armed to defend the royal territory, and to die in its defense if need be, against all kings, princes and peoples of the world; and they recorded their testimony. And those who were present were the following:

The Captain Vasco Núñez de Balboa,
Andrés de Vera, Priest,
Francisco Pizarro
etc.

These twenty-six, and the notary Andrés de Valderrábano, were the first Christians to tread the shore of the South Sea; and they scooped up the water in their hands and tasted it, to see whether it was salt like the water of the North Sea; and finding that it was salt, and remembering where they were, they all gave thanks to God.[12]

Balboa's own despatches, which reached Spain in the middle of 1514, have disappeared, but it is clear from contemporary accounts that they made a considerable stir. 'Our Vasco Núñez . . . was an Antaeus; he has been transformed into Hercules the conqueror of monsters. From being foolhardy, he has become obedient and entirely worthy of royal honours and favours. Such are the events made known to us by letters from him and the colonists of Darién.' So Peter Martyr—never much disposed, before that time, to praise Balboa—made amends. Balboa had indeed deserved well of his King. The expedition to the Other Sea was carefully planned, ably executed and successful. Movement was rapid, there was no unnecessary fighting, and losses were few. Besides the central facts—the existence of the Pacific and the narrowness of the Isthmus—the expedition yielded a crop of native treaties, a considerable haul of gold, and knowledge of the Pacific pearl fishery. Balboa was prevented by rough weather from visiting the Pearl Islands, some twenty miles offshore, but he and his people travelled by canoe along the north coast of the Gulf of San Miguel, learned about pearl fishing, and saw the manner of it demonstrated. They were probably the first Europeans in the New World to acquire any first-hand knowledge of the habits of pearl oysters. All this was eagerly noted by Peter Martyr: 'It is evident from the military style in which Vasco and his men report their deeds, that their statements must be true. Spain need no longer plough up the ground to the depths of the infernal regions . . . in order to draw wealth from the earth. She will find riches on the surface, in shallow diggings; she will find them in the sun-

43 Drawings of early sixteenth-century ships and caravels, details from 'John Rotz, his book of Hydrography . . . 1542'. *British Museum, Royal MS 20.E.ix, fos 25 and 38.*

dried banks of rivers; it will suffice merely to sift the earth. Pearls will be gathered with little effort.'

Pedrarias Dávila had sailed in the spring of 1514, before Balboa's news arrived, with a great fleet in which the Crown had sunk 40,000 ducats. He could be relied on to organise the collection of pearls and gold; but Balboa's despatches also revived hopes of a seaway to the Spicery, which had been laid aside since 1508. The Isthmus was so narrow that it could be surmounted. Supplementary instructions were sent off after Pedrarias, ordering him to have caravels built on the South Sea shore: 'two of Andalusian design, the other two lateen caravels of the Portuguese type, each of eleven or twelve tons'. The smaller vessels were intended, presumably, for pearling or for coastal exploration. Meanwhile an expedition from Spain was to renew the search for a strait. In November 1514 the King signed an agreement with Juan Diáz de Solís for this purpose.[13]

Solís had sailed with Pinzón in 1508, and in 1512 had succeeded Vespucci as pilot-major. His plan on this occasion was for a coasting voyage, south down the Atlantic coast in the direction indicated by

Vespucci in 1501; through the strait, if it existed; north and west up the other coast as far as 'the back of the land where Pedrarias Dávila is governor', and further for another seventeen hundred leagues, or more if possible. He was to search for the entrance of another possible strait, to the north of Pedrarias' territory, and if he found it, was to send messages to Spain via Cuba, while himself continuing to follow the coast. If the shore of the South Sea trended steadily west, like the Great Gulf in the Ptolemaic maps, it might be expected to connect with some part of Asia; presumably the ultimate object of the expedition, though not explicitly stated, was to settle this crucial question. It was a formidable assignment; yet the equipment was modest: three caravels, sixty men, provisions for two and a half years. The cost was estimated at 9,000 ducats, 4,000 to be paid by the Crown (whose resources had been strained to pay for Pedrarias' fleet), the rest to be raised by Solís and his private backers. Departure was delayed by the loss of one of the caravels, which capsized, fully loaded—perhaps overloaded—in harbour at Lepe. A year elapsed before a replacement, bought with borrowed money, could be got ready. Solís finally sailed from San Lúcar in October 1515.

Meanwhile, in July 1514, Pedrarias arrived in Darién and took over from Balboa; though his supplementary instructions, sent off after the receipt of Balboa's despatches, ordered him to consult Balboa and to act on his advice. Balboa was appointed, under Pedrarias' general command, *Adelantado* of the Shore of the South Sea and Governor of Coiba and Panamá. These Indian regional names entered the historical geography of America as the first extension of Spanish designs beyond Atlantic waters. Balboa's appointment might have left Pedrarias—had the old man been more scrupulous and less astute—with an empty title and small profit. Sixteenth-century notions of the chain of command were often dangerously unrealistic; yet it is curious that the King should have allowed such a situation to develop. The two men hated one another, as well they might. Pedrarias could not proceed openly and immediately against so celebrated an explorer, but he worked steadily and vindictively to undermine Balboa's position, and to seize and secure the places allotted to Balboa by the King. He had the advantage of social standing, a numerous following, and the royal commission as governor. Balboa's 'royal honours and favour' were no more, in effect, than a reprieve. His fate was sealed from the moment of Pedrarias' arrival; though five years elapsed before the old vulture felt strong enough to arrest him on a trumped-up charge of treason. Balboa was beheaded in 1519. The officer who arrested him was Francisco Pizarro, who had been with him to the Other Sea in 1513, and who later was to conquer Peru.

Pedrarias was the first royally appointed governor of a mainland territory in America. Historians, from Oviedo to the present day, have treated him severely, contrasting him, to his disadvantage, with Balboa; yet the differences between their methods and achievements did not simply reflect a difference in character and ability. Those who suffered from Pedrarias' misrule were, in a sense, the victims of Balboa's success. Balboa never had more than two or three hundred Spaniards with him; a party large enough to be formidable yet small enough for the local economy to support. Though not picked men in any sense, they came mostly from Hispaniola and had some pioneering experience. Balboa's despatches so gilded Darién, however, that when Pedrarias began recruiting he was overwhelmed with volunteers. He eventually sailed with more than 1500 people. Many were soldiers discharged from the recent wars in Italy. The King warned Pedrarias that he would have trouble with them; an unemployed *soldadesca* was the last thing Darién needed. Like Columbus in 1493 and Ovando in 1502, Pedrarias entered upon his government with too many people, and the wrong kind of people. The consequences, on all these occasions, were famine, devastation and disease.

In Darién the disease, according to Oviedo and Pascual de Andagoya, was *modorra*, which means lethargy. Both authors referred to it casually, without description, implying that it was well known. It attacked only the newcomers; it did not spread to the established residents or the Indians. It may have been a deficiency disease akin to beri-beri, or perhaps a result of

44 Chart of the West Indies, by Joan Martines, c. 1578. *British Museum, Harleian MS 3450, map 14.*

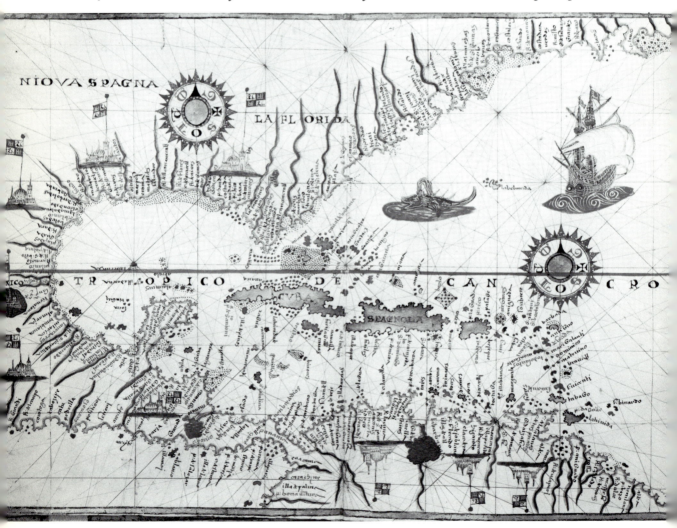

eating contaminated food in the last stages of a long and crowded passage. It did not become endemic, nor re-appear; but in the initial epidemic more than a third of the newcomers died. Those who survived the *modorra* faced the risk of death by starvation. The regulations for Pedrarias' fleet provided that his people, immediately on landing, should cease to draw ship's rations—on the assumption, presumably, that the Spaniards and friendly Indians at Santa María would be able to feed them. In practice the regulation was an instruction to forage. Indian stocks were low, as it happened, because of a recent infestation of locusts. What the locusts left the foragers seized, and still they starved.

The desperate expedients of those early weeks became established habits. The *conquistador* society of Darién was unstable and predatory, and it retained these characteristics throughout Pedrarias' government and later. Pillaging expeditions—*cabalgadas*—ranged out regularly in all directions from Santa María in search of food, gold, pearls and slaves. The governor and treasury officials would contract with an individual captain for a *cabalgada* in a particular area; the captain in turn would contract with a group of *compañeros*, whom he might arm and equip. Payment was by plunder, shared according to the old rules governing *cabalgadas* in frontier areas in mediaeval Spain. The governor and his officials took their share, as recompense for issuing the necessary licence, and might earn an additional dividend by investing. Officials rarely went out on *cabalgadas* in person, but they might contribute, say, a negro slave to help with the trail-cutting and general pioneering, or perhaps a horse. A horse was entitled to a share of plunder, which accrued not to the man who rode the horse, but to the man who owned it. *Cabalgadas* supplied the principal income of the Darién Spaniards in Pedrarias' day. They produced much more gold than direct mining and washing; partly, perhaps, because the slaves brought in, instead of being employed in the gold washings—as Balboa complained—were mostly sold for export. Some went to Spain, more to Hispaniola, where the spread of sugar planting created an acute demand for labour. *Cabalgadas*, of course, were a wasting source of income. The means which Pedrarias employed for exploring and exploiting *Tierra Firme* were also the means of devastating it, so thoroughly that its native economy never recovered.

By 1519 Santa María was already far behind the frontier of devastation, and in that year Pedrarias moved the seat of his government to Panamá, an Indian fishing village on the South Sea with an indifferent harbour, few people and fewer resources, but with access to inhabited and as yet un-plundered areas further west. This change necessitated a new route across the Isthmus, with a Caribbean terminus not at Balboa's settlement of Acla, but further west at Nombre de Dios, where Nicuesa had established himself briefly ten years earlier. This was to be the normal route throughout the sixteenth century. Santa María was abandoned to the bush, and so, a little later, was Acla. Pedrarias explained the move by saying that Santa María was unhealthy, which Oviedo, who had lived there for some years and liked the place, denied. Europeans in the New World brought their diseases with them. There was no yellow fever in Darién in Pedrarias' day—that came later, probably from West Africa—but men who had recently campaigned in Italy must have had malaria in their blood-stream, and there were plenty of mosquitos in Darién to spread it about. Panamá may have been healthier than Santa Mariá at that time simply because it was not yet infected by imported disease.

Health and supply were not the only considerations, however. Pedrarias' duties included the exploration of the South Sea, which he had neglected. He had delegated the shipbuilding project to Balboa, in 1517; but with instructions likely to ensure failure. The timbers were to be cut and shaped near Acla, carried by Indians more than thirty miles to the Río Balsas, assembled and floated down to the Gulf of San Miguel (not Panamá). Balboa—with, we may guess, a resigned shrug—undertook this preposterous task. Pascual de Andagoya, who took part in it, described the operation: 'On this river [Balsas] we made two ships and thereby used up the Indians of that province, who were numerous, by taking them to Acla to carry the materials for the ships and also by taking their stocks of food to feed the carpenters and the people who were building the ships. . . . We took these ships down to the sea with great labour, for there were many shoals through which we dug channels for them to pass. When they were floated in the Gulf of San Miguel they began to fill, because the carpenters did not know the nature of the wood, and all the timbers were rotted and riddled [by termites?]. With great difficulty we crossed in them to the Pearl Islands, where they sank. We had to set to work to build new ones, with better wood.'[14] All this took nearly two years, during which there had been no exploration by sea; perhaps Pedrarias had no other object than to get Balboa out of the way, and to discredit him. Balboa's death, however, changed the situation. Spanish curiosity about the South Sea was growing steadily; it was high time for Pedrarias to show a personal interest, and to provide results. Hence the move to Panamá.

None of the early explorers towards the South Sea had much luck; Juan Díaz de Solís least of all. No eye-witness account of his voyage survives; our knowledge of it comes from the chroniclers, particularly Herrera, who probably had access to a log or journal. Solís duly took his caravels down the coast of Brazil and entered the Río de la Plata, doubtless thinking, as others had before him, that it might be the looked-for strait. Solís was not the first discoverer; the first ships into the Río—though we have no certain evidence—were probably those of the Coelho-Vespucci expedition in 1501. Probably the name of Giordan, which occurs in early Portuguese and Italian maps, dates from this visit. In 1513–14 Cristóbal de Haro, the Fugger agent in Lisbon, mounted a small expedition to search for the strait. His ships also apparently entered the Río, and returned to Lisbon with optimistic reports, reflected in the 1515 Schöner globe. These were both Portuguese ventures. There may have been others. Solís, however, seems to have thought himself the first discoverer, for he gave the river a name, Santa María, now the name of a cape in the estuary. His was certainly the first Spanish expedition. For ten or twelve years thereafter the river was called by Spaniards either Mar Dulce or Río de Solís. The name was Solís' epitaph: 'más famoso piloto que capitán', in Herrera's terse phrase, he landed incautiously with half a dozen companions, was ambushed, killed, and according to some accounts eaten.

The Charrúa Indians on the left bank of the Río were not otherwise reported as cannibals, or as belligerent; possibly they remembered some injury done them by Haro's people. They spared and adopted one of the landing party, a boy apprentice. The people in the ships, shocked and disheartened, left the Río and made for home. One ship, on the way north, was wrecked on Catalina Island off the coast of Brazil. Survivors of this wreck escaped ashore, and lived among the Indians on the island until they were discovered and taken off by Sebastian Cabot's expedition of 1526. Stories of upstream silver told by these men and by the boy adopted

45 Northern and eastern coasts of South America, from a Portuguese *portolano* by Diogo Homem, 1558. Portuguese notions of the courses of the Amazon and the Río de la Plata were drawn at second hand from Spanish reports. *British Museum, Add. MS 5415 A, fos 23 and 24.*

by the Charrúas encouraged Cabot to abandon his project of sailing to the Moluccas, and to explore the Río instead.

The return of Solís' surviving caravels (with a cargo of brazil-wood picked up on the way, and a small Indian girl kidnapped) did nothing to discourage interest in the strait. Since the Río, being fresh water, could not offer a passage to the South Sea, the search would have to be continued further south. Interest was quickened by the arrival in Spain of Cristóbal de Haro, who in 1516 transferred his activities from Lisbon to Seville. Haro was one of the leading proponents of a westward route to the Spicery; no academic geographer, but an experienced and imaginative business man who had made a great deal of money in the spice trade in Lisbon, and expected to make still more in Seville. He and Fonseca quickly found common ground, and in the following year they were joined by two crucial Portuguese defectors: Magellan (Fernão Magalhães), soldier by sea who had served in the East, and Rui Faleiro, mathematician and astrologer, who had a great—though not wholly deserved—reputation for cosmographical learning, and who was a strenuous advocate of the south-western route to Asia. Each of the four men had a valuable contribution to offer; and their fortuitous combination coincided with the accession of an impressionable, glory-seeking youth to the Spanish throne.

Fonseca's planning in 1517–18 was not wholly based on the arguments of Haro and the two Portuguese. In his habitually cautious way, he distributed the risks of failure. The problem of access to the South Sea, and the exploration of that sea, were to be approached simultaneously from different directions, and, as in earlier plans, there were to be two expeditions. One was to be Magellan's; the other was to sail through the Caribbean, cross the Isthmus, take over the ships Pedrarias had been told to build, and follow the north coast of the South Sea westward. The contract for this voyage was given to Gil González Dávila, one of Fonseca's *entourage*, who had served for some years as government accountant in Hispaniola. Andrés Niño—another of the Moguer family—went with him as navigator and second-in-command.

Gil González sailed in 1519, landed at Acla, sought out Pedrarias, and exhibited his instructions. Pedrarias, probably having plans of his own and conscious as always that Spain was far away, refused to turn over Balboa's ships; so Gil González and his men set to work to build their own. This took two years, and the expedition finally left Panamá in 1522. They ran out the whole coast from the Gulf of Panamá to the Gulf of Fonseca, in what is now Honduras, and made some inland forays in Nicaragua, revealing the lake of that name and collecting a quantity of gold. They took the Gulf of Fonseca for a strait leading through to the Atlantic, but were prevented by the condition of their ships from exploring it. Their report may have been the origin of the 'streito dubitoso' which appeared in the world chart by Vesconte de Maggiolo, dated 1527. Apart from that, the chief result of the voyage was a series of armed *entradas* and slave raids which conquered and partly depopulated Nicaragua. Nicaragua was the northernmost conquest of Pedrarias' captains. Along what is now the border with Honduras, the northward advance of the men of Darién was halted by the superior force of Cortés' people moving south from Mexico.

Magellan also sailed in 1519, with five ships and about 270 men. The company were mostly Spaniards. There was a running dispute about this between Magellan, who wanted to man his fleet as far as possible with his own countrymen, and the Spanish authorities, who tried to limit the number of foreigners carried. In the end about thirty Portuguese shipped, including all the navigating officers. Mutual dislike and suspicion between Spaniards and Portuguese was largely responsible for the quarrels and mutinies which were to mar the voyage. There was nothing unusual about the ships; they were small or medium-sized trading vessels—not caravels—purchased for the expedition by the purveyors of the *Casa*, on the open market in Cadiz. The Portuguese ambassador—his wish the father to his thought—reported that they were so rotten as to be unsafe; but their performance gave him the lie. The navigational equipment was adequate, without new or experimental devices, though it included twenty-three charts, some of them drawn specially for the expedition with the help of Magellan's countrymen, Jorge and Pedro Reinel. Armament was heavy, for the type of ship: eighty-two mounted pieces, and a generous supply of small arms and body armour. The cargoes were probably selected by Haro, who invested heavily in them. They included the usual small truck for primitive barter—hawks' bells, 20,000 of them, and brass bracelets—but also more sophisticated articles, such as the Portuguese had found to be in demand in the East Indies: looking glasses (500), a quantity of velvets, and over 2,000 lb. of quicksilver. The fleet was equipped, then, for serious trading and, if necessary, for serious fighting at any stage of the voyage.

Magellan, like Columbus, had good reason to be secretive about his precise destination. In Spanish circles it was assumed to be the Spice Islands, the Moluccas; but more probably Magellan hoped to find other spice-producing islands, not yet visited by his countrymen. A note in his hand, glossing a passage in Duarte Barbosa, suggests that he associated the biblical names of Tarshish and Ophir with reports of the Ryu-kyu Islands, Formosa, or the Philippines. He probably identified South America (which he had not before visited) with the great peninsula of Asia; the South Sea with Ptolemy's *Sinus Magnus*. Access to the Great Gulf was to be by a sea passage, leading from the south-western Atlantic. According to Pigafetta, the chronicler of the voyage, 'the captain-general . . . knew where to sail to find a well-hidden strait, which he saw depicted on a map in the treasury of the King of Portugal, which was made by that excellent man Martin de Boemia'. The only cartographical work of Martin Behaim which survived to modern times is a crude globe, which he completed in 1492. This indeed marks a strait, between the extremity of the great peninsula and a large island (Sumatra?) labelled 'Seilan'; but what appear to be the East Indian islands are east, not west, of the strait. If Magellan ever saw this globe (which is most unlikely) its muddled and archaic depiction of Asia would not have encouraged him to navigate as he did. Behaim, however, may have drawn later, better maps. He died in Lisbon, in 1506. Magellan may have known him.

The first part of the voyage, including the passage of the strait, proceeded according to plan, at least in a geographical sense: across the Atlantic from the Cape Verde Islands to the coast of Brazil, then southwest down the coast; a brief stay in the Río de la Plata, which Magellan— knowing all about the Solís attempt—took for a river and did not pause to explore; the miserable, mutinous months in Port St Julian, the bleak inlet in Patagonia where the fleet wintered; and finally the terrors of the Strait.

Antonio Pigafetta, the Lombard gentleman-volunteer who sailed in the fleet, apparently for the sake of adventure, served Magellan loyally during the voyage, and with his pen afterwards. From his notes, he compiled what is perhaps the best, the fullest and the most moving of all the eye-witness accounts of the great voyages of discovery. Pigafetta was vague about navigational detail—a defect which can be supplied, to some extent, from surviving navigators' logs—and he was reticent about such

46 Coast of Brazil, Río de la Plata and Magellan's Strait, from 'John Rotz, his book of Hydrography . . . 1542' showing Brazilian Indians fighting, dancing, and building and fortifying a village. South is at the top. *British Museum, Royal MS 20.E.ix, fo. 28.*

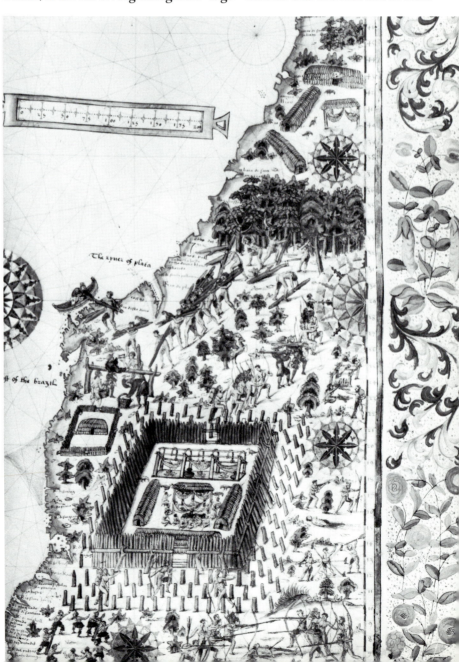

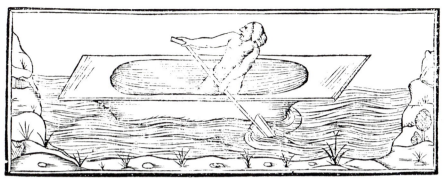

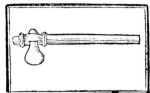

47 Stone axe and dug-out canoe; woodcuts from Oviedo, *Historia General*, fo lxi.

matters as mutiny; but his descriptions of places and people are vivid, immediate, and on the whole convincing. For example, on the Tupinambá Indians of the coast of Brazil:

That land of Verzin is wealthier and larger than Spagnia, Fransa and Italia put together, and belongs to the King of Portugalo. The people of that land are not Christians, and have no manner of worship. They live according to the dictates of nature, and reach an age of one hundred and twenty-five and one hundred and forty years. They go naked, both men and women. They live in certain long houses, which they call *boii*, and sleep in cotton hammocks called *amache* which are fastened to those houses by each end to large beams. A fire is built on the ground under those hammocks. In each of those *boii*, there are one hundred men with their wives and children, and they make a great racket. They have boats called canoes made of one single huge tree, hollowed out by the use of stone hatchets. These people employ stones as we do iron, as they have no iron. Thirty or forty men occupy one of those boats. They paddle with blades like the shovels of a furnace, and thus, black, naked and shaven, they resemble, when paddling, the inhabitants of the Stygian marsh. Men and women are as well proportioned as we. They eat the flesh of their enemies, not because it is good, but because it is a certain established custom.

·   ·   ·

Those people paint the whole body and the face in a wonderful manner with fire in various fashions, as do the women also. The men are smooth shaven and have no beard, for they pull it out. They clothe themselves in a dress made of parrot feathers, with large round arrangements at their buttocks made from the largest feathers, and it is a ridiculous sight. Almost all the people, except the women and children, have three holes pierced in the lower lip where they carry round stones, one finger or thereabouts in length and hanging down outside. Those people are not entirely black, but of a dark brown colour. They keep the privies uncovered, and the body is without hair, while both men and women always go naked. Their King is called *cacich*. They have an infinite number of parrots, and gave us 8 or 10 for one mirror; and little monkeys that look like lions, only yellow and very beautiful. They make round white bread from the marrowy substance of trees, which is not very good, and is found between the wood and the bark and resembles buttermilk curds [could this be an attempt to describe cassava?]. They have swine which have their navels on their backs [peccaries] and large birds with beaks like spoons and no tongues [Muscovy ducks?]. The men gave us one or two of their young daughters as slaves for one hatchet or one large knife, but they would not give us their wives in exchange for anything at all. . . . The women cultivate the fields, and carry all the food from the mountains in panniers or baskets on the head or fastened to the head. But they are always accompanied by their husbands, who are armed only with a bow of brazil-wood or of black palm-wood, and a bundle of cane arrows, doing this because they are jealous. The women carry their children hanging in a cotton net from their necks.

On the first encounter with a Tehuelche Indian in Port St Julian:

One day we suddenly saw a naked man of giant stature on the shore of the port. . . . He was so tall that we reached only to his waist, and he was well proportioned. [Many explorers remarked on the tall stature of the Amerindians, compared with wiry little European sailors; the legend of the Patagonian giants persisted for centuries.] His face was large and painted red all over, while about his eyes he was painted yellow; and he had two hearts painted on the middle of his cheeks. His scanty hair was painted white. He was dressed in the skins of animals skilfully sewn together. That animal has a head and ears as large as those of a mule, a neck and body like those of a camel, the legs of a deer, and the tail of a horse, like which it neighs, and that land has very many of them [guanacos]. His feet were shod with the same kind of skins, which covered his feet in the manner of shoes. In his hand he carried a short, heavy bow, with a cord somewhat thicker than those of a lute, and made from the intestines of the same animal, and a bundle of rather short cane arrows feathered like ours, and with points of white and black flint stones in the manner of Turkish arrows, instead of iron. . . . The captain-general called those people Patagoni [i.e., 'big feet', presumably from the habit of wrapping their feet in guanaco skin]. They all clothe themselves in the skins of the animal above mentioned; and they have no houses, except those made from the skin of the same animal, and they wander hither and thither with those houses just as the Cingani [gypsies] do. They live on raw flesh and on a sweet root which they call *chapae*. Each of the two whom we captured ate a basketful of biscuit and drank one-half pailful of water at a gulp. They also ate rats without skinning them.[15]

Pigafetta was to learn to appreciate rats, at a later stage of the voyage.

Magellan's ships—four of them, he had lost one on the coast of Patagonia—entered the strait which bears his name on St Ursula's day, 21 October 1520; and the cape at the entrance is called Cape Virgins to this day. The most detailed contemporary description of the actual passage of the strait is not Pigafetta's, but that of young Maximilian of Transylvania; not an eye-witness account, but the next best thing. Maximilian used the method of his tutor Peter Martyr, questioning the survivors of the expedition immediately after their return.

As the fleet coasted south from St Julian,

. . . certain inlets of the sea were discovered, which had the appearance of a strait. Magellan entered them forthwith with the whole fleet, and when he saw other and again other bays, he gave orders that they should be all carefully examined from the ships, to see if anywhere a passage might be discovered; and said that he would himself wait at the mouth of the strait till the fifth day, to hear what might happen.

[One ship's company mutinied, deserted and returned to Spain.]

Another discovered nothing but a bay full of shoals and shingle, and very lofty cliffs. The third ship, however, reported that the largest bay had the appearance of a strait, as in three days' sail they had found no way out; but the farther they had gone the narrower the sea was, and they had not been able to sound the depth of it in many places by any length of line, and that they had also noticed that the tide was rather stronger than the ebb, and that so they were persuaded that a passage was open in that direction to some other sea. He made up his mind to sail through it. This channel, which they did not then know to be a channel, was at one place three Italian miles wide, at another two, sometimes ten, and sometimes five, and pointed a little westward. The altitude of the southern pole was found to be 52 deg., and the longitude to be the same as at St Julian's Bay. The month of November was upon them, the night was rather more than five hours long, and they had never seen any human beings on the shore.

But one night a great number of fires were seen, mostly on their left hand, from which they guessed that they had been seen by the natives of the region. But Magellan, seeing that the country was rocky, and also stark with eternal cold, thought it useless to waste many days in examining it, so with only three ships, he continued on his course along the channel until, on the twenty-second day after he had entered it, he sailed out upon another wide and vast sea. The length of the channel they attest to be nearly a hundred Spanish leagues.

There is no doubt that the land which they had upon their right was the continent of which we have spoken, but they think that the land on the left was not a mainland, but islands, because sometimes on that side they heard on a still farther coast the beating and roaring of the sea.

Magellan saw that the continent stretched northwards again in a straight line; wherefore, leaving that huge continent on the right hand, he ordered them to sail through that vast and mighty sea, which I do not think had ever seen either our or any one else's ships.[16]

Nearly two years later, in September 1522, one remaining ship of the original five limped into the Seville river and eighteen enfeebled survivors staggered ashore to give thanks for their deliverance. They had crossed the Pacific; visited the Philippines; lost half their number,

48 Chart of Pacific Ocean by Battista Agnese, 1555: an elegant summary of the results of exploration to that date, from an illuminated atlas, MS on vellum. *National Maritime Museum, Greenwich.*

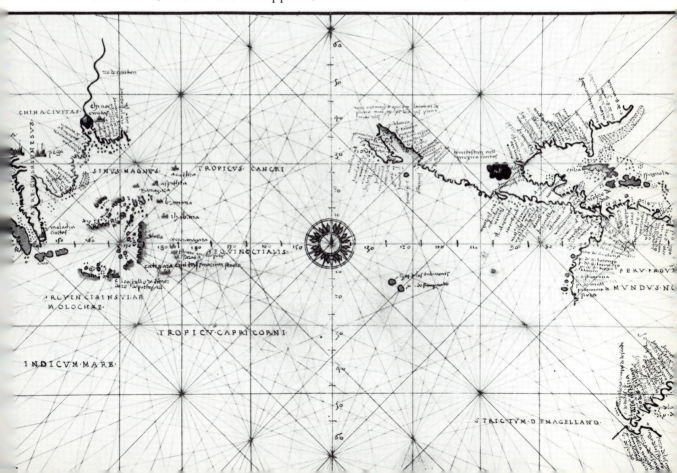

including the captain-general, in needless fighting; loaded cloves in the Moluccas; crossed the Indian Ocean; rounded the Cape; and returned through the Atlantic to tell the tale.

Magellan's voyage was a triumph of endurance, pertinacity and skill, a victory against tremendous natural odds; but it was a Pyrrhic victory. Its results, for Spaniards, were almost wholly discouraging. El Cano, it was true, had sailed round the world; but that was not what the expedition had been sent out to do, and from a narrowly Spanish point of view, it was a pointless exercise. The *Victoria* had brought back 500 hundredweight of cloves; but not enough to cover the costs. More important than cloves, she had brought a great deal of vital geographical information; but to the King of Spain, it was unwelcome information. The world was considerably bigger than Ptolemy, or anyone else, had supposed. America was not connected with Asia; not, at least, in the Tropics or the southern hemisphere—what happened in the north was still anyone's guess. Between them lay an ocean, no Ptolemaic gulf, but an ocean bigger than any that Europeans had hitherto seen. All this was good news for Portugal

49 Map of the world by Diogo Ribeiro, 1529, believed to be based on the *Padrón Real*, the master chart maintained in the *Casa de la Contratación* in Seville, where Ribeiro is known to have worked. One of the most beautiful examples of the cartographer's art. *Biblioteca Apostolica Vaticana.*

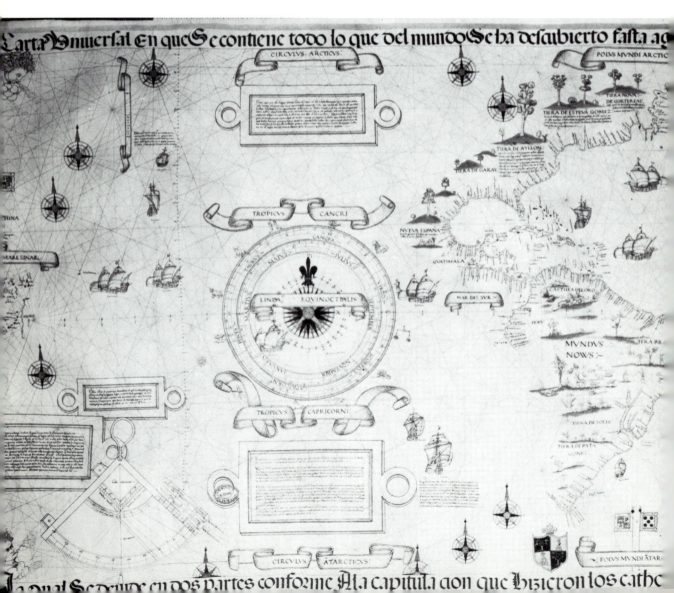

and very bad news for Spain. True, there was a sea passage from Atlantic to Pacific; but what a passage! Magellan's Strait today carries a considerable volume of shipping, nearly all coastal steamers; but before steam became general it rarely saw a ship. For sailing ships it is dauntingly difficult and dangerous, a labyrinthine navigation with strong and variable tidal currents and frequent thick weather. Its western end, especially, is a narrow fjord between abrupt ice-capped mountains, a funnel through which the prevailing west wind drives in savage, unpredictable gusts. Nor were navigational hazards the only difficulties; there was a problem of victualling. It was all very well for explorers to eke out their weevilly biscuit with salted cormorants and seal meat; but this would not do for supercargoes and companies carrying valuable merchandise on regular voyages. The Atlantic coast of South America within the Spanish demarcation, it appeared, was unproductive and worthless, and became worse the further south one went, from the grass plains about the Río de la Plata, to the semi-desert of Patagonia, to the bare rock and hanging glaciers of Tierra del Fuego. The whole region was

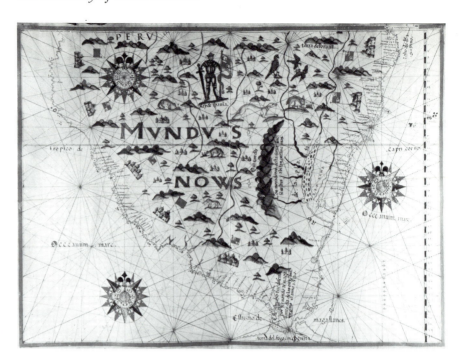

50 Map of southern South America from a Spanish *portolano, c.* 1560. *British Museum, Add. MS 9814, map 7.*

sparsely inhabited by very primitive people, and the prospect of inducing Europeans to settle there seemed remote.

The distances, the dangers and the costs effectively ruled out Magellan's route for regular seaborne trade between Spain and the Spicery. In the euphoria induced by the circumnavigation this unwelcome conclusion was resisted for a few years; but the fate of the follow-up voyages drove the lesson home. Of the seven ships which sailed from Coruña with García Jofré de Loaisa in 1525, only one reached the Moluccas and none returned. Another fleet, in 1526, under the specious Sebastian Cabot, got no further than the Río de la Plata. Meanwhile, hope of an alternative strait in the north was fading fast. In the year Magellan sailed, Alonso Alvarez de Pineda, at the instance of the governor of Jamaica, explored the coast of the Gulf of Mexico from west Florida to Vera Cruz, and closed off that possibility. Over the next five years, Vázquez de Ayllón, Verrazzano and Estevão Gomes between them revealed a continuous continental coast all the way from east Florida to Nova Scotia. As for ship-building on the South Sea coast, that, clearly was a possibility; Cortés in Mexico carried it much further than Balboa and Gil González Dávila had done. In 1527, one of his two ships actually reached the Moluccas; but it never returned. Reluctantly but realistically, the Emperor decided to abandon his depreciating claim to the trade and navigation of the Spicery. In 1529, at the Treaty of Saragossa, he sold it for a tidy sum to the King of Portugal. For Spaniards the gold—or rather, as it later turned out, the silver—of the New World was prize enough.

II

The Indian Empires

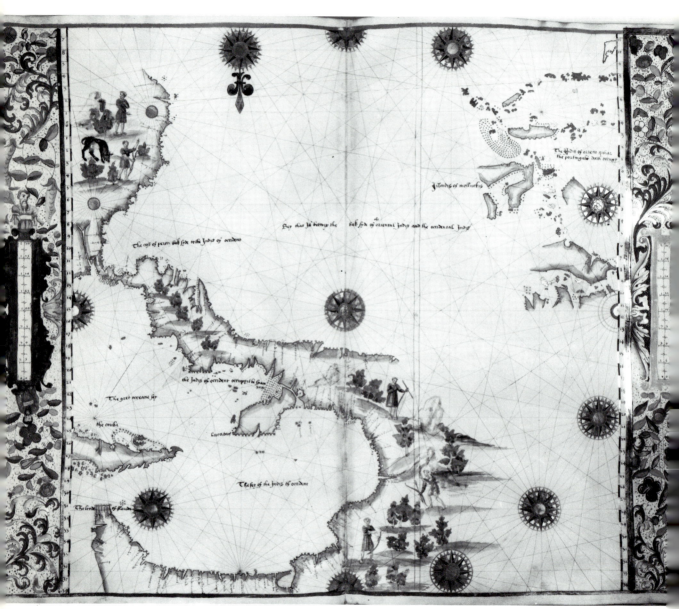

51 Chart of Gulf of Mexico
and Pacific, from 'John Rotz,
his book of Hydrography . . .
1542'. *British Museum, Royal
MS 20.E.ix, fos 7 and 8.*

5 Mexico

Magellan sailed from Seville on the first stage of his great voyage on 15 August 1519. On the following day Hernán Cortés left his quarters at Cempoala, in the coastal plain of Vera Cruz, to march on the capital city of Mexico. Once again, the main thrusts of Spanish oversea endeavour—towards participation in the Asiatic spice trade, and towards conquest and settlement in the New World—moved forward simultaneously.

Magellan's capitulation with the Crown had been sealed in March 1518. In November of the same year Diego Velázquez, the governor—or, more properly, lieutenant-governor—of Cuba, had been appointed (at his own petition, naturally) *adelantado* of Yucatán. This title empowered Velázquez to explore, conquer and settle, independently of the authority of his nominal superior Diego Colón, governor of Hispaniola and hereditary admiral of the Indies. Velázquez' decree and Magellan's contract had both been issued through the effective head of the Indies administration, Juan Rodríguez de Fonseca. After the death of King Ferdinand, while Cardinal Jiménez was regent, Fonseca had been temporarily under a cloud; but Charles I had restored him to office in 1517, apparently as powerful as ever. Velázquez was Fonseca's relative by marriage, his partisan and his creature. He was also, after plundering Cuba, a rich man; circumstances which, added to his ambition and his organising ability, made him a formidable figure in the violent and litigious world of the Indies.

Velázquez did not 'discover' Yucatán. The existence of land west of Cuba had been indicated vaguely in maps from early in the century. The Canerio map of 1502–04, in particular, shows, imprecisely but unmistakably, Florida and the Gulf of Mexico. At the south-east extremity of the Gulf is an island which appears to represent Yucatán. Where this information came from, we do not know; presumably from an early voyage of which no certain record survives. The first voyage in that quarter, of which we have plausible record, was the Pinzón-Solís expedition of 1508, which, according to las Casas, sailed west from the Guanaja islands in the Gulf of Honduras, then north up the mainland coast. The printed map inserted in some copies of the 1511 edition of Peter Martyr, shows a coastline extending far north of the latitude of Cuba. Its features cannot be certainly identified; possibly the promontory which bears the legend Baya de Lagartos may be intended to represent Yucatán; equally possibly, it may be Turneffe Island, off Belize, and the smaller head further north, Cozumel Island. The indications were vague, but at least in 1511, when Velázquez began the conquest of Cuba, there was no doubt among informed Spaniards that Cuba was an island and that a considerable unexplored territory lay not far west of its westernmost point. Further confirmation came in 1513. Ponce de León's 'Bimini' expedition, on its circuitous return from the east coast of Florida to its base

52 Map of the Caribbean, from Peter Martyr d'Anghiera, *Opera . . . Oceani Decas* (Seville, 1511) with vague indications of Florida (Isola de Beimini) and Yucatán.

in Puerto Rico, almost certainly sighted the north coast of Yucatán.

Serious exploration, which included armed landings as well as mere coasting, began in 1517 with the expedition commanded by Francisco Hernández de Córdoba. This venture was organised by a group of *compañeros* of whom Bernal Díaz, the future chronicler, was one. Most of them—so he recalled—had gone out with Pedrarias to Darién, but having no luck there, had removed to Cuba, where Velázquez had given them fair words but no Indians; so they joined together to promote an expedition: 'seeking and exploring new lands where we might find employment'. They approached Hernández, who was a leading settler, with a proposal that he should invest in the expedition and lead it, to which he agreed. Velázquez also invested in the project, and suggested that it should take the form of a slave raid on the Guanaja islands. With the decline in numbers of the native population in Cuba and Hispaniola, slave raiding in neighbouring islands unsettled by Spaniards had become a familiar recourse. The *compañeros*, however, 'answered that it was neither in accordance with the law of God nor of the King, that we should make free men slaves'; this, at least, was Díaz' account of the matter, written many years later. The truth, more probably, was that the *compañeros* were after bigger prizes, and it is tempting to see, in their decision, the influence of Antonio de Alaminos of Palos, their chief pilot. Alaminos was on his way to becoming a distinguished navigator. He piloted the first three expeditions into the Gulf of Mexico. Subsequently, he worked out the best return route from Mexico to Spain, using the Gulf Stream, sailing through the Florida Channel and passing close to Bermuda (which had been discovered by, and named after, another Palos navigator, Juan Bermúdez). This was the route which Spanish convoys were to use for the next two hundred years. Earlier, in 1513, he had been to Florida and thence to Yucatán with Ponce de León.[1] Earlier still, according to Herrera,[2]

140

he had sailed as an apprentice with Columbus. Herrera does not say on which voyage; if, as seems most likely, it was the fourth, Alaminos may have remembered the incident of the trading canoe off the Honduran coast, and drawn from it the conclusion that Columbus failed to draw: that the land of cities and civilised people lay west, not south, of Cuba.

The expedition formed in the sheltered harbour on the north shore then called Catenas (later le Havana), the harbour which, thanks to Alaminos' careful observations of the Gulf Stream, was to become one of the key ports of the Indies. They sailed west along the north coast of Cuba, passed Cape San Antonio, crossed the Yucatán Channel (which, in rough weather, took them nine days) and made their landfall near Cape Catoche. Here they found a town; no haphazard collection of thatched huts, but a town with regular streets, with houses built of *cal y canto*—stone laid in mortar—and stone-faced temple-pyramids, which, at first, the Spaniards took for forts or watch towers. They were reminded of what they had read or heard of the cities of the Levant, and in their excitement called the place Grand Cairo. The people were Maya, the town Ecab. This was the first encounter of Europeans with any of the city-building peoples of the New World.

Once again, however, the *compañeros* had no luck. Upon landing, they were treated initially with courteous curiosity, and hospitably welcomed. They had with them a supply of green glass beads for trading purposes. The Indians apparently took these for jadeite—to them a precious stone, used for ritual objects—and offered in barter for them small trinkets of gold, or a gold-copper alloy, in the shapes of birds and fish. These objects—or the gold of which they were made—must have come in by way of trade, for Yucatán has no gold; but the Spaniards could not have known that, and were naturally delighted. Within a few hours, however, the atmosphere changed abruptly; the Spanish party, lightly armed and off guard, was attacked by a large force of warriors and driven back to the boats. The fleet sailed on, first west, then south, following the Gulf coast of the peninsula; and everywhere they landed the same sequence of events recurred, with particularly fierce fights at Campeche and Champotón. It was unusual anywhere in the West Indies for Indians who had no previous experience of Europeans, to make unprovoked attacks on them. Bernal Díaz, who wrote the only eye-witness account, was clearly at a loss to explain what to him seemed premeditated treachery. Las Casas, more percipient, supplies the clue: it was a question of water. At Catoche,

The Spaniards passed on through the town which contained more than 4,000 houses. As the Indians saw that the Spaniards did not attack them or take their fortresses as they were believed to be but went on, they [the Indians] came to them unarmed with joyful and kindly faces making signs of peace to them. All together they returned, as if they had known each other for a long time and as friends, to the beginning of the town where they had come in and all sat down outside under a large tree. A son of the lord and a woman brought to the captain of the Spaniards a cooked turkey, one of the large ones like peacocks, and some masks of fine gold. . . . When this had been done they asked the captain by signs what he wanted to which he replied 'water to drink'. The Indians showed him a round walled-up well of good water where the Spaniards went to sleep. Then they took all the water needful for the ships. The Spaniards kept guard that night, and no less did the Indians do in their town. When day broke, all the Indians came out of their town armed with bows and arrows, shields and lances. They surrounded the town on the side where the Spaniards were and sent three to tell them to go to their ships. This they did with signs and with threats that if they did not go they would shoot arrows at them and do them harm. The Spaniards obeyed their order and went aboard their boats and thence to their ships.[3]

Similarly at Campeche and Champotón. The Spaniards were accustomed, both in Europe and in the West Indies, to take water where they found it. On the Main coast, and in most of the islands, it is plentiful. Yucatán, however, is formed of porous limestone. Rainfall is seasonal. Rivers are few, and surface water is accessible, for the most part, only where the limestone crust has broken through to form natural wells, *cenotes*. Water, therefore, is precious. When the Spaniards asked for it, their hosts, assuming that they wanted it for immediate drinking, courteously showed them the wells; but when they proceeded, without permission or payment, to take water by the cask-full and carry it off to their ships, the Indians resented the theft and took prompt measures to stop it.

The Maya-speaking peoples of northern and western Yucatán were militarily formidable. For several centuries before the arrival of the Spaniards they had lived under the sway of intrusive warrior groups from central Mexico, and to a considerable extent had accepted Mexican gods, Mexican styles of architecture and decoration, Mexican forms of social and military organisation. They wore Mexican body armour of quilted cotton, and fought with Mexican weapons: the *maquauhuitl*, a terrifying double-edged, obsidian-bladed battle-axe which could decapitate a horse; javelins and javelin throwers; long bows, and slings. Against this array Hernández' people had steel swords, crossbows and a few primitive fire-arms. They had no horses, and the fatigue of fighting hand-to-hand against greatly superior numbers wore them down. At Champotón they lost more than fifty men—nearly half their number—and decided to withdraw. Desperate for water, and unable to return directly to Cuba against the east wind, they made for the west coast of Florida, on Alaminos' advice, and there filled their casks at the cost of another skirmish, this time with Indians who remembered Ponce de León and wanted no more dealings with Spaniards.

The fleet, or what was left of it, limped back to Havana in April 1517, and there, according to Bernal Díaz:

We wrote in great haste to the Governor of the Island, Diego Velásquez, telling him that we had discovered thickly-peopled countries, with masonry houses, and people who covered their persons and went about clothed in cotton garments, and who possessed gold and who cultivated maize fields, and other matters which I have forgotten.

From Havana our Captain Francisco Hernández went by land to the town of Santispíritus, for so it is called, of which he was a citizen, and where he had his Indians; but he was so badly wounded that he died within ten days.

Three soldiers died of their wounds in Havana, and all the rest of us dispersed and went some to one and some to other parts of the Island. The ships went on to Santiago where the Governor was living, and the two Indians we captured at Cape

Catoche, whom we named Melchorejo and Julianillo were sent on shore, as were also the little chest with the diadems and the ducks and little fish and other articles of gold and the many idols. These showed such skilful workmanship that the fame of them travelled throughout the Islands including Santo Domingo and Jamaica and even reached Spain. It was said that better lands had never been discovered in the world; and when the pottery idols with so many different shapes were seen, it was said that they belonged to the Gentiles, and others said that they were the work of the Jews whom Titus and Vespasian had turned out of Jerusalem and sent to sea in certain ships which had carried them to this land, which, as Peru was at yet undiscovered (indeed it was not discovered for another twenty years) was held in high estimation.[4]

Velázquez did more than write letters: he took immediate steps to assert his own right to exploit Hernández' discoveries. This was his purpose in sending agents to Spain to urge his claim to the title of *adelantado*. This, too, was his object—again according to Bernal Díaz—in assigning to Fonseca, to the Secretary Conchillos, and to other members of the Council 'Indian townships in the island of Cuba, so that their inhabitants might extract gold from the mines for them, and for this reason they were ready to do much for Diego Velázquez'. In the meantime, while awaiting the royal answer, Velázquez pushed on with local preparations. He mounted an expedition to be commanded by his kinsman Juan de Grijalva, and provided—Díaz again—'the four ships, crossbows and guns, some beads and other articles of small value for barter, and a small supply of beans'. Some of the participants also invested, and contributed the salt pork and cassava bread with which the ships were victualled. About 240 men volunteered, more than double the number who went with Hernández, most of them with their personal arms; and the ships—unlike Hernández'—carried a few small cannon.

Grijalva's instructions were to trade and to discover, not to conquer or to settle, since Velázquez could not confer an authority which he did not himself, as yet, possess. Velázquez seems to have hoped that Grijalva would, so to speak, read between the lines, and was displeased with him on his return for not having exceeded his instructions. This was unreasonable; the expedition was ably commanded, and successful in accomplishing its set tasks. The first discovery was Cozumel island; a place of importance, both as a centre of pilgrimage and the site of a talking oracle, and as an entrepôt for an extensive network of Maya canoe-borne trade. According to las Casas, Cozumel was famous also for its beehives, and exported large quantities of honey. Spanish occupation dealt hardly with Cozumel; its trade dried up, its population dwindled, and the island entered upon a long sleep, broken only in our own day by the tourist trade.

From Cozumel, Grijalva sailed south down the east coast, as far as the big inlet which he named Bahía de la Ascensión; then back to Cape Catoche, and along the north and west coasts, in the wake of Hernández. At Champotón he was attacked on landing, as Hernández had been, but with a more numerous and better-armed company, came off better. Beyond Champotón the coast was unknown to Europeans. They entered, briefly, the Laguna de Términos, which Alaminos took for a strait connecting with the Bahía de la Ascensión, thus making Yucatán an island; as it was shown in maps for the next ten years or so. They found—having left the territory of the Yucatec Maya—that they were no longer attacked whenever they went ashore. Bernal Díaz, writing years later, explained the natives' restraint in political terms; but a simpler explanation might be that the Spaniards had entered a region of rivers and abundant water. They anchored at the mouth of the Tabasco river, where, though treated with armed circumspection, they were able to trade; and similarly at the Coatzacoalcos. Then on to the anchorage in the lee of the island they called San Juan de Ulúa, which was to become the gateway to New Spain. The people on this coast were Totonacs, tributary to the Mexica of the high plateau, but possessors of a developed culture of their own, 'elegant' people, according to Sahagún's informants.[5] 'The men clothed themselves; they wore capes, breechclouts, sandals, arm-bands, necklaces, quetzal feather devices; they bore fans, they had trinkets. They cut their hair, arranged their hair-dress well, looked at themselves in mirrors. The women wore skirts, embroidered shifts' (as they still do). As others had done, they offered gold trinkets for green glass beads.

From San Juan de Ulúa, Pedro de Alvarado—later to be famous as a reckless and ruthless *conquistador*— was sent back in a fast caravel with the news, the sick and the gold; 20,000 *pesos* of it, according to Gómara. He brought to Cuba the first intimation that the new lands to the west yielded objects of value in significant amount. Velázquez at once set about organising a third expedition, and named Hernando Cortés to command it. Meanwhile the rest of Grijalva's fleet beat up the coast as far as the Río Pánuco, the end of the area of high culture. There, after some half-hearted discussion on the possibility of settlement, they turned back. Their return passage to Cuba took so long that Cortés was instructed to search for them; but they arrived at the western end of the island before he left.

Cortés was an odd choice to command the biggest of the fleets which sailed from Cuba under Velázquez' auspices. It is true that he put money into the project; but although he held an *encomienda* and some gold placers in Cuba, he was not a rich man and his investment cannot have been heavy enough to constitute, in itself, a claim to command. He had no experience of such work, and had shown no interest in the earlier expeditions. Except, indeed, for his part in the settlement of Cuba—not a very exacting campaign—he had been more of a scrivener than a soldier; he had some knowledge of law—how obtained, we cannot be sure—and had practised as a notary or notary's clerk both in Spain and in Cuba. Subsequently he had served as governor's secretary. His relations with Velázquez had been punctuated by violent quarrels and—if Gómara is to be believed—affectionate reconciliations. Velázquez distrusted him, but nevertheless appointed him; probably, as Bernal Díaz suggests, Cortés had rich and persuasive backers or partners among the governor's *entourage*. When distrust reasserted itself and Velázquez changed his mind, he was too late to stop Cortés.

Cortés' instructions required him, besides searching for Grijalva's overdue ships, to investigate a hearsay report of Spanish castaways in northern Yucatán, survivors from a shipwreck several years before;

beyond that he was to trade and discover, like his predecessors. The size of the expedition, however, its equipment and its arms, suggested something more ambitious than trading; and a clause in his instructions allowed him discretion in dealing with unforeseen circumstances. Cortés undoubtedly had settlement in mind as a possibility. More far-seeing than most *conquistadores*, he was acutely aware of the destruction which casual slaving and looting had caused in the islands. Like Balboa, he understood that the profits of *rescate* were soon exhausted; that America could be made to yield permanent revenue to Spain and Spaniards only through planned settlement and careful, responsible exploitation of all its resources. Like any ambitious *conquistador*, he preferred to conquer and settle in his own name, rather than as another's deputy; probably he intended from the beginning to serve Velázquez as Velázquez had served Diego Colón, and as Cristóbal de Olid was later to serve Cortés himself. He was too wily to affront the Crown by a premature and open act of rebellion, if it could be avoided. His tactic, rather, was to carry out the early part of the voyage according to his instructions. When he was beyond Velázquez' reach, he could establish his settlement, and seek authorisation *ex post facto* by direct petition to the Crown over the heads of Velázquez and his influential patrons. Events, however, forced Cortés' hand. Velázquez was becoming suspicious; he might decide to relieve Cortés of his command. Equally serious, the title of *adelantado* was believed to be on its way, and might arrive before Cortés left. In that event, Velázquez would issue his own instructions for conquest and settlement and would claim the credit and the profit of anything Cortés

53 The ruins of Tulum, fortified Maya town on the east coast of Yucatán, opposite Cozumel island. This was probably the town sighted by Grijalva's people, who thought it too strong for them, and did not land. *Photograph, Peabody Museum, Harvard University.*

might achieve. To forestall these possibilities, and at the risk of an open breach, Cortés put to sea hastily and surreptitiously on 18 November 1518.

The Cortés expedition is the best recorded of the major Spanish expeditions in the New World in the sixteenth century. Among eye-witness accounts by participants, two are of outstanding value and interest: Cortés' own *Cartas de Relación*,[6] detailed despatches addressed to Charles v; and Bernal Díaz' *True History*. One early formal history, that of Gómara, is of outstanding merit and exceptionally well informed. In addition, there are a number of accounts from the Indian side. These include, besides pictographic records of the traditional kind, chronicles actually written by hispanicised Indians such as Ixtlilxochitl and Tezozómoc; histories based on Indian information but written in Spanish by Spanish missionaries, such as Motilinía, Durán and Juan de Tovar; and, in a class by itself, the *General History of the Things of New Spain* by the Franciscan Bernardino de Sahagún, who transcribed, or caused to be transcribed, both in Spanish and in Náhuatl, the reports of many Indian informants.[7]

The narratives are not works of objective historiography, naturally. All the writers had their loyalties and their pre-conceptions, and many of them had axes to grind. Cortés, in particular, knew that if his despatches were well received he might be the Emperor's viceroy; if ill received, he would probably be superseded, and might lose his head. He was concerned to justify his assumption of independent command, to magnify the power, wealth and splendour of Mexico, and to emphasize his own courage, skill and wisdom in finding and conquering it. The *Cartas* contain a great deal of skilful special pleading and some deliberate misrepresentation. Gómara served Cortés as private secretary and chaplain during the last six years of the conqueror's life. He was not present—as Bernal Díaz never tired of pointing out—at the events he described; but that is a disadvantage suffered by most historians. He was close to the best possible source of information, Cortés himself, but he also consulted other reliable witnesses, notably Andrés de Tapia. Gómara's *History* was published a few years after Cortés' death, and was dedicated to Cortés' son. Las Casas, who hated Cortés and all he stood for, belittled Gómara as a mere mouthpiece or paid panegyrist; and the same charge was levelled, for different reasons, by Díaz. It is unjust. Gómara clearly admired Cortés and wrote, in part, to extol the memory of a distinguished patron; but he commented on the defects of Cortés' character with the freedom of a privileged chaplain, and used his critical judgement in interpreting what Cortés told him. Gómara's tale is superbly told, with sustained dramatic tension and telling irony. It appears also to be substantially accurate. Díaz, for all his tirades against Gómara, corroborated most of his statements; the principal differences between the two writers are those of emphasis and style. Díaz' own plain tale, despite its author's protestations of unvarnished veracity, is not as plain as it appears. On the contrary, it is distinguished by simple, but highly effective, literary artifice, and by the grinding of axes. Díaz was concerned with fame: his own, and that of the rank-and-file to which, during the conquest, he had belonged. Writing in middle and old age as a comfortable *encomendero*, he remained in spirit a disgruntled old soldier. There is an undercurrent of envious complaint throughout the *True History*; it is of a piece—though on a vastly larger scale—with the *relaciones de méritos y servicios* which poured into Spain with every fleet, describing the value of the writers' services and the inadequacy of their recognition and reward. Bernal Díaz creates—deliberately, no doubt—the strong impression that Cortés' decisions were really made by a sort of soldiers' soviet, of which Díaz himself was a member; but that Cortés got away with an excessive share of the plunder and all the glory. The second impression may have had some basis in fact, the first was nonsense. Nevertheless, the *True History* is the freshest, most detailed and most endearing of the Spanish accounts, a splendid foil and complement to the devious formality of Cortés' own letters and to the dramatic story-telling of Gómara. The Indian accounts have in common, as might be expected, an elegiac quality, a nostalgia for the past; but they are often ambiguous. Most of the writers and informants were, at least formally, Christian converts. Some of them belonged to tribes which had allied themselves with Cortés at an early stage of the invasion, and some had been well rewarded. They differed widely in their interpretation of events, therefore, though all were affected, to a greater or less degree, by their contact with the Spaniards.

These various sources, Spanish and Indian, differ greatly, then, in their treatment of the political and military events of the conquest of Mexico. The concern of the present chapter, however, is not with conquest, but with discovery. This was a less controversial topic, one which lent itself less readily to axe-grinding. Some of the Spaniards—Cortés and Díaz in particular—were acute observers and careful recorders of their observations. So were some of Montezuma's emissaries. The extracts which follow are chosen to illustrate the manner in which Cortés and his companions found their way to Mexico; the impression which the country made upon the Spaniards; and the impression which Spaniards and Indians made upon one another.

The fleet left Santiago short of food, and Cortés had to put in to several of the south coast harbours to buy bread and pork. This proved to be an advantage, because he fell in with Grijalva's ships, recently returned, and recruited many of the men, including Bernal Díaz, into his own fleet. Cortés now commanded a formidable force: eleven ships, over five hundred men, with sixteen horses, thirteen arquebuses and a few small cannon. Antonio de Alaminos, also recruited from Grijalva's fleet, was the chief navigator. Cortés took his final departure from a small harbour near Cape San Antonio in February 1519. Arrived at Cozumel, he inquired through Maya traders after Spanish castaways on the Yucatán coast, and located one of them, Jerónimo de Aguilar, who was living with Indians as a slave and had learned Chontal Maya. For a ransom of green beads, Aguilar was released to join the fleet. A little later, off the Tabasco river, after a sharp fight and a formal 'taking possession', Cortés was presented by the local ruler with another valuable captive, the woman whom the Spaniards called Marina. Marina's parents were said to have been people of consequence in the Vera Cruz region. She was intelligent, and seems to have made a considerable impression on those who met her. All the Indian *codices* depicting the conquest contain drawings of Marina, finger upraised, advising or admonishing Cortés. She spoke Náhuatl as her mother tongue, had learned Chontal Maya, and soon acquired some Spanish. Cortés, unlike his two predecessors, thus had competent interpreters, one of whom was capable of explaining some of the intricacies of Mexican religion and politics. Their help enabled Cortés, on arrival at San Juan de Ulúa, to make the first major discovery of the voyage: that the towns and chiefdoms of the Vera Cruz coast were not independent city states, but were tributary to an overlord people living far inland, beyond the great wall of mountains that could be seen from the coast. The Aztec 'empire' was the first large-scale political unit encountered by Spaniards in America. Its ruler, Motecuçoma or 'Montezuma', seemed, from the reports they heard, to occupy a position analagous, in an American context, to that of Charles v in Europe. Cortés seems to have formed in his mind, at an early stage, a resolve to penetrate inland, and by some means to induce Montezuma to accept the suzerainty of the King of Spain. Seizing the ruler's person would occur to him naturally as a possible way of doing this; during the campaigns in the islands and in Darién, Spanish leaders had often held local chiefs as hostages for the docile behaviour of their people. Montezuma's 'empire', admittedly, was a more formidable proposition than an Island *cacicazgo*; but if Cortés could succeed, his fortune and his reputation would be made and his defiance of the governor of Cuba splendidly vindicated.

Cortés, always conscious of the importance of carrying his people with him step by step, prudently kept to himself, at this early stage, his designs on the person and state of Montezuma. His immediate task was to establish his base: to make a settlement on the coast and to give it a formal structure. The 'rich city of the True Cross' had a legal or quasi-legal existence before it had a geographical location; its exact site cannot now be determined, but the names of its first officials are all meticulously recorded. In these proceedings Cortés made skilful use both of the discretionary clause in his instructions and of a deep-rooted tradition of Spanish law. To give the colour of legitimacy to his own command, he represented it as a surrender to loyal public opinion. The whole body of the army and the municipality was shown rejecting the selfish timidity of Velázquez, demanding in the royal name that Cortés should take charge and organise a settlement in Mexico. It was a classic example of a spontaneous demonstration arranged by a clever, bold and popular leader. As the town council of Vera Cruz explained to the Emperor,

... we in this fleet who were of noble lineage, gentlemen and knights, zealous in the service of God and of Your Royal Highnesses, and most eager to honour the Royal Crown, extend its dominions and increase its revenues, came together and urged the aforementioned captain Fernando Cortés, saying that land was very good and, to judge by the samples of gold which the chieftain had brought, most wealthy also, and, moreover, that the chieftain and his Indians had shown us great goodwill: for these reasons, therefore, it seemed to us not fitting to Your Majesties' service to carry out the orders which Diego Velázquez had given to Hernando Cortés, which were to trade for as much gold as possible and return with it to the island of Fernandina in order that only Diego Velázquez and the captain might enjoy it, and that it seemed to all of us better that a town with a court of justice be founded and inhabited in Your Royal Highnesses' name so that in this land also You might have sovereignty as You have in Your other kingdoms and dominions.[8]

Such sovereignty—so the town councillors assured the Emperor—would be well worth having:

... this land which we have now settled in Your Majesties' name extends for fifty leagues along the coast on either side of this town: the coast is completely flat with sandy beaches which in some places stretch for two leagues or more. The country inland is likewise very flat with most beautiful meadows and streams; and among these are some so beautiful that in all Spain there can be none better, for they are both pleasing to the eye and rich in crops, and well cared for and well situated; and there are places to walk and to graze all kinds of herds.

In this land there is every kind of game, and animals and birds similar to those of our acquaintance, such as deer, and fallow deer, wolves, foxes, partridges, pigeons, several kinds of turtledove, quail, hares and rabbits: so that in the kinds of birds and animals there is no difference between this land and Spain, and there are lions and tigers as well.

Some five leagues inland from the sea, and in certain places less, runs a great range of the most beautiful mountains, and some of these are exceedingly high, but there is one [Orizaba] which is much higher than all the others from which one may see a great part of the sea and land; indeed it is so high that if the day is not fine one cannot even see the summit, for the top half of it is all covered by cloud. At other times, however, when the day is very fine one can see the peak rising above the cloud, and it is so white we think it to be covered in snow, and even the natives say it is snow, but as we have not seen it very clearly, although we have come very close to it, and because this region is so hot, we cannot be certain that it is.

We shall endeavour to see and learn the secret of this and other things of which we have heard so that we may render Your Royal Highnesses a true account, as of the wealth in gold and silver and precious stones which Your Majesties may judge according to the samples we are sending. In our view it cannot be doubted that there must be in this land as much as in that from which Solomon is said to have taken the gold for the temple. ...

The people who inhabit this land, from the island of Cozume[l] and the cape of Yucatan to the place where we are now, are of medium height and of well-proportioned bodies and features. ...

The food they eat is maize and some chili peppers, as on the other islands, and *patata yuca*, just the same as is eaten in Cuba, and they eat it roast, for they do not make bread of it; and they both hunt and fish and breed many chickens such as those found on *Tierra Firme*, which are as big as peacocks.

There are some large towns and well laid out. The houses in those parts where there is stone are of masonry and mortar and the rooms are small and low in the Moorish fashion. In those parts where there is no stone they make their houses of adobes, which are whitewashed and the roofs covered with straw.[9]

While the Spaniards explored the neighbourhood of Vera Cruz, they themselves were under scrutiny. Their arrival off the coast had been promptly reported by runner to Montezuma, and relays of emissaries kept him informed of their subsequent movements. The Florentine Codex contains some vivid samples of the information he received:

. . . strange people have come to the shores of the great sea. They were fishing from a small boat, some with rods and others with a net. They fished until late and then they went back to their two great floating towers and climbed up into them. . . . They have very light skin, much lighter than ours. They all have long beards, and their hair comes only to their ears.[10]

A little later, after the Spaniards had landed:

Their trappings and arms are all made of iron. They dress in iron and wear iron casques on their heads. Their swords are iron; their bows are iron; their shields are iron; their spears are iron. Their deer carry them on their backs wherever they wish to go. Those deer, our lord, are as tall as the roof of a house.

The strangers' bodies are completely covered, so that only their faces can be seen. Their skin is white, as if it were made of lime. They have yellow hair, though some of them have black. Their beards are long and yellow, and their moustaches are also yellow. Their hair is curly, with very fine strands.

As for their food, it is like human food. It is large and white, and not heavy. It is something like straw, but with the taste of a cornstalk, of the pith of a cornstalk. It is a little sweet, as if it were flavoured with honey; it tastes of honey; it is sweet-tasting food.

Their dogs are enormous, with flat ears and long, dangling tongues. The color of their eyes is a burning yellow; their eyes flash fire and shoot off sparks. Their bellies are hollow, their flanks long and narrow. They are tireless and very powerful. They bound here and there, panting, with their tongues hanging out. And they are spotted like an ocelot.[11]

The same report contained the earliest recorded Amerindian account of the firing of a gun:

A thing like a ball of stone comes out of its entrails; it comes out shooting sparks and raining fire. The smoke that comes out with it has a pestilent odor, like that of rotten mud. This odor penetrates even to the brain and causes the greatest discomfort. If the canon is aimed against a mountain, the mountain splits and cracks open. If it is aimed against a tree, it shatters the tree into splinters.

The Spaniards were clearly very formidable by Amerindian standards, and if this is a true summary of a recital which reached Montezuma, it was natural that he should be alarmed. Even so, for a man famous as a seasoned warrior, the degree of alarm attributed to him seems excessive. 'When Montezuma heard this report he was filled with terror. It was as if his heart had fainted, as if it had shrivelled. It was as if he were conquered by despair.'

Montezuma's despair is a constantly recurring refrain in the story of the conquest. From his receipt of the first reports to his death, a captive of the Spaniards, six months later, nearly all the narratives of the conquest represent him as paralysed by fear and indecision. According to Sahagún's informants, he regarded the Spaniards—at least in the early days, before he actually met them—as supernatural beings, and could think of no way of deflecting their approach, save by magic, by sending his own magicians to deal with them. This had no effect; as he sadly remarked, 'It is a natural thing, for almost everyone is a magician.' The next recourse was to make propitiatory oblations. The first gifts that he sent to the Spanish camp were ritual vestments appropriate to various Mexican deities. This may have been an experiment, an attempt to find

54 Ancient Mexican jewellery: a sacrificial knife of chalcedony, the handle inlaid with shell and turquoise mosaic, in the form of an eagle knight, a member of one of the warrior Orders. Mixtec, fourteenth century AD. *British Museum*.

out where the Spaniards stood, so to speak, in the spirit world. The Spaniards—not appreciating Indian craftsmanship nor interested in turquoise, shell mosaic or *quetzal* feathers—were unimpressed: 'and is this all? Is this your gift of welcome? Is this how you greet people?' Then came a ritual meal and sacrifice, which equally failed of its purpose.

He sent out his most gifted men, his prophets and wizards, as many as he could gather. He also sent out his noblest and bravest warriors. They had to take their provisions with them on the journey: live hens and hens' eggs and tortillas. They also took whatever the strangers might request, or whatever might please them.

Motecuhzoma also sent captives to be sacrificed, because the strangers might wish to drink their blood. The envoys sacrificed these captives in the presence of the strangers, but when the white men saw this done, they were filled with disgust and loathing. They spat on the ground, or wiped away their tears, or closed their eyes and shook their heads in abhorrence. They refused to eat the food that was sprinkled with blood, because it reeked of it; it sickened them, as if the blood had rotted.

Motecuhzoma ordered the sacrifice because he took the Spaniards to be gods; he believed in them and worshiped them as deities.[12]

According to Sahagún, Montezuma associated Cortés with the Toltec priest-king or god-hero Quetzalcóatl. This interpretation was widely accepted, in the sixteenth century and later. Sahagún, however, was a missionary. He studied Indian custom and belief for a practical purpose, that of rendering Christian proselytising more effective. Indian religious beliefs in general were for him superstitions to be eradicated; but there were some, he thought, which might have pre-disposed Indians to accept Christian doctrine. For him and for other ethnologist-friars—for Durán, conspicuously—the Quetzalcóatl legend, with its Messianic analogies, had a special fascination. The cult centre of Quetzalcóatl was Cholula, in the fertile plain east of the volcanoes, between Tenochtitlán and the coast. In Montezuma's reign Cholula had been conquered by the Mexica, and its gods humiliated. Montezuma himself was a priest of Huitzilopochtli, the tutelary deity and conquering war-god of the Mexica. He had no reason to accord any particular reverence to Quetzalcóatl. Sahagún's informants were trying to recall, in the 1560s, events which had occurred forty years earlier. They may themselves partially have lost contact with their tribal histories, and have read into their own recollections ideas acquired through contact with Spanish missionaries. Most probably the association between Cortés as a divinely appointed agent, and Quetzalcóatl as a prophetic figure, was a Spanish invention.

Nothing in Cortés' despatches suggests that he was conscious of receiving divine honours; if he did in fact receive them, either he missed their significance, or tactfully did not mention them. Nor does Bernal Díaz mention the sacrifice incident. Months later, however, in the second *Carta de Relación*, Cortés put into Montezuma's mouth a speech pledging allegiance to Charles v, on the ground that Charles was the descendant or the reincarnation of an earlier Mexican ruler who had gone into exile across the sea, but had promised to return one day to resume his kingdom. Montezuma thus, according to Cortés, acknowledged himself to be a usurper or, at best, a *locum tenens*. Such a speech, employing conventional Spanish concepts of kingship, is obviously implausible in the mouth of an Amerindian war-chief. At the time the despatch was written, Cortés, having been expelled from Tenochtitlán with heavy loss, was about to lay siege to the city. He wished to show that the defeat of the *noche triste* was a transitory revolt; that the Mexica were *de jure* the Emperor's subjects, and that through Cortés' efforts they would soon be his subjects *de facto*. Possibly, having heard some account of the Quetzalcóatl tradition, or of some similar myth, he adapted it for his own political ends.

It is not certain, then, nor even very likely, that Montezuma associated Cortés with any particular divinity. He may have credited the Spaniards with supernatural powers of some sort; magic abounded in the mental world he inhabited. Equally possibly, his patience in dealing with them arose from traditional respect for the immunity of ambassadors; or else, perhaps, he thought the Spaniards, with their guns and their horses, too formidable to be resisted in the open. If they insisted—though obviously unwelcome—in visiting the capital, let them come; entrapped behind the drawbridges, hampered by the crowded buildings and the intersecting canals, they could be captured, sacrificed and eaten at leisure.

Whatever the explanation, the Spaniards remained unmolested at Vera Cruz. No swift expedition came to destroy their camp and to punish the people who harboured them. During the four months of their stay they were able not only to explore their geographical surroundings in the coastal plain, but also to make political inquiries. They were well received at Cempoala, the Totonac capital; and there discovered in conversation that the Aztec empire was less united than at first sight it appeared. Many towns and tribes on the plateau and in the coastal plain, including Cempoala itself, had been subdued only recently by the Mexica, and resented their subjection the more bitterly because the tribute exacted from them included a regular supply of captives for sacrifice to the gods of Tenochtitlán. More promising still, Cortés learned in Cempoala of one Indian *pueblo* which, though surrounded by tributary peoples, still held out against the Mexica: the city-state of Tlaxcala, up on the plateau a few days' march from Tenochtitlán. Meanwhile, the embassies came and went. Montezuma's gifts, and the equivocations of his emissaries, suggested uneasiness. The Mexican state, indeed, seemed to display all the characteristics most likely to attract the attention of a pious predator such as Cortés: evident wealth, all-too-evident wickedness, political weaknesses which a judicious alliance might exploit. According to his own account, Cortés' mind was made up very early; but to persuade his companions to march on Tenochtitlán required both rhetoric and ruthlessness. There was an attempt at mutiny by the adherents of the governor of Cuba (adherents, in their own view perhaps, of lawful government) some of whom, as Gómara bitingly expressed it, 'were servants of Velázquez, others his debtors, and a few were his friends'. The mutiny was put down, and talked down. Even so, Cortés found it necessary to scuttle the ships in which they had all come from Cuba, so removing the temptation to desert, and freeing the sailors to march with the army. He saved the guns and the gear for future use. What he did with the hulls is not explained; probably he sank them in the shallow water. Later legend had it that, like Julius Caesar, he burned them.

The army set out from Cempoala accompanied by Totonacs, both warriors as guides and fighting allies, and porters to carry the baggage. It was a rough march. The Sierra Madre is a formidable obstacle, especially in the wet season when the march began, and the route followed by Cortés seems to a modern eye almost perversely difficult. It was chosen, probably on Totonac advice, to avoid towns tributary to the Mexica. First came the long steady climb from the coastal plain up to the escarpment shelf where Jalapa—a Totonac town—stood and stands. From Jalapa the easiest route west (the route of road and railway today) passes north of the Cofre de Perote; but the Spaniards instead climbed directly up to the bleak saddle, at over 10,000 feet, between the Cofre and Orizaba: a rough climb for the horses, wrote Bernal Díaz, and no doubt for the men too. Three Indians died in a hailstorm on the saddle. The west slope of the Cofre is a desert of sand and volcanic ash, with salt ponds and marshes in the depressions— high, wind-swept, uninhabitable. After several days of floundering north through the ash, the army found a way out through the defile which they called Puerto de la Leña, the Firewood Pass, down to the fertile Tlaxcala table-land, then west through Zocotlán (modern Zautla) to the marches of Tlaxcala. Here they met their first armed resistance. The border was fortified by a dry-stone wall (fragments of which remain, near the town of Tecoac) and defended by Otomí settlers. Tlaxcala, like many Mexican states, was a composite society; the Otomíes were regarded as barbarians by the Nahua majority, but they were noted fighting men, much prized by the Mexica as sacrificial captives. Sharp fighting ensued before the Spaniards could enter Tlaxcala town and negotiate.

Cortés compared Tlaxcala—to its advantage—with Granada. Spaniards often likened Mexican buildings to Moorish, perhaps because they usually had flat roofs, and the snowy ridge of Ixtaccíhuatl may have reminded Cortés of the Sierra Nevada; but the physical resemblances cannot have been very close. There was, however, a political resemblance between the Tlaxcala of 1519, and Granada a generation earlier, before its conquest by Castille: each was threatened by a powerful neighbour, and each had long survived in hostile, but tolerated, independence.

153

Independent Granada, in the intervals of fighting which suggested the tournament rather than serious war—until Isabella put a stop to the pretence—had paid tribute to Castille. Tlaxcala paid no stated tribute, but was bound by treaty to engage at intervals in tournaments of another sort: formal pre-arranged battles with the Mexica, to provide, on both sides, prisoners for sacrifice. The Mexica, with extensive conquered territories and a big population at their disposal, could easily afford these 'flower wars'; among them, human life was cheap. The rulers of Tlaxcala were less well placed; in effect, they bought a precarious independence with a wasting tribute of their subjects' lives. Cortés' arrival offered them a way of escape. Once convinced, by experience, of Spanish fighting capacity, they entered into a firm alliance.

Cortés now had a base for his final advance. His easiest route lay over the northern shoulder of Ixtaccíhuatl to Texcoco, and along the lake shore. His first move, however, was in the opposite direction: fifty miles south to Cholula, a major religious and commercial centre which had only recently become tributary to the Mexica. From Cholula there was a direct route to the coast, passing through Tepeaca and south of the Orizaba *massif*; a much easier route than that by which Cortés had come. Probably, having heard in Tlaxcala of the existence of this route, he decided to seize Cholula in order to secure his communications with the

55 The negotiations for peace and alliance between the rulers of Tlaxcala and the Spaniards; from *Antiguedades Mexicanas publicadas por la Junta Columbina de Mexico en el cuarto centenario del Descubrimiento de América* (Láminas), ed. A. Chavero (Mexico, 1892), plate 4. This is a facsimile copy of the post-conquest codex known as the *Lienzo de Tlaxcala*: a pictorial narrative, drawn in Tlaxcala in the sixteenth century, presenting the Spanish conquest from a Tlaxcalan point of view. Marina is seen interpreting for Cortés.

veyotlipan. oncáqnamicq3 mtlatoque qmaca q̃yxq̃ch qualom.

56 Cortés welcomed in
Tlaxcala after his retreat
from Tenochtitlán: corn cobs
in tall baskets, tortillas in
low baskets, turkeys live
and dressed, corn stalks for
the horses; from Chavero,
Lienzo de Tlaxcala facsimile,
plate 28.

coast; but he was also impressed by the place itself, as well he might be. It remains prosperous and beautiful to this day; and from the platform of the great pyramid, now surmounted by a huge baroque church, the surrounding plain can still be seen dotted with many lesser mounds.

This state is very rich in crops, for it possesses much land, most of it irrigated. The city itself is more beautiful to look at than any in Spain, for it is very well proportioned and has many towers. And I can assure Your Highness that from a temple I counted more than 430 towers, and they were all of temples. From here to the coast I have seen no city so fit for Spaniards to live in, for it has water and some common lands suitable for raising cattle, which none of those we saw previously had, for there are so many people living in these parts that not one foot of land is uncultivated, and yet in many places they suffer hardships for lack of bread. And there are many poor people who beg from the rich in the streets as the poor do in Spain and in other civilized places.[13]

Cortés was dissatisfied with his reception at Cholula. He and Bernal Díaz both explain that Marina discovered a conspiracy, inspired by Montezuma, to ambush and kill the Spaniards; and that Cortés decided to strike first. He did so by convening an assembly of notables in an enclosed court, and having them massacred. The soldiers, accompanied by several thousand Tlaxcalteca, then ran through the streets for several hours, killing and setting fire to shrines. Cortés mentions staked pits in the streets and piles of stones on the house roofs. It was natural enough that the Cholulteca, expecting a self-invited guest at the head of a formidable army, should take precautions; but in the event, there was no resistance. The plot seems to have been imaginary. Possibly the Tlaxcalteca, who were on bad terms with Cholula, invented it, and so made use of the Spanish army to pay off old scores; possibly, as las Casas asserts, Cortés deliberately adopted a policy of exemplary terror in order to discourage

57 Pyramid at Cholula; from A. von Humboldt and A. Bonpland, *Voyage aux régions équinoxiales du nouveau continent: Vue des Cordillères et monumento des peuples indigènes de l'Amérique* (2 vols.; Paris, 1810), plate 7.

the Mexica from resisting the Spaniards, on the last stage of their long march to Mexico. According to Sahagún's informants:

When the massacre at Cholula was complete, the strangers set out again toward the City of Mexico. They came in battle array, as conquerors, and the dust rose in whirlwinds on the roads. Their spears glittered in the sun, and their pennons fluttered like bats. They made a loud clamour as they marched, for their coats of mail and their weapons clashed and rattled. Some of them were dressed in glistening iron from head to foot; they terrified everyone who saw them.

Their dogs came with them, running ahead of the column. They raised their muzzles high; they lifted their muzzles to the wind. They raced on before with saliva dripping from their jaws.[14]

They went by the most direct, though not the easiest route, east to Ixcalpán, up to the high pine-clad saddle between the volcanoes, known then as the Eagle Pass (now as the Paso de Cortés); and thence down by way of Amecameca into the central valley. There is no road over the pass today, scarcely even a foot track, and probably it is much less used now than in Cortés' time. The Spaniards were not wholly ignorant of this wild, remote mountain area; there had been tentative exploration during their stay in Tlaxcala. Popocatépetl at that time was an active volcano (its last recorded eruption was in 1665; an eruption in 1519 after a long dormant period may have been associated by Aztec augurers with the arrival of the Spaniards). Cortés was puzzled by the spectacle of flame and smoke pouring from a snow-clad peak, and sent Diego de Ordaz up the mountain with a small party to investigate. The climb is not technically difficult, but it is long and arduous and the last four thousand feet or so are over hard permanent snow. Ordaz—without climbing equipment, in an age when mountaineering as a sport was unheard of—did well to reach almost to the rim of the crater. He was driven off by rumbling and shaking and a shower of hot stones; but he saw, from near the summit, the valley with its lakes, its cities and its causeways. He found also the Amecameca track, which Cortés—always fearful of ambush—chose in preference to the easier, more frequented and recommended road to Chalco.

At some point on the long, rough descent, the Spaniards met yet another embassy. Montezuma had given up trying to please them by ritual offerings. Knowing by now what they most wanted, he sent a gift of gold jewellery, with the suggestion—peremptorily worded but weakened by excuses—that they should take the bribe and depart. Nothing, naturally, could have been better calculated to ensure that they would press forward. Soon the little army, making its best attempt at martial pageantry, was marching along the causeway which separated Lake Chalco from Lake Xochimilco, to Iztapalapa. This march inspired Bernal Díaz' most famous passage of descriptive recollection.

The next day, in the morning, we arrived at broad Causeway, and continued our march towards Iztapalapa, and when we saw so many cities and villages built in

58 The massacre at Cholula; from Chavero, *Lienzo de Tlaxcala* facsimile, plate 9. Marina is looking on.

59 Scarped hill near Atlixco; probably a temple mound, with the cone of Popocatepetl behind it, from a water-colour by Adela Breton. 1890s, *Bristol City Museum, no. 8147.*

the water and other towns on dry land and that straight and level causeway going towards Mexico, we were amazed and said that it was like the enchantments they tell of in the legend of Amadis, on account of the great towers and cues and buildings rising from the water, and all built of masonry. And some of our soldiers even asked whether the things that we saw were not a dream? It is not to be wondered at that I here write it down in this manner, for there is so much to think over that I do not know how to describe it, seeing things as we did that had never been heard of or seen before, not even dreamed about. . . . I say again that I stood looking at it and thought that never in the world would there be discovered other lands such as these, for at that time there was no Peru, nor any thought of it. [Of all these wonders that I then beheld] to-day all is overthrown and lost, nothing left standing.[15]

From Iztapalapa the causeway led straight across the salt lake of Texcoco to the island city, Tenochtitlán. Montezuma himself came out to meet them on the causeway, in ceremonial welcome. In the city, lodging, food, firewood and fodder for the horses were generously provided. For some generations, each successive *uei tlatouani* had built his own palace compound, to be occupied during his reign and left empty as a monument after his death. The compound used by the Spaniards was that of Axayacatl, Montezuma's father, which covered an extensive site on the west side of the great temple enclosure (now the Zócalo). It says much for Aztec powers of organisation, that in a city where all transport was by canoe or on men's shoulders, a whole army, four hundred Spaniards and three or four thousand of their Indian allies, could be housed and fed at relatively short notice. Bernal Díaz, for one, was delighted with the accommodation, as well he might be, after the rigours of the Eagle Pass. Cortés' account of the city is less wide-eyed but all the more impressive— as it was meant to be—by being matter-of-fact.

This great city of Temixtitan is built on the salt lake, and no matter by what road you travel there are two leagues from the main body of the city to the mainland. There are four artificial causeways leading to it, and each is as wide as two cavalry lances. The city itself is as big as Seville or Córdoba. The main streets are very wide and very straight; some of these are on the land, but the rest and all the smaller ones are half on land, half canals where they paddle their canoes. All the streets have openings in places so that the water may pass from one canal to another. Over all these openings, and some of them are very wide, there are bridges made of long and wide beams joined together very firmly and so well made that on some of them ten horsemen may ride abreast. . . .

This city has many squares where trading is done and markets are held continuously. There is also one square twice as big as that of Salamanca, with arcades all around, where more than sixty thousand people come each day to buy and sell, and where every kind of merchandise produced in these lands is found; provisions as well as ornaments of gold and silver, lead, brass, copper, tin, stones, shells, bones, and feathers. They also sell lime, hewn and unhewn stone, adobe bricks, tiles, and cut and uncut woods of various kinds. There is a street where they sell game and birds of every species found in this land: chickens, partridges and quails, wild ducks, fly-catchers, widgeons, turtledoves, pigeons, cane birds, parrots, eagles and eagle owls, falcons, sparrow hawks and kestrels, and they sell some of the skins of these birds of prey with their feathers, heads, and claws. They sell rabbits and hares, and stags and small gelded dogs which they breed for eating. . . .

They sell honey, wax, and a syrup made from maize canes, which is as sweet and syrupy as that made from the sugar cane. They also make syrup from a plant

60 Montezuma; water-colour drawing by a *tlacuilo*, an Indian scribe, but with obvious signs of European influence, from Juan de Tovar 'Historia de la venida de los Indios . . .' MS, *c.* 1585. *John Carter Brown Library, Providence.*

Overleaf
61 'Tipus sacrificiorum'; engraving purporting to show an Aztec temple and rites; from Diego Valadés, *Rhetorica Christiana* (Perugia, 1579). A European impression of Mexican culture.

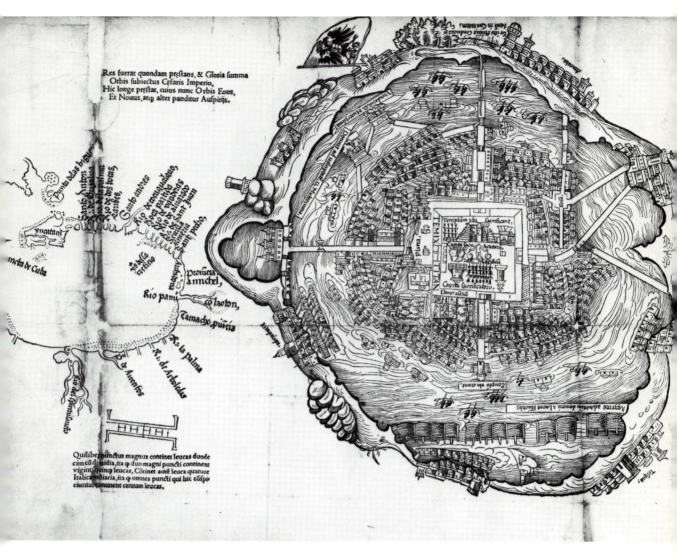

Res fuerat quondam preftans, & Gloria fumma
Orbis fubiectus Cefaris Imperio,
Hic longe preftat, cuius nunc Orbis Eous,
Et Nouus, atq; alter panditur Aufpitijs.

Quilibet punctus magnus continet leucas duode
cim cū dimidia, ita q̄ duo magni puncti continent
viginti quinq; leucas. Cōtinet autē leuca quatuor
Italica miliaria, ita q̄ omnes puncti qui hic cōfpi
ciuntur continent centum leucas.

which in the islands is called *maguey*, which is much better than most syrups, and from this plant they also make sugar and wine, which they likewise sell. There are many sorts of spun cotton, in hanks of every color, and it seems like the silk market at Granada, except that there is a much greater quantity. They sell as many colors for painters as may be found in Spain and all of excellent hues. They sell deerskins, with and without the hair, and some are dyed white or in various colors. They sell much earthenware, which for the most part is very good; there are both large and small pitchers, jugs, pots, tiles, and many other sorts of vessel, all of good clay and most of them glazed and painted. They sell maize both as grain and as bread and it is better both in appearance and in taste than any found in the islands or on the mainland. . . .

There are, in all districts of this great city, many temples or houses for their idols. . . .

Amongst these temples there is one, the principal one, whose great size and magnificence no human tongue could describe, for it is so large that within the precincts, which are surrounded by a very high wall, a town of some five

Above
62 Map of City and Lake of Mexico; from *Praeclara Ferdinandi Cortesii de Nova Maris Oceani Hispanica Narratio* (Nürnberg, 1524), the first German publication of Cortés' second despatch, or *Carta de Relación*. It was accompanied by this map and plan which Cortés said had been given him by Montezuma.

63 European impressions of Mexican culture: engraving purporting to show a Mexican Cú or temple; from G. B. Ramusio, *Delle Navigationi e Viaggi* (Venice, 1556), III, 307 r.

hundred inhabitants could easily be built. All round inside this wall there are very elegant quarters with very large rooms and corridors where their priests live. There are as many as forty towers, all of which are so high that in the case of the largest there are fifty steps leading up to the main part of it; and the most important of these towers is higher than that of the cathedral of Seville. They are so well constructed in both their stone and woodwork that there can be none better in any place, for all the stonework inside the chapels where they keep their idols is in high relief with figures and little houses, and the woodwork is likewise of relief and painted with monsters, and other figures and designs. All these towers are burial places of chiefs, and the chapels therein are each dedicated to the idol which he venerated.[16]

In general,

I will say only that these people live almost like those in Spain, and in as much harmony and order as there, and considering that they are barbarous and so far from the knowledge of God and cut off from all civilized nations, it is truly remarkable to see what they have achieved in all things.[17]

This, despite its air of judicious condescension, was calculated to mislead. The innocuous word 'almost' concealed a world of differences: the huge technical gap, for example, represented by hard metals, wheeled vehicles and beasts of burden, all unknown to the Mexicans. More serious still, in Spanish eyes, was the social and spiritual barrier raised by Mexican devotion to 'idols', by human sacrifice and ritual cannibalism. Cortés, in writing to his Catholic and imperial master, simply ignored the technical gap, and explained away the idols and the sacrifices as aberrations which could be remedied.

The most important of these idols, and the ones in whom they have most faith, I had taken from their places and thrown down the steps; and I had those chapels where they were cleaned, for they were full of the blood of sacrifices; and I had images of Our Lady and of other saints put there, which caused Mutezuma and the other natives some sorrow.[18]

As might be expected, Cortés also used his temporary ascendancy, during his first few days in the city, to demand gold, ostensibly as a tribute to the Emperor. In this matter also, Montezuma proved helpful. Cortés' account is substantially corroborated by Sahagún's informants:

When the Spaniards were installed in the palace, they asked Motecuhzoma about the city's resources and reserves and about the warriors' ensigns and shields. They questioned him closely and then demanded gold.

Motecuhzoma guided them to it. They surrounded him and crowded close with their weapons. He walked in the center, while they formed a circle around him.

When they arrived at the treasure house called Teucalco, the riches of gold and feathers were brought out to them: ornaments made of quetzal feathers, richly worked shields, disks of gold, the necklaces of the idols, gold nose plugs, gold greaves and bracelets and crowns.

The Spaniards immediately stripped the feathers from the gold shields and ensigns. They gathered all the gold into a great mound and set fire to everything else, regardless of its value. Then they melted down the gold into ingots. As for the precious green stones, they took only the best of them; the rest were snatched up by the Tlaxcaltecas. The Spaniards searched through the whole treasure house, questioning and quarreling, and seized every object they thought was beautiful.

Next they went to Motecuhzoma's storehouse, in the place called Totocalco [Place of the Palace of the Birds], where his personal treasures were kept. The Spaniards grinned like little beasts and patted each other with delight.

When they entered the hall of treasures, it was as if they had arrived in Paradise. They searched everywhere and coveted everything; they were slaves to their own greed. All of Motecuhzoma's possessions were brought out: fine

64 'El modo de baylar de los Mexicanos': a Mexican ceremonial dance; from a water-colour in Juan de Tovar 'Historia de la venida de los Indios . . .' MS, *c.* 1585. *John Carter Brown Library, Providence.*

bracelets, necklaces with large stones, ankle rings with little gold bells, the royal crowns and all the royal finery—everything that belonged to the king and was reserved to him only. They seized these treasures as if they were their own, as if this plunder were merely a stroke of good luck. And when they had taken all the gold, they heaped up everything else in the middle of the patio.[19]

According to Cortés the gold extorted from Montezuma amounted to more than 150,000 *pesos*. The honoured, though unbidden, guest seemed to be making himself master of the household; yet his position was precarious. It depended on Montezuma's co-operation, which could not be relied on so long as Montezuma was a free agent. At the end of a week of sight-seeing, therefore, Cortés kidnapped Montezuma, as he had long planned to do, and installed him, as puppet ruler and hostage, in the Axayacatl compound. Probably, with his European notions of hereditary kingship, he did not foresee that such humiliation would destroy Montezuma's authority. Shortly afterwards, Velázquez' lieutenant Narváez landed at Vera Cruz with an army considerably larger than Cortés' and with instructions to take over. This, to Cortés, was a far more serious threat than anything the Mexica seemed likely to attempt, and he turned his back on them in order to deal with Narváez. By a combination of force, bribes and promises, he induced most of Narváez' people to change sides; but in Cortés' absence Alvarado, left in charge with a small garrison, became alarmed by rumours of an intended rising in the city. He forestalled it, much as Cortés had done at Cholula, by a massacre of notables assembled for a ceremonial dance. The result of the massacre was the reverse of that intended. Cortés, re-entering the city with a greatly enlarged army, marched unopposed through silent streets; but once inside the Axayacatl compound, he was entrapped and closely besieged. A new *uei tlatouani* had already been chosen and installed. Montezuma, now a worthless hostage, was killed, probably by an Aztec missile. Cortés broke out of the trap, but at the cost of many men and horses, and all the baggage and the loot. Forced back on Tlaxcala, he had no recourse—other than accepting defeat, disgrace, perhaps execution—but systematic siege. His Indian allies, faced with the prospect of Aztec revenge if he should be

65 Two men playing at the ceremonial ball game: from water-colour drawing of the Mexican Indians who accompanied Cortés to Spain in 1529. 'Das Trachtenbuch des Christoph Weiditz', *MS, Germanisches National Museum, Nürnberg.*

66 Water-colour drawings of
the Mexican Indians who
accompanied Cortés to Spain
in 1529. 'Das Trachtenbuch
des Christoph Weiditz', *MS.
Germanisches National
Museum, Nürnberg*:
This page Man with parrot
Opposite left Warrior with
spear
Opposite right Chief wearing
feather-tapestry cloak

defeated, fielded a great army in his support. He invested the causeways.
He cut off the water supply. His *bergantines*, patrolling the lake, cut off the
supply of food. A sinister ally, smallpox—brought in with Narváez'
army—thinned the defenders. To avoid the hazards of street fighting and
to make the most of the horses, the advancing army destroyed the
buildings, street by street, and shovelled the rubble into the lake. When
the starving survivors finally surrendered, Cortés possessed himself of a
devastated ruin. Even the loot extorted from Montezuma was lost, sunk in
the lake on the *noche triste*. In the beautiful Spanish city which grew up on
the site, few visible traces remained of the Aztec past. The place was built
over as completely as the Roman cities of Europe.

No one knew how many more Mexicos remained undiscovered. Some
of Cortés' more enterprising captains led *entradas* of their own into the
lands bordering New Spain. Cortés himself never forgot that the discovery
of New Spain had originated in attempts to find a route to the Pacific and
so to the Far East. He continued to press the search, either for a strait
between the oceans, or for harbours which could become bases for Pacific
exploration. Between 1522 and 1526 Michoacán and most of the Pacific
coast area as far as the Santiago river were explored and conquered. The
great area known as New Galicia, north of the Santiago and of Michoacán,
was added in 1530–31 by Cortés' arch-enemy, the lawyer-*conquistador*
Nuño de Guzmán. New Galicia later became an immensely productive
source of silver, but Cortés and Nuño de Guzmán were both dead before
the silver veins were found.

Cortés sent two of his ablest captains on exploring and conquering expeditions to the south. Pedro de Alvarado led a well-equipped force through Tehuántepec into the highland region of Guatemala. Cristóbal de Olid was sent by sea to make a settlement on the north coast of Honduras. This was unknown territory; the Honduras coast had not been examined since 1502, when Columbus beat painfully west from Cape Honduras to Cape Gracias a Dios, and the head of the Gulf of Honduras had never been visited at all. It was the one remaining place in central America where a sea passage to the Pacific might be found, and Olid was instructed to look for such a strait. On landing near Puerto de Caballos, however, he repudiated Cortés' authority, set up an independent command, and became embroiled with some of Pedrarias' people exploring north from Darién. Cortés thought it necessary to deal with this explosive situation in person. We have Bernal Díaz' account, as well as Cortés' own, of how he managed it. His army—140 Spaniards and 3,000 Indians—marched from Espíritu Santo on the Gulf coast of Tehuántepec, across Tabasco, southern Campeche and northern Petén, to Nito at the head of the Gulf of Honduras. Much of this route ran through the classical Maya heartland, and in the area just west of the Golfo Dulce the Spaniards found several large towns; but most of the country was deserted. Everywhere ruined temple mounds stood as monuments to the long decay of the lowland Maya culture. It was appallingly difficult and quite unknown country, in which abrupt mountain ranges alternated with dense rain forest. One river and its riparian swamps had to be crossed by means of a floating bridge, whose

construction required the felling of over a thousand trees. Few horses survived the march, and the men who survived emerged from the forest like emaciated ghosts; yet Cortés' presence sufficed to restore order, of a sort. Olid had been murdered, and the men of Darién were willing to come to an agreement. Cortés found time to explore the Golfo Dulce, and prove that there was no strait. He returned to Mexico, where he had been given up for dead, by sea.

Meanwhile Alvarado had carried out a successful and ruthless campaign in highland Guatemala. We know very little about the initial impact of Spaniard on Maya, Maya on Spaniard, in that area. Alvarado was wholly a man of action, decisive, incurious, not very intelligent. The despatches which he sent to Cortés are simply curt accounts of military operations. The highland Maya, vigorous, intelligent, with a developed though decaying culture, lacked political unity, and Alvarado profited by the enmity between two principal peoples, Cakchiquel and Quiché, to support one against the other and eventually to subdue both. The Spanish city of Guatemala, on the first of its three successive sites, was founded in 1524. The country, though not productive of great wealth, was pleasant and prosperous enough. Bernal Díaz eventually secured an *encomienda* there, and lived in reasonable comfort, though he never ceased to complain of poverty.

The most vigorous branch of the Maya people in the sixteenth century

67 Drawings from the Florentine Codex, facsimile. *Florentine Codex: General History of the Things of New Spain*, by Fray Bernardino de Sahagún, translated from the Aztec into English . . . by Arthur J. O. Anderson and Charles E. Dibble, in 13 parts (Santa Fe, N.M., 1950–): *Opposite above* Parts V and VI (1957) Book 4, The Soothsayers, no. 57: Uitzilopochtli. *Opposite below* Part XI (1961) Book 10. The People, no. 58: The weaver. *Above* Part XI (1961) Book 10. The People, no. 70: The good farmer.

68 Drawings from the Florentine Codex, facsimile. *Florentine Codex: General History of the Things of New Spain*, by Fray Bernardino de Sahagún, translated from the Aztec into English . . . by Arthur J. O. Anderson and Charles E. Dibble, in 13 parts (Santa Fe, N.M., 1950–): *This page* Part XIII (1955) Book 12, The Conquest of Mexico, no. 1: The landing of the Spaniards. *Opposite* Part XIII (1955) Book 12, The Conquest of Mexico, no. 2: Spaniards on the march.

was in Yucatán. A number of large towns in the peninsula were still occupied, and resistance to Spanish intrusion was stubborn and prolonged. Since the initial coastings in 1517–19, Yucatán had been by-passed and neglected by the Spaniards hurrying to Mexico; but in 1526 Francisco de Montejo—one of Cortés' ablest captains, who had twice served him as *procurador* in Spain—secured a patent from the Crown to settle the 'islands of Yucatán and Cozumel'. Montejo began operations on the east coast in 1527 and by 1528 had explored the Bahía de Chetumal and established that Yucatán was a peninsula, not an island. This discovery led him to claim, as part of his *adelantamiento*, large areas of contiguous coastal territory, in Higueras to the east and Tabasco to the west. In 1528–29 he retired to New Spain to raise more men, and began his second Yucatán expedition from a base in Tabasco. For a few years, exploration and settlement went forward in Yucatán, both on the coast and inland. One settlement was planted among the ruins of the ancient city of Chichén Itzá. Montejo's followers, however—never more than about three hundred—were too few for their many undertakings. In 1534 a widespread Maya rising put all the Spanish settlements in peril, and Montejo, after discussing the situation in a general council, reluctantly agreed to withdraw. His subsequent activities were concentrated in Higueras-Honduras. The final conquest and settlement of Yucatán was

chiefly the work of his son and his nephew, in one of the most prolonged military efforts the Spanish Indies ever witnessed.

The *Adelantado* Montejo explained his own initial failure in Yucatán in a dispirited letter to the Crown in 1534:

In these provinces [of Yucatán] there is not a single river, although there are lakes, and the hills are of dry rock, dry and waterless. The entire land is covered by thick bush and is so stony that there is not a single square foot of soil. No gold has been discovered, nor is there anything [else] from which advantage can be gained. The inhabitants are the most abandoned and treacherous in all the lands discovered to this time, being a people who never yet killed a Christian except by

69 Portrait medal of Hernán Cortés, made by Christoph Weiditz during Cortés' visit to Spain in 1529. One of the very few portraits of an early conquistador probably drawn from life, and in sharp contrast with the sentimental piety of the many posthumous portraits of Cortés. *Staatliche Museen zu Berlin.*

70 The ruins commonly known as Las Monjas, at Chichén Itzá, Yucatán; from F. Catherwood, *Views of Ancient Monuments in Central America, Chiapas and Yucatan* (London, 1844), plate 21. Montejo, in his campaign of conquest in Yucatán, encamped with his army among the spectacular ruins of this Toltec-style city in Maya territory. The city had been abandoned some years before, and the ruins probably appeared to Montejo much as they did to Catherwood.

foul means and who have never made war except by artifice. Not once have I questioned them on any matter that they have not answered, 'Yes', with the purpose of causing me to leave them and go somewhere else.

Having become thoroughly acquainted with the land, and in seven years of hardship and danger having achieved no reward nor found gold, with the arrival of news from Peru the soldiers will remain no longer.[20]

There were no more Mexicos. The minds of the adventurous were turning to Peru.

6 Peru

Discovery and conquest, though difficult to separate in historical narrative, were in their nature distinct activities. Throughout the story of discovery there were moments when successful explorers paused to gaze in wonder at what they had found, before proceeding to attack it, plunder it, and often enough—in so far as it was the work of man—destroy it. These were the moments of climax in the story of discovery, hard for anyone save a participant to recapture, hard even for participants to describe. Some participants managed it. In Mexico Bernal Díaz, whether by nature or design, succeeded in conveying the experience of those breathless moments. Cortés too, in his more calculated account, allowed the excitement to show through. Similar moments occurred in the discovery of Peru; but they are less easily shared. Most of the chroniclers—Zárate was the only significant exception—were themselves fighting men, whether by choice or by force of circumstance. They concentrated their attention on the drama, the hazards and the rewards of conquest, and upon the savage faction fights which broke out between the conquerors. For the most part they wrote only perfunctory summaries of the processes of exploration and discovery.

Francisco Pizarro wrote nothing comparable with Cortés' *Letters*; he could not write. He dictated, when necessary, to a secretary; but he was a strictly practical predator, unimaginative and taciturn, and probably the idea of recording his impressions for posterity, of describing for description's sake, never entered his head. Moreover, unlike Cortés, he secured his contract with the Crown beforehand (travelling to Spain for the purpose in 1529); he entered Peru with a governor's commission in his pocket, and had no need of plausible writing to excuse irregular proceedings.

None of Pizarro's followers wrote anything comparable with Bernal Díaz' *True History of the Conquest of New Spain*. Pedro Pizarro, perhaps, came nearest to it. He was Francisco's cousin, and accompanied him from Spain in 1530 as a page, at the age of fifteen. Like Díaz, he wrote in old age, but apparently with undimmed memory. His *Relación* has the freshness of eyewitness report, and in places recalls the author's adolescent wonder. It conveys admirably, for example, the nervous tension of the long wait before the fight in the square at Cajamarca. Pedro Pizarro, however, lacked Díaz' gift of description; his meaning is often obscure; and though he was present throughout the early stages of the conquest, he did not experience the long and arduous years of exploration before the conquest could begin. The fullest and most detailed of the early accounts of Peru are by Cieza de León who arrived in the Indies as a boy of fourteen in 1532. He did not reach Peru until 1547, however, and so was an eyewitness neither of the discovery nor of the early stages of the conquest. Nor was Zárate, whose admirable chronicle covers the whole story and contains the most convincing of all the descriptions of the principal personalities. Zárate was an accomplished historian; the Gómara, one might say, of Peru. He was actually in Peru only a year, on an official mission in 1544–45; though he made excellent use of his time. Indeed the only eyewitness account of those exploring years is the *True Relation* of Francisco Jérez who took part in all three of Pizarro's exploratory voyages, latterly in the capacity of secretary to Pizarro; though he returned to Panamá in the course of the second voyage and so missed the crucial moment of discovery at Tumbes. His narrative is an official account, in the sense that Pizarro told him to write it, and is admirably terse and businesslike; but it is brief, and ends with the affray at Cajamarca. Jérez never saw high Cuzco.

Nor have we any contemporary accounts of the reactions of Peruvians to their first encounter with Europeans, comparable with those which Sahagún's informants supplied for Mexico. The *Royal Commentaries* of the Inca Garcilaso de la Vega provide, it is true, a principal source of information about pre-conquest Peru. His asides, scraps of personal reminiscence, recollections of conversations with old men, are of especial interest and value. But for the events of discovery and conquest, which took place before he was born, Garcilaso relied on Gómara and Zárate. He was a prominent *mestizo*, brought up as a Spaniard; he left Peru as a young man, and though he occasionally thought of returning, never did so. He certainly felt the pull of both loyalties; but he wrote in Spanish, for a Spanish public, many years after the event.

The conquest of Peru followed, at least superficially, a pattern similar to that of Mexico: the establishment of a coastal base; the march inland towards the centres of power; the exploitation of internal divisions, including, in Peru, a succession dispute; the capture of the ruler in a surprise attack; the extortion of ransom; the use of the captive as hostage and puppet; his elimination when his usefulness was exhausted; and finally the naked take-over of power by force. This was not necessarily conscious imitation. Many of the stratagems employed by both Cortés and Pizarro, the seizure of the 'cacique' as hostage, for example, had been for some years familiar—one might almost say standard practice—on the Isthmus and in the islands.

The stories of discovery had less in common. In Mexico the processes of exploration and conquest were closely connected. The attack on the Aztec empire followed almost immediately upon the discovery of its existence. The route to Mexico lay along coasts inhabited by settled people, where food for a substantial armed force was available. Most of the discoverers participated in the conquest. In Peru the conquest was preceded by long and arduous exploration, south from Panamá, by years of search, with frequent failures and disappointments, in pursuit of vague rumours gathered from Indians. The formidable personality of Pizarro gave the enterprise its unity; but few of the men who accompanied him in his preliminary explorations marched also in the conquest. The conquerors of Peru, except for a few leaders, were recruited in Panamá, in Nicaragua or in Spain, after the existence of the Inca empire had been discovered and made known. The rhetoric, the seeming spontaneity, the general air of rapid improvisation which marked the course of events in Mexico, were lacking in Peru. To some extent this reflected the personalities of the leaders: the dour, self-centred determination of Pizarro, and Almagro's abilities as planner and business manager; but even more it reflected geographical fact.

Peru was vastly more remote, less accessible to explorers from Europe or the Caribbean, than Mexico. The Inca dynasty in the early sixteenth century governed a territory stretching through thirty-five degrees of latitude, approximately from the Equator south to the Maule river in central Chile. Despite its great extent, however, the empire was isolated within its boundaries. The Incas were mountain people, and their centres of power lay inland, in the high, bleak depressions between the Cordilleras. The great mountain system of the Andes, in its double and triple parallel ranges, ran throughout the empire from north to south. West of it lay the narrow Pacific coastal desert, east the *montaña* jungle, into which the Inca armies rarely ventured; further east still the Amazonian rain forest, wide as the Atlantic and far more difficult to cross. Scarcely less formidable, the jumbled mountains and precipitous valleys of Colombia lay between Peru and the Caribbean. Colombia, it is true, had big navigable rivers, draining north into the Caribbean, but their headwaters were in wild mountain country and they gave no easy access to Peru. For practical purposes, Peru was inaccessible from the Atlantic and the Caribbean, and could be approached only from the Pacific, where the fringes of the empire touched the coast. South of the Equator a series of short rivers, flowing from the western Cordillera, irrigated narrow parallel strips of the coastal desert and created ribbon oases. For many centuries, long before the Incas began their career of conquest, the oases had been inhabited by settled, city-building peoples. Some of these people were sea-farers, using canoes and large sailing rafts both for fishing and for coastwise trade. They found materials for these craft about the Gulf of Guayaquil, which was normally the northern limit of their voyaging. They had no inducement to go further north: the coast from Guayaquil to the Isthmus was a thousand miles of sparsely inhabited mangrove swamp.

Balboa's expedition of 1513 (in which Pizarro was a leading participant) brought Spaniards to the shore of the South Sea; but there was no immediate rush to explore this unattractive coast. Pedrarias, shortly after his arrival, sent an expedition under his cousin Gaspar de Morales, with Pizarro as second-in-command, to follow up Balboa's discovery, but its purpose was limited: to secure control of the Gulf of San Miguel and the off-shore Pearl Islands. This object achieved, the expedition turned to slaving and plunder. Systematic exploration of the Pacific coast had to await the establishment of a permanent base and the construction of adequate ships. Ship-building began, not very efficiently, in 1517; Pedrarias moved the seat of his government to Panamá in 1519; Gil González Dávila sailed westward from Panamá in 1521, Pascual de Andagoya eastward in 1522.

It is surprising, at first sight, that neither of these commands was given to Pizarro. He was an old hand in the Indies, having come out to

Hispaniola in 1502 and moved on to *Tierra Firme* with Ojeda in 1509. He was an experienced captain, not dashing nor brilliant, but capable, tough, dependable. He had often been a trusted second-in-command and had led minor expeditions himself. He was too suspicious, too vindictive, too narrow in his loyalties, to be much loved; probably he never fully trusted anyone outside the tight circle of men from his home town in Extremadura; but he could be genial in a tight-lipped fashion, and was widely respected. He was a town-councillor of Panamá and an *encomendero*. *Encomiendas* on the Isthmus were not much by the later standards of Mexico or Peru, but Pizarro's was one of the best. He had capital, therefore, to finance *entradas*; or at least could command credit. His part in Balboa's arrest had made him, in a grimly ironic sense, Balboa's successor; traditionally the man who captured a rebel was often rewarded with the captive's property or command. Yet Pizarro was passed over; probably the reason was his very seniority, the *antigüedad* by which he himself set store. There was a standing jealousy throughout Pedrarias' government between the old hands, the survivors of the Ojeda-Nicuesa expeditions, and the more sophisticated crowd who came out with Pedrarias in 1514. Pedrarias himself always preferred his own people to command when he could.

Gil González, it is true, was one of Fonseca's favourites, and had come out with a royal commission; Pedrarias could not prevent his using it, though he tried to obstruct. But when Gil González returned with reports of Nicaragua—populous, accessible, exploitable—Pedrarias promptly appointed one of his own men, Francisco Hernández de Córdoba, to command the conquest, which he conducted with swift and brutal efficiency.

Andagoya was Pedrarias' man. He was a gentle creature by the standards of that time and place, intelligent, well-read, with an observant eye and ear for ethnographic detail. His *Relación*[1] contains much interesting information about the Darién Indians. He was appointed to several important commands during his Indies career, but something always went wrong; either he fell sick, or he was ousted by a more powerful rival—Benalcázar, for example, had no difficulty in getting rid of him in Popayán in 1541. In 1522—according to his own somewhat sketchy account—he seems to have sailed two or three hundred miles down the coast of what is now the Chocó province of Colombia. The population of this mangrove-lined coast today is mainly Negro, but then there were several Indian groups, including people of Cuevan speech similar to those about the Gulf of San Miguel, besides the Chocó, who were shy forest dwellers. Andagoya had Cuevan guides with him, and learned from them of a more powerful and warlike people further south. He landed (probably) somewhere south of Baudo and marched inland for six or seven days, till he came to the country which he called Birú. He 'ascended a great river for twenty leagues, and met with many chiefs and villages, and a very strong fortress at the junction of two rivers, with people guarding it'. After some skirmishing Andagoya 'pacified' the country and 'received accounts both from the chiefs and from merchants and interpreters, concerning all the coast, and everything that has since been discovered, as far as Cuzco; especially with regard to the inhabitants of each province, for in their trading these people extend their wanderings over many lands'. With this information, he travelled down-river to the coast, spent some time exploring the 'ports' (the delta?) in a canoe; fell ill; and returned to Panamá.[1]

The 'great river' was probably the San Juan; the 'strong fortress' probably guarded the confluence with the Río de Calima; and 'Birú' may have denoted the area of the Calima culture, which stretched from the San Juan valley over the western Cordillera into the upper Cauca valley. It was a cultural rather than a political grouping, containing many small chiefdoms, and though still populous and prosperous was already in decline in Andagoya's time. It had in the past a notable tradition of gold working, and many spectacular gold objects have been found in tombs throughout the area. Andagoya, however, makes no mention of gold. Whether the people of 'Birú' had any direct contact with, or knowledge of, the area which Spaniards later knew as Peru, is uncertain. Andagoya said they had, and claimed that many of the difficulties of the ensuing search for Peru could have been avoided if his directions had been followed; but Andagoya's *Relación* was written with the advantages of hindsight, twenty years after his visit to 'Birú' and ten years after the Spanish invasion of Peru. Possibly the reports he collected were merely part of a general current of rumour concerning rich kingdoms further south; rumours such as led Enciso in the *Suma de Geografía* to place in the South Sea 'islands where there are many pearls and much gold . . . and lands where, the Indians say, they have books and read as we do'.

Whatever the source of these reports, Pizarro seems to have taken them seriously. He was one of the few who did, probably *faute de mieux*. The hopes of ambitious captains in Darién at that time were fixed on Nicaragua, and Pizarro did not stand well enough with the governor to expect a command there; so he asked, and received, the command which Andagoya was too ill to exercise, and formed a partnership to exploit it. Among the sleeping partners was Pedrarias; he expected to be 'cut in' on any serious expedition organized within his jurisdiction, though there is no evidence that he contributed much by way of investment. A prominent backer was the judge Gaspar de Espinosa who came from an important banking family in Spain. His judicial office did not prevent him from playing the *conquistador*. He had financed a number of *cabalgadas*, and had himself taken part in some of them. Others made investments, including Bartolomé Ruiz of Moguer, chief pilot of all three of the exploring voyages. The enterprise, however, was Pizarro's. He was always clearly the principal partner. His active partner was Diego de Almagro, an associate of long standing who possessed a smaller *encomienda* adjoining Pizarro's. Though a fighting man as Pizarro was, he made his chief contribution as business manager, recruiting the men, provisioning the ships, arranging the finances; tasks for which Pizarro had neither taste nor aptitude. Pizarro was well aware of his dependence on Almagro, but always treated him as an inferior, as a trusted *mayordomo* rather than as an equal partner. By the social criteria of the time, of course, he *was* inferior. Pizarro, despite his illegitimate birth, his illiteracy, his plebian upbringing and tastes, had some claim to lineage and standing; enough to qualify him, when the time came, for the habit of Santiago. Almagro was a nameless foundling.

The partners acquired Andagoya's ships and made their first voyage in 1524, with about eighty fighting men, recruited on a profit-sharing basis, besides the sailors, who probably received wages. The voyage was a failure. The expedition did not even go as far as Andagoya had done. Landings were made at two unidentifiable places in the Chocó, 'Port Famine' and 'Burned Village', and Almagro lost an eye in a shoreside skirmish. There were no profits. Pizarro's mistake lay in underestimating the obstacles and the sheer distance which separated him from the kingdoms of rumour. He did not know that before he found anything worth conquering he would have to spend many months, in an area of unreliable winds and contrary currents, exploring an unhealthy coast where 'living off the country' was out of the question. To embark on such service with a substantial force of fighting men crowded into small, inadequately provisioned ships was to court disaster. Pizarro's people— those who survived the voyage—returned with discouraging tales of the Chocó.

Espinosa naturally hesitated to throw good money after bad, and there were difficulties over financing a second attempt. It was probably at this stage that the priest, Hernando de Luque—whom some chroniclers mention as a full partner in the enterprise—became important, whether as an investor in his own right, or as Espinosa's agent. Allegations by the heirs of both men in subsequent litigation make Luque's role difficult to define precisely; but late in 1526 the expedition got away, with two ships, 160 men, and a few horses; and with a more realistic appreciation of the obstacles to be encountered.

The settlers of the Isthmus had developed a technique for countering the high mortality which most expeditions suffered in exploring unhealthy coasts. An expedition would go as far as practicable by sea; the main body of men would then land, and proceed along the coast on foot, picking up what food and plunder they could find. If enough ships were available, one might be sent ahead to reconnoitre; the others would return to their home base, pick up more supplies and—more important—more men, and carry them to a rendezvous at the point the main body was expected to reach. By this means the expedition could be reinforced regularly with fresh men, and the sick could at intervals be shipped home. Pizarro tried this on his second voyage; he himself, with his main body, landed at the mouth of Andagoya's Río de San Juan; Almagro took one ship back to Panamá for supplies and reinforcements; Ruiz sailed on south beyond the Equator.

It was in the course of this reconnaissance that Ruiz found the first reliable evidence of a high culture to the south: a big sea-going raft, the first native sailing vessel encountered by Europeans in the New World. The wondering, almost breathless description of it, which eventually reached the King, is plausibly attributed to Francisco Jérez:

They took a ship carrying about thirty men, of whom eleven dived into the sea. The rest were captured; the pilot detained three of them, and treated them well,

71 The Pacific coast of the Americas, from a *portolano* by Diogo Homem, 1558. *British Museum, Add. MS 5415 A, fos 21 and 22.*

intending to use them as interpreters; the others he put ashore.

This ship . . . seemed to be of about thirty tons. The keel and bottom were made of reed stems as thick as posts, lashed together with *henequén* [sisal], a fibre resembling hemp. There were raised platforms made of lighter stems, lashed in the same way, on which the cargo was stowed and the people sat, to keep dry, because the hull was awash. It had slender masts and yards of wood, well-cut cotton sails, of much the same design as those in our ships, excellent rigging made of the same *henequén*, and stone anchors shaped like grindstones.

They carried as trade goods many personal ornaments of gold and silver, including crowns, diadems, belts and bracelets; armour, such as greaves and breastplates; tweezers and rattles; beads and rubies in strings and clusters; silver-mounted mirrors, cups and other drinking vessels. There were quantities of woollen and cotton mantles, tunics . . . and other garments, most of them lavishly embroidered with designs of animals, birds, trees and fish, in scarlet, purple, blue, yellow, and other colours. They had little weights for weighing gold . . . beaded bags containing small emeralds, chalcedonies and other stones, pieces of crystal and amber. They were taking all these to barter for coral and white shells, which they make into counters. The whole ship was loaded with these goods.[2]

The raft altered the whole aspect of the voyage; but the voyagers were still a long way from the source of all these treasures. When Ruiz rejoined Pizarro at the San Juan he found the army in desperate straits. They had been unable to move along the coast. They had exhausted their supplies, and many had died. Almagro, long delayed, brought some food but no reinforcements: the reputation of the coast had reached Panamá. He was sent back to try again. Ruiz ferried the rest of the people on down the coast of Ecuador. At Atacames they found a fair-sized Indian settlement (the town still exists) but the people were truculent and the Spaniards, in their enfeebled state, dared not attack. Finally the expedition retired to recuperate on an uninhabited island—Gallo Island—in the Tumaco estuary, which Ruiz had reconnoitred. Here they received, in the first ship from Panamá, not reinforcements, but an order from the governor (Pedrarias' successor, Pedro de los Ríos) that any men who wished to return should be given passage back to Panamá. Most of them— disillusioned, weary of privation, sick and afraid—accepted; though some of the sick—Francisco Jérez was one—rejoined the expedition later. Only a handful—thirteen, according to most accounts—remained; either they were braver, fitter or more optimistic than the rest, or were under personal obligations to Pizarro, or had invested more in the enterprise than they could afford to write off. The key man, Ruiz, the seaman—taciturn, capable, indispensable—decided to continue; his sailors, so far as we know, were offered no choice.

Los Ríos in fact rendered Pizarro an unwitting service. The drastic reduction of his following, in numbers and in baggage, changed its character from a hungry itinerant army looking for something to conquer, to a serious exploring expedition, which was what the circumstances required. Early in 1527 they sailed rapidly on down the coast, entered the Gulf of Guayaquil and came to anchor before Tumbes, a well-built, well-ordered city. Too few to appear threatening, they were civilly received. Visits and gifts were exchanged. There was no shooting, except a target demonstration by Pizarro's gunner, Pedro de Candía, which the Inca notables acknowledged with polite admiration. Pizarro's people grasped that they were on the fringes of a sophisticated, highly organised society. They made a rapid cruise of reconnaissance down the coast, as far as the Santa river in about 9°S, and then returned to Panamá, taking with them more Indian boys to be trained as interpreters and a small collection of local products, obtained either in barter or as gifts: vessels of gold, silver and pottery, samples of textiles, and (according to Zárate, though it seems unlikely) live 'sheep of the country'—llamas.

The evidence of Peruvian wealth seemed to the partners strong enough to justify a direct approach to the Crown, and they scraped together enough money for Pizarro to travel to Spain. He was fortunate, in that his visit coincided with Cortés' triumphant appearance at court, fresh from Mexico; the official mind was thus prepared for the kind of application Pizarro had to make. His *capitulación* empowered him to conquer 'Peru', with the title of governor and captain-general which rendered him independent of that rapacious sleeping partner, the governor of Panamá, and gave him unequivocal military command and civil authority over his other associates. Luque was offered a somewhat vague prospect of becoming bishop of Tumbes; Almagro, bitterly resentful of an arrangement which emphasized his own subordinate standing, had to be pacified, with difficulty, by promises. Meanwhile recruitment went forward. During Pizarro's absence Almagro continued to solicit investment and encourage recruits in Panamá. Ruiz went up the coast to Nicaragua, to take advantage of disappointed expectations there, and opened negotiations with several prominent captains, to persuade them to bring their ships and their following south, to join in the invasion of Peru. Pizarro himself brought a big party from Spain, mostly from his home country, from Trujillo-Cáceres, the harsh, arid and backward area of eastern Extremadura. The party included a cousin and four half-brothers: the Pizarro ascendancy in the conquest of Peru was not based solely on natural leadership or royal appointment. The Pizarros and their Extremaduran following formed a *bloc* within the army of conquest, often at loggerheads with men from other parts of Spain, especially when those others had long experience in the Indies. Only Francisco Pizarro himself— both an Extremeño and a veteran of Indian fighting and jungle marches on the Isthmus—could bridge the gap and hold the army together.

The main body of Pizarro's expedition, about 180 men, left Panama at the beginning of 1531, expecting other contingents to follow. The destination was Tumbes, where Pizarro proposed to establish the capital of his new government. Ruiz had by this time mastered the peculiarities of the navigation, and at first they made remarkably good time. Within two weeks they had passed the Tumaco; but in the neighbourhood of Cape San Francisco they ran into persistent head winds, and decided to put into San Marco Bay (in northern Ecuador), send the ships back for supplies and reinforcements, and march overland. This proved to be a mistake. The march was slow and arduous, through thick forest and coastal swamps, under incessant rain. They found few settlements and only a little loot, chiefly emeralds, with which they were unfamiliar. They suffered a severe attack of *verruga peruana*, an insect-borne disease peculiar to the western foothills of the Andes, which causes ugly and painful swellings and can cause death. They looked for a place where they could rest and dry out, on Puná island in the Gulf of Guayaquil; but there they were fiercely attacked by the primitive and belligerent inhabitants. Reinforcements arrived from time to time, however: at Puerto Viejo (Manta), Benalcázar from Nicaragua with thirty men, and at Puná, Hernando de Soto with a hundred. Eventually the whole force crossed from Púna to Tumbes in a flotilla of balsas; only to find the town in ruins. A series of misfortunes had afflicted the area since the last Spanish visit: a devastating epidemic, almost certainly of smallpox, an Old-World disease new to Peru, which had probably travelled overland from the Caribbean; and a savage civil war between the adherents of two sons of the last *Sapa Inca*, Huayna Capac—'the Old Cuzco' as the Spaniards called him—who had died in the great sickness and left the succession in doubt.

For some months Pizarro's people explored the arid north-west corner of Peru, moving mostly by sea and meeting little resistance. They established a base, a Spanish 'city', about a hundred miles south of Tumbes, in the Chira valley, and called it San Miguel. The town was subsequently moved to another site, in the Piura valley, where it stands today, the modern town of Piura. It was not a place of much promise or importance. The Pizarros may have had difficulty, at this stage, in preventing some of the newcomers from seizing ships and returning to Nicaragua. They were in a remote corner of the Inca empire; the towns, and the river valleys in which they stood, were small oases in an immensity of desert and seemed to have no mineral wealth. The intelligence which the Spaniards received, however, was in other respects hopeful. They learned that one of the contenders in the civil war, Huáscar, ruler of Cuzco, had been defeated and captured by the other, Atahuallpa, whose power base was in Quito and the northern provinces. These northern regions had only recently been incorporated into the Inca realm and their inhabitants were still foreigners to the people of central Peru; like frontier provinces in other empires, they had become recruiting grounds for the imperial armies. Cuzco, however, was the venerated heart of the empire, the political and religious capital; and the *Sapa Inca*, whatever the basis of his support might be, must reign in Cuzco. As it happened, even as the Spaniards sweated and grumbled on the coast, Atahuallpa was encamped with a powerful force not far inland, at the agreeable hill town of Cajamarca, in the course of a leisurely progress towards Cuzco in the wake of his armies. There at Cajamarca, it seemed, was the key to a complex and still changing political situation. Pizarro decided to seek out the Inca. His little army left San Miguel in September 1532: about 170 men, a smaller force than Cortés had led into Mexico, but better equipped; about sixty of them were mounted. Their route lay first along the coast, by way of Piura, Motupe and Saña; then inland, probably up the valley of the Chancay, broad and fertile near the coast, narrowing to a deep canyon with steep terraced sides as they climbed through the Andean foothills. Above the source of the Chancay, at about 13,000 feet, they would have come out on to the watershed, and turned south, across a great expanse of treeless savannah, covered by wiry grey-green grass and swept by cold winds. Here and there Inca watchtowers looked down on them; but their passage was not opposed. Atahuallpa may have been curious to see them; he probably considered them too few to be dangerous, and thought he was luring them into a trap. According to some Spanish accounts, he later confessed that he had intended to kill the Spaniards in order to gain possession of their horses.

Cajamarca today is a pleasant small town in a beautiful and fertile valley; a huddle of red-tiled roofs surrounded by pastures full of cattle and shaded by eucalyptus groves. These features are all introductions from the Old World. In Inca times the buildings were grey and severe and the roofs were of thatch; but Jérez and Pedro Pizarro, despite a natural nervous tension, both noticed the beauty of the place. The town had a big central plaza; the Spaniards occupied the flanking buildings, which were deserted, and despatched their envoys to the Inca's quarters outside the town. Hernando de Soto, always in the forefront, characteristically tried to impress the Inca by a display of horsemanship. Atahuallpa—who had never before seen a horse—remained, to all appearance, stonily unmoved. He agreed, nevertheless—with a self-confidence which in retrospect seems astonishing—to a meeting with Pizarro in the plaza. In that confined space, the Spaniards emerged at a pre-arranged signal, massacred his retinue and seized his person. On that day—16 November 1532— discovery merged into conquest.

The Spanish chronicles all remarked on Atahuallpa's shrewdness, and the speed with which he reacted to a hitherto unimaginable predicament. As soon as he discovered—with some surprise, apparently—that the Spaniards intended to keep him captive and hostage instead of killing him out of hand, he began to reassert himself. He had powerful armies on foot, under capable generals; Inca discipline was deeply ingrained; even as a captive he could command obedience. He used his authority for three main purposes: to dissuade his adherents from any immediate attempt at rescue, which might cost him his life; to prevent his captive rival, Huáscar, from taking advantage of the turn of events; and to buy his own liberty. He ordered his generals, accordingly, to remain on guard where they were; he sent secret orders to have Huáscar killed; and—noticing the Spaniards' obsessive love for gold—he offered them an immense, an almost unimaginable quantity of gold and silver objects by way of ransom. This ransom was duly collected, by Atahuallpa's orders, melted down and distributed; enough to make every man in the army rich for life, if he survived. Humble foot-soldiers at Cajamarca got more than famous captains amassed in years, in Mexico or the Isthmus.

Through the early months of 1533 Pizarro's people, with the captive Inca in their midst, waited at Cajamarca, while the ransom instalments trickled in, and Almagro, daily expected from Panamá with reinforcements, made his slow way up from the coast. Pizarro dared not scatter his forces; but some small parties went out to reconnoitre and to hurry the payments. Atahuallpa himself urged that a party of Spaniards should go to Cuzco, to supervise the stripping of gold plates from the walls of the Coricancha, the temple of the sun. Volunteers were sought for this

¶ Uerdadera relacion de la conquista del Peru
y prouincia del Cuzco llamada la nueua Castilla: Conquistada por el magnifico
y esforçado cauallero Francisco piçarro hijo del capitan Gonçalo piçarro caua
llero de la ciudad de Trugillo: como capitan general de la cesarea y catholica
magestad del emperador y rey nuestro señor: Embiada a su magestad por Francisco
de Xerez natural de la muy noble y muy leal ciudad de Seuilla secretario de
sobredicho señor en todas las puincias y conquista de la nueua Castilla y vno
de los primeros conquistadores della.
¶ Fue vista y examinada esta obra por mandado de los señores inquisidores
del arçobispado de Seuilla: z impressa en casa de Bartholome perez en el mes
de Julio. Año del parto virginal mil z quinientos y treynta y quatro.

72 Title page of Francisco
Jérez (Xeres) narrative of the
conquest of Peru, showing
the scene in the plaza at
Cajamarca, Pizarro, the priest
Valverde, and Atahuallpa in
his litter. Francisco de Xeres,
*Verdadera relación de la
conquista del Peru* (Seville,
1534).

frightening mission, and three comparatively expendable foot-soldiers selected. They travelled in litters, with native guides and carriers, and were received with frigid acquiescence by Quisquis, the commander of the Quiteño occupying force, who 'liked the Christians very little, though he marvelled greatly at them'.[3] Quisquis' people refused to help in stripping the temple, as Atahuallpa suspected they might; the three men themselves prised off the plates with copper crowbars. They returned to Cajamarca with many llama loads of gold; but—alas for history!—left no first-hand record of their impressions. Another and larger party—twenty-five horse under Hernando, the only Pizarro who was both legitimate and literate—did better in this respect. Hernando was given two main tasks. The first was to collect the accumulated treasure of the temple-shrine of Pachacámac. The ruins of Pachacámac, in the coastal desert near Lima, remain today one of the principal archaeological sites of coastal Peru. They housed a famous oracle, widely revered and consulted in pre-Inca times, whose prestige and wealth had spread more widely still as a result of the Inca conquest of the coast. The second task was to find, and if possible, capture the Inca general Chalcuchima or Chilicuchima, who was supposed to be bringing down an instalment of the ransom gold by way of Jauja. Hernando was outwitted by the priests of the Pachacámac oracle, and the loot from the shrine was disappointing; but Chalcuchima was intercepted at Jauja and induced by 'sweet talk' to accompany Hernando to Cajamarca.

Hernando Pizarro's journey was a considerable feat. He and his companions rode for hundreds of miles over country completely unknown to them. Their route took them over high *puna* from Cajamarca to Huamachuco, then up the immense ravine now known as the Callejón de Huaylas, with the snows of Huascarán on their left and the rushing Santa in its deep hot canyon on their right. Huascarán, at 22,000 feet, was by far the highest mountain that any of them had ever seen. At Huaraz they turned west, crossed the Cordillera Negra, and rode down the steep foothills to the coast. Then south, crossing in succession stretches of desert and open irrigated valleys, the homeland of an orderly, sophisticated culture, the Chimú, until they arrived at Pachacámac. On the return journey, they retraced their steps up the coast as far as Chincha (Patavilca), then toiled inland up the Patavilca valley to Cajatambo at its head—a substantial town then as now. They planned to intercept Chalcuchima on the highland road between Jauja and Huánuco, and to reach it had to cross a particularly desolate part of the coastal Andean range, the Cordillera Huayhuash, by a 15,000 foot pass. Because they carried credentials from Atahuallpa, they were supplied, everywhere they went, with food, porters and guides. Hernando himself wrote a concise account. A somewhat fuller account, which follows, was written by the notary Miguel Estete, who was one of the party, and this narrative was later incorporated in Francisco Jérez' *Verdadera relación*. It gives a fascinating glimpse of Inca organisation, as it worked at the local level, on the eve of its disintegration.

He commenced his journey on the 14th of January, and on the same day he

73 Indians conscripted as porters by a Spanish expedition; engraving from Theodor de Bry, *America*, Part IV (Antwerp, 1594), plate iv.

crossed some difficult passes, and two rivers, passing the night at a village called Totopamba, which is on a steep declivity. The Indians received him well and gave him good food and all he required for the night, and men to carry his baggage. Next day he left this village, and reached another called Corongo, where he passed the night. Half way there was a great pass of snow, and all the way there were many flocks with their shepherds, who have their houses in the mountains, as in Spain. In this village they were given food, and all they required, and Indians to carry the loads. This village is subject to Guamachoco. Next day they started and came to another small village called Piga, where they passed the night. They found no inhabitants, as they had run away from fear. This was a very severe march, for they had to descend a flight of steps cut out of the stone, which was very dangerous for the horses. Next day, at dinner time, they reached a large village in a valley, and a very rapid river flowed across the road. It was spanned by two bridges close together, made of network in the following manner. They build a foundation near the water, and raise it to a great height; and from one side of the river to the other there are cables made of reeds like osiers, but as thick as a man's thigh, and they are fastened to great stones. From one cable to the other is the width of a cart. Smaller cords are interwoven between the cables, and great stones are fastened beneath, to steady them. By one of these bridges the common people cross over, and a porter is stationed there to receive transit dues; while the lords and captains use the other, which is always closed, but they opened it for the Captain and his followers, and the horses crossed over very well. . . . All this land has abundant supplies of maize and many flocks; and, as the Christians marched along the road, they saw the sheep crossing it. Next day, at dinner time, the Captain reached a great town called Huaras, the lord of which was called Pumacapllai. He and his people supplied the Christians with provisions, and with Indians to carry the loads. This town is in a plain, and a river flows near it. Other villages were in sight, with flocks and maize fields. They had two hundred head of sheep in a yard, merely to supply the wants of the Captain and his men. . . . Here the Captain left the royal road which leads to Cuzco, and took that of the coast valley. Next day he stopped for the night at a place called Marcara, the chief of which was named Corcara. Here there are pastures, and at a certain time of the year they bring the flocks to browse, as they do in Castile and Extremadura. From this village the rivers flow to the sea, which makes the road very difficult, for all the country inland is very cold, and with much water and snow. The coast is very hot, and there is very little rain. The rain is not sufficient for the crops, but the waters that flow from the mountains irrigate the land, which yields abundant supplies of provisions and fruits.

Next day they departed from this village, and marching along the banks of a river, following its downward course through fields and fruit gardens, they stopped for the night at a village called Guaracanga. Next day they stopped at a large place near the sea called Parpunga. It has a strong house with seven encircling walls painted in many devices both inside and outside, with portals well built like those of Spain, and two tigers at the principal doorway. The inhabitants were filled with fear at the sight of a people never before seen, and of the horses, which astonished them still more. The Captain spoke to them through the interpreter who accompanied him, to reassure them, and they then did good service.

In this village they came upon another broader road, made by the people of the coast, and bounded by walls on either side. . . . On the following day the Captain stopped at a village called Llachu, to which he gave the name of 'the town of partridges', because there were many partridges kept in cages in all the houses. The Indians of this village were friendly and did good service. . . .

The next day was Sunday, the 30th of January [*sic*]. The Captain departed from this village, and, without leaving groves and villages, he reached Pachacama, which is the town where the mosque stands. Halfway there is another village, where the Captain dined. The lord of Pachacama and the principal men came out to receive the Captain and the Christians, and showed a desire to be friends with the Spaniards. The Captain went to lodge, with his followers, in some large chambers in one part of the town. He said that he had come, by order of the Governor, for the gold of that mosque, and that they were to collect it and deliver it up, or to convey it to where the Governor then was. All the principal men of the town and the attendants of the Idol assembled and replied that they would give it, but they continued to dissimulate and make excuses. At last they brought a very little, and said they had no more. The Captain dissimulated also, and said that he wished to go and see the Idol they had, and he went. It was in a good house, well painted, in a very dark chamber with a close fetid smell. Here there was a very dirty Idol made of wood, and they say that this is their God who created them and sustains them, and gives them their food. At the foot of the Idol there were some offerings of gold, and it was held in such veneration that only the attendants and servants, who, as they say, were appointed by it, were allowed to officiate before it. No other person might enter, nor is any other considered worthy even to touch the walls of the house. The Captain ascertained that the Devil frequented the Idol, and spoke with his servants, saying diabolical things, which were spread all over the land. They look upon him as God, and offer many sacrifices to him. They come to this Devil, from distances of three hundred leagues, with gold and silver and cloth. Those that arrive go to the porter and beg that their gift may be accepted. He enters and speaks with the Idol, who says that he consents. Before any of his ministers may enter to minister to him, they say that they must fast for many days and refrain from women. In all the streets of the town, and at its principal gates, and round this house, there are many wooden Idols, which they worship as imitations of their Devil. It was ascertained from many lords of this land that from the town of Catamez [Atacames] which is at the commencement of this government, all the people of this coast serve this mosque with gold and silver, and offer a certain tribute every year. There were houses and superintendents to receive the tribute, where they found some gold, and there were signs that much more had been taken away. Many Indians deposed that the gold was removed by order of the Devil. I omit many things that might be said touching the worship of this Idol, to avoid prolixity. But it is believed among the Indians that this Idol is their God, that he can destroy them if they offend him and do not serve him well, and that all things in the world are in his hands. The people were so shocked and terrified at the Captain having merely gone in to see it, that they thought the Idol would destroy all the Christians. But the Spaniards gave the Indians to understand that they were in a great error, and that he who spoke from the inside of the Idol was the Devil, who deceived them. They were told that from henceforth they must not believe him, nor do what he advised them, and were taught other things touching their idolatries.

The Captain ordered the vault, in which the Idol was, to be pulled down, and the Idol to be broken before all the people. He then told them many things touching our Holy Catholic Faith, and he taught them the sign of the cross✝, that they might be able to defend themselves against the Devil. The town of Pachacama is very large. Adjoining the mosque there is a house of the Sun, well built, and situated on a hill, with five surrounding walls. There are houses with terrace roofs as in Spain. The town appears to be old, judging from the ruined houses it contains; and the greater part of the outer wall has fallen. The name of the principal lord is Taurichumbi. The neighbouring lords came to the town to see the Captain, with presents of the products of their land, and with gold and silver. They wondered greatly that the Captain should have dared to enter where the Idol was, and to see it broken. . . .

The Captain then set out from the town of Pachacama, to form a junction with Chilicuchima. He marched by the same road as he had come, until he reached Huara, which is on the coast near the sea. Then he left the coast and marched into the interior. . . .

On the 5th of March he passed the night at a village belonging to Caxatambo, called Chinca. On the road they had to cross a pass where the snow was very deep, reaching to the girths of the horses. This village has large flocks. The Captain remained there for two days. On Saturday, the 7th of March, he set out, and passed the night at Caxatambo. This is a large town, situated in a deep valley, where there are many flocks, and all along the road there were sheepfolds. The chief of this village is called Sachao, and he did good service to the Spaniards. At this town the Captain changed his route, in order to take the broad road by which Chilicuchima would come, which entailed a flank march of three days. Here the Captain made inquiries whether Chilicuchima had passed, in order to form a junction. All the Indians said that he had passed with the gold; but it afterwards appeared that they had been told to say this, that the Captain might be induced to march onwards; while he remained in Xauxa, with no intention of moving. The Captain, however, considered that these Indians seldom spoke the truth; so he determined, although it entailed great trouble and danger, to march to the royal road by which Chilicuchima must go, in order to ascertain whether he had already passed. If he had not gone on, the Captain resolved to seek him out, wherever he might be, as well to secure the gold as to disperse his army. . . .

As soon as the Captain arrived [at Jauja], and before he dismounted, he asked for Chilicuchima, and the people answered that he was at some other village, and that he would return next day. . . . The Captain had with him a son of the old Cuzco who, when he heard of the absence of Chilicuchima, said that he wished to go where he was, and set out in a litter. All that night the horses were saddled and bridled, and the lords of the town were told that no Indian was to appear in the square, because the horses were angry and would kill them. Next day that son of the Cuzco returned with Chilicuchima, both in litters, and numerously attended. On entering the square they alighted, and, leaving their servants, they went on foot, with a few attendants, to the house occupied by the Captain Hernando Pizarro, for Chilicuchima to see him and offer his excuses for not having fulfilled his promise, or come to receive him. He said his business had prevented him from doing more. . . . Next morning Chilicuchima came to the Captain's lodgings and said that, as he desired him to accompany the Spaniards, he could not refuse to obey, and that he was ready to go, leaving another captain with the troops at Xauxa. On that day he got together about thirty loads of gold; and after marching for two days they met thirty or forty loads. During these days the Spaniards kept a good look out, the horses being kept saddled night and day; for this captain of Atababila had so large a force that if he had made a night attack on the Spaniards he would have done much mischief.

The town of Xauxa is very large. It is situated in a beautiful valley, and enjoys a temperate climate. A very large river flows near the town. The land is fertile. The town is built like those of Spain, with regular streets, and many subject villages are in sight. The town and district are very populous, and the Spaniards saw one hundred thousand people assemble every day in the principal square. The market places and streets were also crowded. There were men whose duty it was to count all these people, and to know who came in for the service of the troops; and other men had to watch and take note of all who entered the town. . . .

On Friday, the 20th of March, the Captain Hernando Pizarro departed from that city of Xauxa to return to Caxamalca, accompanied by Chilicuchima. He marched by the same road to the village of Pompo, where he stayed for the day he arrived, and one more. On Wednesday he set out from this village of Pompo, and marching over plains covered with flocks, he passed the night at some large buildings. On that day it snowed heavily. Next day he came to a village amongst the mountains called Tambo, which is near a large and deep river, where there is a bridge. There is a flight of stone steps to descend to the river, and if the position was defended, much mischief might be done. The Captain received good service from the lord of this village, and was supplied with all that he and his party required. They made a great festival out of respect for the Captain Hernando Pizarro, and because Chilicuchima accompanied him. Next day they came to a village called

Tomsucancha, the lord of which, named Tillima, received them well. There were plenty of Indians fit for service; for, though the village was small, many had assembled from the surrounding country to see the Spaniards. In this village there are small sheep [vicuñas], with very fine wool, like those of Spain. Next day they reached the village called Guaneso, a march of five leagues, the greater part over a paved road, with channels of water by the side. They say the road was paved on account of the snow, which, at a certain season of the year, falls over that land. This town of Guaneso is large. It is situated in a valley, surrounded by steep mountains, the valley being three leagues in circuit. On the side leading to Caxamalca there is a long and very steep ascent. The Captain and his followers were very well received, and during the two days that they remained, the inhabitants celebrated several feasts. This town has other surrounding villages under its jurisdiction. It is a land of many flocks. . . .

Next day the Captain set out, and, after a march of five leagues, he passed the night at a village called Guacango. Next day he reached the large town of Piscobamba, which is on the side of a mountain. The chief is called Tauquame; and he and his people received the Captain well, and did good service to his followers. Halfway to this town, at Huacacamba, there is another deep river with two bridges of network close together, resting on a foundation of stone rising from the water; like those I have mentioned before. From one side to the other there are cables of reed, the size of a man's thigh, and between are woven many stout cords; to which larger stones are fastened, for the purpose of steadying the bridge. The horses crossed this bridge without trouble; but it is a nervous thing to pass over it for the first time, though there is no danger, as it is very strong. There are guards at all these bridges, as in Spain. Next day the Captain departed from Piscobamba, and reached some buildings, after a march of five leagues. Next day he came to a village called Agoa, which is subject to Piscobamba. It is a good village among the mountains, and is surrounded by fields of maize. The chief and his people supplied what was required for the night, and next morning provided porters for the baggage. Next day the Captain marched for four leagues over a very rugged road, and passed the night at Conchuco. This village is in a hollow. Half a league before reaching it, there is a wide road cut in steps in the rock, and there are many difficult passes, and places which might easily be defended. Next day they set out, and reached a place called Andamarca, which is the point where they diverged to go to Pachacama. At this town the two royal roads to Cuzco unite. From Andamarca to Pombo there are three leagues over a very rugged road; and stone steps are cut for the ascents and descents; while on the outer side there is a stone wall, to protect the traveller from the danger of slipping. If any man fell, he would be dashed to pieces; and it is an excellent thing for the horses, as they would fall if there was no flanking wall. In the middle of the road there is a bridge of stone and wood, very well built, between two masses of rock. At one end of the bridge there are well-built lodgings and a paved court, where, according to the Indians, the lords of the land had banquets and feasts when they travelled by that road.

From this place the Captain Hernando Pizarro went by the same stages as he came, until he reached the city of Caxamalca, which he entered, with Chilicuchima, on the 25th of May, 1533. Here a thing was seen that had never been witnessed before since the Indies were discovered. When Chilicuchima passed through the gates of the place where his master was imprisoned, he took a light load from one of the Indian porters and put it on his back, an example which was followed by many chiefs who accompanied him. Thus laden, he and the others entered where their Lord was; and when Chilicuchima saw him, he raised his hands to the Sun, and gave thanks that he had been permitted to enjoy the sight. Then, with much reverence, and weeping, he approached his Lord, and kissed his face, hands, and feet. The other chiefs, his companions, did the same. Atabaliba maintained a mien so majestic that, though there was not a man in the kingdom that he loved more than Chilicuchima, he did not look in his face or take more notice of him than of the vilest Indians that came into his presence. This taking up of a load to enter the presence of Atababila is a ceremony which was performed for all the Lords who have reigned in that land.[4]

When Hernando Pizarro entered Cajamarca with Chalcuchima, he found the size of the Spanish army almost doubled; Almagro had arrived during his absence with 150 fresh men. Shortly afterwards, the emissaries from Cuzco returned with news of the Coricancha gold. Atahuallpa's ransom was becoming a reality; in May the melting and weighing began. Atahuallpa gained nothing by it. He could not grasp that Pizarro was playing for higher stakes, for the entire empire. Pizarro was impatient to move on to Cuzco and complete the conquest. His men were bored and restive with the long wait at Cajamarca, and doubtless apprehensive of the future; if he could not lead them quickly on to new successes, they might demand to go back to Spain with the loot they already had. What was he to do with Atahuallpa? He dared not release him to resume command of his armies; to leave him behind under guard at Cajamarca would invite attempts at rescue; to take him to Cuzco would encumber the advance, and might equally invite attack. A decision was forced by the arrival of Almagro and his men. The newcomers had not been present at Atahuallpa's capture and had no claim to share in his ransom. They feared that if Atahuallpa remained a captive, the old hands might claim future plunder—that of Cuzco, in particular—as further instalments of the ransom; especially since Atahuallpa's own reaction, when he found himself still held captive, was to raise his offer. They clamoured, therefore, for Atahuallpa's death. Even to the Pizarro interest, the captive Inca was becoming an embarrassment. His value as a hostage depreciated with every day of his captivity. A report—subsequently proved false—reached the camp, of an Inca army advancing on Cajamarca at Atahuallpa's instigation; and Pizarro, in a moment of panic, ordered his execution. There was no delay: the 'trial' of Atahuallpa was an invention by later apologists for the conquerors. The Inca was offered, and accepted, baptism in order to avoid burning, and was promptly strangled.

Chalcuchima, after his moving audience with the captive Inca, had himself been made captive and kept under strong guard. He was almost as important a hostage as his master Atahuallpa. Later his value in that capacity diminished, as Atahuallpa's did, and then, like Atahuallpa, he was killed. By then, Hernando Pizarro was on his way to Spain and was unable, if he had wished, to speak for the man who had been, for several arduous weeks, his companion and his host. Chalcuchima refused baptism and was burned alive on the road to Cuzco.

By killing Atahuallpa and Chalcuchima, the Spaniards took sides in the civil war, and ranged themselves with the Cuzco faction, the faction of Huáscar and his successors, against the Quiteño faction, the faction of Atahuallpa and his generals. The attitude of both factions towards the invaders was coldly realistic. The Peruvians did not attribute supernatural powers to the Spaniards. To the Peruvian leaders, the Spaniards were rapacious and formidable barbarians; barbarous, because of their destructive indifference to works of art, formidable because their steel swords and steel-tipped lances, their fire-arms, above all their horses, gave them immense advantages over the Peruvians in war. This, again, was not a matter of superstitious dread; horses were initially objects of fear, but Peruvians soon learned that they were both vulnerable and usable, a vastly more efficient form of llama. The Peruvians naturally treated the Spaniards with great circumspection; but they allowed themselves to be deceived by the small numbers of the Spaniards and their greed for gold. They thought of them as bandits, rather than as invaders and potential conquerors; and in troubled times bandits might have their uses. To Atahuallpa, of course, the Spaniards were daring and successful kidnappers, to be bought off if possible; the immediate problem for him was to raise enough ransom to satisfy them and induce them to go away. To Huáscar's successors, however—especially to the 'young Cuzco', the surviving son of Huayna Capac, Manco Inca, who joined the army voluntarily on its march to Cuzco—the Spaniards were potential mercenaries, who could be employed to place Manco on the throne, and then paid off. Atahuallpa's surviving generals, also, after their master's death, seem to have regarded the Spaniards in this light, as the hatchet men of the Cuzco party rather than as conquerors in their own name. As for the Spaniards themselves, they needed a plausible puppet ruler whom they could manipulate, but whom the people would obey, and they thought that in Manco they had found the right man.

These considerations help to explain why Pizarro's band reached Cuzco in relative safety. The inhabitants of the country they had to cross were either loyal to the Cuzco house, or else indifferent, wanting only to be left alone. They all feared and hated the Quiteños. The forces commanded by Atahuallpa's generals were occupying armies among a hostile population. They had limited mobility, therefore, and could not bring their whole strength to bear against the advancing Spaniards. In some places, indeed—in Jauja, and even to some extent in Cuzco itself—the Spaniards were initially welcomed as deliverers; so deep was the fatal rift in the Inca polity, superficially so strong, so well-disciplined and calm.

The distance from Cajamarca to Cuzco in a straight line is about 700 miles. The direct route lies along the line of the central Cordillera, crossing and re-crossing the watershed between the Amazon basin and the Pacific; but the Spaniards, hoping perhaps for easier going, made a long descent to the west of the main Inca highway, down into the Callejón de Huaylas, the great valley already explored by Hernando Pizarro. They followed it south to the headwaters of the Santa river, and then climbed painfully out again over snow-covered passes on to the central highlands. They suffered from exposure and mountain sickness, but were not resisted until they reached the highland city of Jauja, sheltered in a shallow and fertile valley surrounded by bleak hills, as Miguel de Estete had described it. Jauja was a big town and a major staging post on the Inca road, with huge storehouses for supplying armies on the move. Here a Quiteño force— part, presumably, of the army Chalcuchima had commanded—occupied the far bank of the Mantaro river, and a detachment crossed into the town to burn the stores before the Spaniards arrived; but they were not quick enough, and before the fire could spread the Spanish cavalry caught them and drove them across the river. The Indian forces retreated along the road to Cuzco, pursued by about eighty lancers, and many were ridden down and speared. The Huanca inhabitants—whether from loyalty to the Cuzco Incas or from a resurgent local independence—gave the Spaniards an enthusiastic welcome.

At Jauja the Spaniards were half-way to Cuzco; but the worst part of the journey lay ahead, through wild, deeply broken mountains. The nature of the country in this central section of the Andes varies abruptly with altitude, ranging from snow peaks, through bare misty *puna*, through sheltered valleys full of maize fields, down to the dense tropical growth and suffocating heat in the canyon bottoms. For some distance the road runs beside the Mantaro, constantly climbing in and out of the valleys of its tributaries; but then the river turns north to join the Amazon, and the road continues east across a succession of great rivers separated by mountain ridges. The country would have been almost impassable, but for the Inca roads; though these, well engineered as they were, and paved in many places, were designed for marching men, not for horses. As for the fibre-cable suspension bridges, which spanned the rivers, the retreating Quiteños destroyed them systematically as they

74 A fanciful picture of a battle between Spaniards and Indians; engraving, from Theodor de Bry, *America*, Part V (Antwerp, 1595), plate xvi.

went. Fortunately for the Spaniards, they were travelling at the end of the dry season in an unusually dry year, and the rivers were low. Even the mighty Apurímac—whose Quechua name means Great Speaker—was forded with the water only to the horses' chests. Two months later, all these rivers would be swirling grey torrents rising high up the canyon walls. The Quiteños did not contest the fords; but they repeatedly prepared ambushes in the mountain defiles. Soto, riding ahead too far and too fast with the vanguard he commanded, was caught by one of these ambushes as his people straggled, leading their horses, across the steep slope of Vilcaconga. He lost five men, and his squadron would have been annihilated had not Pizarro, warned perhaps by some sixth sense, sent a second party racing after them. Ambushes were the Indians' only tactical hope, until such time as they could acquire swords, crossbows and horses. In open fighting, Indian warriors armed with slings, longbows, and bronze or wooden clubs, could make little impression on armoured, mounted men, using lances and slashing swords, backed by crossbowmen and arquebusiers. In the last fight of the march, a hotly contested pitched battle outside the gates of Cuzco, the Quiteño army was defeated. That night the warriors, leaving their camp fires burning,

75 The cyclopean masonry of the fortress of Sacsahuaman at Cuzco, from a photograph by Hiram Bingham. *Peabody Museum, Harvard University.*

slipped away in the darkness and began the long migration back to the north whence they had come.

Pizarro entered Cuzco on 15 November 1533, and Manco Inca, who rode in with him, received a rapturous welcome. The Spaniards were impressed by Cuzco, especially—as well they might be—by the great fortress Sacsahuamán which overlooks the city. Even today, in ruins, the Cyclopean walls of Sacsahuamán retain their look of serene indestructability. Unfortunately for history, no eye-witness wrote a description of the entry into Cuzco comparable with Bernal Díaz' account of Mexico. Some of the more articulate of Pizarro's men missed the occasion. Hernando Pizarro and Francisco Jérez were already on their way to Spain; Miguel de Estete was present, but left soon after. Pedro Pizarro was present, but wrote only a cursory description. Jérez' successor as secretary was Pedro Sancho, who continued the semi-official record which Jérez had begun; his description of Cuzco is factual, flat, and lifeless, but it is the best we have:

The city of Cuzco, being the capital city and the seat of the rulers, is so large and so beautiful that it would be remarkable even in Spain. It is full of palaces; no poor people live in the city, but each ruler in turn builds his own house, and so do all the nobles, though they do not live there permanently. Most of these buildings are of stone, or else faced with stone, but there are also many adobe houses, very well built, arranged in straight streets on a rectilinear grid. All the streets are paved, and each has running water in a stone-lined gutter down the middle. The only drawback of these streets is that they are narrow, and allow only one mounted man to pass on either side of the gutter. . . .

The plaza is square, level over most of its area, and paved with cobble-stones. It is flanked by four rulers' palaces, the biggest in the city, all built of dressed stone, and painted. The best of them is the palace of Huayna Capac. Its gateway is of red, white and variegated marble, and it has very striking flat-roofed buildings. There are many other splendid buildings and monuments in the city. There are two rivers, one flowing each side of the city. They rise a league upstream from Cuzco, and from their sources to a point two leagues downstream they run in paved channels, so that the water is always clean and clear, and although the level sometimes rises, it never overflows. The streams are crossed by bridges at the entrances to the city.

On a nearby hill, with an abrupt face towards the city, there is a very splendid fortress of earth and stone. It has big embrasures looking over the city, which makes its appearance more impressive still. Inside there are extensive living quarters, with a strong tower in the middle, square, four or five storeys high. The individual rooms inside are all small. The stones of which it is built are very well cut, as smooth as planed boards, and so well fitted together that the joints can hardly be seen. The courses are laid in the same way as in Spain, with the spacing of the joints alternating from one course to the next. There are so many towers and other buildings in the fort that one could not inspect them all in a day. Many Spaniards who have travelled in Lombardy and other foreign countries, say that they have seen no other building equal to this fortress, and no stronger castle. It could hold a garrison of five thousand Spaniards. It could not be breached by gunfire, nor could it be sapped from below, because it is built on solid rock.

On the side of the fort which overlooks the city the slope of the hill is very steep and there is only one curtain wall, but on the far side, where the slope is gentler, there are three lines of fortification of different heights, the innermost being the

76 Cuzco; engraving from Georg Braun and Franz Hogenberg, *Civitates Orbis Terrarum* (6 vols.; Antwerp, 1574), vol. I, fo 59. No *conquistador*, so far as is known, made drawings of Cuzco. The engraver did his best, from the cursory descriptions available, and produced something reminiscent of a Roman camp.

highest. These walls . . . are built of stones so huge that one can hardly believe they were placed there by human hands. They are boulders, lumps of mountain-side, ten, fifteen, twenty feet high, and broad in proportion. None is so small that three ox-carts could carry it. These are not dressed stones; but they are shaped sufficiently to fit firmly together.

The Spaniards who have seen it say that neither the aqueduct at Segovia, nor any other building erected by the Romans, or by Hercules himself, can compare with this. . . .[5]

Neither Sancho nor Pedro Pizarro mentions the Coricancha, 'place of gold', the great temple of the sun, part of whose walls now support the colonial church and convent of Santo Domingo; but presumably it had lost its interest for them, since the plates of gold which sheathed its walls had been stripped away to augment Atahuallpa's ransom.

The taking of Cuzco did not, of course, complete the conquest of Peru. The process of conquest was delayed by murderous fighting between Spanish factions, who thus perpetuated the Inca civil wars by which they had initially profited. Manco Inca did not prove a manageable puppet; in 1536 he came near to retaking Cuzco and driving the Spaniards out. He

196

and his descendants maintained a diminished but independent royal state in the forests of Vilcabamba for some forty years. Nor did the entry into Cuzco complete the process of discovery. There was still a great deal of exploring to be done; some parts of Peru remain unknown and almost inaccessible to this day. The capture of Cuzco can be taken in a real sense, however, as marking the end of the discovery of Inca Peru, of Peru as the Spaniards first found it. Possibly Inca Peru was already breaking up when the Spaniards landed; certainly its society and polity disintegrated very quickly after 1533. It became undiscoverable, one might say, except by the methods of history and archaeology. Early Spanish descriptions of Peru—except for the few written by men who took part in the initial invasion—have an elegiac quality. The best and fullest, that of Cieza de León, completed about 1550, already refers to Inca society in the past tense. Cieza's narratives of conquest are conventionally pious and triumphant; but in his descriptions he often includes a lament for lost splendour and an acid comment on Spanish destructiveness. Of Cuzco he writes:

Cuzco was grand and stately, and must have been founded by a people of great intelligence. It had fine streets except that they were narrow, and the houses were built of solid stones, beautifully joined. These stones were very large and well cut. The other parts of the houses were of wood and straw, but there are no remains of tiles, bricks, or lime amongst them. In this city there were many grand buildings of the Yncas in various parts, in which he who succeeded to the lordship celebrated his festivals. Here, too, was the solemn and magnificent temple of the sun, called Ceuri-cancha, which was rich in gold and silver. Most parts of the city were inhabited by *Mitimaes*, and laws and statutes were established for their conduct, which were understood by all, as well regarding their superstitions and temples as in matters relating to the government. This city was the richest of which we have any knowledge, in all the Indies, for great store of treasure was often brought in to increase the grandeur of the nobles; and no gold nor silver might be taken out, on pain of death. The sons of the chiefs in all the provinces came to reside at court, with their retinues, for a certain time. There were a great many gilders and workers in silver, who understood how to work the things ordered by the Yncas. The chief priest, called Huillac-Umu, lived in the grand temple.

At present there are very good houses, with upper storeys roofed with tiles. The climate, although it is cold, is very healthy, and Cuzco is better supplied with provisions than any other place in the kingdom. It is also the largest city, and more Spaniards hold *encomiendas* over Indians here than elsewhere. The city was founded by Manco Capac, the first King Ynca; and, after he had been succeeded by ten other lords, the Adelantado Don Francisco Pizarro, governor and captain-general of these kingdoms, rebuilt and refounded it in the name of the Emperor, Don Carlos, our Lord, in the month of October of the year 1534.[6]

On Pachacamac:

Four leagues from the City of the Kings, travelling down the coast, is the valley of Pachacamac, which is very famous among these Indians. This valley is fruitful and pleasant, and in it there was one of the grandest temples that is to be seen in these parts. They say of it that, although the Kings Yncas built many temples besides the temple of Cuzco, and enriched them greatly, yet none were equal to this temple of Pachacamac. It was built on the top of a small hill, entirely made of earth and *adobes* (bricks baked in the sun). The edifice had many doors, and the doors and walls were painted over with wild beasts. Within the temple, where they placed the idol, were the priests, who feigned no small amount of sanctity. When they performed sacrifices before the people, they went with their faces towards the doors and their backs to the idols, with their eyes to the ground, and they were filled with a mighty trembling. Indeed, their perturbation was so great, according to the accounts of those Indians who are still living, that it may almost be compared with that of which we read concerning the priests of Apollo when the gentiles sought for their vain replies. The Indians further relate that they sacrificed animals, and some human blood of persons whom they had killed, before the figure of this devil, which, at their most solemn festivals, gave replies, and when the people heard them, they believed them to be true. In the terraces and lower parts of this temple a great sum in gold and silver was buried.

The priests were much reverenced, and the chiefs obeyed them in many of the things which they ordered. Near the temple many great buildings were erected for the use of those who came on pilgrimage, and no one was considered worthy to be buried in the vicinity of the temple except the chiefs, or those who came as pilgrims bringing offerings to the temple. When the annual festivals of the year were celebrated, a great concourse of people assembled, rejoicing to the sound of such instruments of music as they use.

When the Lords Yncas, in extending their sway, came to this valley of Pachacamac, and saw the grandeur and great antiquity of the temple, and the reverence paid to it by all the people in the neighbourhood, they knew that it would be very difficult to put aside this feeling, although it was their general practice to order temples to the sun to be built in all the countries they had conquered. They, therefore, agreed with the native chiefs and with the ministers of this god or devil, that the temple of Pachacamac should continue with the authority and reverence it formerly possessed, and that the loftiest part should be set aside as a temple of the sun. This order of the Yncas having been obeyed, the temple of the sun became very rich, and many virgins were placed in it. The devil Pachacamac was delighted with this agreement, and they affirm that he showed great satisfaction in his replies, seeing that his ends were served both by the one party and the other, while the souls of the unfortunate simpletons remained in his power.

Some Indians say that this accursed demon Pachacamac still talks with the aged people. As he sees that his authority and credit are gone, and that many of those who once served him have now formed a contrary opinion, he declares that he and the God of whom the Christians preach are one, and thus with other false and deceitful words induces some to refuse the water of baptism. Nevertheless God, taking pity on the soul of these sinners, is served by many coming to His knowledge and calling themselves sons of the church. Thus every day some are baptised. The temple is now so completely dismantled that the principal edifice is gone altogether, and in the place where the devil was once so served and adored, a cross is planted to increase his terror, and to be a comfort to the faithful.

The name of this devil is intended to signify 'creator of the world', for *camac* means 'creator', and *pacha* 'the world'. When the governor Don Francisco Pizarro (God permitting it) seized Atahuallpa in the province of Caxamarca, he heard wonderful reports of this temple, and of its great riches. He, therefore, sent his brother, the captain Hernando Pizarro, with some Spanish troops, with orders to seek out the valley, and take all the gold he could find in the accursed temple, with which he was to return to Caxamarca. Although the captain Hernando Pizarro succeeded in reaching the temple of Pachacamac, it is notorious among the people that the priests had already taken away four hundred loads of gold, which

Opposite left
77 Tomato plant, 'apple of love'; from John Gerard, *The Herball or generall historie of plantes* (London, 1633). The tomato is native to tropical America, one of many such plants introduced into Europe in the sixteenth century.

Opposite right
78 Cotton plant; engraving from P. A. Matteoli, *Compendium de plantis omnibus* (Venice, 1571). Various species of cotton are widespread in the Tropics, some being native to the Old World, some to the New. Most of the commercial cottons in use today are hybrids. The species *gossypium peruvianum*, or 'Peruvian full rough', was the principal raw material for textile weaving in pre-conquest coastal Peru; an area which produced some of the finest textiles ever made.

have never yet appeared, nor do any Indians now living know where they are. Nevertheless Hernando Pizarro (the first Spanish captain who came to this place) found some gold and silver. As time passed on, the captain Rodrigo Orgóñez, Francisco de Godoy, and others, took a large sum of gold and silver from the burial places. It is considered that there is much more, but as the place where it is buried is unknown, it was lost. From the time that Hernando Pizarro and his Christians entered the temple, the devil has had little power, the idols have been destroyed, and the temple and other edifices have fallen into ruins. Insomuch that very few Indians now remain in the place.[7]

In the valleys of the central coast the most striking impression is of the spread of introduced Old World crops—wheat, citrus fruits, grapes and sugar:

All the land of these valleys, which is not reached by the sand, forms one of the most fertile and abundant regions in the world, and the one best suited for cultivation. I have already mentioned that it does not rain, and that the water for

irrigation is drawn from the rivers which descend from the mountains and fall into the South Sea. In these valleys the Indians sow maize, which is reaped twice in the year, and yields abundantly. In some parts they grow *yucas*, which are useful for making bread and liquor when there is want of maize. They also raise sweet potatoes, the taste of which is almost the same as that of chestnuts, besides potatoes, beans, and other vegetables.

Throughout the valleys there is also one of the most singular fruits I ever saw, called *pepinos*, of very pleasant smell and taste. There are great quantities of *guayavas*, guavas, and *paltas*, which are like pears, *guanavanas*, *caymitos*, and the pines of those parts. About the houses of the Indians many dogs are seen, which are very different from the Spanish kind, and about the size of ordinary curs; they call them *chonos*. The Indians breed many ducks. In the thickets of these valleys there are *algarobas*, somewhat long and narrow, and not so thick as the pods of beans. In some parts they make bread of these *algarobas*, and it is considered good. They are very fond of drying such of their fruits and roots as are adapted for it, just as we make preserved figs, raisins, and other fruits. Now there are many great vineyards in these valleys, where large harvests of grapes are gathered. No wine has yet been gathered from them, and I cannot, therefore, certify to its quality; but, as the land is irrigated, it will probably be weak. There are now also fig-trees and pomegranates, and I believe, and hold for certain, that all the fruits of Spain may be grown here.

Wheat is raised, and it is a beautiful sight to see the fields covered with crops,

79 '(Bolivia), Une Balsa ou Bateau de Jonc, sur le Lac de Titicaca'. Alcide d'Orbigny, *Voyage dans L'Amérique Méridionale* (Paris & Strasbourg, 1835–47). Coutumes et Usages, Plate 8. These raft-canoes, made of bundles of *totora* reeds, are still used for fishing on Lake Titicaca; one of the few places in the world where reed craft survive.

in a region devoid of natural supplies of water. Barley grows as well as wheat, and lemons, limes, oranges, and citrons are all excellent and plentiful. There are also large banana plantations; and besides those which I have already enumerated, there are many other luscious fruits which I do not mention, because it seems sufficient to enumerate the principal ones.

As the rivers descend from the mountains and flow through these valleys, and as some of the valleys are broad, while their whole extent is, or was, when the country was more thickly populated, covered with flocks, they led channels of water in all directions, which is a remarkable thing, for these channels were conducted over high and low places, along the sides of hills and over them, some in one direction, and some in another, so that it is a great enjoyment to travel in those valleys, and to pass their orchards and refreshing gardens.

The Indians had, and still have, great works for drawing off the water, and making it flow through certain channels. Sometimes it has chanced that I have stopped near one of these channels, and before we had finished pitching the tent the channel was dry, the water having been drawn off in another direction, for it is in the power of the Indians to do this at their pleasure. These channels are always very green, and there is plenty of grass near them for horses. In the trees and bushes many birds fly about; there are pigeons, doves, turkeys, pheasants, and some partridges, beside many deer in the thickets. But there are no evil things, such as serpents, snakes, and wolves. There are, however, many foxes, which are so cunning that, although great care is taken to watch the things where the Spaniards or Indians encamp, they come to steal, and when they can find nothing better, they make off with the bridles or switches for the horses. In many parts of the valleys there are extensive fields of sweet cane, and they make sugar, treacle, and other things from it.[8]

In the southern coastal valleys the picture is darker:

From this valley of Yca the road leads to the beautiful rivers and valleys of Nasca, which were also very populous in times past, and the streams were made to irrigate the fields. The late wars destroyed by their cruelty (as is well known) all these poor Indians. Some Spaniards of credit told me that the greatest harm to the Indians was done during the dispute of the two governors Pizarro and Almagro, respecting the boundaries of their jurisdictions, which cost so dear, as the reader will see in the proper place.

In the principal valley of those of Nasca (which by another name is called Caxamalca) there were great edifices built by order of the Yncas. I have nothing to say of the natives than that they also assert that their ancestors were valiant, and esteemed by the Kings of Cuzco. I have heard that the Spaniards took a quantity of treasure from the burial-places, or *huacas*. These valleys being so fertile, as I have said, a great quantity of sweet canes have been planted in one of them, of which they make much sugar for sale in the cities of this kingdom. The great road of the Yncas passes through all these valleys, and in some parts of the desert signs may be seen to indicate the road that should be taken.

Beyond these valleys of Nasca is that of Acari, and further on are those of Ocoña, Camana, and Quilca, in which there are great rivers. Notwithstanding that at the present time these valleys contain few inhabitants, in former times they were populous, but the wars and calamities have reduced their numbers of late years until there are now few left. These valleys are as fruitful and abundant as the others, and are well adapted for breeding stock.

Beyond this valley of Quilca, which is the port of the city of Arequipa, are those of Chuli, Tambopalla, and Ylo. Further on are the rich valleys of Tarapacá. Out of the sea, in the neighbourhood of these valleys, rise some islands much frequented

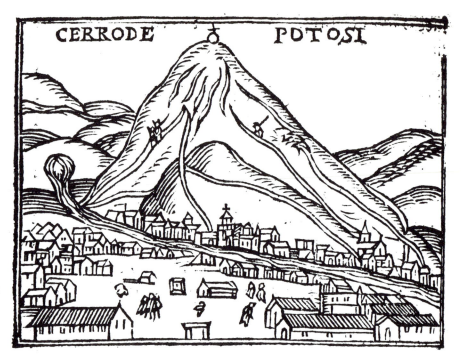

80 The hill and town of Potosí, woodcut, from Agustín de Zárate, *Historia del descubrimiento y conquista del Perú* (Antwerp, 1555). The earliest surviving picture of a New World mining establishment.

by seals. The natives go to them in *balsas*, and bring a great quantity of the dung of birds from the rocks, to apply to their crops of maize, and they find it so efficacious that the land, which formerly was sterile, becomes very rich and fruitful. If they cease to use this manure they reap little maize. Indeed the people could not be supported if the birds, lodging on the rocks near these islands, did not leave that which is afterwards collected, and considered so valuable as to become an article of trade between the natives.

It does not appear to me necessary to dwell longer on the things concerning these valleys, for I have already written down the principal things I saw or was able to obtain notice of. I will conclude, therefore, by saying that there are now few natives, and that in ancient times there were palaces and store-houses in all the valleys, the tribute rendered to the King Yncas being conveyed partly to Cuzco, partly to Hatuncolla, partly to Vilcas, and partly to Caxamalca. The principal grandeur of the Yncas was in the *Sierra*.[9]

Of Potosí, the prodigious mountain of silver ore in what is now Bolivia, Cieza writes:

The mines of Porco, and others in this kingdom, have been open since the time of the Yncas, when the veins whence they extract the metal were discovered; but those which they have found in the hill of Potosí (concerning which I now desire to write) were never worked until the year 1546. A Spaniard named Villaroel was searching for veins of metal with some Indians, when he came upon this wealth in a high hill, being the most beautiful and best situated in all that district. As the Indians call all hills and lofty eminences Potosí, it retained that name. . . . They discovered five very rich veins on the upper part of the hill, called the 'rich vein,' the 'vein of tin,' etc. This wealth became so famous, that Indians came from all parts to extract silver from the hill. The climate is cold, and there are no inhabited places in the vicinity. When the Spaniards had taken possession, they began to extract the silver, and he who had a mine gave each Indian who entered it a marc, or, if he was very rich, two marcs every week. So many people came to work the mines, that the place appeared like a great city. . . . It may with truth be asserted that in no part of the world could so rich a hill be found, and that no prince receives such profits and rents as this famous town of Plata. From the year 1548 to 1551 the royal fifths were valued at more than three millions of ducats, which is more than the Spaniards got from Atahualpa, and more than was found in the city of Cuzco, when it was first occupied.[10]

This leads Cieza to a disquisition on llamas, beasts which fascinated all the early Spanish writers:

The silver is conveyed by the royal road to Cuzco, or to the city of Arequipa, which is near the port of Quilca. Most of it is carried by sheep, without which it would be very difficult to travel in this kingdom, owing to the great distance between the cities, and the want of other beasts.

It appears to me that in no part of the world have sheep like those of the Indies been found or heard of. They are especially met with in this kingdom and in the government of Chile, as well as in some parts of the province of the Río de la Plata. It may be that they will also be found in parts that are still unknown. These sheep are among the most excellent creatures that God has created, and the most useful. It would seem that the Divine Majesty took care to create these animals, that the people of this country might be able to live and sustain themselves, for by no others means could these Indians (I speak of the mountaineers of Peru) preserve

81 General view of the hill of Potosí, with Spanish smelting works in the foreground. The hammers for crushing the silver ore are driven by an over-shot water wheel. Drawing in an atlas of sea charts, *c.* 1584. *The Hispanic Society of America, New York.*

their lives without these sheep, or others which would supply them with the same necessaries. In this chapter I shall relate how this is.

In the valleys on the coast, and in other warm regions, the natives sow cotton, and make their clothes from it, so that they feel no want, because the cotton cloth is suitable for their climate.

But in the mountainous parts, such as Collao and Charcas, no tree will grow, and if the cotton was sown it would yield nothing, so that the natives, unless they obtained it by trading, could have no clothing. To supply this need, the Giver of all good things, who is God our Lord, created such vast flocks of these animals which we call sheep, that, if the Spaniards had not diminished their number in the wars, there would be no possibility of counting them, such would have been their increase in all parts. But, as I have already said, the civil wars of the Spaniards have been like a great pestilence, both to the Indians and to their flocks.

The natives call these sheep *llamas*, and the males *urcos*. Some are white, others black, and others grey. Some of them are as large as small donkeys, with long legs, broad bellies, and a neck of the length and shape of a camel. Their heads are large, like those of Spanish sheep. The flesh of these animals is very good when it is fat, and the lambs are better and more savoury than those of Spain. The *llamas* are very tame, and carry two or three *arrobas* weight very well. Truly it is very pleasant to see the Indians of the Collao go forth with their beasts, and return with them to their homes in the evening, laden with fuel. They feed on the herbage of the plains, and when they complain they make a noise like the groaning of camels.

82 Llama (*this page*) and Vicuña (*opposite*); from Georg Margraf, *De Quadrupedibus* (bound in W. Piso and G. Margraf, *Historia Naturalis Brasiliae*; Leyden and Amsterdam, 1648), pp 243 and 244.

There is another kind, called *huanacus*, of the same shape and appearance, but they are very large and wander over the plains in a wild state, running and jumping with such speed that the dog which could overtake them must be very swift. Besides these, there is another sort of *llamas*, called *vicuñas*. These are more swift than the *huanacus*, though smaller. They wander over the uninhabited wilds, and eat the herbage which God has created there. The wool of these *vicuñas* is excellent, and finer than the wool of merino sheep in Spain. I know not whether cloth can be made from it, but the cloths that were made for the lords of this land are worth seeing. The flesh of these *huanacus* and *vicuñas* tastes like that of wild sheep, but it is good. In the city of La Paz I ate a dinner off one of these fat *huanacus*, in the inn kept by the captain Alonzo de Mendoza, and it seemed to me to be the best I ever had in my life. There is yet another kind of the tame *llamas*, which are called *alpacas*, but they are very ugly and woolly. They are of the shape of *llamas*, but smaller, and their lambs when young are very like those of Spain. Each of these *llamas* brings forth once in the year, and no more.[11]

Finally, on Piura in the north, the first Inca province to be invaded by the Spaniards:

There used to be great flocks of *llamas*, the sheep of Peru, but now there are very few, owing to the way the Spaniards have destroyed them. . . . There are priests in most of these districts, who, if they live well and abstain from evil, as their religion requires, will reap great fruits. By the will of God, this is done in the greater part of the kingdom, and many Indian lads have become Christians, who, by their example, attract others.

The ancient temples, which are generally called *huacas*, are now ruined and desecrated, the idols are broken, and the devil is thus badly wounded in these places. Where he was once, for the sins of man, so reverenced and esteemed, the cross is now planted. Truly we Spaniards should ever give infinite praise to our Lord God for this.[12]

7 Quito, Chile and New Granada

The withdrawal of Quisquis and his Quiteño army from Cuzco in November 1533 was the beginning of an arduous retreat of well over a thousand miles. At Jauja his passage was resisted both by the Spanish garrison and by the local people. He was pursued first by Pizarro and Manco Inca with a combined force of Spanish cavalry and native levies from Cuzco, subsequently by Soto. He had to fight a series of delaying actions all the way north. Eventually he reached the Quito highlands, with his army intact but weary; only to find the hated Spaniards already there before him.

This most northerly province of the Inca empire, which the Spaniards called the Kingdom of Quito, and which is now known as the Republic of the Equator, displays in its highland area a majestic symmetry. The Cordillera of the Andes, here running almost due north and south, divides into two chains of high peaks, many of which are shapely volcanic cones, some active, all snow-capped. The symmetry of the scene is more apparent on the map than on the ground, partly because of the huge size of the mountains, making it impossible to see more than one or two at a time, partly because although the western chain is almost a straight line, the eastern is irregular. The two chains, *pace* the popular geographies, are not parallel; but for most of their length they are only thirty or forty miles apart, well within sight of one another. Between them is a winding plateau-corridor, about 300 miles long from north to south, divided by transverse ridges into a series of shallow upland basins. Of these the southernmost, now called the Cuenca basin, is the lowest—about 8,000 feet—and the most arid; the northernmost, in which the city of Quito stands, is the highest—about 9,500 feet—and the most fertile. All were populated, in Inca times, by settled peoples. As the last major Inca conquest, the province had received a great deal of attention in the reigns of Atahuallpa's two predecessors: military occupation, the establishment of colonies of settlers from central Peru and extensive royal building in the towns of Quito and Tumibamba. Atahuallpa himself had regarded the northern provinces as the base of his power. Spanish rumour, after his capture, had it that Tumibamba and Quito approached Cuzco in splendour and that Atahuallpa had stored great quantities of treasure there.

These rumours circulated not only among Atahuallpa's captors—who in any event were too busy with the Cuzco campaign to investigate them—but also outside Peru. There was some doubt as to whether Pizarro's capitulation with the Crown included territory north of Tumbes, and the possibility of a new and profitable conquest attracted an already famous predator, the ruthless and reckless Alvarado, Cortés' old companion, who raised in his government of Guatemala an army of five hundred experienced men and 120 horses—by far the biggest Spanish force to enter South America up to that time—and brought them south by sea early in 1534. They landed in February at Puerto Viejo (Manta) on the Ecuador coast. This was a mistake, of the kind Pizarro had made in 1526. The southern jaw of the Gulf of Guayaquil marks the northern limit of the influence of the Humboldt current. The coast to the south is desert, except in the river valleys; to the north, mangrove swamps and rain forest. Alvarado thus inadvertently chose for his approach an extremely difficult terrain. He behaved on arrival with characteristic impatient brutality, conscripting the coastal Indians to carry loads, and hanging chiefs who failed to produce the numbers demanded. His people had no idea of the best route inland and could obtain no reliable guides. They cast about, first south-east towards the Gulf of Guayaquil, then north-east along the bank of the Macul river, hacking their way through the tangle, their arms rusting in the damp heat. They had to plough through a rain of ash from an erupting volcano, presumably Cotopaxi. They chose the wrong route to penetrate the Andes and climbed one of the highest passes, that between Chimborazo and Carihuairazo, in deep snow. They lost most of their horses. Tropical fevers, exhaustion and lack of food caused the death of some eighty Spaniards, and nearly all the conscripted coastal Indians died in the icy passes. It was a weakened and disheartened, though still formidable army which in July stumbled on the Inca highland road half-way between Tumibamba and Quito; only to find in the dust the hoofprints of Spanish horses.

Shortly after the affray at Cajamarca, Pizarro had sent Sebastián de Benalcázar back to San Miguel-Piura with a consignment of loot for

83 The volcanoes Chimborazo and Carihuairazo; from A. von Humboldt and A. Bonpland, *Voyage aux régions équinoxiales du nouveau continent: Vue des Cordillères et monuments des peuples indigènes de l'Amérique* (2 vols.; Paris, 1810), plate 25.

84 Ship, *c.* 1532, from a drawing attributed to Holbein. The ships which carried Alvarado's army south may have looked something like this— including the general air of carousal. *Science Museum, South Kensington, London.*

shipping to Panamá, and with orders to remain and guard the northern approach to Peru. Benalcázar had only a handful of men with him, mostly old and sick, and San Miguel had only a dozen *vecinos*; but he found the little settlement swollen by more than two hundred new arrivals, all clamouring to be led to conquest and plunder. To Benalcázar—removed, doubtless against his will, from the main scene of action—the attractions of an expedition into the Quito highlands were obvious. A comparatively loyal ruffian, he hesitated to move without orders from Pizarro, who certainly regarded Quito as within his own grant of government; but his reluctance vanished at the news of Alvarado's arrival, brought to Piura by Alvarado's chief pilot, Juan Fernández, who after landing the army at Puerto Viejo had sailed on south. Fernández was an old associate of Benalcázar; he had indeed navigated Benalcázar's original voyage from Nicaragua in 1531, and his putting into Piura may have been, in part, an act of friendship. Benalcázar reacted promptly; in March 1536 he set out for Quito with two hundred men and sixty horses.

Inca authority was then represented in the province by Ruminavi, the commander of the northern garrison. Ruminavi, like his colleague Quisquis, recognised the Spaniards as ruthless invaders and would-be conquerors, and was adamantly opposed to any dealings with them. He was in a strong position, with a powerful and loyal army, and with possession of Atahuallpa's two infant sons. The Spaniards, on the other hand, after the death of Atahuallpa and Chalcuchima, had no hostages for Ruminavi's conduct; he had a free hand. His only serious competitor for power would have been Atahuallpa's brother Quilliscacha; but Quilliscacha was compromised by collaboration with the Spaniards.

Rumiñavi had him murdered at a drinking ceremony, and to drive the point home, had his body flayed and his skin made into the membranes of a drum. In these circumstances both Alvarado and Benalcázar could expect determined and united resistance; Benalcázar especially, since he proposed to approach Quito through—so to speak—the front door. No eyewitness account survives of the first Spanish invasions of what is now Ecuador. Benalcázar, like his master Pizarro, could not write. Alvarado was literate, but wrote only when he had to, for some practical purpose. Neither was accompanied by a chronicler. The story of their expeditions has to be pieced together from later accounts, particularly that of Cieza de León, who travelled by Benalcázar's route, in the opposite direction, some fifteen years later. He was an observant traveller, and from his descriptions an impression can be formed of the country as it appeared to the first Spanish invaders. Benalcázar had further to go than Alvarado, but he had easier going and moved faster. The flat semi-desert of north-western Peru, featureless save for occasional water-holes surrounded by stunted trees, offered no topographical obstacles. In most parts of the Andes, north-south travel is much easier than east-west; and from Saraguro onward Benalcázar marched along the central highland road of the Incas. 'In the time of the Incas', according to Cieza de León, 'there was a royal road made of the force and labour of men, which began at . . . Quito, and went as far as Cuzco, whence another of equal grandeur and magnitude led to the province of Chile, which is more than one thousand two hundred leagues from Quito. On these roads there were pleasant and beautiful lodgings and palaces every three or four leagues, very richly adorned. These roads may be compared to that which the Romans made in Spain, and which we call the silver road'.[1] Some sections of the road can still be traced today. The Pan-American highway follows roughly the same route through Ecuador.

The first important town on Benalcázar's route was Tumibamba (modern Cuenca). The Inca conqueror Tupac Yupanqui had tried to make this place a second Cuzco, and to some extent succeeded, according to Cieza:

The famous buildings of Tumibamba are in the province of Cañaris, and they are among the richest and most splendid in the whole kingdom of Peru. . . . The temple of the sun is built of stones very cunningly wrought, some of them being very large, coarse and black, and others resembling jasper. Some of the Indians pretend that most of the stones . . . have been brought from the great city of Cuzco by order of the King Huayna Capac, and of the great Tupac Inca his father, by means of strong ropes. If this be true it is a wonderful work, by reason of the great size of the stones and the lengths of the road. The doorways of many of the buildings were very handsome and brightly painted, with precious stones and emeralds let into the stone; and the interior walls of the temple of the sun, and of the palaces of the Incas, were lined with plates of the finest gold stamped with many figures. The roofs were of straw, so well put on that no fire would consume it, while it would endure for many ages. . . . Now these buildings of Tumibamba are in ruins, but it is easy to see how grand they once were.[2]

Today not even ruins remain.

The natives of the country round Tumibamba, the Cañari, had suffered heavily at the hands of the conquering Incas and still resented their subjection. In the recent civil war they had risen in the name of Huáscar—the only important tribe in the north to do so—and had suffered for it again at the hands of Atahuallpa. Now at Benalcázar's approach they offered him their alliance against Rumiñavi.

The natives of this province, called Cañari [wrote Cieza], are good-looking and well grown. They wear their hair very long, so much so, that by that and a circular crown of wands, as fine as those of a sieve, the Cañaris may easily be known, for they wear this head-dress as a distinguishing mark. . . . The women are very pretty, amorous, and friendly to the Spaniards. They are great labourers, for it is they who dig the land, sow the crops and reap the harvests. . . . When any Spanish army passed through their province, the Indians at that time being obliged to supply people to carry the baggage of the Spaniards on their backs, many of these Cañari sent their wives and daughters, and remained at home themselves. . . . Some Indians say that this arises from the dearth of men and the great abundance of women, owing to the cruelty of Atahuallpa to the people of this province, when he entered it after having killed the captain-general of his brother Huáscar at Ambato, whose name was Atoco. They affirm that, although the men and boys came out with green boughs and palm leaves to beg for mercy, he, with a haughty air and severe voice ordered his captains to kill them all. Thus a great number of men and boys were killed, and they say that now there are fifteen times as many women as men.[3]

Nevertheless, the Cañari contributed three thousand fighting men to Benalcázar's army, besides women to carry the loads, and gave him important help, not only in battle, but in gathering intelligence of intended ambushes and in springing the traps that Rumiñavi laid for him.

Between Saraguro and Tumibamba Rumiñavi had confined himself to harassing tactics and minor testing raids; north of Tumibamba, however, the Inca road climbed a 14,000 foot pass, and beyond the head of the pass, at Teocajas on the chill hail-lashed *páramo*, Rumiñavi awaited the Spaniards with—according to Oviedo—fifty thousand men, in full view, tempting the cavalry to charge across concealed trenches set with stakes. The Cañari, on this and many subsequent occasions, detected the stratagem and enabled the horsemen to outflank the entrenchments, and a major pitched battle ensued. It was indecisive; Rumiñavi's army was neither scattered nor destroyed, Benalcázar's march on Quito, though delayed, was not prevented. The battle was remarkable for the discipline and persistence with which Rumiñavi's warriors kept up their attacks, so that the invaders came near defeat through sheer weariness; it confirmed, on the other hand—if confirmation were needed—that Indians on foot, armed with traditional weapons, were no match for Spanish horsemen. Benalcázar's men were attacked on many other occasions as they pursued their northward advance, always with the same result. On one occasion their attackers were dispersed by the ash from an eruption of Cotopaxi, probably the same eruption which was impeding the advance of Alvarado's army, far below them. As they marched through the high upland basins, approaching the equator, with the great volcanoes bounding the horizon on either side, they found the country growing steadily greener, better watered and more fertile. Finally in June, four months after leaving San Miguel, they entered Quito. The town was empty; Rumiñavi had sent the people away, removed all food and valuables and burned many of the buildings. He mounted one major counter-attack, which the Spaniards and the Cañari beat off with some difficulty and loss. Thereafter his army split into separate bands, attacking isolated parties of Spaniards but unable to face their main force. Benalcázar's people spent the next few weeks pursuing an elusive enemy, foraging, and trying to extract information about hidden treasure from any Indian leader they could catch. Eventually they caught Rumiñavi himself, tortured him and killed him. Organised Indian resistance, though it did not cease entirely, retreated to defensible crags or isolated jungle camps.

Meanwhile fresh threats to Benalcázar's position had developed as army after army marched up the Inca highway towards Quito. First, Almagro; Almagro was at Vilcashuamán, mid-way between Cuzco and Jauja, when he heard of Alvarado's invasion. He hurried north to counter the threat; found Benalcázar gone from his post; and set out in pursuit. Having only a few men with him, he found his way repeatedly barred by Indian war parties, which he had either to fight or to elude. By the time he reached Quito the main battles were over and mopping-up operations had begun. Benalcázar, however, had not repudiated Pizarro's authority—indeed he professed to have conquered Quito in Pizarro's name—and Almagro, no doubt regarding Alvarado as the greater threat, accepted his assurances. Alvarado's men, meanwhile, were marching north in an ugly mood, knowing themselves forestalled, envious, frustrated and ready for a fight. The two armies met near Ambato, in an atmosphere of intense suspicion and latent hostility. There was no fight, however; after several days of threats and posturing, the leaders settled down to discuss terms, and a deal was arranged. Alvarado agreed to sell his claim, his ships and his equipment, and to return to Guatemala, for a payment of 100,000 *pesos* in gold. His men got nothing. Most of them stayed in Peru and sought service with established captains there.

Finally Quisquis: he entered southern Ecuador, with his retreating army in good order, in August 1534, completely ignorant of the events of the previous few months. If he had arrived earlier and established contact with Rumiñavi, they might between them have inflicted serious damage on the invaders; but Rumiñavi was already defeated. Quisquis was surprised on the march by the combined forces of Almagro and Alvarado; eluded their attack; and continued his march to Quito, only to suffer the second shock of finding Benalcázar in possession. He tried to rally his forces for an attack on the town; but his people, weary and by now disheartened, mutinied and killed him, and then dispersed to their homes.

Alvarado and Almagro rode on south to join Pizarro in Peru, where Alvarado was to be paid, leaving Quito, for a time, to Benalcázar. He soon extended his government to the coast of the Gulf of Guayaquil, and Guayaquil itself became an important harbour; but the heart of the Spanish Kingdom of Quito was always in the highlands. Cieza de León, who marched through it fifteen years after its conquest, described it appreciatively:

The city of Quito is under the equinoctial line, indeed only seven leagues distant from it. The surrounding country appears to be sterile, but in reality is very fertile, and all kinds of cattle are bred on it plentifully, besides other provisions, corn and pulse, fruit and birds. The country is very pleasant, and particularly resembles Spain in its pastures and climate, for the summer begins in April, and lasts until November, and, though it is cold, the land is no more injured by it than in Spain.

In the plains they reap a great quantity of wheat and barley, so that there is a plentiful supply of provisions in the province, and in time it will yield all the fruits of our Spain, for even now they begin to grow some of them. The natives are in general more gentle and better disposed, and have fewer vices than any of those we have passed, and indeed than all Indians of the greater part of Peru. . . . They are a people of middle height, and very hard workers. They live in the same way as the people of the Kings Yncas, except that they are not so clever, seeing that they were conquered by them, and now live by the rules which were ordered to be observed by the Yncas. For in ancient times they were, like their neighbours, badly dressed and without industry in the erection of buildings.

There are many warm valleys where fruit trees and pulses are cultivated all the year round. There are also vineyards in these valleys, but as the cultivation has only lately commenced, I can only mention the hope that they will yield; but they already have large orange and lime trees. The pulses of Spain yield abundantly, and all other provisions may be had that man requires. There is also a kind of spice, which we call cinnamon, brought from the forests to the eastward. It is a fruit, or kind of flower, which grows on the very large cinnamon trees, and there is nothing in Spain that can be compared to it, unless it be an acorn, but it is of a reddish colour inclined to black, and much larger and rounder. The taste is very pleasant, like that of real cinnamon, and it is only eaten after it has been pounded, for, if it is stewed like real cinnamon, it loses the strength of its flavour. It makes a warm cordial, as I can affirm from experience, for the natives trade with it, and use it in their illnesses, particularly for pains in the bowels and stomach. They take it as a drink.

They have great store of cotton, which they make into cloth for their dresses, and also use it for paying tribute. In the neighbourhood of the city of Quito there are many flocks of what we call sheep, but they are more like camels. . . . Of provisions, besides maize, there are two other products which form the principal food of these Indians. One is called potato, and is a kind of earth nut, which, after it has been boiled, is as tender as a cooked chestnut, but it has no more skin than a truffle, and it grows under the earth in the same way. This root produces a plant exactly like a poppy. The other food is very good, and is called *quinoa*. The leaf is like a Moorish rush (amaranth?), and the plant grows almost to the height of a man, forming a very small seed, sometimes white and at others reddish. Of these seeds they make a drink, and also eat them cooked, as we do rice.[4]

The Kingdom of Quito never rivalled central and southern Peru as a source of silver and gold; but it was prosperous and productive and clearly, in Spanish eyes, a pleasant place to live and hold Indians.

Quisquis' retreat to the north had left the whole central area of the Inca empire, which had been Huáscar's—roughly the area of the modern republic of Peru—under the nominal rule of Manco Inca. Manco lost no time in exercising his prerogatives as *Sapa Inca*, and some of the manifestations of his authority made a great impression on Spanish observers. At Jauja, for example, where he and Pizarro broke off their pursuit of Quisquis, he ordered the local people to organise a *chaco* or royal hunt, an elaborate *battue* in which the game animals of an extensive mountain area—vicuñas, guanacos, deer, hares, even sometimes pumas— were surrounded by lines of thousands of beaters and driven into a confined space for the Inca and his guests. Not all the game was killed; vicuñas, for example, were shorn and released. The *chaco* was not only a royal sport, a source of meat, and an occasion of local festivity; it served also as a rough-and-ready form of game management. Several Spanish writers—Cieza, Zárate, Cobo—described it. More central to the functioning of Peruvian society was the Inti Raymi ceremony, which marked the beginning of the agricultural year. Manco, with the approval of his Spanish mentors, performed this ceremony in April 1535, and a detailed description has survived, written by a young priest, then recently arrived in Peru, Cristóbal de Molina:

The Inca opened the sacrifices and they lasted for eight days. Thanks were given to the sun for the past harvest and prayers were made for the crops to come. . . . They brought all the effigies of the shrines of Cuzco on to a plain at the edge of the city in the direction of the sun's rise at daybreak. The most important effigies were placed under very fine, beautifully-worked feather awnings. These awnings were arranged in an avenue with one canopy a good quoit's throw from the next. The space [between] formed an avenue over thirty paces wide, and all the lords and chiefs of Cuzco stood in it. . . . These were all magnificently-robed orejones wearing rich silver cloaks and tunics, with brightly-shining circlets and medallions of fine gold on their heads. They formed up in pairs . . . in a sort of procession . . . and waited in deep silence for the sun to rise. As soon as the sunrise began they started to chant in splendid harmony and unison. While chanting each of them shook his foot . . . and as the sun continued to rise they chanted higher.

The Inca had a canopy in an enclosure, with a very rich stool for a seat, a short distance from the route of these men. When the time came for the chanting he rose with great dignity, placed himself at their head, and was the first to open the chant. They all followed his lead. After he had been there for some time he returned to his seat and dealt with those who came up to him. From time to time he would go to his choir, remain there for a while and then return. They all stayed there, chanting, from the time the sun rose until it had completely set. As the sun was rising towards noon they continued to raise their voices, and from noon onwards they lowered them, keeping careful track of the sun's course.

Throughout this time, great offerings were being made. On a platform on which there was a tree, there were Indians doing nothing but throwing meats into a great fire and burning them up in it. At another place the Inca ordered ewes [llamas] to be thrown for the poorer common Indians to grab, and this caused great sport.

At eight o'clock over two hundred girls came out of Cuzco, each with a large new pot of one and a half arrobas [six gallons] of chicha, plastered and with a cover. The girls came in groups of five, full of precision and order, and pausing at intervals. They also offered the sun many bales of a herb that the Indians chew, whose leaf is like myrtle.

There were many other ceremonies and sacrifices. It is sufficient to say that when the sun was about to set in the evening the Indians showed great sadness at its departure, in their chants and expressions. They allowed their voices to die away on purpose. As the sun was sinking completely and disappearing from sight they made a great act of reverence, raising their hands and worshipping it in the deepest humility. All the apparatus of the festival was immediately dismantled and the canopies were removed. Everyone returned to their homes and the effigies and terrible relics were returned to their houses and shrines.

These effigies that they had under the awnings were those of former Incas who had ruled Cuzco. Each had a great retinue of men who stayed there all day fanning away flies with fans like hand mirrors, made of swans' feathers. Each also had its mamaconas, who are like nuns: there were some twelve to fifteen in each awning.

They came out in this same way for eight or nine days in succession. When all the festivals were over, they brought out on the last day many hand ploughs—these had formerly been made of gold. After the religious service the Inca took a plough and began to break the earth, and the rest of the lords did the same. Following their lead the entire kingdom did likewise. No Indian would have dared to break the earth until the Inca had done so, and none believed that the earth could produce unless the Inca broke it first.[5]

During these early months of his reign Manco remained on good terms with the formidable allies to whom he owed his throne, especially to Almagro, whom he seems to have liked personally. He needed their support; there were other possible claimants to the succession, and the Inca aristocracy was by no means united in loyalty to him. Initially he was not ungrateful. Besides lavish entertainments and gifts to the Spanish leaders, he lent his authority to Spanish actions which might otherwise have been insupportable. While Pizarro busied himself with laying the groundwork of Spanish government, founding municipalities and granting *encomiendas* to those of his followers whom he thought he could trust, Manco ordered his officials to provide native labour for municipal building and to co-operate in collecting the *encomenderos'* tribute. Pizarro, for his part, was convinced of the value of the alliance. He insisted that Spaniards should treat Manco with respect, and should refrain from robbing and insulting his subjects; at least—as he repeatedly told them—until there were enough Spaniards in the country to make the conquest secure and indirect rule unnecessary. In the early stages of the conquest that day seemed remote, and Pizarro showed no great impatience for it. Enough Spaniards to hold the country secure, as he well knew, meant too many importunate claimants for the available rewards.

The difficulty of matching rewards with services was inherent in the initial organisation of the conquest. The core of Pizarro's personal following, including his brothers, had been recruited in Spain; but other leaders—Benalcázar, Soto, Cristóbal de Mena, Juan de Salcedo—had joined him on the coast, coming from Nicaragua or the Isthmus, each with his own band. They had been welcome additions to the expedition before the conquest, but were embarrassing sharers in success after it. The army, small as it was, had too many captains. Some of these men had distinguished themselves in the fighting. They had no particular reason for loyalty to the Pizarro interest; they were ill content with the conventional officer's reward—an *encomienda* and one or more horsemen's shares of the loot; they wanted governments of their own. 'Finders keepers' was the rule of the Pizarros, as of most *conquistadores*; so Francisco Pizarro sought to get rid of his semi-independent captains before they could try to carve up the vast territory which he claimed as his own. His behaviour in the months after Cajamarca is instructive in this regard. Many of the rank and file of his army wanted to go back to Spain, with their share of the loot, while they still had whole skins. Only prominent and ambitious captains had a strong motive to remain. Pizarro, who at first needed every fighting man, in general refused leave to all save the old, the sick and necessary messengers; but he positively encouraged Mena and Salcedo to go. Both, grumbling, took the hint and retired, each to his home town in Spain. A year later, Soto received broad hints that there was no future for him in Peru. He went to Spain, organised an expedition to North America, suffered great and unrewarding hardships, and died beside the Mississippi. Benalcázar was a tough old Indian fighter, illiterate, plebian in his origin and habits. He had spent all his adult life in the Indies, and Spain had little attraction for him. Pizarro got rid of him temporarily by sending him—as he thought—to dull garrison duty in an unrewarding corner of the empire.

While the Pizarros worked, with some success, to remove from the scene of action those captains who might take an independent line, they found themselves faced, from the spring of 1534, by a different, though related problem: a rapid increase in the number of rank-and-file adventurers—*soldados*, in the phrase of the time—clamouring for employment. Tales of plunder in Peru attracted them from all round the Caribbean and from Spain itself. Despite the shortage of shipping, despite the obstacles which governors placed in the way of people leaving for Peru, they crowded every south-bound ship. They came too late to share in the initial loot and, as newcomers, had no claim on the perquisites—*encomiendas* and the like—which were in Pizarro's gift. They had to pick up what they could, which—in a Peru full of tales of hidden treasure—meant robbing living Indians or plundering the tombs of dead ones. Even Manco and his entourage were not exempt from their rapacity. During much of 1534–35 Francisco Pizarro was down at the coast organising his new city of Lima, and left Cuzco in the charge of his younger brothers Juan and Gonzalo. This irresponsible pair did nothing to protect Manco either from Spanish violence or from jealous Peruvian intrigue, and forced him into reliance on Almagro, who had his own reasons for seeking the Inca's alliance. So far from making the country secure, then, the influx of newcomers represented a potential threat to Pizarro's authority, and caused a rapid deterioration in the relations between the Inca aristocracy and the Spanish command.

The obvious way of getting rid of these trouble-makers was to employ them in new expeditions of exploration and conquest; but such expeditions would have to be in new territory, to which the Pizarros could advance no claim. The remedy had therefore to await a royal definition of the boundaries of Pizarro's Peru. This was especially urgent, because the obvious candidate for command of a major new *entrada* was Almagro. Almagro regarded himself as a partner rather than as a subordinate, and bitterly resented the arrogance of the Pizarro clan. The Pizarros despised him as a man with no name, and distrusted him as a semi-foreigner—he came from New Castille; Hernando once went so far as to call him a circumcised Moor. On the other hand, they recognised him as a formidable competitor. He could not be pushed out like Soto and Mena; he was too prominent in the conquest; much respected both as an organiser and as a fighting man, generally popular because of his careless generosity and his convivial ways. Like Benalcázar he had no wish to return to Spain, but wanted his own government in the Indies.

When, after Cajamarca, Hernando Pizarro went to Spain to report and to negotiate for the honours and offices which were to be Francisco's reward, he promised to do what he could for Almagro also; but Almagro, with previous experience of Pizarro promises, gave his power of attorney to Cristóbal de Mena. Throughout the early months of 1534 the two agents worked, with petitions and counter-petitions and a lavish distribution of Peruvian gold, to promote the interests of their respective principals. The result was a compromise. A series of decrees in the early summer of 1534[6] divided the new Pacific territory into four parallel bands, each running east from the Pacific, either to the Atlantic or to the line of demarcation. The northernmost was Pizarro's territory. Originally it was to extend 200 leagues from north to south, measured (presumably) from the point at which the Spaniards first landed; but Pizarro asked and obtained an additional seventy leagues to the south. Almagro was to govern an area, as yet unconquered and unexplored, extending 200 leagues south from the southern boundary of Pizarro's. South of Almagro's grant came that of Pedro de Mendoza and further south again that of Simón de Alcazaba. Mendoza and Alcazaba were both new to the Indies and procured their grants by importunity at the court. Both made abortive attempts to take possession. Alcazaba tried, but failed, to reach his government by sea through Magellan's Strait, and was killed by mutineers on the coast of Patagonia. Mendoza made a first, short-lived attempt to found a settlement on the Río de la Plata, and died shortly afterwards on his way back to Spain.

The boundaries of 1534 were obviously arbitrary, and could not be fixed on the ground. Only one of them was of practical importance: that between Pizarro and Almagro. When the news of the division arrived in Peru, early in 1535, Almagro was persuaded that, even with Pizarro's additional seventy leagues, the line passed north of Cuzco. He claimed the city for himself, a claim which naturally led to high words and would have led to fighting, had Almagro persisted in it. He could not hope, however, to hold Cuzco against the Pizarros, and at the same time explore and conquer a vast unknown region in the south. After several uneasy months he allowed himself to be talked into giving up Cuzco, at least for a time. In return he received valuable help in preparing an expedition to the south; into the *Collasuyu*, the southern quarter of the Inca empire, which included not only the Pacific province known vaguely to the Spaniards as Chile, Almagro's ultimate destination, but also a vast area of highland country in what is now western Bolivia. Almost everyone's interests appeared to converge on the success of this undertaking. Almagro himself had his kingdom to conquer; as Cristóbal de Molina sourly put it, he was 'so obsessed by greed and by ambition to rule great kingdoms, and so full of the tales that lying Indians told him about the riches of Chile, that he thought nothing of the country he was actually in'. The Pizarros, for their part, had the strongest possible motive for hurrying Almagro out of Peru, and for encouraging him to take with him as many as possible of the unemployed and undisciplined newcomers. Francisco Pizarro gave him much help to this end, and invested heavily in the expedition. Manco Inca, still clinging to the pretence of sovereign authority, probably saw in the expedition an opportunity to extend his own control over the southern third of Huayna Capac's empire. He acceded willingly to Almagro's request for a major chief to accompany the expedition, and sent two: his half-brother Paullu—always a favourite with the Spaniards— and the temple dignitary Villac Umu, whom the Spaniards variously described as Pope or High Priest. There was even a possibility that the Inca—whose life in Cuzco was becoming more and more a humiliating captivity—might accompany the expedition himself. The Pizarros moved swiftly to prevent this; but Manco contributed fighting men and porters, some twelve thousand Indians in all. As for Spanish participants, there was no lack of volunteers. Many of those who had come with Alvarado attached themselves to Almagro. His total Spanish strength was between five and six hundred; much larger than the force which originally invaded Peru, and initially probably better equipped. About half were mounted. Many of Alvarado's men had lost their horses in the Ecuadorean forest; they borrowed from Almagro to replace them, at Peruvian prices. (The number of horses and mules in Peru was growing steadily, partly through natural increase, partly through shipment from southern Mexico, where some breeders—the Cortés estate in particular—made a business of it; but riding animals still fetched extravagant prices.) Besides horses, the expedition used several thousand llamas for carrying baggage, and the usual dogs for hunting down recalcitrant Indians. Arms were the usual swords, pikes and lances, some body armour, a few cross-bows, very few fire-arms. The most serious lacks were warm clothing, and iron for all purposes, so that horses had sometimes to be shod with copper.

The first expedition to Chile is much less fully chronicled than the earlier invasion of Peru, or than the savage civil war which broke out in Peru after Almagro's return. There is one eye-witness narrative, that of Fray Cristóbal de Molina,[7] and several *relaciones de méritos y servicios* submitted by survivors.[8] These last, though designed to appeal to the royal bounty rather than to inform, contain interesting details and are in substantial agreement one with another. Oviedo, whose son took part in the expedition and was drowned in one of the river crossings when returning, wrote a full and moving account; Zárate a shorter one. The expedition offered more examples of physical endurance—which did not particularly interest chroniclers—than of feats of arms; and for its immediate purposes—conquest and plunder—it was a failure. As a feat of exploration and discovery, however, it was one of the most interesting, one of the longest, certainly one of the most arduous, of all the Andean expeditions.

Almagro's army did not move as a single united column. As was customary with expeditions of that size and complexity, he divided his people into several parties, which set out from occupied Peru at considerable intervals of time. Almagro knew from his Indian informants that the road to Chile passed through big stretches of uninhabited desert. He sent Juan de Saavedra off in the spring of 1535 with a hundred

Spaniards, to establish an advanced base at the edge of the first major desert stretch. There he was to collect provisions for the crossing of the *despoblado*. Almagro himself, with fifty men, left Cuzco in July. He left his second-in-command, Rodrigo Ordóñez, in Cuzco to organise a support party to follow later. In addition, two parties were despatched from Lima by sea. Neither accomplished much; the navigation was dauntingly difficult, more than a thousand miles against wind and current, and the ships were none of the best. The coast was arid, and the few water-courses jealously guarded; watering parties were often attacked, and men killed on the beaches. García de Alfaro, sent off in the early stages of planning with a single ship on a voyage of coastal reconnaissance, reached the neighbourhood of Arica, returned north with his ship in a sinking condition, and got back to Peru after Almagro had left. The ship had to be sent to Panama for refit, and returned to Peru too late to be of any help to the expedition. Ruy Díaz, in command of a powerful force, left about the same time as Almagro, with three ships and with instructions to join the main body on the coast of Chile. After about a hundred miles of maddeningly slow progress, however, he landed his men and marched to Chile by the same highland route as Almagro, whom he eventually succeeded in joining, though with his force attenuated by hardship. One of his ships, the *San Pedro*, pushed on down the coast as far as Arica, where her exhausted company beached her, and encamped on the shore in the unlikely hope of rescue. The other two ships returned to Callao; but one of them, the *Santiago*, refitted and set out once more for the south. This ship reached the coast of central Chile, found Almagro—almost incredibly—at some point, possibly Los Vilos, on his long march from Copiapó to Aconcagua, and delivered to him some much-needed supplies, including horse shoes. The *Santiago* was commanded by her navigating officer, Alonso Quintero, her master having been killed in a shore-side skirmish. Of Quintero, Oviedo wrote: 'I knew him well. . . . He was a skilful seaman, not so much with the quadrant, as by dead-reckoning experience, and rule of thumb. He was much addicted to cards. Of the astrolabe he was wholly ignorant'.[9] Quintero, in other words, could not observe the latitude of the places he visited, and so could not estimate their distance—a matter of some moment to Almagro—from Magellan's Strait. No matter, he could find his way, and served Almagro well.

Almagro's own route took him over the Moina pass immediately south of Cuzco and across the Collao, the great highland basin in southern Peru and western Bolivia at whose centre lies Lake Titicaca. Almagro passed west of the lake, crossed the Desaguadero, the swift river which drains it, using native canoes, and marched on south-east to Paría—modern Poopó, near the north-eastern margin of the lake of that name. Along the march—three hundred miles or so—from one lake to the other, the land deteriorated steadily, becoming bleaker, more arid, increasingly impregnated with salt. The area round Lake Titicaca, though cold and windswept, is fertile, with extensive fields of small mountain potatoes, *quinoa* and today even barley and a little wheat here and there. The lake itself is always brimming full, fed by the snow of the Cordillera Real, and its water, though slightly brackish, can be drunk, and contains fish which are caught for food. Round its edge are great beds of *totora* reeds from which Indian fishermen fashioned—and fashion still—their raft-canoes. Lake Poopó, through evaporation, is salt and sterile, its margin a stinking saline marsh. It has no outlet except south to the Salar de Uyuni, an immense dried-out salt pan more than 5,000 square miles in area. The town then called Paría lay at the edge of the first stretch of desert. Saavedra had made his base camp there and had assembled great stores of grain and herds of llamas; and from there the army began its first march through *despoblado*. The destination was Tupiza, and the way lay south-south-east, skirting the chain of high peaks now called Cordillera de los Frailes, and passing close to Potosí where, ten years later, a prodigious hill of silver was to be found. Tupiza, then as now, was an oasis and a primitive market. It lay some 3,000 feet lower than the *páramo* through which the army had passed, and was correspondingly warmer and more genial. There Almagro rested his people for two months; and there, probably, word reached the camp of a general Indian rising in the Cuzco area led by Manco Inca himself. Almagro ignored the reports or rumours, and Paullu Inca—who apparently had decided to throw in his lot with the conquerors—clung steadfastly to Almagro; but the Villac Umu escaped, and hurried north to join his lord. Mounted parties sent in pursuit failed to catch him, and he duly played his part in the war which ensued. Many others ran away, or tried to. The Indians—both those who accompanied Almagro and those through whose territory he passed—had been very roughly handled, if Cristóbal de Molina is to be believed. A young and impressionable priest might be expected to exaggerate; the story of foals, dropped on the march by Spanish mares, being carried in litters by Indians, seems improbable; but Almagro's men, especially those who had come to Peru with Alvarado, were a very rough lot. It was they who, on the expedition, first coined the word *ranchear* for the systematic process of foraging, looting, and impressment of native carriers. 'Any natives who would not accompany the Spaniards voluntarily', says Molina, 'were dragged along bound in ropes or chains. The Spaniards shut them up in makeshift prisons at night, and led them by day heavily laden and dying of hunger'. The Spaniards themselves were to experience hardship enough before long, and possibly the Villac Umu's anxiety to get away from the expedition may in part have arisen from his knowledge of what lay ahead.

Almagro, on Indian advice, proposed to approach the coast by way of the valley and province known then, and now, as Copiapó. The Copiapó river is the northernmost river in Chile with a reliable (if fluctuating) flow of water. North of it, stretching for hundreds of miles, lies the waterless coastal desert of Atacama. Inland is the *Puna* of Atacama, a vast highland area flanked on either side, east and west, by ranges of high peaks. Between the cordilleras lies the *Puna* proper, at an average height of 11,000–12,000 feet, broken by minor mountain chains, the depressions filled with salt pans, the whole area arid, windswept, bitterly cold, and for the most part uninhabited. Between Tupiza and Copiapó the *Puna* had to be crossed. There were—and are—ancient roads, or rather trails, one of which leads more or less directly in a general south-south-west direction;

but the distance by that route is over 800 miles, the oases far apart, and their water supply sufficient only for small parties. A big force such as Almagro's would have to carry its own water, and so must try to make a dash across the *Puna* at the narrowest point.

Almagro's guides took him south, through what is now the Argentinian province of Jujuy, into the broad plain where the modern town of Salta stands. They lost much height in the process—Salta is at only 4,000 feet—and marched through hot, wooded valleys of rivers descending from the eastern scarp of the *Puna*, on the right flank. These rivers form part of the immense Río de la Plata drainage. The people of the region had never been subject to Inca discipline. They were hunters, primitive but formidable, skilled—like many primitive Amerindian groups but unlike the settled town and village dwellers—in the use of the bow. Six Spaniards and several horses were killed in brushes with these people. Almagro himself had a horse killed under him by an arrow; the priest Molina lent him a spare horse as a replacement, and was remembered for it in Almagro's will.[10] Wild people were not the only danger. The rivers were swollen by the melting snows of late summer, and one of them, the Huachipas, had flooded the whole of its valley. In floundering through this broad flood Almagro lost many of his llamas—which had been intended to carry water-skins across the *Puna*—and a large part of his baggage and provisions. The army was poorly equipped, after that disaster, for the rough climb up the escarpment, and for the saline wastes and chill winds of the *Puna*. Their worst hardships were in the Paso de San Francisco, the high pass by which they crossed the western Cordillera. The head of the pass is over 15,000 feet, and the peak which flanks it on the south, Ojos del Salado, is probably, at 23,200 feet, the highest in the Andes. Winter was setting in. At least four of the *relaciones de méritos* mention loss of toes by frost-bite. Ruy Díaz with his support party, following Almagro later in the winter, suffered worse, and lost many of his people. Zárate gives grisly details:

Many men and many horses froze to death, for neither their clothes nor their armour could protect them from the piercing wind. . . . Many of those who had died remained, frozen solid, still on foot and propped against the rocks, and the horses they had been leading also frozen, not decomposed, but as fresh as if they had just died; and later expeditions following the same route, short of food, came upon these horses, and were glad to eat them.[11]

The Copiapó valley, where Almagro descended from the Cordillera, is little more than an oasis. It was inhabited by settled people, and the army procured food there; but otherwise it had few attractions. Almagro's men found no indication of the silver which, in modern times, became the chief product of the area. Almagro turned south, marching parallel with the coast, climbing in and out of river valleys, with the icy wall of the Cordillera always in sight, until he reached the valley of the Aconcagua, the river at whose mouth modern Valparaíso stands. The country here was less inhospitable—the central valley of Chile, indeed, is fertile and beautiful—but as the country improved, so native resistance stiffened, and still there was no sign of gold or silver. At Aconcagua, then, Almagro admitted failure and began his retreat. From Copiapó he marched north, preferring the dangers of the unknown to a second crossing of the Cordillera; so the army trudged for hundreds of miles through the nitrate desert of Atacama, travelling in small parties with a day's interval between them to avoid exhausting the scanty springs and water-holes. Early in 1537 they reached the southern confines of Peru, re-formed near the site of modern Arequipa, and marched on Cuzco, which then was closely invested by the forces of Manco Inca. With his frustrated but still formidable army, Almagro dispersed the besiegers and entered the city, which he claimed as his own; so inaugurating the decade of savage fighting in which he and three of the four Pizarro brothers, and many other captains, came to a violent end.

The expedition was a remarkable feat of courage, endurance and leadership; losses, at least among Spaniards, were relatively light, thanks largely to Almagro's organising ability. From the point of view of the organisers, the project had been a costly failure, and few of the participants showed any desire to return to Chile. Pizarro nevertheless thought the discovery worth pursuing, and after Almagro's death found in Pedro de Valdivia a captain willing to attempt conquest and settlement. This proved a slow and arduous process. The *encomiendas* distributed by Valdivia were small and scanty, the Indians intractable; the Spanish settlers, never numerous, had to grow food for themselves—an unwelcome necessity, unusual in the annals of the conquest—and fight to defend their fields. Valdivia put a brave face on it, and wrote optimistic reports to the King:

I can truly say of the goodness of this land, and all those of Your Majesty's subjects here who have seen New Spain agree, that there are far more people here than there. The whole country is one settlement, one corn-field, one gold mine. Unless the houses were to build one above the other, there is no room for more. There are great flocks of sheep, as in Peru, with wool that hangs to the ground. The Indians grow abundant crops of maize, potatoes, quinoa, madia, peppers and beans. The people are well-built, domestic in their habits, friendly, of light complexion and handsome, men and women alike. They wear clothes made of coarse woollen cloth. They are terrified by horses. They are devoted to their wives and children, and to their dwellings, which are strongly built of massive timbers, some of them very big, with two, four or eight entrances. The houses are well stocked with food of all kinds and with wool, and are furnished with elegantly decorated vessels of pottery or of wood. They are expert farmers and great drinkers. Their law is in arms; they all keep weapons in their houses, ready to defend themselves against their neighbours or to attack those weaker than themselves. The country has a fine temperate climate, so that Spanish plants of all kinds would grow better here than in Spain itself. This is what we have so far discovered about these people.[12]

One characteristic, at least, of the natives of Chile was mentioned without exaggeration in this otherwise somewhat implausible description: their pugnacity. The Araucanians were among the few settled Amerindian peoples who maintained a steady resistance to Europeans over a long period; more than two hundred years in the south of the country. Valdivia himself met his death in a skirmish with them in 1553.

He was one of the few major captains of the conquest to be captured and killed by Indians, and one of the very few to be suitably commemorated in epic verse. The *Araucana* of Alonso de Ercilla has been praised—over-praised, perhaps—by Cervantes, Voltaire and others. It quickly became famous in its own day, and is still read. It is not an eye-witness account of discovery; the author does not even mention Almagro. He arrived in Chile in 1556, three years after Valdivia's death, and remained there six years, years largely occupied in fighting the Araucanians. He knew many of Valdivia's associates and wrote of Valdivia himself with warm, though not uncritical admiration. The main part of the work is a vigorous account of the war, full of vivid scenes and episodes. In his preface, Ercilla pays a fighting man's tribute to the Araucanian enemy:

Some may think that I have praised the Araucanians more highly than such barbarians deserve, and have devoted too much attention to their customs and their exploits; but if we study their martial traditions, their training for war, and their manner of conducting it, we have to agree that in these respects they have few equals. Few nations have shown such bravery and persistence, in defending their land against such formidable enemies as the Spaniards. Their courage has been amazing. The long wars with the Spaniards have destroyed almost all they had; there are three Spanish settlements on their borders and two Spanish forts within their territory; they do not control more than twenty leagues of land, and that open, without natural barriers; they have no fortifications, no adequate reserve of arms; yet by sheer courage and stubborn resolution they have redeemed and maintained their freedom, with such losses, both of their people and of ours, that almost all the land is soaked in blood and strewn with bones. . . . The boys take up arms before their time . . . and even the women fight by the side of the men and cheerfully meet death. I have wished to record all this, as tribute and testimony to the valour of these people, which is worthy of much greater praise than my verse can give.[13]

Benalcázar in the north, and Almagro in the south, had penetrated to the extremities, or almost the extremities, of the Inca empire. Their exploits marked the end of a chapter, a transition, in the areas they traversed, from discovery to conquest, to quarrelling over the spoils, and eventually to a settled colonial administration. This did not mean, however, that they had exhausted the possibilities of discovery elsewhere. No one knew how many Perus there might be. Spaniards and others pursued the search, both in the mountains and in the *montaña* forest to the east, for kingdoms neither subject to the Incas nor—and this was more to the point—pre-empted by the Pizarro clan. The cold damp forests of southern Chile were unpropitious for the search, as Valdivia discovered; and the eastern *montaña* was daunting to the searcher. In the northern Andes, however, Benalcázar, having established his administration in Quito, moved hopefully north, partly because it was his restless nature to move, partly to find new kingdoms, partly to put as much distance as possible between himself and the Pizarros. Late in 1537, Francisco Pizarro, suspecting that Benalcázar was developing ideas above his station, sent Lorenzo de Aldana and a party of horsemen in pursuit, with instructions to arrest Benalcázar and bring him back; but Aldana's movements were slowed by lack of supplies, caused by Benalcázar's depredations, and Benalcázar moved on. He moved slowly, driving a large and doubtless very destructive herd of pigs along with his army for food on the way, foraging for grain and potatoes and fighting with those who disputed his passage. He passed through Popayán—high, rough, but settled country, site of an ancient culture long vanished save for its monuments—into the fertile Neiva valley on the upper Magdalena. After a long halt and rest at Neiva, he moved on north-east, and found himself in an agreeable, cool and fertile upland area, dotted with settlements: the sort of place he had been looking for; but here—just as he had forestalled Alvarado in Quito—he found himself forestalled by Spaniards who had hacked their way, incredibly, from the Caribbean coast, in the *entrada* led by Gonzalo Jiménez de Quesada.

All the settled territories of the Andes were difficult of access, and none more so than the highland areas of what is now Colombia, which the Spaniards called New Granada; Granada being Quesada's home in Spain. The Pacific coast is uninviting, with vast mangrove swamps. Its rivers offer access, with difficulty, to the western Cordillera, but after Andagoya's journey up the San Juan no other Spanish explorer felt tempted to enter the country by that route. Much of the Caribbean coast is also lined with mangrove swamps, at least in the western section, west of Cabo de la Aggia, by modern Santa Marta. From Santa Marta east to Punta Gallinas, at the extremity of the Goajira peninsula, the coast is dry and rocky, with many sandy coves; but the way inland is blocked by the Sierra Nevada de Santa Marta, an isolated bold mountain *massif* running up directly from the coast to 19,000 feet—a barbican, so to speak, of the ramparts of the Andes. Inland the country is extraordinarily broken, even by Andean standards. East-west travel is almost impossible; even today nearly all the roads run north and south. In Pasto the great chain of the Andes fans out into three distinct ranges—Cordilleras Oriental, Central, Occidental—separated not (as in the central Andes) by high, cold, grassy basins, but by two great rivers, the Magdalena and its tributary the Cauca, flowing north to the Caribbean through deep-cut valleys choked with rain forest. The central and eastern cordilleras are further sub-divided at their northern ends, the central into several minor ridges which finally dip into the lowlands, the eastern into two well-defined ranges, the Cordillera de Mérida and the Sierra de Perija, a huge pair of pincers almost enclosing the Gulf of Maracaibo. Of the three major cordilleras, the central is the most abrupt, containing many high peaks, though none as high as the giants further south. The eastern is the most extensive, and contains great areas of hilly upland savannah. Of these, the plateau of Cundinamarca, 'Land of the Condor', is the southernmost. Here the north-bound and south-bound streams of Spanish exploration met in 1537.

The settled cultures of this vast region were as diverse as the terrain, and had grown up over the centuries in many scattered localities. Of those which were flourishing in the early sixteenth century some, such as the Sinú, south of the Gulf of Morosquillo, were situated in coastal lowlands, others in the valleys of the major rivers. The Calima and Quimbaya cultures, for example, both notable for their gold work, occupied restricted areas in the upper Cauca valley. There had been a tendency, however, in the centuries preceding the Spanish invasion, for settled populations to move on to higher ground, possibly for reasons of defence. To do this they had to change their food habits, abandoning characteristic lowland staples such as 'sweet' cassava, and developing upland crop complexes. In the northern and western foothills of the Sierra Nevada, the Tairona developed a highly individual culture based on maize cultivation and showing many signs of Meso-American influence. They had among them skilled potters, stone carvers and workers in soft metals. They lived in scattered villages, but some of these were big enough to be called towns, were fortified, and had large public works—temple enclosures, agricultural terraces, paved roads and irrigation. They had no general political cohesion, however; and the area which they occupied was relatively small. The Cundinamarca-Boyacá plateau in the eastern cordillera covered a much bigger area, then as now an area of high population density. The people who inhabited it—Chibcha, or more precisely Muisca, the name they gave themselves—were the subject of many enthusiastic descriptions by Spanish chroniclers; naturally enough, since the early Spanish invaders of the area were anxious to persuade their countrymen, and to persuade themselves, that they had found another Peru. On archaeological evidence, the attainments of the Chibcha are more difficult to assess. They were not stone-masons, and left no monuments. Their dwellings were of wood and thatch, but their stockaded villages impressed the Spaniards by their orderliness and strength. They were skilful farmers; besides maize they grew quinoa, several varieties of potato, and many minor highland crops. They were weavers, grew cotton,

Below
85 Anthropomorphic figurine in gold, Tairona. *Museo del Oro, Bogotá, Colombia.*

Below right
86 Ear-rings in gold, Tairona. *Museo del Oro, Bogotá, Columbia.*

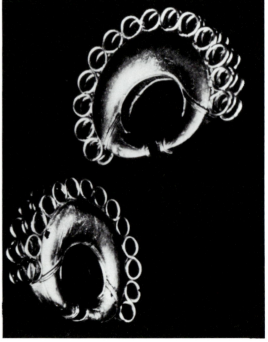

and wore clothes made of it. They were traders; like most of the settled peoples of the region, they valued gold and were skilled in working it; but having none in their own area, they bartered for it with cotton cloth, emeralds and salt. The Zipaquirá salt mines near Bogotá, which the Chibcha used, are still being worked, and Colombia is still a major source of emeralds. The largest political units in the area, which the chroniclers called kingdoms, were federations of villages, of which the two most powerful, when the Spaniards arrived, were centred respectively on Tunja and Bogotá. The plateau was isolated, cut off from other settled areas by great areas of dense forest and by wild people who lived in the forest—hunters and gatherers, sometimes head-hunters and cannibals, so the chroniclers said. This, then, was an island of settled culture; not a second Inca empire, nor in the way of becoming one.

Exploring and trading expeditions had followed the Caribbean coast from Cumaná to the Isthmus in the early years of the sixteenth century; but the propensity of the explorers to vary trade with looting and slaving produced hostile reactions, which in turn discouraged attempts to settle. In 1529, however, old Rodrigo de Bastidas, who had explored the coast in 1501–02, and since then had lived in Hispaniola, established a settlement at Santa Marta. In 1528 a small force, despatched from Santo Domingo to assert the authority of the *audiencia* on the coast, chose Coro, a hundred miles east of the Gulf of Maracaibo, as the site for a town. Coro became, in 1529, the headquarters of the German agents despatched by the House of Welser, under contract with the Emperor to settle Venezuela, and a port of shipment of Indian slaves to the islands. In 1533 Pedro de Heredia, coming directly from Spain, founded Cartagena. Thus by the mid 1530s there were three settlements—however, rudimentary and precarious—which might serve as bases for expeditions into the interior, in search of sources of gold. News of the conquest of Peru naturally quickened interest in such enterprises. Some, at least, of the early expeditions had the object, among others, of finding a direct overland route to Peru—Cieza de León, who took part in one of them, is specific on this point. If other Perus should be discovered on the way, so much the better.

The New Granada expeditions were all made by relatively large Spanish forces, mostly considerably larger than the original armies of conquest in Mexico and Peru, with a substantial proportion of mounted men. They made little use of Indians, except as guides, since the tribes of the area had no tradition of organised forced labour and could not—even if they would—produce large bodies of docile porters. They all had to traverse great areas of swamp and rain forest, largely uninhabited, before they reached the mountains; and all suffered unprecedentedly high losses, more from sickness and starvation than from fighting. A few, in particular those who found their way to the Chibcha highlands, acquired substantial loot and valuable *encomiendas*, though nothing comparable with Peru. Most found nothing they thought worth finding, and failed to cover their costs.

Cieza's expedition, commanded by a lawyer-*conquistador* named Vadillo, set out from Cartagena in 1536 with about 350 men. They went nowhere near the Chibcha 'kingdoms', but made their way slowly and painfully through the Sinú country and up the Cauca valley, losing about a hundred men and many horses. After nearly two years of travel the survivors reached the newly founded town of Cali, only one year old; and there fell in with Pizarro's lieutenant Aldana. They deserted their own leader and attached themselves to Aldana, who was about to return to Peru, as Cieza relates. This was the basis of his claim, that the expedition was the first to find a direct way from the Caribbean to Peru; though it was a way far too arduous to compete with the route through Panama and down the Pacific coast.

The Venezuelan Germans explored assiduously, usually in jealous competition one with another and without much attempt to concert their plans. At Coro they were poorly placed to find anything of interest to them. Ambrose Ehinger, the governor in 1531, led an expedition across the Maracaibo Gulf in canoes, and on to the coast at Riohacha. The arid Goajira offered no rewards, so he turned south, climbed to the rough saddle which separates the César valley from the Ranchería, crossed the ridge of the Sierra de Perija, and followed the high ground south, roughly to the site of modern Pamplona. There—as Aguado, the chronicler of Venezuela remarks—he was not far from the confines of the Chibcha; but he turned back, and was killed by Indians shortly afterwards. Only a tattered remnant of his Spanish followers got back to Coro. His successor Hohemut—George of Speyer, Jorge Espira, as the Spaniards called him—died in the course of a similar attempt. Ehinger's and Hohemut's deputy, Nicholas Federmann, passed over as Ehinger's successor, mounted an *entrada* of his own in 1535, with about five hundred men. Marching south from Coro, they wandered for two years in the labyrinth of the Llanos, a vast plain covered in horse-high grasses and intersected by hundreds of water-courses, not adequately mapped to this day. Their saddles rotted, their clothes dropped away in rags, and had to be replaced by substitutes made of horse-hide and deerskin. Eventually they reached the Meta river, one of the principal tributaries of the Orinoco, and followed it upstream to the high steep scarp of the eastern Cordillera. About a hundred and sixty tattered scarecrows, survivors of the original five hundred, leading or dragging the remaining horses, climbed up to the crest and down into the Bogotá savannah—'this treasure casket' as Castellanos called it, 'only to be approached by the roughest ways'. There they found, as Benalcázar was to find a few weeks later, Quesada's army already ensconced.

The expedition which Quesada commanded was mounted and financed by Pedro Fernández de Lugo, first governor of Santa Marta, who borrowed part, at least, of the money from Hispaniola merchants, and from the Welsers through their agent in Santa Marta.[14] Lugo had come from Tenerife, where he was hereditary governor, in 1535, bringing Quesada with him in the capacity of *alcalde mayor*, chief magistrate. Immediately on arrival he set about organising a series of *entradas* in search of gold. That he should have entrusted the most ambitious of them to Quesada is at first sight surprising; not because Quesada was a lawyer—there had been lawyer-*conquistadores* before, some of whom, such as Nuño de Guzmán and the Vadillo mentioned above, distinguished themselves by their brutal determination—but because he was new to the

Indies and had no training or experience to guide him. He must have been a remarkably impressive personality; certainly he had a gift for leadership and for attracting loyalty. He was better educated than most of the *conquistadores*, intelligent, observant, articulate. He was a humane man, as *conquistadores* went; he murdered no rivals and committed few atrocities, even against Indians (though he did not always prevent his followers from committing them). He was one of a few *conquistadores* who made testamentary provision for masses to be said for the souls of Indians killed in the conquest. In general, he displayed remarkable tact and skill, both in negotiating with other Spanish captains and in placating the conquered Indians. The governor of Santa Marta made a good choice.

We do not know whether the Chibcha highlands were specifically among the objects of Quesada's search. He probably had heard tales— Castellanos says he was guided by 'vague rumours and faint echoes of a report'. In any event, whether he were looking for Bogotá or Peru, or— though this is unlikely—merely exploring at random, Santa Marta was a much better base for the *entrada* than Coro or Cartagena. Today it is the only coastal city connected directly by a good road to Bogotá. This route, however, skirts the western foothills of the Sierra Nevada, which then were inhabited by formidable people. It took the Spaniards the best part of a century to subdue the Tairona; they rose again and again, undeterred by defeat and repression. Like the Araucanians, they never assimilated. Their descendants the Coquí, who inhabit the Sierra today and who inherited what little remained of Tairona culture, still reject and resist European influence. In 1535, the year before Quesada's departure, Lugo, accompanied by his son Luis Alonso, had led an expedition into the Tairona country, and had met stubborn resistance everywhere. Luis Alonso had taken one of the principal *pueblos*, Bonda, and acquired some loot, but not enough to tempt others to imitate him. Quesada had taken part, in a civil capacity, in this operation, and these considerations probably weighed with him in planning his own expedition. He decided to enter the country not by marching through Tairona territory, but by ascending the Magdalena river.

This proved a mistake, though a natural one. The Magdalena valley indeed led in what appeared to be the right direction, and it had indeed been for millennia a route of southward migration; but not—and this was the essential point—not for armies. Quesada, like many other *conquistadores*, was confronted by a dilemma of scale. He proposed to explore a vast area totally unknown—save for the 'faint echoes of report'—to him and to his countrymen; he proposed also, if he found kingdoms worth conquering, to conquer them. Exploration, especially in the kind of terrain which Quesada proposed to enter, was best carried out by relatively small parties, well-equipped, mobile, adaptable, able to live off the country and to support themselves, if necessary, on wild game. Obviously such parties must be well armed to defend themselves against attack; though in areas where Europeans were unknown, small parties, because less threatening, were often less likely to provoke attack than large ones. The most efficient and most economical technique of conquest was to explore first with a few picked men and subsequently, if anything worth conquering were discovered, to follow up the discovery with more substantial forces, as Pizarro had done. The risk here, however, was that when a successful explorer returned with good news—and nothing could be kept secret in those small gossiping settlements—others, with better access to the centres of power and the sources of capital, would move in and exploit what he had discovered. So, finders keepers: intending *conquistadores* would take whole armies into the unknown without adequate reconnaissance. If they found anything of value, they seized it at once; but often they found nothing and lost hundreds of men in the search.

The Magdalena is a broad, powerful river, still a mile wide 300 miles from the sea, unimpeded by falls or rapids in its lower course, navigable—though not without difficulties and dangers—for several hundred miles. There are no roads, even today, along its banks; the people who live there have developed a specialised riverine craft, the *bongo*, which, with its high bow and stern and low freeboard in the waist, recalls the sixteenth century. This awkward-looking vessel—some still survive in use—sets a big lateen sail when the wind serves, but can also be quanted against wind and current, by gangs of *bogas*—men with long poles stationed in the waist. In Quesada's day the local Indians did most of their travelling by water. Quesada might have been expected to do the same; but he had too many men: about eight hundred Spaniards, a hundred of them mounted, with Indian guides and presumably—though the chroniclers do not mention them specifically—Indian porters. He managed to procure five launches—*bergantines*—capable of carrying, perhaps, forty men each, and sent them by sea from Santa Marta to a rendezvous about 150 miles up the river, on the right bank, opposite the site of modern Mompós. Three of them were wrecked at the river mouth. The other two arrived late at the rendezvous. Replacements, procured in Hispaniola, arrived months later. The little makeshift fleet so assembled was employed in ferrying the men across tributary rivers, and in a slow, unreliable shuttle between the army and its base, bringing up tardy, scanty supplies and returning with the sick, until the limit of navigation was reached. The main body marched overland to the rendezvous, crossed the César, and advanced up the right bank of the Magdalena, at a rate of four or five miles a day, hacking through matted jungle and floundering in the riparian swamps. Significantly, one of the officers who received high praise from the chroniclers of the expedition was Jerónimo de Inza, captain of *macheteros*.

The army followed the river for 300 miserable miles. In that high dense bush, the banks appeared uninhabited, as they do today. They found in all that distance only one settled village, the place they called Tora, on the site of modern Barranca Bermeja, now a considerable port serving a productive oil field. The inhabitants had fled, leaving a ripening maize crop and some canoes, all of which were promptly commandeered. Tora was not much of a settlement, but the bluff on which it stood (and which gives its name to the present town) made a break in the wall of vegetation and showed a distant glimpse of the mountains to the east. The army wintered there for three months. Further progress up the Magdalena was prevented by rapids in the river and floods along the banks. After much

87 An ant bear; engraving from Georg Margraf, *De Quadrupedibus* (bound in W. Piso and G. Margraf, *Historia Naturalis Brasiliae*; Leyden and Amsterdam, 1648), p. 225.

display of rhetoric from Quesada, and several weeks of reconnaissance, it was then agreed to follow a tributary—either the Opón or the Carare—which appeared to descend from the cordillera. In this river they encountered trading canoes loaded with salt, not the loose sea salt to which they were accustomed, but hard quarried lumps; an indication that they were on the right track.

The importance which Quesada attributed to the salt suggests that he had some information about Chibcha society and was deliberately making for Chibcha territory. Before they could reach it, the Spaniards still had to travel more than a hundred miles through wild, hilly country inhabited by primitive people, where travel even today is difficult and can be dangerous. The river became too shallow and too swift for the launches, which went back to Santa Marta to take a final load of the sick and eventually return with reinforcements. Their departure left the army dependent for food on what they could steal from the wild inhabitants, and on such wild game as they could kill; though all their powder and most of the crossbow strings had been spoiled by water. Game was easier to find in the foothills than in the dense wet forest along the river; good horsemen on agile horses can kill such animals as peccaries with spears, and according to Castellanos they sometimes got even deer in that way; but a marching army cannot be fed adequately on the product of hunting. On one occasion they were glad to eat an ant bear; and still they starved. Finally they had to ascend the high rocky scarp of the cordillera, by cliff tracks so precipitous that the horses had to be steadied by ropes of twisted lianas. Only 166 men eventually emerged on to the high level plateau of Cundinamarca. More than three quarters of the original force had died during the ten-month journey, or had returned sick to Santa Marta. Pizarro had invaded Peru with about 160 men; but Quesada, unlike Pizarro, had no Almagro hurrying behind with reinforcements. The horses did better than the men. Quesada's care for the horses had amounted almost to obsession; he once hanged a man who, in the extremity of his hunger, had slaughtered his horse for food. Sixty horses had survived. Saddles and bridles had rotted, so that many of the cavalry rode bare-back, with halters made of lianas; but this did not diminish their moral effect upon people who were unfamiliar even with llamas.

Quesada's people passed from discovery to conquest almost at a bound. There was no central government with which they could negotiate, and they had no interpreters. They dealt with each situation as it appeared, using the methods which had become traditional. At Tunja they kidnapped the paramount chief, who, though treated with courtesy, died shortly after. In the Bogotá area—the paramount chief having fled—they supported a pretender, and later, when he failed to reward them adequately, tortured and killed him. They had no need for puppet rulers. The Chibcha were settled people; they lacked the jungle craft, the skill with the bow and the knowledge of arrow poisons which made the forest peoples formidable; yet on the other hand they had no large-scale military organisation, such as the Incas possessed. They fought in local bands, at close quarters, with clubs and fire-hardened javelins. Against mounted lancers and armoured infantry with steel swords, they were helpless. The conquest of the plateau, indeed, though it took a long time, was less difficult than the search for it had been. Quesada lost only two men: one was killed in the fighting; the other, one Juan Gordo, Fat John, was hanged by Quesada's orders for unauthorized looting. Most of the Chibcha villages, after the initial sharp encounters, submitted one by one. Tribute was levied; of food, cotton garments, and such treasure as the Indians had no time to hide. The haul, in gold and emeralds, was substantial; not comparable with that of Cuzco or Cajamarca, but enough to 'make' the expedition, especially since so many participants had died, including—though this was not known at the time—the principal investor, Pedro Fernández de Lugo. Lugo's son and heir was living, estranged from his father, in Spain, where—so his enemies alleged—he had fled in 1535, having embezzled some of the loot of the Tairona expedition; and where he had married the sister-in-law of the royal secretary, Francisco de los Cobos. Quesada witheld payment of the Lugo dividend, and thus acquired, in Luis Alonso de Lugo, a dangerous enemy.

The plunder was collected, the royal fifth set aside, and a rudimentary administration set up by the time Federmann and Benalcázar, coming from opposite directions, arrived on the plateau. Federmann, with his starveling followers and a few emaciated horses, presented no serious threat. Benalcázar was a more formidable figure, his force more numerous, fresher and better equipped. There was a possibility that the newcomers might make common cause against Quesada, but this was averted by a lavish and timely present to Federmann. After some preliminary rhodomontade, the three chieftains came to terms. They shared, to some extent, common problems; all three had superior officers—Pizarro, Lugo, Hohemut—to whom they were expected to report; all three hoped to escape from this subordination by appealing directly to Spain for confirmation of their conquests; so they agreed to leave the question of the governorship of New Granada to be settled in Spain, and to travel to Spain together. No doubt Quesada's personality and negotiating skill contributed to the agreement; but he also had an indispensable asset. The only way to reach the coast quickly was by water, and the only boats plying on the river, other than Indian canoes, were controlled by Quesada. So off to Spain they went in 1539, avoiding Santa Marta and taking ship from Cartagena. Benalcázar became governor of Popayán, Federmann of Coro. Only Quesada was unlucky: the governorship of New Granada went to Luis Alonso de Lugo. Quesada, for complicity in the murder of the last chief of Bogotá, was disqualified for five years from holding any office. He spent this time travelling about Europe, selling his emeralds (so his detractors said) at better prices than he could have got in Spain, and writing.

Almost all Quesada's writings are lost, and we have no eye-witness account of his exploits. Oviedo knew him in Spain, talked with him, and borrowed from him 'un gran cuaderno' (notebook? journal?) describing the discovery of New Granada. Oviedo's account, based—as he says—on this volume, must be considered the most authoritative, the nearest to the events described.[15] Next in point of time is that of Juan de Castellanos. Castellanos was one of the literary curiosities of his time: an adventurer who went to the Indies as a young man, fought in many *entradas* round the Caribbean, without sharing in any of the major prizes of the conquest lottery; took Holy Orders and wandered for some years from diocese to diocese; and finally settled, in 1561, as parish priest at Tunja, where he spent the last forty years or so of his long life. There he wrote the series of works which he called *Elegías de Varones Ilustres de Indias*, at once funerary eulogies, chronicles and epic poems, a torrent, a tidal wave of verse amounting in all to some 150,000 lines. Castellanos proclaimed Ercilla and Oviedo to be his models. His writings lack the vivid imagery and the polish of Ercilla—his verse is both rough and pedestrian—nor have they the comprehensive precision of Oviedo; but they have an endearing simplicity, and contain a good deal of information not recorded elsewhere. They include a lengthy *History of New Granada*, in blank verse.[16] The author was not a participant in the Quesada expedition, but he knew many of the participants, and was familiar with the country (which Oviedo was not). Castellanos was one of the sources, along with others now lost, used by the principal seventeenth-century chroniclers of New Granada, Fray Pedro Simón and Lucas Fernández Piedrahita, Bishop of Santa Marta. Both wrote valuable and interesting works.[17] Piedrahita was a historian of some sophistication and polish (and, it must be said, some pomposity). Simón was a simpler soul, but his *Noticias* have occasional flashes of ironic humour, rare among the chroniclers and reminiscent of Bernal Díaz.

On the march up the Magdalena valley, Oviedo has this to say:

. . . I have been thirty-four years in the Indies, and know whereof I speak. I make bold to say that nowhere in the world have Christians endured greater labours and worse discomforts than did the Spaniards in the Indies; and certainly these soldier-sinners, fighting by land and water against savages, against sickness, against hunger and thirst, against heat and cold, often half naked, without shoes for their horses or themselves, through deserts and swamps, through thorny scrub and tangled forest, cutting their way with knives and axes, bruised and weary, suffered daily more hardships than I can adequately describe.

The Indians in that area travel mostly by water. On land, the forest is so thick and so tangled with underbush and creepers, that at best one can make only about two leagues in a day; and each day of this arduous march, more men died or fell sick, without any possibility of remedy, having no beds and no shelter against the incessant rain; for this was winter, the season of rains, which lasts from May to September.

Besides these hardships, they were constantly harassed by the forest Indians; a number of Spaniards were killed in these skirmishes. The rivers they had to cross were infested with crocodiles, and the forests were full of jaguars. Three Spaniards were dragged down by the crocodiles, and another three carried off by jaguars.

The advance party under Quesada which ascended the Opón from Tora fared even worse:

The general set out up the tributary which the canoes had already explored, in order to discover the source of the salt which they had seen. All the land for thirteen or fourteen leagues, up to the place where they had found the store of salt, was uninhabited and covered with thick forest. They were caught by a flash flood, caused by heavy rain upstream, which put them in great danger, not only because of the water, but because of lack of food. They had to spend the nights in trees, because the ground was flooded, and the horses were up to their girths in water. This state of affairs lasted ten days. They lived on roots and leaves of trees, of kinds unknown to them, and could not travel more than a league in a day. The best meal they had in those ten days was a dog, one of those which accompanied the army, which had followed the party; but the dog did not last long, and they were reduced to gnawing the leather of their shields. . . until they came to the place where the salt was stored, and found some grain still standing in the fields.[18]

But they still had to scale the Sierra. The relief of these much-tried soldiers of fortune, when at last they emerged on the populous savannah, can easily be imagined. The doggerel chant, with which the reconnoitring scouts announced the promised land, has come down to us. Its jingle would not survive translation:

> Tierra buena, tierra buena,
> Tierra que hará fin a nuestra pena,
> Tierra de oro, tierra abastecida,
> Tierra para hacer perpetua casa,
> Tierra con abundancia de comida,
> Tierra de grandes pueblos, tierra rasa,
> Tierra donde se ve gente vestida. . . .

Of all the chroniclers, the poetaster Castellanos best captured the excitement of the moment:

. . . The hungry found themselves standing among ripening crops . . . the naked saw themselves surrounded by people dressed in gaily coloured cottons, orderly settled people—how different from the savages of the swamps and forests they had left! Some, as I have heard, thought that with their weakened forces, far from help and reinforcements, they could not hope to conquer so numerous a people. Some were frightened and dismayed; but our valiant man of law, with the weary people he had with him, felt able to conquer the entire world.

Of the kingdom he in fact conquered, Castellanos writes ecstatically:

All the land within the confines of this hidden country is under a benign influence. It has gold and silver, copper, lead and precious stones. Its climate is always temperate and pleasant. There may occasionally be frosts or hailstorms, but it is rarely cold enough to call for fires or braziers. Though much of the land is high and open, it easily grows wheat and corn, vegetables and fodder, and now also we have all manner of cattle in abundance; which, together with the use of the plough, have rendered even the most unpromising land useful and fertile. . . . There are warmer areas too, equally fertile and pleasant, where all kinds of fruit trees grow, some of them native to the area and others recently introduced, each fruit welcome in its season to the people who live in the cool highlands.

This is a recognisable description, even today, of the agreeable country surrounding that most genial and cultivated of American cities, Bogotá. Our poet continues:

In this remote and walled-in land, there were once many petty rulers, to whom their subjects paid tribute. Most of these little chiefs were subject in their turn to one or another of the two high Kings, Bogotá and Tunja, both proud and powerful monarchs with many vassals. Between these two was constant war, but neither was strong enough to subdue the other. The feud between them was very ancient, and has passed down from generation to generation. I do not know what the causes of it were. The Indians themselves have little sense of history, and know nothing of the origins of their forebears. I believe that they were people who originally migrated from the lowlands into the mountains, and that it was to protect themselves from increasing cold that they took to wearing clothes.[19]

According to Oviedo—presumably quoting Quesada himself—these perpetual feuds between Bogotá and Tunja represented, for the Spaniards, a missed opportunity.

The conquest of the Indies was achieved by animals as well as by men, and the annals of conquest are full of tales and descriptions of animals. The story of New Granada is particularly rich in anecdotes of this kind. One from Oviedo concerns horses, and suggests that to people unfamiliar with them, riderless horses can be as terrifying as mounted men:

One night when the Spaniards were encamped near a hostile Indian band, three or four stallions broke out of the picket lines, trying to get at the mares. They galloped near the enemy camp, screaming and neighing. The Indians, who knew nothing of horses, were aroused by the clamour and thunder of these monsters approaching their camp. They assumed that the creatures were coming to eat them, took fright, and bolted up into the hills. The Spaniards, hearing the Indians stirring, thought that an attack was imminent, and stood to arms. They did not discover until the following morning that some of the horses were missing. They found them eventually, grazing within the enemy camp, and not an Indian in sight.[20]

Next to horses, the animals which the Spaniards found most useful in Indian fighting were dogs. Every conquering band was accompanied by a pack of dogs, formidable brutes of mastiff type. They were trained to

88 Spanish dogs attacking Indians; engraving from Theodor de Bry, *America*, Part IV (Antwerp, 1594), plate xxii.

attack, and were employed to guard the camps and to cow or track down recalcitrant Indians. Quesada had dogs with him; some were killed for food on the way, but some evidently survived, and multiplied so rapidly that they became a pest, especially when Indians acquired them and loosed them on Europeans. In 1547 Quesada, restored to favour and with the title of marshal, was sent back to New Granada to help and advise the judges of the newly created *audiencia*. A long report which he wrote to the King, probably in 1549, includes the following passage:

I have to inform Your Majesty that the dogs which the Spaniards brought with them, when I conquered this New Kingdom, have multiplied excessively. The Spaniards themselves, in order to show courtesy to the chiefs and leading Indians, gave them dogs and bitches for breeding, so that now every Indian village, big or small, has five hundred or a thousand dogs and any Indian, however poor, can keep as many as he likes. This is a great nuisance and danger. If an Indian chief were to renounce his allegiance to Your Majesty, and rebel, it would be difficult to bring him to book, because his people, having all these dogs to guard their villages, would have good warning of the approach of Spaniards, and would be able to escape to the hills. If the country as a whole were to rise this would be the more serious, because they could use their packs of dogs against us. . . . I therefore pray Your Majesty to order that no Indian in this Kingdom be allowed to keep dogs and that all dogs in the possession of Indians be confiscated or destroyed; except that chiefs may be permitted one or two dogs. In no circumstances should any Indian be allowed to keep bitches. . . .[21]

The royal annotation on this document is perfectly characteristic of the colonial bureaucracy with which, by that date, the *conquistadores* had to deal: 'Let the *audiencia* report further on this matter.'

An anecdote about the humblest of the beasts which Spaniards brought to the New World, a donkey, is related by the good Father Simón. The episode occurred during the expedition which Luis Alonso de Lugo led against the Tairona in 1535. A Spanish party led by Indian guides approached a remote mountain village by night, intending to attack at first light:

. . . At dawn, as they lay hidden in the cornfields which surrounded the village, awaiting the moment to attack, they heard an ass bray. They knew that the Indians did not possess such animals, and did not believe that an ass could have climbed the high crags which barred the way from the coast. Some maintained that there was no ass there—unless it had wings—and that the noise was made by the Indians in mockery; the sentries, perhaps, had detected their presence, and were proclaiming that they would give the invaders such a drubbing as one might give an ass. One man, a foreigner named Malatesta, who had some knowledge of the classics, said that it must be the ass in the story of Silenus which, because it had helped Jupiter against the giants and served well in the war, had been taken up to Heaven; but had fallen again because it was too heavy, and had landed in these mountains . . . and was urging the Spaniards to get up from among the cornstalks and attack, so that if all went well it might get something to eat.

So they launched their attack, which was successful.

When the place had been pacified and looted, they inquired about the ass. . . . The Indians said that it had come in a ship, which had been wrecked on the coast. . . . They had killed those of the ship's company who got ashore, but had kept the ass, and had carried it up into the mountains, trussed with ropes and slung between two poles, along with all the other loot they found in the ship, which included shirts, doublets, coloured bonnets, hatchets, picks and shovels; of which there were indeed great quantities, adorning the persons of the Indians or lying about the village. So our soldiers, deeming it inappropriate and contrary to native custom that such articles should be in the hands of Indians, collected them all up, along with everything else that took their fancy, including the ass, and took it back to the coast. But the trails were rough, more suited to cats than men, and the descent was as hard as the ascent had been, so they made the Indians carry the donkey down just as they had brought it up; and very useful it turned out to be. Surely, as the first of its race to penetrate those mountains, it deserved to be numbered among the *conquistadores*. It served in other *entradas* later, and finally in the expedition which Hernando de Quesada, brother and deputy of Gonzalo Jiménez de Quesada the discoverer, led in search of El Dorado. It was ridden by Fray Vicente Requejada of the Order of Saint Augustine. . . . The ass served the friar well until, on the return march, they all ran out of food and, in the extremities of hunger, killed it for food. They left not a scrap of it. They collected its blood, made sausages of its guts, and even devoured its hide, well boiled. It had served them well in life, and served them better still in death, by its timely rescue from starvation; a salutary reminder of the hardships which in those days were the daily lot of discoverers.[22]

III

The Empty Spaces

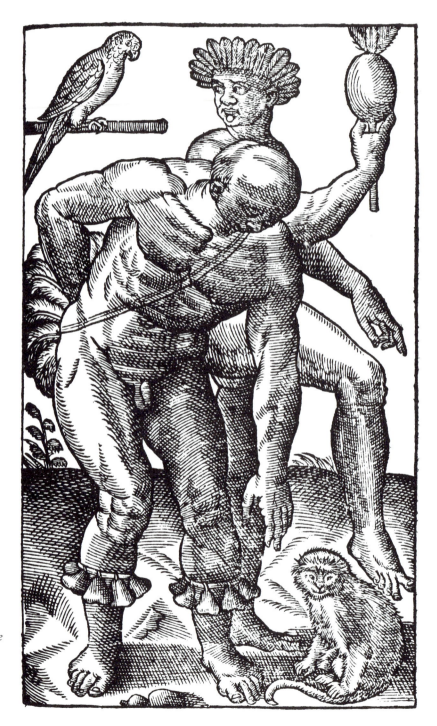

89 Tupinambá Indians
dancing, one with a gourd
rattle; engraving from Jean
de Léry, *Histoire d'un voyage
fait en la Terre du Brésil
autrement dite Amérique*
(Geneva, pour Antoine
Chuppin, 1578), facing
p. 274.

8 The Rivers

Quesada's expedition to the Chibcha highlands was the last successful major *entrada* of the traditional type. Thereafter, for the rest of the sixteenth century the story of South American discovery was, in the main, one of diminishing returns and disappointment; disappointment, that is, in view of what the explorers hoped to find. The successes of Cortés and Pizarro had set a pattern of expectation in terms of loot and lordship. The hope of the ambitious explorer in the interior of South America was to find a pleasant and habitable land, unknown to other Europeans and so available for conquest; rich in natural resources, especially precious metals; governed by autocratic rulers whose power, centred in major cities, could be paralysed by a swift decisive blow; inhabited by a numerous, industrious and settled people who—once their own rulers had been subdued—would be susceptible to Europeanising, Christianising influences, available as a labour force, and capable of rendering tribute to the conqueror.

Expectations were not only high; they were stereotyped and relatively rigid. The various characteristics of the dream land were closely interconnected in the European mind, and to answer fully the hopes of the discoverer, all must be present. A pleasant, habitable land had little attraction if it was uninhabited, or inhabited only by primitive hunters and gatherers; for what was the use of land without labour? A land tilled by peasants was more attractive; but the inhabitants would be difficult to conquer and control if (as in central and southern Chile) they had no central government, and hardly worth conquering if (as in Paraguay and many parts of Brazil) they farmed only for subsistence and possessed no objects of value to Europeans. Every explorer hoped, of course, to find lands yielding gold or silver; but even these metals were of no obvious value unless they were already being exploited by the natives. If they existed only as a potential resource hidden in the ground, the discoverers, lacking prospecting skill and mining experience, might never find them. It is worth noting, in this connection, that the silver veins of Zacatecas in New Galicia and Potosí in Upper Peru—perhaps the most important discoveries made by Europeans anywhere in the world in the 1540s— were additional (though of course very large) sources of supply, in regions where the inhabitants were already familiar with silver working and knew what silver ore looked like. In primitive Minas Gerais, by contrast, Europeans travelled back and forth through the area for a hundred and fifty years before they noticed that the gravel of the stream beds was rich in gold.

Some captains in the later 1530s—Benalcázar in Quito and Popayán, Quesada in New Granada—succeeded in emulating Pizarro in finding and seizing places which answered some or all of these expectations. Others, who made more modest but still acceptable discoveries, concealed whatever disappointment they may have felt, and exaggerated the value of what they had found in order to attract settlers, as Valdivia did in central Chile. The successes, or reputed successes, were numerous enough to keep alive the heady optimism inspired by the discovery of Peru. No one knew how many more Perus awaited discovery, and many would-be Pizarros (including some people thoroughly unsuited to such enterprises) came to the Indies to search for them.

By 1540 or thereabouts, the main inhabited areas in the northern and central Andes had been cursorily explored, and claimed by one *conquistador* or another: all the more habitable portions of the coastal strip west of the mountains, similarly, were in process of conquest and settlement; and as for the southern Andes, the tales of the Puna de Atacama, which Almagro's people brought back, effectively discouraged endeavour in that direction. If there were other Perus—and busy rumour constantly reported them—they must be east of the Andes. Here was an immense area comprising—though this was not yet known—at least nine-tenths of the South American continent. So far as Europeans were concerned, this area was almost unexplored, except for its coasts which had been traced in outline at least down to the Río de la Plata, early in the century. From the 1520s a number of small European settlements had grown up, Spanish on the Caribbean Main coast, Portuguese in what is now Brazil. The Portuguese establishments were very modest, little more than camps where brazil-wood was cut and stacked for shipment, at long intervals, to Lisbon. One of them, Pernambuco, was later to become the city of Recife; another was São Vicente, on the site of modern Santos. In 1531 Martim Afonso de Sousa, with five ships, explored the Atlantic coast in greater detail than his predecessors had done, in order to select sites for further settlement. He put briefly into Bahia de Todos os Santos, and made a longer stay—more than three months—at anchor in Guanabara Bay, where the city of Rio de Janeiro now stands. Sousa preferred São Vicente, however, and Guanabara Bay was settled initially not by Portuguese, but by Frenchmen, in 1555 under the (temporary) Huguenot Durand de Villegagnon. Villegagnon was not, of course, a discoverer, but an organiser of settlement, and on the whole a successful one. He maintained good relations with the local Indians and his colony paid its way by shipping dyewood, cut with Indian help, to France. His troubles, like those of Alvar Núñez Cabeza de Vaca at Asunción a few years earlier, arose from his puritanism and from his ill-advised attempts to enforce stricter standards of conduct, in dealing with Indians, than most settlers were willing to accept. His frustrations probably affected the balance of his mind. In 1559 he bolted; and in the following year the settlement was dispersed by a Portuguese force under Mem de Sá. Those who survived the attack sought—and found—refuge among the Indians. 'Antarctic France' thus lasted less than five years. Its principal legacy was a literary one: Jean de Léry, a young theological student from Geneva, one of a group of Calvinist divines sent to Brazil at Villegagnon's request, quarrelled with Villegagnon shortly after arrival, was expelled from the settlement, and lived for a year among the Indians. His account of his experiences is perhaps the best-informed, most sympathetic and most

readable of all sixteenth-century works on South American Indians. It is superior in all these respects to the much better known work of Léry's rival, also a missionary at the settlement, the Franciscan André Thevet; though Thevet had a longer acquaintance with the coast, having been there previously, with Guillaume le Testu, in 1551.

The exploration of the interior was a more difficult matter. The country presented obstacles to penetration no less formidable than the ramparts of the Andes, though of a different character, and most explorers came early to the conclusion that their only hope was to follow the rivers. The map of South America east of the Andes is dominated by its rivers: by the three immense river systems—the Orinoco, the Amazon and the Río de la Plata—whose head-waters interlace in the centre of the continent. All three draw part of their flow of water from the Andean snows; all three discharge into the Atlantic. They are therefore among the longest river systems in the world. The Amazon is usually reckoned second to the Nile in this respect; though it greatly exceeds the Nile in the area of its drainage and in the volume of water which it carries. The South American rivers, indeed, are so big that they do not look like rivers. Spanish explorers, as a rule, were relatively insensitive to natural phenomena, or at least were

90 Cannibal butchery in Brazil; a characteristic flight of imagination on the part of André Thevet, the Franciscan missionary. *Les singularitez de la France antarctique* (Paris, 1558), fo 77 r.

241

reticent in describing their own reaction to them; but one may imagine the impression that these vast moving seas of muddy water made, upon men whose notions of big rivers were drawn from the Guadalquivir, the Tagus or the Rhine. The South American rivers are navigable for great distances. They afforded, before the advent of air travel, the only routes into most parts of the interior of the continent. They were not easy routes, however; all three discharge through extensive and intricate deltas, the Amazon and the Orinoco at their outfalls, the Río de la Plata in the area where the Uruguay and the Paraná enter the Plata estuary. These mazes of mud and mangroves, with their hundreds of channels and islands, presented baffling problems of navigation to ships entering from the sea. Even when the main channel had been found, the strong currents of these mighty streams, the floods, the shoals, the floating tree-trunks, the falls and rapids (especially in the Orinoco), the insects, all obstructed travel. Worse still, the explorers starved. Expeditions reaching the coast after a two-, three- or four-month passage from Europe, were often, already on arrival, short of food and suffering from scurvy. The countries through which the rivers passed—the *llanos* of the Orinoco, the rain forest of the Amazon, the grassy *pampa*, the savannas, the Chaco forest of the Río de la Plata and its tributaries—were, for the most part, relatively sparsely inhabited by relatively primitive people. Over great stretches of river, hundreds of miles in length, food was not to be found; and if found, was to be had only by ruthless foraging, which of course provoked resistance. In general, the story of the early attempts to enter South America by ascending its major rivers was a story of hardship, disappointment and heavy loss of life.

The rivers had attracted the notice of early coasting explorers because of the volume of fresh water they discharged, which discoloured the sea for miles offshore. The many mouths of the Orinoco and the island-studded estuary of the Amazon were early recognised as rivers, though of prodigious size. Short-lived hopes that the Río de la Plata might be a strait, connecting the Atlantic with the South Sea or the Great Gulf, were terminated (at least in Spain) by the reports of the survivors of the Solís expedition in 1515–16. Solís was the first casualty of river exploration. His cursory reconnaissance of the Río estuary had a curious sequel ten years later. Sebastian Cabot—son of John, the Genoese-turned Venetian-turned Englishman who discovered Newfoundland—had himself been brought up in England, but failing to find employment under Henry VIII, had removed to Spain, where—partly, perhaps, on the strength of his father's achievements—he had succeeded Solís as pilot-major. In 1524 he put up a proposal for a voyage by a western route to the Moluccas and to sundry other places, real and imaginary—Tarshish, Ophir, Cipango and eastern Cathay, according to his *capitulación*, which was issued in March 1525. The Moluccas, of course, were a definite group of islands, whose position was known and which Spanish ships had visited. The mention of Tarshish and Ophir, however, suggested a desire on the part of the explorer to keep his options open; a hope of finding other spice-producing territories, hitherto undiscovered, somewhere in the East. Magellan had used the same formula six years earlier, probably for similar reasons. The voyage was intended to be a private venture financed by commercial investors in Seville, but the Emperor's advisers seized eagerly upon the proposal. Cabot received from the Crown not only the necessary authorisation, but also royal backing in money and in dockyard services, which made his venture at least semi-official. This generosity may have been connected with Cabot's office of pilot-major; but there were other reasons. In July 1525 García Jofré de Loaisa sailed with seven ships, to follow up the Magellan-Elcano voyage, reinforce the Spanish garrison at Tidore in the Moluccas, and open a regular trade in spices. Shortly after his departure a survivor from Magellan's *Trinidad* turned up in Spain, bringing news of the fate of that unlucky ship and of the sufferings of her people at the hands of the Portuguese. This suggested that Loaisa, when he arrived at Tidore, might find himself with a local war on his hands. In November, accordingly, Cabot was instructed by the Emperor to proceed with all speed to the Moluccas, postponing all other projects of discovery, in order to reinforce Loaisa.[1]

Cabot sailed in April 1526, with three ships and a caravel. Our knowledge of the voyage comes partly from records of the litigation to which it gave rise, partly from a long letter which one of the crew, Luis Ramírez, wrote to his father from 'San Salvador in the River of Solís'. Ramírez was Cabot's page and cabin servant, and obviously admired his master. His letter shows him to have been an educated boy, literate, intelligent, and affectionate. It contains the only account we have of the up-river exploration, which was the main achievement of the voyage.

Like most foreigners in command of Spanish fleets, Cabot had trouble with his captains. He suspected them—almost to the point of paranoia—of disloyalty. They resented his overbearing manner and doubted his competence. He was, indeed, something of an armchair navigator, and this—though it may not have been his first sea-going command—was his first command in Spanish service. The outward passage was unpromising; the fleet sighted the coast of Brazil too far north and at a bad time of year— in June, a season of prevailing southerly winds. After beating about for some days in the neighbourhood of Cape São Agostinho, they put into the little Portuguese settlement of Pernambuco (Recife) for refreshment. This was long before the great days of Pernambuco sugar; the local Portuguese numbered only a dozen or so, mostly engaged in supervising the cutting of brazil-wood for shipment to Europe. They did their best to be hospitable, however; and they provided Cabot with some interesting information or rumour, to the effect that some Spanish castaways were living on an island near the Río de Solís, and that these men knew of a rich country which produced silver somewhere up the river. Some of Cabot's officers, when consulted, were inclined to dismiss the whole story as Portuguese romancing; but the majority agreed that it was worth investigating.

The island was Catarina Island—in Spanish, Catalina, the name Cabot himself gave it, in honour of his wife. It is now a beach resort, connected by a bridge with the city of Florianopolis; then it was thickly wooded, with abundant wild fruits, fish and game. The Indians who inhabited it must have been tolerant people, for living among them were indeed a dozen or more castaways. Most of these had sailed in one of Loaisa's ships, the *San Gabriel*. Loaisa's fleet—so they told Cabot—had been scattered by

S.Catherina
Ins.

a gale off the coast of Patagonia; and the captain of the *San Gabriel* had
given up and made for home. Those of his people who objected to this
course had been put ashore, not—fortunately for themselves—in
Patagonia, but on Catarina Island, where they had remained. Two other
castaways on the island had been there still longer; they were survivors
from the wreck of one of the ships of the Solís expedition in 1516, and so

had some knowledge of the Río estuary. One of them, indeed, had sailed a second time into the Río—so he told Cabot—as interpreter in a Portuguese expedition. Why he had then returned to the island was not explained; possibly he was a beachcomber by choice, and preferred life among the Indians to cutting dyewood in a Portuguese camp. These two men independently—for they had been living apart—repeated to Cabot Indian reports of a mountainous country inland, ruled by a 'white king', whose people produced and worked gold and silver in quantity. Some of the silver was traded downstream, and its source could be reached by ascending a tributary of the Río, the Paraná.

All this while the ships lay at anchor off the southern end of the island; but two of the Loaisa survivors undertook to guide them into a more sheltered harbour, Puerto de los Patos, 'Duck Bay' (probably modern Rio Messianbu). Cabot accepted this offer; rashly, as it turned out, for the volunteer pilots ran the flagship on to a reef, where she stuck and eventually broke up. The other ships anchored safely in Puerto de los Patos; and there, almost certainly, Cabot finally reached the decision towards which he had been tending for weeks, to change the whole plan of the expedition. Cabot was a determined man, especially—his contemporaries remarked—in pursuit of gain, and brave enough on occasion; but he was no man for a forlorn hope. On several occasions in his career he was accused of actual cowardice (he was one of the first into the boat when his flagship grounded). He had heard much, no doubt, of the perils of Magellan's Strait and the rigours of the Pacific crossing. He knew that Loaisa's ships had been scattered before even entering the Strait; they might never reach the Moluccas (in fact only one did). The loss of his flagship provided him with a reason, or an excuse, for declining to expose his weakened fleet to similar danger. He had heard circumstantial reports, from presumably well-informed people, of a rich and rewarding country nearer at hand, awaiting discovery. He did not know, of course, that the Emperor would soon decide to cut his losses in the Moluccas by selling the Spanish claim to Portugal; but he might reasonably expect the Emperor and the investors to forgive his departing from his instructions if he brought his ships back loaded with treasure from the Río de Solís.

This explanation of Cabot's change of plan has not been universally accepted. Some of his enemies alleged, after his return to Spain, that he had been persuaded, perhaps suborned, by Braga, the Portuguese factor at Recife, with whom Cabot had been all too friendly. Braga may well have thought it his duty to try to divert Cabot from the Moluccas by telling him any story he could think of; but Cabot would have been a fool to accept the story without the corroborative evidence which he received off Catarina Island. Some modern historians have produced more ingenious theories. Medina thought that Cabot intended from the beginning to explore the Río de Solís, and that he announced the Moluccas as his destination in order, fraudulently, to attract support. The late J. A. Williamson suggested that he had a secret understanding with the Emperor, to the same effect. No evidence supports either suggestion. The simplest explanation is the most probable. Luis Ramírez, for one, states clearly that the decision to explore the Río was made and announced at

91 Imaginary view of Catarina Island; engraving from Theodor de Bry, *America*, Part III (Frankfurt, 1592), p. 18. The ship in the engraving is lying off the southerly tip of the island, where Cabot's ship was wrecked. The point is known as Punta dos Naufragados today.

245

Puerto de los Patos. Some of Cabot's people objected, and urged him to continue the voyage he had set out to make. For this, eight or ten of them, including several senior officers—in general, those who had been most critical of Cabot from the start—were marooned on Catarina Island. Some died there; the rest, led by Francisco de Rojas, one of the original captains, crossed to the mainland and made their way to São Vicente. They built a boat, and eventually reached Spain where, like many others, they brought suit against Cabot. Meanwhile Cabot set his people to work building a *galeota*—a sailing vessel equipped with sweeps, of shallow draft for river navigation—to replace the lost flagship. They sailed from Puerto de los Patos in February 1527 for the Río.

Of the river voyage, Luis Ramírez should speak for himself:

As soon as the galliot was completed and the people re-distributed in her and in the remaining ships . . . we left the said harbour [Río de los Patos] on 15 February 1527, and six days later sighted Cape Santa María, at the mouth of the Río de Solís. This is a very powerful river, twenty-five leagues wide at its mouth. We were to encounter many difficulties and dangers in the river; it is full of shoals, and we did not know the channel; it is subject to violent storms, and since there is very little shelter along the banks, even a moderate wind can raise dangerous waves. I assure Your Honour that we encountered the worst dangers of the whole voyage in the fifty leagues from the river mouth upstream to the harbour which we called San Lázaro. I had sailed from Catarina Island in the galliot. I was sick with fever, and since she gave us very little protection from the weather, I suffered severely on this passage, and even more later on . . . but I give thanks to God that after all these sufferings, He brought us to the discovery of this rich land, as Your Honour will see. . . . We arrived here on . . . 6 April 1527.

The captain-general stayed for a month in this harbour. During this time the interpreters made inquiries among the local natives, and heard of a Christian captive who had been living among them ever since the death of Solís. This man, who called himself Francisco del Puerto, when he heard of our arrival, came to talk with the captain-general, and told him a good deal about the nature of the country. He confirmed that precious metals could be found there in great quantity, and explained how to reach the tribe which possessed the metals by ascending the rivers. He said that big ships could not navigate the Paraná because of frequent shallows; so the captain-general left the ships behind, and thirty seamen as ship-keepers, with instructions to lay the ships up in a sheltered harbour. With them he left a further dozen men as an armed guard, to protect the ships and all the property, public and private, in them. I was one of these, because I was still unwell and exhausted from my fever. The captain-general divided the rest of the people between the caravel and the galliot, and left San Lázaro on 8 May 1527 to ascend the Paraná. Before he left . . . in clear calm weather, about the third hour of the night, there arose a sudden storm, so violent that even those of us who were on shore thought our last hour had come. The ships were in great danger; the mainmast of one of them had to be cut away to prevent a total wreck, and . . . the galliot, which was lying to two anchors, parted both cables and was driven a quoit's throw up the beach, so that they had to use tackles to get her back into the water. However, as I said, the captain-general got away from San Lázaro. Those of us who stayed behind were very short of food, and suffered more from hunger than I can ever describe. . . . We killed and ate one of the dogs we had with us; and mice were valued as if they had been capons. . . . Two men died, whether of hunger or of some other cause—they were ill anyway—and so we remained, until . . . August . . . when the captain-general sent the galliot back to pick us up, with the gear we were guarding, and take us to his camp sixty leagues up the Paraná, at the mouth of the Carcarañal, a tributary which, according to the Indians, rises in the mountains. [The Carcarañá enters the Paraná about fifty miles north of (modern) Rosario. Its headwaters are in the Sierra Grande of (modern) Córdoba province, a minor range unconnected with the Andes.] We found that the captain-general had established his headquarters there and built a fort strong enough for protection against local attack. All the Indians of the surrounding country, of various tribes and languages, had come in to see the captain-general, including some people who live out in the grass plains, who are called Quirandíes. They are very nimble people, who live by hunting, and who drink the blood of the game they kill, because there is little or no water in their country. These people gave us a detailed description of the mountains and of the white king. They are very nimble people, who live by hunting, and who drink the blood of describe until I have seen them for myself, because otherwise you would think I was repeating tall stories.

These Quirandíes are so quick that they can run down a deer on foot. They are armed with bows and arrows, and also with a device consisting of round stones, about the size of one's fist, attached to a long cord, by means of which they can sling the stones with great accuracy. Besides the mountains and the white king, as I said, they told us about a tribe of people with ostriches' feet, and other tales of monsters, so unlikely that I will not write them down. They said that on the far side of the mountains was the shore of a sea. The captain-general thinks, from their description of the rise and fall of its tides, that it must be the South Sea. If this is true, it will be a discovery as valuable to His Majesty as the silver mountains themselves.

There are other tribes in the neighbourhood of the fort: Carcarais, Chamoes, Beguas, Chanaes-Timbús and Timbús, all of whom speak different languages. They all came to see the captain-general; they are well-disposed people; all of them, men and women, have their noses pierced, both septum and nostrils, also their ears, and the men pierce their lower lips. The Carcarais and Timbús grow maize, squashes and beans. The other tribes do not raise crops, but live on meat and fish. There is yet another tribe, spread over a wide area, friendly to us, called Gaurenís, or Chandris. They are hostile to all the other tribes, and exploit them. They are treacherous people, everything they do is by treachery. They rule a large part of these Indies, and their territory extends to the mountains. They bring down gold and silver in the form of plates, or as ear ornaments, or hatchets, which they use to clear the scrub for growing their crops. They are cannibals.

Our food here, since May when our supplies from Spain ran out, has been *cardos* [literally thistles; wild artichokes perhaps?], fish and meat, as much as we can eat. The fish is especially good and plentiful, the best food man could wish. When we arrived here we were ill and half-starved, but after two months of this diet we are all as fit and well as when we first left Spain, and no one has fallen sick. The country itself is healthy; very flat, and without trees. There are many kinds of wild animals—deer, wolves, foxes, ostriches and tigers, these last very formidable. There are many wild sheep about the size of yearling mules, weighing two hundredweight or so, with long necks like camels—extraordinary looking animals. The captain-general is sending one to His Majesty.

Sixteenth-century Spaniards were not much interested, as a rule, in describing wild animals accurately. Ramírez' effort is fairly typical. There are no wolves in South America, and the most wolf-like of the foxes, the so-called maned wolf (*Chrysosyon brachyurus*) does not occur so far south.

Ramírez' wolf was probably the big pampa fox (*Dusicyon gymnocerus*), a grey animal of the size and general shape of a jackal; his fox, the chilla, the small grey fox of temperate South America. The ostriches were rheas; the tigers, presumably pumas, though the name was more commonly applied to jaguars, which do not occur in the pampa. The wild sheep were guanacos, once common all over Argentina but now confined to the Andean foothills and to Patagonia.

While we were in this place the captain-general sent out parties to explore the surrounding country and to see whether it was possible to travel overland; but they reported that much of the land was uninhabited, and without water for more than forty leagues. The captain-general also told the interpreters to inquire what was the shortest route to the mountains; they said that the best way was to follow the Paraná upstream to its junction with a big tributary called the Paraguay, and then to ascend the Paraguay. So the captain-general gave orders for departure by river; supplies and gear, other than what was needed for the journey, were to be stored in the fort, and captain Gregorio Caro was to remain with thirty men as a garrison. The rest were to embark in the galley and in a launch that had been built on the site. On 23 December of that same year [1527] . . . we made sail, and in a few days arrived at an island which we called Año Nuevo, because we discovered it on that day.

From there the captain-general sent Miguel Rifos with thirty-five men in the launch to punish the Timbús, the tribe whom I mentioned before, who were on bad terms with the Indians who accompanied us. The trouble arose because some of the Timbús had come to the island to see the captain-general and had brought him some maize; so he had given each of them some small trinkets (the amount of maize they brought being very small) and they had complained, saying that they should have had more and better presents. They made as if to shoot our accompanying Indians with arrows, and even threatened the captain-general himself, shouting that they were angry with him and that he ought to pay them. So he sent off the launch, as I said, because he was afraid that, unless they were taught a lesson, they might cause trouble back at the fort and catch the garrison unprepared. The launch approached their village at dawn; we landed, surrounded them in their houses and marched in. There was very little resistance; they saw we were Christians and had no stomach for a fight. We killed many of them and captured many more, took all the corn in the village and loaded the launch with it, and burned all the houses. Our accompanying Indians kept the captive Timbús as slaves, and made them carry the corn; and so we returned to where we had left the galley, and were welcomed with much joy, especially when they saw the food we brought.

. . .

We went on from there, sailing from island to island. On one island there were so many herons that we could have filled the ships with them; we took a few, but did not stay long, because the wind was favourable. We went on up the river, which in some places was twelve or fourteen leagues wide, and never less than five . . . sometimes sailing, sometimes rowing, sometimes tracking from the bank, weary and hungry . . . because the canoe Indians who had accompanied us and caught fish for us now left us and returned downstream with the Timbús they had captured. The captain-general broached a barrel of flour which he had reserved for emergencies, and issued three ounces per man per day. . . . We could only make a league, or half a league in a day by tracking, so worn-out and hungry we were. . . . Whenever the boats approached the bank we would jump ashore like starving wolves to scour the woods for food . . . always afraid of being devoured ourselves by some lynx or tiger. . . . Some people made themselves ill by eating poisonous fruits; we gave them oil to drink, to relieve their pain and to make them vomit. . . . The flour ran out, and then all we had was two ounces of chick-peas and two ounces of bacon a day, and sometimes half a pig's foot. . . . We killed and cooked poisonous snakes and enjoyed them as if they had been capons. . . . We ate grass boiled in water . . . we broke off fronds from palm trees, chopped them up small with our knives, and cooked them; the result was just like sawdust, and I swear I ate more than an *arroba* of the stuff myself.

So the narrative flows on, slow, detailed, repetitive, remarkably cheerful (all things considered), unavoidably monotonous like the broad river itself. Near the confluence of Paraguay and Paraná prospects brightened. They found a friendly village and obtained food, 'twenty canoe loads . . . of maize, squash, manioc roots, sweet potatoes, and very good bread made of manioc flour', and fish, which the natives caught by netting, trapping in shallow water or shooting with arrows.

The captain-general stayed some days in this harbour, which he called Santa Ana, and collected a great quantity of food. . . . We saw that the Indians there had ear ornaments and plaques of good silver and gold. . . . The captain-general told the interpreter Francisco del Puerto to find out from the Indians where and from whom they obtained this metal. . . . He reported that the Chandules, who are a branch of this same tribe and who live sixty or seventy leagues up the Paraguay, bartered it for beads and for canoes; and that the territory of the Chandules was six days' journey by land, though the road passed by many lakes and through country that was often flooded.

The captain-general could have obtained a quantity of silver and gold by barter, but he did not do so, because he did not wish these Indians to know that this was the chief purpose of our journey; he wished, rather, to push on to the territory of the Chandules, because—according to what the Indians told Francisco the interpreter—these Chandules had plenty of precious metal, and sent their women and children up into the mountains to fetch it. So the captain-general gave the order to prepare to leave for the ascent of the Paraguay, since the way by land, according to the information we received, was too difficult. Before we left the harbour we heard from the Indians that some ships had entered the Río de Solís and had encountered our own ships; but we dismissed the report as a story made up by the Indians, for we had often found them to be incorrigible liars. . . . So we entered the Paraguay . . . and went upstream, sometimes sailing, sometimes tracking, for the river has so many bends that no wind will serve for more than two or three leagues, and we had constantly to track or row round the bends.[2]

They did not get very far, however; the rumour of ships in the estuary was confirmed by some down-river Indians who had come up to trade with the Chandules. This might be serious, especially if the newcomers— as Cabot at first feared—were Portuguese; so down the river they went at their best speed, to protect their title to the discoveries they had made and hoped to make. The vessels turned out to be Spanish: a ship and a *bergantina*, commanded by Diego García of Moguer. The small harbours of the Odiel and the Río Tinto were still providing seamen for trans-Atlantic voyages. García had been with Solís in 1515–16, and after Solís' death had claimed somewhat more than his share of credit for the discoveries then made. Almost certainly—García is a common name and we cannot be quite sure—he had sailed with Magellan and returned with Elcano. He was thus a practical mariner of some note. In 1526 he had organised, for the first time, an expedition of his own. Cristóbal de Haro was one of his backers. He sailed from La Coruña, with licence from the Emperor specifically to explore the Río de Solís.

García had supposed Cabot to be in the Moluccas or on his way there, and was mightily surprised to learn of his presence in the Río. Leaving his ship at San Lázaro, where Cabot's ships also lay, he started upstream in his launch. The two captains met in the Paraná somewhere between the Carcarañá and the Paraguay. Each demanded, with the outward forms of courtesy, that the other should withdraw. García had the better title, Cabot the stronger force; and the officer in charge of Cabot's ships, acting on urgent instructions sent down the river by Cabot, boarded García's ship and took away the sails, so preventing García's people from moving except on Cabot's terms. They came to terms, as usually happened on such occasions: each would forward his case separately to Spain, and while awaiting a royal decision they would explore the river in partnership.

Cabot sent his report, with a request for reinforcement and some silver ornaments obtained by barter, home in the caravel *San Gabriel*, which sailed in July 1528. Luis Ramírez' letter went in the same vessel, so our only eye-witness narrative ends at this point, and we have little detailed information about the subsequent movements of the uneasy partnership in the river. Cabot's world map of 1544 is curiously unrevealing on the process of discovery, and indeed in some respects seriously misleading on the whole geography of the Río de la Plata drainage. It was compiled many years after the event, and possibly memory had faded. Our knowledge of the later stages of the discovery comes chiefly from the depositions of witnesses in the subsequent *pleitos*. The partners—who regarded one another with mutual dislike and contempt—followed the Paraná and the Paraguay upstream and went some way up a tributary, probably the Pilcomayo. Cabot's people had outworn their welcome among the riparian tribes, so that even in the populated areas they had difficulty in finding food. Though the river was full of fish, they could never catch enough. Their incessant foraging provoked retaliation. Many were killed by arrows or *boleadoras*. Eventually, despairing of reaching the silver mountains, they decided to retreat. They found that 'Sancti Spiritus', the makeshift fort at the mouth of the Carcarañá, had been sacked by Indians, many of the garrison killed, and some of the corpses partly eaten. For years afterwards the ruins of the mud walls were known as 'Cabot's tower', and a village near the site is called Gaboto to this day.

The partnership broke up in the estuary, and García left for home with his grievances against Cabot. Discipline in Cabot's fleet appears to have broken down under the pressure of constant Indian attacks, which prevented his people from fishing or foraging. Cabot's departure at the end of 1529—even allowing for the prejudice of hostile witnesses—had all the appearance of panic. He abandoned one ship as unseaworthy, and left behind some of his people who had been sent off to kill seals for food and were late in returning. When they got back to the Río and found Cabot gone, they patched up the abandoned ship and sailed her back to Spain, where they arrived a month or so after Cabot himself. Cabot called at

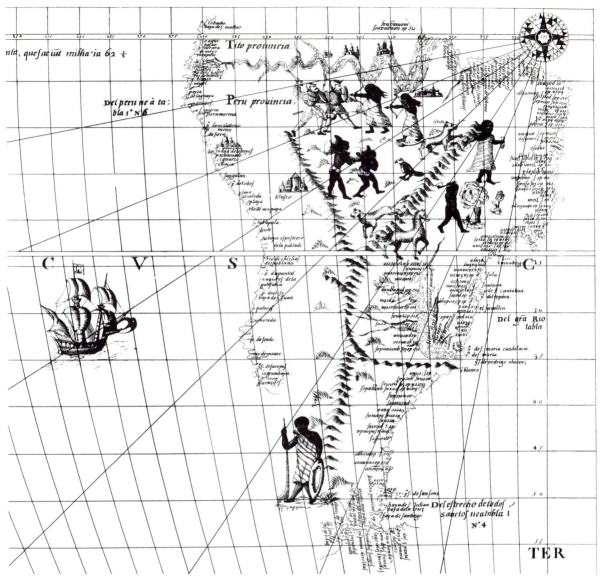

various places on the Brazilian coast for water and provisions. At São Vicente he encountered the marooned Francisco de Rojas, but refused to take him on board. He loaded a cargo of Indian slaves for sale in Spain (as García had also done) but most of them died on the voyage. He reached Seville in July 1530;

and that [says Oviedo] was the end of the expedition of Sebastian Cabot. He squandered the money of those who financed him and the lives and persons of those who served with him . . . for they wasted years, coveting what they never found, longing for what they never saw, and returning in the end without profit or honour.[3]

Cabot defended himself successfully against the many suits and charges brought against him. After a short imprisonment he was exonerated by

92 South America, from the world map by Sebastian Cabot, 1544. It displays many of the 'properties' of South American legend, including the fighting Amazons. Some of the tribal names recorded by Ramírez are inscribed along the Río de la Plata. In general a crude and misleading production. *Paris, Bibliothèque Nationale; facsimile in Harvard College Library.*

the Emperor and reinstated in his office as pilot-major. He and García both
sought contracts for new expeditions, Cabot to the Moluccas, García once
more to the Río. Cabot's application was refused, not surprisingly; apart
from his own record in the matter, access to the Moluccas was now denied
to Spaniards by the Treaty of Saragossa. Cabot's later career in Spain and
in England was distinguished and influential, but he never again served at
sea. García's proposal may have been more seriously considered,[4] though
nothing came of it. There was no doubt that exploration of the Río would
go forward. Cabot's reports, and the scraps of silver he brought back—the
first Peruvian silver to reach Spain—gave the river the name it still
retains, Río de la Plata, Silver River. Shortly after Cabot's return, news of
Cajamarca and Cuzco began to arrive. It required little imagination—
especially since the longitudinal width of South America was unknown,
and commonly under-estimated—to identify Cabot's 'white king' with
the *Sapa Inca*, and to consider the possibility that the Silver River might
be a short cut to his kingdom—as indeed it proved to be, in later centuries.
Perhaps this was thought to be too big a proposition for a relatively
obscure man such as García. In any event, in 1534—it will be
remembered— the Crown divided South America, from the beginning of
Pizarro's conquest southward, into four latitudinal belts running from
Atlantic to Pacific. The third belt, south of Almagro's, was granted to
Pedro de Mendoza, cadet of a noble house, a fighting man experienced in
the wars in Italy (and in the distempers spread by those wars). The Río de
la Plata fell within Mendoza's grant, and he decided to enter by that route.
He sailed from Seville in 1535. García, denied his own expedition, signed
on with Mendoza, but died on the southward passage.

The Mendoza expedition was one of the biggest to leave Spain for the
New World in the sixteenth century: eleven ships, between 1200 and
1500 men and women (estimates vary and some are wildly exaggerated), a
hundred horses, and pigs and horned cattle. Some of the ships must have
been floating barnyards. In size the expedition was comparable with those
of Columbus (1493) Ovando (1502) and Pedrarias Dávila (1514); like those,
it was intended to exploit and settle rather than to explore. Just as Balboa
had done the pioneering for Pedrarias, so Cabot had explored the land
Mendoza was to settle. The expedition was privately financed, the Crown
contributing nothing but its authorisation. Tales of silver up the river
were circumstantial enough, apparently, to attract investment. Two
German houses, the Fugger and the Welser, each provided a ship with its
cargo and complement, and Mendoza himself invested a substantial sum.
Like Pedrarias, Mendoza had the standing and the reputation to attract a
following among his own kind—'gentlemen and persons of honour',
including 'some that I knew', says Oviedo. It was proposed, in order to
avoid pioneering hardships, to ship two hundred slaves in the Cape Verde
Islands, as an initial labour force. Mendoza, therefore, set out with too
many people, some of them the wrong sort of people, for the task in hand.
Few of them saw Spain again.

Of the course of the expedition, we have an eye-witness account in
German by Ulrich Schmidt, or Schmidel as the Spaniards called him, who
spent sixteen years in the area as a guard or mercenary soldier in the

Vera historia,
ADMIRANDÆ CVIVS-
dam nauigationis, quam Hul-
dericus Schmidel, Straubingenſis, ab Anno 1534.
uſque ad annum 1554. in Americam vel nouum
Mundum , iuxta Braſiliam & Rio della Plata, confecit. Quid
per hoſce annos 19. ſuſtinuerit, quam varias & quam mirandas
regiones ac homines viderit. Ab ipſo Schmidelio Germanice,
deſcripta: Nunc vero, emendatis & correctis Vrbium, Regio-
num & Fluminum nominibus, Adiecta etiamtabula
Geographica, figuris & alijs notationi-
bus quibuſdam in hanc for-
mam reducta.

NORIBERGÆ.
Impenſis Levini Hulſij. 1599.

93 Title page of Ulrich Schmidt's account of his travels, the Latin edition: *Vera historia, admirandae cuiusdam navigationis, quam Huldericus Schmidel, Straubingensis, ab anno 1534 usque ad annum 1554, in Americam vel novum Mundum, iuxta Braziliam & Rio della Plata, confecit* (Nürnberg, 1599). It shows Schmidt heading for home, mounted on a llama, with two Indians on foot carrying the baggage.

employ of the house of Welser. The narrative which this fellow compiled—or, more probably, which someone else compiled from his reminiscences—is muddled and trivial; but it contains the only surviving first-hand account of the adventures of Mendoza's people in the first stage of the enterprise, from their departure from Seville in 1535 to the arrival of the relief expedition at Asunción in 1542.

The settlers first established themselves on the south bank, at the mouth of the Riachuelo, the little river which today serves as an open sewer for parts of Buenos Aires. They sheltered in mud huts thatched with reeds, for the site had neither wood nor stone. Their ships' provisions exhausted, they relied on the local Indians for food; but being so many, they soon wore out their welcome. Foraging provoked retaliation, and attempts at coercion failed. The pampa Indians, unlike those of the Andes, did not fear horses. They were accustomed to hunting large animals. They were good archers and their *boleadoras*, designed to disable running rhea or guanaco, were equally effective for bringing down horses. In the first year of settlement they killed over two hundred Spaniards and twenty-five horses, burned four ships at their moorings, and on one occasion came near to over-running the settlement itself. The settlers held out, but their situation remained precarious; and in the spring of 1537 Mendoza, incapacitated by syphilis, left for home. He died at sea before reaching Spain.

Before his departure Mendoza despatched several parties up the river in search of places described by Cabot. One of these parties, commanded by Juan de Salazar, achieved the only permanent success of the whole expedition by establishing, on a bluff on the left bank of the Paraguay, the little stockaded fort which they called Asunción. When the news of its foundation, and of Mendoza's death, reached Spain, a relief expedition was organised under the command of Alvar Núñez Cabeza de Vaca, already famous as the man who had walked, naked and unarmed, from Florida to Mexico. The expedition sailed from Cadiz in November 1542 and reached Catarina Island in the following March. Núñez sent his ships on down the coast to take what relief they could to Buenos Aires; he himself decided to march with the main body—250 men and twenty-six horses—overland. The march took four and a half months. In its way it was a triumph, though fraught with hardship; a triumph both of path-finding and of diplomacy. There was no fighting; Núñez had a way with Indians, and relations were good throughout. No horses were lost, and only one man—drowned in the Paraná. Part of the journey was made in canoes, down the Iguaçú river and across the Paraná, with a long portage round the Iguaçú Falls, hitherto unknown to Europeans; the manner in which the chronicler of the march describes this mighty *cirque* of cataracts, merely as an obstacle, is a good example of Spanish indifference to scenic splendour.

The last day of January, continuing to advance into the interior of the province, they arrived at the river Yguazú, and before arriving at this river they traversed an uninhabited region without finding any settlement of Indians. This is the same river they crossed at the beginning of their journey, when they left the coast of Brazil. It is also called in that part Yguazú. It flows from east to west, and there are no settlements on its banks. Here they took the altitude and found it to be twenty-five and a half degrees. Before arriving at the river Yguazú, they learned from the natives that it fell into the Paraná, also called Río de la Plata; and that between this river Paraná and the Yguazú the Indians killed the Portuguese whom Martin Alfonso de Sosa had sent to discover that land, who were slaughtered while crossing the river in canoes. Some of these Indians who had so killed the Portuguese warned the governor that the Indians of the Pequiry river were bad people and our enemies, and they were lying in wait to seize and kill us during our passage of the river. Because of this the governor held a council, and decided to secure both banks of the river, he with part of his people descending the Yguazú in canoes, and entering the Paraná, while the remainder of the people with the horses went by land, and took up a position on the bank in order to overawe the Indians; all the people were then to pass to the other side in the canoes, and this was accordingly effected. The governor himself with eighty men embarked in the canoes and descended the Yguazú, the remainder of the people and the horses proceeded by land, as we have said, and all joined on the river Paraná. The current of the Yguazú was so strong that the canoes were carried furiously down the river, for near this spot there is a considerable fall, and the noise made by the water leaping down some high rocks into a chasm may be heard a great distance off, and the spray rises two spears high and more over the fall. It was necessary, therefore, to take the canoes out of the water and carry them by hand past the cataract for half a league with great labour. Having left that bad passage behind, they launched their canoes and continued their voyage down to the confluence of this river with the Paraná. And it pleased God that the people and the horses that went by land, as well as those in the canoes with the governor, all arrived at one time. On the bank of the Paraná there had assembled a great number of Indian Guaranís, all decked with parrots' feathers, painted red and a variety of other colours, holding their bows and arrows and all massed together for battle. The arrival of the governor and his people in the manner we have described caused much fear among them and threw them into confusion. We began to speak with them through interpreters and to distribute a number of presents among their chiefs; and as they were covetous people, delighting in novelties, they began to be appeased and to approach us. And many of them helped us to cross to the opposite bank. When we had passed, the governor ordered rafts to be made by lashing the canoes by twos together; and in two hours they were ready, all the people and the horses reaching the other side without being interfered with by the natives. This river Paraná, at the place where we crossed it, was a long cross-bow shot wide, very deep and rapid; in passing it one of the canoes upset and one Christian was drowned, the current having drawn him under, and he never rose to the surface. The strength of the current and great depth form many whirlpools. . . .

The governor and his people advanced across the country, passing settlements of the Guaranís, all of whom received him well, and came forth to meet him laden

94 Brazilian Indian women making beer, by chewing grain and spitting it into a pottery vat for fermentation; engraving, from André Thevet, *Les singularitez de la France antarctique* (Paris, 1558), fo 46 v.

with provisions, as usual. In this march they crossed large marshes, and other bad places, and rivers, and had to build bridges and overcome many difficulties. After the passage of the Paraná the Indians accompanied them from village to village, showing them great friendship and goodwill; they did them many good offices, both in serving as guides, and providing them with food. For this the governor rewarded them generously, and made them well satisfied. . . .

They cleared and swept the road, formed processions with their wives and children, waited his arrival with presents of provisions: maize, wine, bread, potatoes, fowls, fish, honey, and game, all prepared; and they distributed these gifts among his men. In token of peace they raised their hands, and, in their own language, some, too, in ours, welcomed the governor and his people. Along the route they entered into conversation with us, and were as cordial and familiar as though they were our own countrymen, born and bred in Spain.

Travelling in this way, it pleased God that on the eleventh of March, being one Saturday, at nine o'clock in the morning, in the year of grace 1542, we arrived at the city of Ascension, where we found the Spaniards living whom we had come to relieve.

This town is situated on the bank of the Paraguay, in twenty-five degrees south latitude. Before entering it the governor was met by all the captains and people resident there, who showed incredible joy at his arrival, declaring they had never believed, or even expected that they would be relieved, so great were the dangers and difficulties of the road never before explored; as for the sea-route *via* Buenos Ayres, by which they had hoped succour might have reached them, their expectations from this quarter had also vanished since the Indians had taken the aggressive with the idea of soon capturing and making an end of them. Moreover, so long a time had elapsed since any Spaniards had landed there, that they were in despair.[5]

The gratitude of the settlers of Asunción did not last long. Alvar Núñez' austere personality, and his determination to protect the local Indians against settler exploitation, roused angry resentment. Schmidt, as might be expected, had no good word to say for him. In 1545 he was seized by a mutinous cabal and shipped off to Spain, where he received the shabby treatment commonly accorded the well-meaning but unsuccessful. His notion of a direct route from the Brazilian coast bore fruit, however. A small herd of European cattle, the first to enter the La Plata region, was driven from the coast all the way to Asunción in 1554. Today a paved road, thronged with heavy commercial vehicles, connects Asunción with the Brazilian port of Paranaguá, and crosses the Paraná by a bridge a few miles upstream from the place where Alvar Núñez crossed in 1542.

Asunción survived the disturbance of 1545, and even modestly prospered. The Guaraní Indians of the area, unlike the pampa Indians, were settled cultivators and, *pace* Luis Ramírez, comparatively tolerant, even biddable. The egregious Schmidt wrote appreciatively of their food and their women, and in general the life of the Spanish inhabitants was not intolerable. In 1541, while Alvar Núñez was on the march, the miserable remnant of settlers on the estuary shore had moved up to Asunción. Núñez' ships, on arrival at Buenos Aires, had found the site abandoned. It remained deserted for more than forty years. Asunción, the Spanish capital of the La Plata region, thus lost what direct contact it had with the Atlantic; for many years it was tied to Europe, precariously and tenuously, by way of Peru. Most of the surviving early settlements in the La Plata drainage—Santiago del Estero, Tucumán, Salta, Santa Fe—were established by little bands of pioneers who came from Upper Peru. Even Buenos Aires was founded a second time, and permanently, in 1580, by an expedition coming down the river from Asunción. The great river, gateway to a continent, was effectively opened to European traffic not from its mouth upstream, but from its headwaters down.

95 A Brazilian Indian dance; engraving from Theodor de Bry, *America*, Part III (Frankfurt, 1592), p. 228. Two of the cloaked figures in the centre are puffing tobacco smoke at the dancers. The feather ruffs worn on the dancers' backs were characteristic of many Brazilian tribes, and are mentioned in many surviving European accounts.

The exploration of the Amazon followed a similar pattern, though in different circumstances and for more compelling reasons. The mouth of the river is difficult of approach. The coast, for hundreds of miles on either side, is unattractive, forbidding even, with many reefs and shallows, and with winds and currents which tend to drive ships into the Caribbean. The outfall is not a true delta, but an archipelago formed by the eastward tilting of the continent in some remote geological time; its channels are flooded valleys, its islands the summits of what was once a coastal upland, the whole pattern complicated by shifting banks of silt. For sailing ships entering from the sea in the absence of navigational aids, the lower river was a baffling and dangerous maze. Vicente Yáñez Pinzón, probably the first discoverer of the river, penetrated fifty miles or so inland in 1500, but found nothing of interest; Vespucci, a few months later, spent several weeks exploring the channels and commented on the difficulty of landing anywhere. Both explorers pursued their voyages into the Caribbean, and for a generation thereafter the river was undisturbed by Europeans.

Throughout the sixteenth century the Amazon was usually thought to be a Spanish river, in the sense that its course, or most of it, lay west of the Tordesillas line. That arbitrary line could not, of course, be fixed with any precision; but the Portuguese were usually content to leave the river to their rivals. An attempt was made in the 1530s to settle the coastal territory east of the river mouth—João de Barros the historian was one of the donatories—but the leader, the navigator Aires da Cunha, was wrecked and drowned off the coast, and those of his people who got ashore were mostly killed by Indians. The first attempt to settle on the river itself was made by Spaniards led by Diego de Ordaz, with four ships, in 1531. Ordaz was a captain of note, who had been with Cortés in Mexico; it was he who had led the climbing party which reached the crater of Popocatépetl. The Amazon was too much for him. He spent many weeks in the delta, in a baffling and fruitless search for the main channel. He lost three of his ships by wreck or grounding, and for years afterwards stories circulated to the effect that some of the survivors had escaped ashore and taken up residence with the Indians. Ordaz finally sailed away in the remaining ship, to try his luck in the Orinoco instead.

The first discoverers of the Amazon called it Mar Dulce, the Freshwater Sea. The alternative Marañón or Maranhaõ came into use about 1515, possibly commemorating an explorer of that name; though no record of such a person now survives. The name Marañón on modern maps is usually attached to the upper reaches of the river, before its junction with the Ucayali; in the early 1540s it denoted the outfall, the only part of the river of which the Europeans had any knowledge. In 1541–42, however, a boatload of Spaniards travelled the length of the river from near its headwaters to its mouth. Thereafter the river became known to Spaniards either as the Río de Orellana, from the name of the leader of the party, or as the Río de las Amazonas, from the fighting women whom Orellana said he encountered. Amazonas, in Spanish and in Portuguese, it remains to this day.

Orellana's exploit was unplanned, the result of unexpected, probably accidental circumstance. The war of Las Salinas, the first of the civil wars among the conquerors of Peru, had ended in 1538 with the defeat of Almagro's partisans and his own death. It was followed by a series of exploring expeditions beyond the eastern frontier of the Inca dominions, into the *montaña* forest east of the cordilleras; country into which Inca armies had rarely ventured, and of which nothing was certainly known. Francisco Pizarro, victor in the war, encouraged these enterprises on the familiar principle of finding employment, preferably distant employment for those in a position to cause trouble. The leaders included Pedro de Candía (the Greek gunner who had been at the original landing at Tumbes); Alonso de Alvarado; Pedro Anzures; Gonzalo Díaz de Pineda; and Alonso de Mercadillo. Alvarado's venture was the most ably conducted, and the only one to have any lasting results. He crossed the cordillera east of Cajamarca, founded the town of Chachapoyas on the edge of Inca territory, and descended through the forests, by way of Moyabamba, to the banks of the Huallaga, a principal affluent of the Marañón. The fact that this great river, and others like it, flowed east from the cordillera and presumably discharged into the 'North Sea', the Atlantic, was a discovery of great importance. Alvarado returned to Chachapoyas as its governor; the town survives to this day. The other expeditions were all failures, at least from the point of view of the participants; some were disasters; almost all suffered heavy losses in men and horses. Pedro de Candía, exceptionally, brought all his Spaniards back alive (nothing was said about the Indians) but only because his people insisted on turning back at an early stage. Mercadillo, more persistent, was brought back a prisoner by his own men. All the expeditions used horses (Candía, incredibly, had also a few llamas) but horses were encumbrances in such country. Sooner or later they were eaten by their starving owners. Peranzures' people consumed 220 horses, in an expedition which cost the lives of 143 Spaniards and 4,000 Indians. The survivors of all these ventures told similar stories: of steep, muddy declivities; dense forests; swamps; big, swift rivers; incessant rain—'the noise of the rain on the thick woods was so great they could not hear one another' says Oviedo of the Peranzures venture—of starvation, of insects, sickness and death. None of them brought back anything of value. They did, however, bring back tales told them by Indians who wished to be rid of unwelcome visitors, tales of every kind of wealth, a few weeks' or a few days' journey further on through the forest. Of course the *conquistadores* were credulous; if they had not been credulous they would not have found Peru; and so the search for new Perus went on.

One of those for whom employment had to be found was Gonzalo Pizarro; not because of any doubt of his loyalty—like all the Pizarros he was aware of the importance of hanging together—but because his brutality, his arrogance and his greed tended to make enemies for the clan. With his brother Juan—who died fighting at Sacsahuamán—he had been largely responsible for alienating Manco Inca. Arrogance, brutality and greed were characteristic, in varying degrees, of all the Pizarro brothers, certainly of Hernando; but Hernando was an intelligent man, and had the education of a gentleman—if not the instincts of one—so that he could be employed on diplomatic missions to Spain. Gonzalo had very limited talent for anything except horsemanship and fighting. After Las Salinas, he spent most of 1539 in fruitless pursuit of Manco Inca in the wilds of Vilcabamba. In 1540 he sought and obtained from his brother Francisco the office of governor of Quito, La Culata and Puerto Viejo: roughly the area, mountain and coastal, of modern Ecuador.

Gonzalo, needless to say, had no intention of settling down as an administrator; indeed he handed over to a deputy within three months of his arrival. His purpose in going to Quito was to organise another and bigger expedition east of the Andes, in an area further north than that explored by Alvarado. The objects of his search, by his own account, were two: La Canela, the land of cinnamon, and the lake of El Dorado, the gilded king, both of which figured prominently in Indian report. Both stories had some foundation in fact. *Canellum winteriana*, a congener of the oriental cinnamon tree of commerce, is native to the American Tropics and grows in the *montaña* of the Andes. The Pineda expedition was the first to report it, in 1536. It is not very common, and the trees tend to be widely scattered. It is used today as a drug in native medicine, and for throwing into streams to stupefy fish. Cieza de León says that in his day the flower buds were infused to make an aromatic drink. Its aroma is short-lived and its commercial value—as Gonzalo was to discover—is small.

The El Dorado story is more complex. The lake of Guatavita where, almost certainly, the story originated, is a desolate tarn in the mountains not far from Bogotá. The crater which holds the lake is, in geological terms,

96 Gold model of a raft, with a ruler enthroned and surrounded by his attendants. A superb example of Muisca craftsmanship, thought to represent the Guatavita accession ceremony. *Museo del Oro, Bogotá, Colombia.*

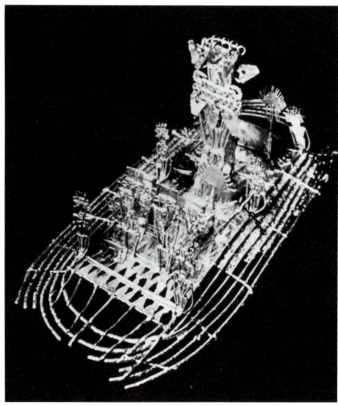

of recent origin, having been formed by the impact of a huge meteorite at a time when the area was already inhabited by man. It is possible that the curious ceremony associated with Guatavita was undertaken in order to derive power from the fiery golden god at the bottom of the crater. Each Guatavita ruler, upon his accession, performed this rite, while his people gathered on the bank by night and lit great fires on the surrounding hills. The ruler's naked body was coated with a resin and powdered with gold dust; he was paddled in a raft out to the centre of the lake, where he threw sacrificial offerings into the water and then immersed himself, so that the gold dust, washed from his body, descended in a gleaming shower to the bottom. One of the finest surviving examples of Muisca gold work, preserved today in the Museo del Oro in Bogotá—a raft in gold, bearing a king enthroned, with attendant figurines—appears to represent this solemn and splendid scene. About fifty years before the arrival of the Spaniards Guatavita became tributary to the Zipa of Bogotá and the ceremony was abandoned; but the memory of it survived. Benalcázar's people heard the story in 1539. It may have been known in Quito earlier still; there is some evidence of communication between Atahuallpa and the Chibcha chiefs, and emissaries would have passed through Quito. The story spread about in a garbled form, in which El Dorado was a living monarch, performing his extravagant ritual not once in a reign, but annually, monthly, even (as in Oviedo's semi-mocking account) daily. The geographical location of the story varied greatly; it was not firmly associated with Guatavita, in Spanish versions, until the seventeenth century (when the lake was visited by Spaniards and strenuous attempts were made to drain or dredge it). In the sixteenth century El Dorado showed a tendency to move east, possibly because of confusion with tales of fugitive Incas. Manco Inca had fled to the hot and forested region of Vilcabamba, north of Cuzco; other and earlier Incas might similarly have established courts in exile somewhere to the East. For whatever reason, Gonzalo Pizarro sought El Dorado in the *montaña* of the Andes, Antonio de Berrío and Sir Walter Ralegh in the Orinoco basin, Keymis in the Rupununi highlands of Guiana.

Gonzalo set out with 220 Spaniards, almost all mounted, and 4,000 Indians (whom he kept shackled, to prevent their running away, until the expedition was well into the forest). He took also a large herd of pigs (Cieza says, incredibly, 5,000) to provide food on the way. It was a smaller force than Almagro's in Chile or Quesada's in New Granada, but formidable in relation to the small Spanish population of Quito, and very well equipped. 50,000 *castellanos* of the loot of the Incas went to make it so; that, at least, was Gonzalo's estimate of what he spent on the expedition. He lost it all; the expedition was a disaster, like its predecessors. When the pigs had been consumed or had run away, the men ate their horses, and then starved. All the Indians died, and half the Spaniards. The survivors staggered back into Quito 'with nothing but our swords' as Gonzalo explained to the King; and all this, or much of it, he blamed on Orellana.

Orellana was an adherent and a relative of the Pizarros and came from their home town, Trujillo. After Las Salinas, Francisco Pizarro made him lieutenant-governor of La Culata, where he was instrumental in the foundation of the city of Guayaquil. When he heard of Gonzalo's arrival in Quito he marched up from the coast with a small body of men, some of them probably sailors, to join the proposed expedition. Finding Gonzalo already gone, he overtook him on the way and became his adjutant, bearing to him, apparently, somewhat the relation which Almagro had borne to Francisco. After some ten months of arduous forest travel the expedition—already short of food—arrived on the banks of the Coca, a tributary of the Napo, itself a major affluent of the Amazon. They knew that Indian cultivations, in that endless wet forest, clung to the banks of rivers; so Gonzalo decided to build a launch in order to facilitate transport and the search for food, and also (according to his own account) with a vague idea of sailing through to the Atlantic, if a return to Quito should prove too difficult. Orellana apparently organised the work; and when it was completed, volunteered to take a party of about sixty men downstream in the launch, at least as far as the next confluence, in the hope of finding food. This was agreed; but when, after some days of fruitless search, the party tried to return to the camp, they found the current too strong for them, so were obliged, perforce, to continue downstream. That, at least, was Orellana's own account of the matter; and though Gonzalo complained bitterly (and understandably) of what he deemed a deliberate desertion, Orellana's account was corroborated by Fray Gaspar de Carvajal, the Dominican friar who accompanied him; and was subsequently accepted by the authorities in Spain.

Carvajal wrote a full narrative of the voyage down the river. It is inevitably monotonous and repetitive, as the voyage was, as the river is; but it is full of vivid detail, and is the only eye-witness account. It reveals an Amazon whose banks, in some places at least, were far more populous and more cultivated than they are today.

> . . . after taking counsel as to what should be done, talking over our affliction and hardships, it was decided that we should choose of two evils the one which to the Captain and to all should appear to be the lesser, which was to go forward and follow the river . . . and so it was that, it being Monday evening, which by count was the eighth [day] of the month of January, while eating certain forest roots they heard drums very plainly very far from where we were, and the Captain was the one who heard them first and announced it to the other companions, and they all listened, and they being convinced of the fact, such was the happiness which they all felt that they cast out of their memories all the past suffering because we were now in an inhabited country and no longer could die of hunger. The Captain straightway ordered us to keep watch by quarters with great care, because . . . [*torn*] it might be that the Indians had caught sight of us and would come at night and attack the party, as is their custom; and so that night a very heavy watch was kept, the Captain not sleeping, it being considered that that night transcended all the rest, because all were so eager for day to come, for they had had their fill of [living on] roots. No sooner had morning come than the Captain ordered the powder and the arquebuses and crossbows to be made ready and all the men to be alert for arming themselves . . . and so in the morning, everything being made quite ready and put in order, we started to go in search of the village. At the end of two leagues of advancing down the river we saw coming up the river to look over and reconnoiter the land four canoes filled with Indians, and, when they saw us, they turned about at great speed, giving the alarm, in such a manner that

in less than a quarter of an hour we heard in the villages many drums that were calling the country to arms . . . [later] the Indians began to come on the water to see what was going on, and thus they kept moving about on the river like simpletons; and, this having been observed by the Captain, he got up on the bank of the river and in their language (for to a certain extent he could understand them) he began to speak to them and tell them to have no fear and to come near, for he wished to speak to them; and so two Indians came right up to where the Captain was, and he cajoled them and took away their fear and gave them something from his supplies and told them to go get the overlord (for he wished to speak to him) and to have no fear that he would do him any harm whatsoever; and so the Indians took what was given them and went at once to inform their overlord, who came right away, very much decked out, to where the Captain and the companions were and was very well received by the Captain and by all, and they embraced him, and the Chief himself manifested great contentment at seeing the good reception that was given him. At once the Captain ordered that he be given clothes and other things, with which he was much pleased, and thereafter he became so happy that he told the Captain to decide on what he needed, for he would give it to him, and the Captain told him to order nothing to be furnished him but food; and straightway the Chief ordered his Indians to bring food, and in a very short time they brought, in abundance, all that was needed, including meats, partridges, turkeys, and fish of many sorts; and after this, the Captain thanked the Chief heartily and told him to depart with God's blessing and to summon to him all the overlords of that land, of whom there were thirteen, because he wished to speak to them all together and announce the reason for his coming. . . . When the Captain perceived that he [now] had all the inhabitants and the overlords accepting peace and friendly toward him [and] that kind treatment was the proper procedure to be followed, [he took advantage of the fact that] they were all glad to come with peaceful intentions; and in this way he took possession of them and of the said land in the name of His Majesty. . . .

It was here that they informed us of the existence of the Amazons and of the wealth farther down the river, and the one who gave us this information was an Indian overlord named Aparia, an old man who said he had been in that country, and he also told us about another overlord who lived at some distance from the river, far inland, who, he said, possessed very great wealth in gold. . . .

After the companions had somewhat recovered from the effects of the hunger and suffering that they had undergone, being [now] in a mood to work, the Captain, seeing that it was necessary to make plans for what was ahead, gave orders to call all the companions together and repeated to them that they could see that with the boat which we were using and the canoes, if God saw fit to guide us to the sea, we could not go on out to a place of rescue and [that] for this reason it was necessary to apply our wits to building another brigantine of greater burden so that we might sail on the sea, and this [he advised] in spite of the fact that among us there was no skilled craftsman who knew that trade, for what we found most difficult [of all] was how to make the nails . . . and there was found among us a woodworker named Diego Mexía, who, though it was not his trade, gave instructions as to how the task was to be done; and thereupon the Captain ordered an apportionment [of the work] among all the companions whereby each man [in one group] was to bring one frame and two futtocks, and others [in another] to bring the keel, and others the stem pieces, and others to saw planks, so that all had enough to occupy themselves with, not without considerable physical toil, because, as it was winter and the timber was very far away, each had to take his ax and go to the woods and cut down the amount that he was supposed to and bring it in on his back, and, while some carried, others formed a rear guard for them, in order that the Indians might not do them any harm, and in this way within seven days all the timber for the said brigantine was cut; and when this task was finished another was immediately assigned, for he ordered [some of the men] to make charcoal in order to manufacture nails and other things. It was a wonderful thing to see with what joy our companions worked and brought the charcoal, and in this same way everything else needed was supplied. There was not a man among all of us that was accustomed to such lines of work as these; but, notwithstanding all these difficulties, Our Lord endowed all of them with [the proper] skill for what had to be done, since it was in order to save their lives, for, had we gone on down from there using [only] the [original] boat and the canoes, coming, as we afterwards did, upon warlike people, we could neither have defended ourselves nor gotten out of the river in safety. . . . Such great haste was applied to the building of the brigantine that in thirty-five days it was constructed and launched, calked with cotton and tarred with pitch, all of which the Indians brought because the Captain asked them for these things. Great was the joy of our companions over having accomplished that thing which they so much desired to do. . . .

We departed from the stopping-place and the village of Aparia aboard the new brigantine (which was of nineteen *joas*, quite [large] enough for navigating at sea) on the eve of the Evangelist Saint Mark's day, the twenty-fourth of April of the year mentioned above, and we came on down past the settlements belonging to that dominion of Aparia, which extended for more than eighty leagues, without our finding a single warlike Indian; on the contrary, the Chief himself came to talk to and bring food to the Captain and to us, and in one of his villages we celebrated the above-mentioned Saint Mark's Day, whither the same overlord came to bring us abundant food, and the Captain gave him a good reception, and no ill treatment was meted out to him because it was the purpose and desire of the Captain, if it was possible, that that land and that barbaric people should continue in its friendly attitude as a consequence of our having come to know them. . . . Because of this, although we found the villages abandoned, seeing the kind treatment that was being given to them, throughout the whole aforesaid province they provided us with sustenance. Within a few days the Indians ceased [to appear], and by this we recognized that we were [now] outside the dominion and tribal domains of that great overlord Aparia; and the Captain, fearing what might come to pass on account of the small food supply, ordered that the brigantines proceed with greater speed than had been the custom. . . .

From here on, we endured more hardships and more hunger and [passed through] more uninhabited regions than before, because the river led from one wooded section to another wooded section and we found no place to sleep and much less could any fish be caught, so that it was necessary for us to keep to our customary fare, which consisted of herbs and every now and then a bit of roasted maize.

Aparia's generosity—or simplicity, or timidity—was exceptional. The Spaniards' reputation for foraging preceded them. Many tribes of the Middle Amazon, more numerous or less amenable than Aparia's people, guarded their food stocks, resisted attempts at landing, and disputed the passage of the river.

When twelve days of the month of May had gone by, we arrived in the provinces belonging to Machiparo, who is a very great overlord and one having many people under him, and is a neighbor of another overlord just as great, named Omaga, and they are friends who join together to make war on other overlords who are [located] inland, for they [i.e. the latter] come each day to drive them from their homes. This Machiparo has his headquarters quite near the river upon a small hill and holds sway over many settlements and very large ones which together contribute for fighting purposes fifty thousand men of the age of from thirty years up to seventy. . . .

Before we had come within two leagues of this village, we saw the villages glimmering white, and we had not proceeded far when we saw coming up the river a great many canoes, all equipped for fighting, gaily colored, and [the men] with their shields on, which are made out of the shell-like skins of lizards and the hides of manatees and of tapirs, as tall as a man, because they cover them entirely. They were coming on with a great yell, playing on many drums and wooden trumpets, threatening us as if they were going to devour us. Immediately the Captain gave orders to the effect that the two brigantines should join together so that the one might aid the other and that all should take their weapons and look to what they had before them.

The Spaniards succeeded in forcing a landing, and in collecting a number of turtles from the village but were subsequently driven off, with the loss of one dead and many wounded. There ensued several days of running battle,

the Indians still not ceasing to follow us and force upon us many combats, because from these settlements there had gathered together many Indians and on the land the men who appeared were beyond count. There went among these and the war canoes four or five sorcerers, all daubed with whitewash and with their mouths full of ashes, which they blew into the air, having in their hands a pair of aspergills, with which as they moved along they kept throwing water about the river as a form of enchantment, and, after they had made one complete turn about our brigantines in the manner which I have said, they called out to the warriors, and at once these began to blow their wooden bugles and trumpets and beat their drums and with a very loud yell they attacked us; but, as I have already said, the arquebuses and crossbows, next to God, were our salvation; and so they led us along in this manner until they got us into a narrows in an arm of the river. Here they had us in a very distressful situation, and so much so that [if luck had not favoured us] I do not know whether any one of us would have survived, because they had laid an ambuscade for us on land, and from there they would have surrounded us. Those on the water resolved to wipe us out, and they being now quite determined to do so, being now very close [to us], there stood out before them their captain-general distinguishing himself in a very manly fashion, at whom a companion of ours, named Celis, took aim and fired with an arquebuse, and he hit [him] in the middle of the chest, so that he killed him; and at once his men became disheartened and they all gathered around to look at their overlord, and in the meantime we seized the opportunity to get out into the wide part of the river; but still they followed us for two days and two nights without letting us rest, for it took us that long to get out of the territory occupied by the subjects of this great overlord named Machiparo, which in the opinion of all extended for more than eighty leagues. . . .

In this manner and in spite of these hardships we made our way out of the province and great dominion of Machiparo and came to another no smaller [than that one], for here was the beginning of [the land ruled over] by Oníguayal, and at the approach and entrance to this land stood a village on the model of a garrison, not very large, on an elevated spot overlooking the river, where there were many warriors; and the Captain, aware that neither he nor his companions could [any longer] endure the great hardship, which consisted not only of fighting but, in addition to this, of hunger (for the Indians, although we did have something to eat, did not leave us free to do so because of the excessive amount of fighting which they forced upon us), decided to capture the said village and so gave orders to steer the brigantines towards the harbor . . . thereupon they [i.e. the Indians] made way and rendered it possible for the brigantines to get our companions up on the beach and for them to leap out on land, and after that they fought on land in such a way that they made the Indians take flight, and so the village was left in our hands along with the food that it possessed. This village was fortified, and, because it was so, the Captain said that he wished to rest there three or four days and get together some ship-stores for farther along, and so we relaxed in this way and with this idea in mind, although not without having to do some fighting, and [this] of such a dangerous sort that one day at ten o'clock there came a great number of canoes bent on seizing and unmooring the brigantines which were in the harbour, and, if the Captain had not had at his disposal crossbowmen to leap quickly on board, we believe that we should have been unable to defend them; and so, with the help of Our Lord and thanks to the great skill and luck of our crossbowmen, some damage was done among the Indians, who thought it best to go off and return to their homes; so we remained resting, regaling ourselves with good lodgings, eating all we wanted, and we stayed three days in this village. There were many roads here that entered into the interior of the land, very fine highways, for which reason the Captain was wary and commanded us to get ready, because he did not wish to stay there any longer, for it might come about that from our staying there some harm would result.

This idea having been voiced by the Captain, all began to get ready to depart when they should be ordered to do so. We had gone, from the time we left Aparia to this said village, three hundred and forty leagues, of which two hundred were [country] without settlements. We found in this village a very great quantity of very good biscuit which the Indians make out of maize and yucca, and much fruit of all kind.

To return to the story, I [next] state that on Sunday after the Ascension of Our Lord we set out from this said village and began to move on, and we had not gone more than two leagues when we saw emptying into the river another very powerful and wider river on the right; so wide was it that at the place where it emptied in it formed three islands, in view of which we gave it the name of Trinity River; and at this junction of the two [rivers] there were numerous and very large settlements and very pretty country and very fruitful land; all this, now, lay in the dominion and land of Omagua, and, because the villages were so numerous and so large and because there were so many inhabitants, the Captain did not wish to make port, and so all that day we passed through settled country with occasional fighting, because on the water they attacked us so pitilessly that they made us go down mid-river; and many times the Indians started to converse with us, and, as we did not understand them, we did not know what they were saying to us. At the hour of vespers we came to a village that was on a high bank, and as it appeared small to us the Captain ordered us to capture it, and also because it looked so nice that it seemed as if it might be a recreation spot of some overlord of the inland; and so we directed our course with a view of capturing it, and the Indians put up a defense for more than an hour, but in the end they were beaten and we were masters of the village, where we found very great quantities of food, of which we laid in a supply. In this village there was a villa in which there was a great deal of porcelain ware of various makes, both jars and pitchers, very large, with a capacity of more than twenty-five *arrobas*, and other small pieces such as plates and bowls and candelabra of this porcelain of the best that has ever been seen in the world, for that of Málaga is not its equal, because it is all glazed and embellished with all colours, and so bright [are these colours] that they astonish, and, more than this, the drawings and paintings which they make on them are so accurately worked out that [one wonders how] with [only] natural skill they manufacture and decorate all these things [making them look just] like Roman [articles]; and here the Indians told us that as much as there was made out of clay in this house, so much there was back in the country in gold and silver, and [they said] that they would take us there, for it was near; and in this house there were two idols woven out of feathers of diverse sorts, which frightened one, and they were of the stature of giants, and on their arms, stuck into the fleshy part, they had a pair of disks resembling candlestick sockets, and they also had the same thing on their calves close to the knees; their ears were bored through and very large, like those of the Indians of Cuzco, and [even] larger. This race of people resides in the interior of the country and is the one which possesses the riches already mentioned, and it is as reminders that they have them [i.e. the two idols] there; and in this village also there were gold and silver; but, as our intention was merely to search for something to eat and see to it that we saved our lives and have an account of such a great accomplishment, we did not concern ourselves with, nor were we interested in, any wealth. . . . We continued onward in our journey and always through settled country, and one morning at eight o'clock we saw on a high spot a fine looking settlement. . . . In this village there were seven gibbets [which] we saw were at certain distances apart from one another throughout the village, and on the gibbets [were] nailed many dead men's heads, because of which [circumstance] we gave to this province the name of Province of the Gibbets [Picotas], which extended down the river seventy leagues. There came down to the river from this village roads made by hand, and on the one side and on the other [were] planted fruit trees, wherefore it seemed probable [to us] that it was a great overlord who ruled over this land.

We proceeded onward and the next day we came upon another village of the same sort, and, as we were in need of food, we were forced to attack it, and the Indians hid in order to let us leap out on land, and so our companions did leap out, and, as soon as the Indians saw that they were on land, they came out from their ambuscade with very great fury. At their head came their captain or overlord spurring them on with a very loud yell. A crossbowman of ours took aim at this overlord and shot him and killed him; and [some of] the Indians, on seeing that, decided not to wait, but to flee, and others to fortify themselves in their houses, and there they put themselves on the defensive and fought like wounded dogs. The Captain, seeing that they did not want to surrender and that they had done us injury and wounded some of our companions, gave the order to set fire to the houses where the Indians were, and consequently they came out from them and fled and gave us a chance to collect some food, for in this village, praised be Our Lord, there was no lack of it, because there were many turtles and parrots and a very great abundance [of all things], for bread and maize do not require any special mention; and we departed from here and straightway went off to an island to rest and enjoy what we had seized. There was captured in this village an Indian girl of much intelligence, and she said that nearby and back in the interior there were many Christians like ourselves and that they were under the rule of an overlord who had brought them down the river; and she told us how there were two white women among them [as wives of two of these Christians], and that others had Indian wives, and children by them; these are the people who got lost out of Diego de Ordaz's party, so it is thought from the indications which were at hand regarding them, for it lies off to the north of the river.

We proceeded on down our river without seizing any village, because we had food on board, and at the end of a few days we moved out of this province, at the extreme limit of which stood a very large settlement through which the Indian girl told us we had to go to get to where the Christians were; but, as we were not concerned with this matter, we decided to press forward, for, as to rescuing them from where they were, the time for that will come . . . we kept on going, picking up food wherever we saw that they could not protect it, and at the end of four or five days we went and captured a village where the Indians offered no resistance. Here was found a great quantity of maize (and there was also found a great quantity of oats) from which the Indians make bread, and very good wine resembling beer, and this [sort of beer] is to be had in great plenty. . . . In this manner we were proceeding on our way searching for a peaceful spot to celebrate and to gladden the feast of the blessed Saint John the Baptist, herald of Christ, when God willed that, on rounding a bend which the river made, we should see on the shore ahead many villages, and very large ones, which shone white. Here we came suddenly upon the excellent land and dominion of the Amazons. These said villages had been forewarned and knew of our coming, in consequence whereof they [i.e. the inhabitants] came out on the water to meet us, in no friendly mood, and, when they had come close to the Captain, he would have liked to induce them to accept peace, and so he began to speak to them and call them, but they laughed, and mocked us and came up close to us and told us to keep on going and [added] that down below they were waiting for us, and that there they were to seize us all and take us to the Amazons. The Captain, angered at the arrogance of the Indians, gave orders to shoot them with the crossbows and arquebuses, so that they might reflect and become aware that we had the wherewith to assail them; and in this way damage was inflicted on them and they turned about towards the village to give the news of what they had seen.

Tales of Amazons never failed to appeal to the European imagination. The descriptions of these warrior women, which Carvajal attributed to Indian informants, merely rehearse the stories of Greek mythology; perhaps they were prompted by leading questions. This part of Carvajal's narrative was received sceptically by the chroniclers; Oviedo treated it with heavy sarcasm; Gómara pointed out that in many Indian tribes women fought alongside the men, but that this did not make them Amazons. Carvajal's own eye-witness account of the encounter with fighting women is, in fact, relatively restrained:

. . . the Captain began to cheer up the men at the oars and urge them to make haste to beach the brigantines, and so, although with hard work, we succeeded in beaching the boats and our companions jumped into the water, which came up to their chests; here they fought a very serious and hazardous battle, because the Indians were there mixed in among our Spaniards, who defended themselves so courageously that it was a marvellous thing to behold. More than an hour was taken up by this fight, for the Indians did not lose spirit, rather it seemed as if it was being doubled in them, although they saw many of their own number killed, and they passed over them [i.e. their bodies], and they merely kept retreating and coming back again. I want it to be known what the reason was why these Indians defended themselves in this manner. It must be explained that they are the subjects of, and tributaries to, the Amazons, and, our coming having been made known to them, they went to them to ask help, and there came as many as ten or twelve of them, for we ourselves saw these women, who were there fighting in front of all the Indian men as women captains, and these latter fought so courageously that the Indian men did not dare to turn their backs, and anyone who did turn his back they killed with clubs right there before us, and this is the

97 Title page, *Historia Naturalis Brasiliae . . .* [Willem Piso, *De Medicina Brasiliensi,* and Georg Margraf, *Historia Rerum Naturalium Brasiliae,* bound together; Leyden and Amsterdam, 1648]. This sumptuous book was commissioned by Prince Johan-Maurits of Nassau, who governed Pernambuco for the Dutch West India Company between 1630 and 1643. It is an encyclopaedic and lavishly illustrated treatise on the anthropology and natural history of Brazil. Margraf's work is divided into separate sections, *De Quadrupedibus, Historia Avium, Historia Plantarum,* etc., cited separately in plates 98–107.

reason why the Indians kept up their defense for so long. These women are very white and tall, and have hair very long and braided and wound about the head, and they are very robust and go about naked, [but] with their privy parts covered, with their bows and arrows in their hands, doing as much fighting as ten Indian men, and indeed there was one woman among these who shot an arrow a span deep into one of the brigantines, and others less deep, so that our brigantines looked like porcupines. . . .

We had now traveled, from the spot from which we had started and at which we had left Gonzalo Pizarro, one thousand four hundred leagues, rather more than less, and we did not know how much there still remained from here to the sea. . . . [And so they went on, until one day] we recognized that we were not very far from the sea, because the flowing of the tide extended to where we were, whereat we rejoiced not a little in the realization that now we could not fail to reach the sea. . . .

Here we began to leave [behind us] the good country and the savanas and the high land and began to enter into low country with many islands, although not so thickly inhabited as those farther back. Here the Captain turned away from the mainland and went in among the islands, among which he gradually made his way, seizing food wherever we saw that that could be done without damage [to us]; and, owing to the fact that the islands were numerous and very large, never again did we manage to reach the mainland either on the one side or on the other all the way down to the sea, during which [part of our voyage] we covered, in and out among the islands, a distance of some two hundred leagues, over the full length of which, and a hundred more, the tide comes up with great fury, so that in all there are three hundred of tidewater and one thousand five hundred without tide; consequently the total number of leagues that we have covered on this river, from where we started out as far as the sea, is one thousand eight hundred leagues, rather more than less.

[Somewhere in the maze of the delta, the smaller of the launches was stove in by a floating log. Repairs took eighteen days. When they were completed] we went on in our journey, continually passing by settled country, where we secured a certain amount of food, although only a small amount, because the Indians had carried it off, but we found a few roots which they call 'inanes' [yams], [and so we remained alive], for, if we had not found these, we should all have perished from hunger; thus we came out of there very short of supplies. In all these villages the Indians met us without weapons, because they are a very docile people, and they gave us to understand by signs that they had seen Christians [before]. These Indians are at the mouth of the river through which we came out, where we took on water, each one a jarful, and some half an *almud* of roasted maize and others less, and others [supplied themselves] with roots, and in this manner we got ready to navigate by sea wherever fortune might cast us, because we had no pilot, nor compass, nor navigator's chart of any sort, and we did not even know in what direction or toward what point we ought to head. . . .

We passed out of the mouth of this river from between two islands, the distance from the one to the other being four leagues measured across the stream, and the whole [width], as we saw farther back, from point to point must be over fifty leagues; it sends out into the sea fresh water for more than twenty-five leagues; it rises and falls six or seven fathoms. We passed out, as I have said, on the twenty-sixth of the month of August, on Saint Louis' Day, and we [always] had such good weather that never in our course down the river or on the sea did we have squalls, and that was no small miracle which Our Lord God worked for us . . . at the end of nine days that we had been sailing along, our sins drove us into the Gulf of Paria, we believing that that was our route, and when we found

98

99

100

98 Jaguar; engraving from
Margraf, *De Quadrupedibus*,
p. 235.

99 Tapir; engraving from
Margraf, *De Quadrupedibus*,
p. 229.

100 Sloth; engraving from
Margraf, *De Quadrupedibus*,
p. 221.

ourselves within it we tried to go out to sea again; getting out was so difficult that it took us seven days to do so, during all of which [time] our companions never dropped the oars from their hands, and during all these seven days we ate nothing but some fruit resembling plums, which are called 'hogos'; thus it was that with great toil we got out of the Mouths of the Dragon (for so this may [well] be called for us), because we came very close to staying inside there [forever]. We got out of this prison; we proceeded onward for two days along the coast, at the end of which [time], without knowing where we were nor whither we were going nor what was to become of us, we made port on the island of Cubagua and in the city of Nueva Cádiz.[6]

This astonishing voyage, in improvised boats, took nine months. Carvajal, naturally enough, attributed the survival of the party to the special favour of Providence. He himself was twice badly wounded: he lost an eye, pierced by an arrow, and had another arrow, fortunately for him not poisoned, between his ribs. He was lucky to survive; so were they all. Even the sardonic Oviedo called the story 'miraculous'. Orellana's feat of leadership in holding the party together—sixteenth-century Spaniards being what they were—certainly verges on the miraculous. If there were murmurs, attempts at desertion, threats of mutiny, Carvajal did not record them. In power of command, in versatility, in energy and cheerful determination, Orellana has few equals in the annals of discovery. His luck did not last. He succeeded in chartering a small vessel to take him to Spain, but was forced by bad weather to land in Portugal, where he was closely questioned, as Columbus had been fifty years earlier. His story aroused interest in some circles in Portugal and rumours soon circulated of a projected Portuguese expedition. Probably they were baseless; but the Spanish government, concerned over relations with Portugal, at first hesitated to pursue the matter; for though Orellana's river was identified by most people with the Marañón, and though most of its course clearly ran on the Spanish side of the Tordesillas line, the Council of the Indies was advised that its mouth probably lay on the Portuguese side. Eventually, reassured that the Portuguese had no serious designs on the

102

103

104

105

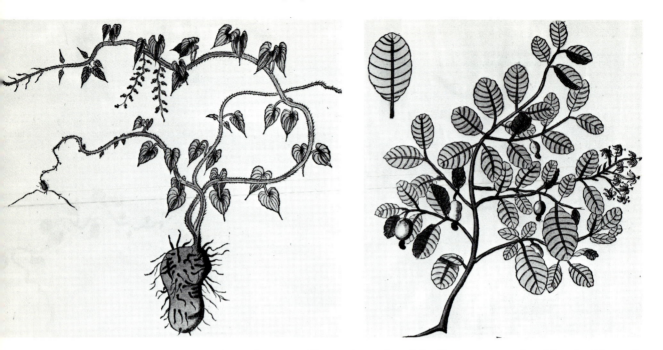

Above
106 Yam; engraving from Margraf, *Historia Plantarum*, p. 93.

Above right
107 Cashew; engraving from Margraf, *Historia Plantarum*, p. 95.

river, the councillors relented and Orellana procured a title of *adelantado* and a contract to settle, at his own expense, an area on the south bank, to be called New Andalusia. He had difficulty in raising money—one of his few backers was a Portuguese—and men; the reports of his river voyage cannot have been very encouraging, and most of his old companions had returned to Peru. It was a poorly equipped, ill-manned expedition which set out for the river in 1549. Like others before him, Orellana, entering from the sea, could not find the main channel; he and many of his companions died somewhere in the delta; only a few enfeebled survivors, including his wife, succeeded in reaching Margarita and safety.

The next attempt to descend the river from the Peruvian *montaña* was that of Ursúa and Aguirre, in 1558, which ended in mad, bloodstained disaster. Responsible Spaniards were obsessed with Peru, and the great river, whatever other attractions it might offer, was clearly not a highway to Peru; so they lost interest. After 1580, moreover, Portuguese rivalry—so far as the government was concerned—ceased to be a serious consideration. In the early seventeenth century the Crown, alarmed by English and Dutch activities in Guiana, positively encouraged Portuguese expeditions to the Amazon valley. The fort which became Belém was built in 1616. In 1623 Luis Aranha de Vasconcelos sailed more than a thousand miles up the main channel and established that the Amazon and the Grão-Pará were branches of the same river. In 1636 two Franciscans, accompanied by half-a-dozen soldiers, succeeded in emulating Orellana's feat. From a remote mission on the Napo they travelled the whole length of the river to Belém. They were both Spaniards; but the first expedition to cover the same distance travelling upstream was Portuguese, that commanded by Pedro Teixeira, which left Belém in October 1637, reached Quito a year later, and in 1639 returned by the way it had come. Teixeira

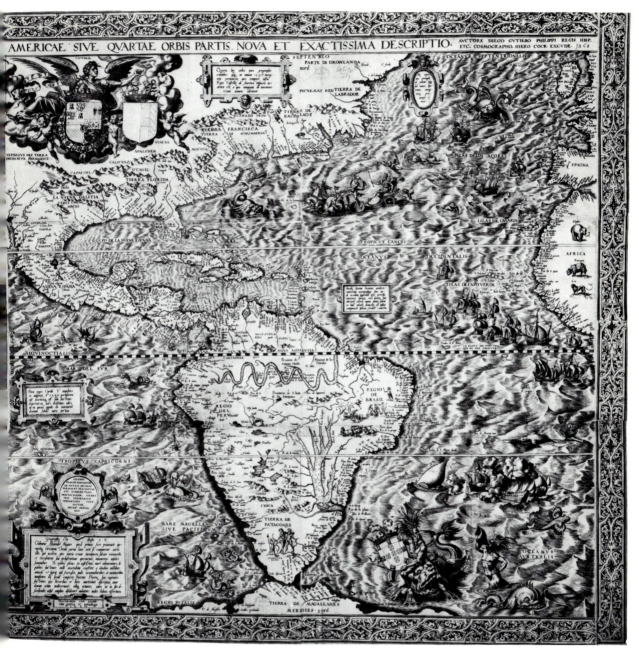

was accompanied on the return journey by the Jesuit Cristóbal de Acuña, whose *New Discovery of the Great River of the Amazons*, published in 1641—if not precisely a 'new discovery'—is the best of all early descriptions of the river. Acuña urged the Spanish Crown to lose no time in occupying the Amazon valley—Portugal being in rebellion even as he wrote—but his advice went unheeded. The river remained Portuguese, and Portuguese missionaries, traders and slavers were thenceforward its explorers.

·   ·   ·

108 Map of South America, 1562, by Diego Gutierrez. The most authoritative summary of the progress of inland exploration to that date. *British Museum.*

Of the three great rivers of South America the Orinoco is the most difficult to navigate, and was the last to yield its secrets. As with the Amazon, it was initially investigated by men in search of El Dorado. Diego de Ordaz, in 1531, entered the delta by one of the channels opening into the Gulf of Paría, using boats built on the coast for the purpose. He reached the confluence with the Meta; ignored his Indian guides who advised him to follow the Meta (which, in the dry season, may indeed have been too shallow for his boats) and stuck to the main stream, but was soon stopped by cataracts. He returned to the coast; planned a second expedition overland; but was murdered before he could set out. His camp-master, Alonso de Herrera, in 1533, penetrated some distance up the Meta in the wet season, in conditions of appalling hardship, until he was killed by a poisoned arrow. Both expeditions were notorious for atrocities against the Indians whom they encountered.

The most famous and most successful of sixteenth-century explorers of the Orinoco basin was Antonio de Berrío, a tough old soldier of conquest, connected by marriage with Gonzalo Jiménez de Quesada. Berrío made three Orinoco voyages between 1584 and 1591, all starting from bases in New Granada and proceeding down the Meta to meet the main stream. He convinced himself that El Dorado's kingdom lay somewhere in Guiana, in the immense, mountainous forested area between Orinoco and Amazon; and that the Caroní, entering the Orinoco from the south, was the route by which it could best be reached. Berrío was never able to test his theory, because the passage of the Caroní is blocked by cataracts; but the accident whereby he, waiting all unsuspecting in Trinidad for orders from Spain, fell into the hands of Sir Walter Ralegh, put Ralegh in possession of his theories, his information, and a good deal of misinformation too. The story of Ralegh's two Guiana voyages, and their tragic sequel, is well known. More poet than economist, more courtier than *conquistador*, he discovered nothing new, but produced from his endeavours a masterpiece of English prose. The *Discovery of the Large, Rich and Bewtiful Empire of Guiana* accurately describes Ralegh's own experiences and incorporates a great deal of information both from Berrío and from his own observation; but it is almost heartbreaking in its lyric optimism. 'Guiana is a country that hath yet her maidenhead, never sacked, turned nor wrought, the face of the earth hath not been torn, nor the virtue and salt of the soil spent by manurance, the graves have not been opened for gold, the mines not broken with sledges, nor their images pulled down out of their temples.' But there were no temples, no mines, and the soil—save in the saline mud of the estuaries—has little virtue. Guiana was to be England's Peru. 'If there were but a small army afoot in Guiana, marching towards Manoa the chief city of the Inca, he would yield Her Majesty so many hundred thousand pounds yearly, as should both defend all enemies abroad and defray all expenses at home.' But it was all mirage, all hallucination. The Orinoco, in fact, led to nothing—nothing that sixteenth-century explorers thought worth finding. When Humboldt visited the area two hundred years later, it was still almost unexplored.

9 The South Sea

One of the most remarkable features of the European discovery of South America was its rapidity. Orellana emerged from the mouth of the Amazon almost exactly fifty years after Columbus' first landfall. During those fifty years the main centres of settled population had all been located and seized. Of the three great continental river systems, two had been navigated along their main streams almost from end to end. The third great river, the Orinoco, it is true, defied navigation; for many years people could still seriously hope to find another Peru in the vast area of its drainage. Its rough configuration, nevertheless, could be surmised; if the source of the main stream in the Serra Parima was unknown, and long remained so, the principal tributary, the Meta, was known to rise in the Cundinmarca highlands, and had been used by Federmann in 1537 in his march to Bogotá. Even this most mysterious and intractable of river systems, therefore, was not wholly unknown to Europeans in 1542.

In the same fifty years, or slightly less, coasting ships had completed the circuit of South America, except only the territory—whether island, archipelago or continent—to the south of Magellan's Strait. About half the circuit—the immense stretch of coast from the Isthmus of Panamá to the Río de la Plata—had been roughly traced at a very early date, in the first ten years of New World discovery. Thereafter there had been a pause—attributable to the greater attractions of Central America, and broken only by the attempts of Solís and others to find a strait in the Río de la Plata area—until Magellan sailed along the Patagonian coast and penetrated the Strait. After passing Cape Pillar, Magellan headed north-west and soon lost sight of land. On the third day out, pressed back by westerly winds, he sighted it briefly again—a mountainous headland, probably Cape Tres Montes in 47°S—but the wind changed and he made no attempt to investigate. The southern Chilean coast—complex, dangerous, a maze of channels and islands—remained unvisited by ships for another twenty years. During those years a series of expeditions explored the Pacific coast further north: from Tehuántepec to Lower California, from Panamá to Nicaragua, and from Panamá southward, in search of the Inca empire and its tributary provinces, as far as the northern coast of Chile. In 1536 Almagro's pilot Alonso Quintero, trying to make contact with Almagro marching south from Copiapó, found him on the Aconcagua coast in 32°S or thereabouts. In 1540 Pedro de Valdivia undertook the conquest and settlement of Chile, and in 1541 he founded the town of Santiago, inland, but with a convenient harbour at Valparaíso.

These developments naturally prompted reconsideration of Magellan's Strait as a commercial route, not to southern Asia but to Pacific South America. In 1539 a fleet of three ships left Seville in an attempt to inaugurate this route. The fleet sailed with royal licence, but was organised and financed by the bishop of Plasencia in Extremadura; an unlikely undertaker for such a project, except that he was the viceroy of Mexico's brother-in-law. Our knowledge of the expedition is scanty, derived from a fragment of a ship's log, from the testimony of two survivors, and from references in early secondary accounts. One ship was lost, one returned to Spain without entering the Strait; the third ship—we do not know her name, nor that of her captain—passed the Strait and sailed up the west coast—presumably outside the islands—in the (southern) summer of 1540–41. She touched at Valparaíso (Valdivia, then beginning his settlement of Chile, was mightily surprised to learn of her presence) and at Quilca in southern Peru. According to one account she eventually, in an extremity of distress, reached Callao, where she was hauled out and for a time preserved as a monument; with justice, for this nameless ship was the first, coming from Spain, to enter a Pacific port, and the first to close the circuit of the coasts of South America.

The ill-success, or very limited success, of this episcopal venture did not discourage the authorities in Chile and Peru from further attempts to find a pattern of sailing, at a propitious time of year, which might make the commercial use of the Strait a practicable proposition. On the contrary, their interest increased, especially after the discovery, in 1545, of the *Cerro* of Potosí, the prodigious mountain of silver ore which in a few decades was to make Potosí a synonym for extravagant wealth and probably the biggest concentration of European population in the Indies. Arica, the nearest port for Potosí, is nearly two thousand nautical miles from Panamá. The portage across the Isthmus was troublesome and expensive, and sometimes dangerous because of the hostility of the local Indians and of *cimarrones*, runaway slaves. The Pacific navigation, especially southward-bound against current and prevailing winds, was slow and difficult. In the worst months, from April to September, a ship might take six months or more from Panamá to Callao, more still to Arica or the ports of Chile. The ships in use were built on the coast, perforce, in the little bush harbours of Tehuántepec or Nicaragua, or later in the century at Guayaquil. Their sails and metal fittings had to be imported from Europe and carried across—ships putting into Nombre de Dios or Vera Cruz could make a handsome profit by selling old and worn-out sails. For cordage they used sisal, made from the fibres of various species of *agave*; an inferior substitute for hemp. Some of these Pacific-built vessels were large—the *Santa Ana* taken by Cavendish in 1587 was said to have been of 700 tons—but they may well have been awkward and unreliable, or reputed to be so. How great the attraction, then—at least in theory—of a route affording a continuous passage between Spain and Peru. One of the officers of the expedition which discovered Potosí, curiously enough, was Alonso de Camargo, who had come to Peru in the bishop of Plasencia's ship—he may have been her captain—and had stayed on. No doubt he could have warned of the difficulties of shipping Potosí silver through Magellan's Strait.

Warnings notwithstanding, the attempts continued. Pedro de Valdivia, throughout his government of Chile encouraged exploration by sea to the south; he was the original founder of all the major port towns on the

central Chilean coast: Valparaíso, Concepción, Valdivia. In 1553 he sent
two ships under Francisco de Ulloa and Francisco Cortés Hojea from
Valdivia to explore the Strait from the western end. On the outward
passage they investigated in some detail the coasts of Chiloé Island and the
intricate sounds of the Chonos archipelago. They found the Strait, and
sailed into it as far as Cape Froward, where the condition of their ships, the
depletion of their stores and the hostility of the local people forced them to
turn back. On their return they found Pedro de Valdivia dead. His
successor as governor, García Hurtado de Mendoza, the son of the third
viceroy of Peru, took over his government with explicit instructions to
pursue the exploration of the Strait, and selected for the task Juan
Fernández Ladrillero of Moguer (how constantly the little ports of the
Odiel and Río Tinto recur in the story of American discovery!). Ladrillero
was a navigator of long experience. He had made more than twenty
Atlantic passages, and had navigated the ship which carried Hurtado de
Mendoza from Callao to Chile; this, presumably, had brought him to the
governor's notice. Ladrillero sailed from Valdivia with two ships and a
bergantín in November 1557. Hojea, who had accompanied Ulloa four
years earlier, went as master of one of the ships, but became separated
early in the voyage; he failed on this occasion to find the entrance to the
Strait, and eventually returned, with considerable difficulty, to Valdivia.
Ladrillero himself spent the first three months of 1558 exploring the
islands and channels of the southern coast of Chile. He wrote a detailed
Relación, so that his route can be followed without much difficulty on a
modern chart. He sailed past the entrance to the Strait, and entered an
unidentified harbour south of Desolation Island where—for reasons he
does not explain—he stayed until late July. He eventually entered the
Strait, therefore, in the middle of winter; but once inside, had a
prosperous passage and reached Cape Virgins in August 1558. He turned
round at once, returned through the Strait much more slowly (as was
usual) and re-entered the Pacific (probably) early in 1559. Of his return to
Valdivia there is no certain record. Some early historians state that his ship
foundered, and even that he himself died in an attempt to return
overland; but since his *Relación* survived, it seems probable that he did
too. In 1574 one Juan Ladrillero, residing in Mexico, addressed a letter to
the King offering, though old and weary, to search for a strait through
North America; but we have no means of knowing whether this was the
same man. However that may be, our Ladrillero was the first explorer to
pass through Magellan's Strait from west to east and the first to return by the
same route.

Ladrillero's *Relación* is not so much a narrative of his own experiences
and impressions, as a set of sailing directions, practical and impersonal.
Descriptions of places, people, animals and plants are few and terse; the
language in which they are couched is often obscure and involved. Visits
to the Strait over three hundred years were so infrequent that every
navigator gave new names to the features that caught his attention. Few of
the names used by Ladrillero (or indeed by Magellan himself) have
survived on modern charts. From his descriptions, however, brief though

they are, and from his record of bearings and distances, many of the places described can be identified with reasonable confidence. The *Relación* ends with several pages of general advice on the navigation of the Strait:

The characteristics by which Cape Deseado [Cape Pillar, at the Pacific entrance to the Strait] may be recognised, are as follows: it is a high, bare mountain, extending a short distance east-south-east, with many deep ravines. There are no other mountains to the south of it, because the coast trends south-east. The land [Desolation Island] of which it forms the tip is narrow, not more than five leagues across thirty leagues inside the Strait. On the seaward side of the Cape are two high, slender rock stacks, the one nearer the sea lower than the other; the higher one formed of black rock; and seaward of these two stacks, a low promontory of black rock.

.   .   .

The best order for the navigation of the Strait is as follows: those who come from Chile or Peru should arrange to sail from Valdivia in September or early October. As soon as they have a north wind they should proceed twenty or thirty leagues out to sea, and run south-south-west in the open sea as far as 51°S. In that latitude they should close the land and make landfall at Cape San Francisco. They can find anchorage off La Campana Island, in the bay which Francisco de Ulloa discovered; or else in a harbour about two leagues from the latter, in a channel opening to the south-south-west. Here they can careen, if necessary.

Alternatively they can find shelter in the Bay of San Lázaro [Nelson Strait] and if necessary can anchor there, or else on the seaward side of a group of islands further up the same inlet, seven or eight leagues from the sea. To make the entrance to the Strait from either of these bays they will have to wait for an east or south-east wind. With these winds the navigation is straightforward. They will know when they are approaching the Strait, because from about ten leagues off the current sets strongly towards the entrance. The east or south-east wind usually holds for two or three days, enough to enable them to reach the Strait and be well inside before the wind changes. Once inside, they should be safe, even if the wind goes round to the north; but if they are caught by a change outside the Strait, they may find themselves in trouble. A norther is often accompanied by dense fog; and there is a string of islands [The Evangelists, etc.] near the mouth of the Strait, twelve leagues long and extending four leagues out to sea.

To a ship sailing into the Strait the mountains seem to close in so that it appears to be a dead end, and one would not venture into it without previous knowledge; but when one is sailing out, it appears straight and open, like an arm of the sea. . . . One can pass through the Strait from the South Sea to the North, in six or seven days, because the prevailing wind is from the north-west and blows directly along the Strait. The best time of year for this passage is in December, January or February, because then the weather is temperate; though even then there may sometimes be a cross-wind from the north. These northers usually last for a day and a night, but sometimes for two days or more. . . . While they last, the visibility is bad, with heavy rain.

In winter, though there may be periods of south or south-east wind and of relative calm most of the time the wind blows with gale force from the north-west, west or south-west, with freezing temperatures and snow. The days are short: in the Strait in July only about six and a half hours. The gales last eight, ten or twelve days. A ship going out into the open sea in that area between the middle of March and the end of September is likely to encounter trouble, because the coast is broken and rocky and one can anchor only in sheltered harbours. . . .

Ships coming from Spain and making the passage of the strait from east to west, should enter the Strait at the Atlantic end between October and February. . . .

They should pass through, as I explained in my narrative, making westing with the help of the tides. When they reach the Pacific end of the strait, they should wait for an east or south-east wind; though this may mean a wait of twenty days or more. . . . They should sail in the open sea, parallel to the coast, as far as 40°S, which is the latitude of Valdivia. . . . From there on they will find southerly winds, and can make their passage north without risk or trouble. If, however, they cannot leave the Strait before the middle of March, they should winter in the Strait and not attempt to put out to sea, because . . . from April onwards the prevailing wind off the coast of Chile is from the north.

The Strait is the most impressive of all the inlets in that region. . . . It is possible to anchor almost anywhere within it . . . but it is important to keep well clear of the sides where the mountains are covered with snow. The snow may be up to ten fathoms deep . . . and breaks off in huge lumps a hundred, sometimes a thousand *estados* across [*estado* equals the height of a man] . . . and hard as rocks . . . which come crashing down with a noise like thunder . . . and fall into the water. . . . Because the channels are deep, ships tend to navigate close to the shore; but this can be extremely dangerous. . . . I have seen places where the channel was a league and a half in width, and too deep for sounding . . . yet so thickly strewn with these lumps [icebergs] that a launch could not thread a way through them. They float in the water, like floating islands, often two, three and four *estados* above the surface and an equal depth below. . . . I give this warning, at the risk of being disbelieved and ridiculed, for the safety of those who navigate the Strait in future.[1]

Icebergs notwithstanding, Ladrillero clearly thought that the Strait was a practicable route between Spain and Peru. His countrymen thought otherwise. Communication continued to follow the route by which it had begun, across the Isthmus of Panamá. Vested interest, as well as the Strait's evil reputation, may have had something to do with this; but in commercial reckoning the sceptics were probably right, Ladrillero wrong. In those days of small ships and slow passages, sheer distance mattered much more, portages and trans-shipments much less, than they do today. In any event, so far as is known, for twenty years after Ladrillero no Spanish ship visited the Strait. Not until 1578 did the authorities in Peru become aware that other Europeans might use the back door to the South Sea, which Spaniards were neglecting. In that year Francis Drake passed through the Strait, in the course of the voyage which was to become the second circumnavigation of the globe.

The original purposes of this celebrated enterprise have been matters of dispute from Drake's day to our own. They probably did not include a search for *Terra Australis*, a visit to the Moluccas, a circumnavigation; they may have included a search for the 'Strait of Anian'; they almost certainly did include a reconnaissance of the coasts of Patagonia, the Strait, and the southern coast of Chile; and Drake being what he was, his backers must have expected that he would try to make his voyage pay, by plundering Spanish shipping, as indeed he did. In most respects the voyage was a costly success; costly, because Drake, like Elcano, brought home one ship of an original five. It added little to European geographical knowledge; only a tentative conclusion that there was nothing but open sea to the south of Tierra del Fuego. This was the result of accident, the *Golden Hind*, on emerging from the Strait, being driven south by a 'norther'. It is unlikely that Drake actually sighted Cape Horn. Until his discovery had been confirmed by actual navigation, its significance was limited, and it aroused no widespread interest at the time.

Drake's own account of the voyage is lost. *The World Encompassed*, compiled by his nephew and namesake and published in 1628, makes splendid reading. It is not strictly contemporary, nor always wholly reliable. It was based on the notes and recollections of Francis Fletcher, chaplain to the expedition, whose manuscript, illustrated by his own sketches, has survived. Fletcher's account of the passage of the Strait, which follows, is in interesting contrast with the bald and sometimes cryptic comments of Ladrillero.

Wee thus arieueing at the northerly cape or headland of the aforesaid streight, wee struck sale & made som stay for a tyme tell we had performd among ourselues that dewty & seruice to God who had safely brought vs thither which we had so long desired & honor to her Highnes fitting for Subjects of so gratious & seuenfold blessed princes praying for the continuance of her dayes to be as the dayes of Heauen as long as the Sonn & Moone indureth those things thus accomplished wee joyfully entered the Streight w:th hope of Good success. at our first Entrance we conjectured that from the cape whence wee departed to the oposite land one the other side against it being a grat Iland & high & seemeth to make the mouth of a streight that it was about 10 Leagues or there about by Estimacō but afterwards we found the passage in som place 4 in other places 3 & 2 leagues broad & where it was narrowest it was as a large league. In passing alongst wee plainly discouered that the same terra australis left & sett downe to bee terra incognita before we cam there to bee no continent (& therfore no streight) but broken Ilands. & large Passages amongst them Within small tyme continueing our way we chanced w:th 3 Ilands a little. distant one from another at 2 wherof wee ariued & gaue the names to all of them the first wee named Elizabeth, the 2 bartholomew the day being called by this name, & the last George his Iland according to custom of our Country: In these Ilands we found great releife & Plenty of good victualls for Infinite were the Numbers of the foule, w:ch the Welch men name Pengwin. & Maglanus tearmed them Geese, This fowle cannot flye, hauing but stubb wings without feathers, couerd ouer w:th a certaine downe as it were young Goslings of 2 monthes old, as are allso all their body besides in their head eyes & feet they be like a Duck but allmost as a goose. They breed and lodge at land & in the day tyme goe downe to the sea to feed being so fatt that they can but goe & their skinns cannot be taken from their bodyes without tearing of the flesh because of their Exceeding fatnes they digg earth in the ground as Conyes doe, wherein they Lay their eggs & Lodge themselues: & breed their young ones. It is not Possible to find a bird, of their bignes, to haue greater strength then they; for our men putting in cudgells into their Earths to force them out they wold take hold of them w:th their Bills & would not lett goe their hold fast & yet tryeing all their strength could not in long tyme draw them out, of their holes being large & wide within som of them haue vpon their heads standing vpright a little Tuft of fethers like a Peacock & haue Redd Circles about their Eyes w:ch becom them well: The fatt w:ch came from their bodyes is most peirceing & of the nature & quallity of the oyle of the sea Calues. or seales wherof wee haue spoken; wee departeing from these Ilands had somwhat a hard passage & with difficulty many tymes did proceed in our way & that for diuers causes. first The Mountains being verry high & som reaching into the frozen Region did euery one send out their seuerall windes: somtymes behind vs to send vs in our way. sometymes one the starrborde side to driue vs to the Larborde & so the contrary.

109 Penguin; engraving from Johan de Laet, *Nieuwe Wereldt ofte Beschrijvinghe van West-Indien* (Leyden, 1630), p. 459.

282

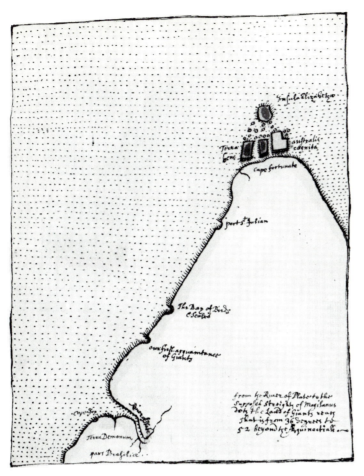

Map labels (as drawn):
Insula Elizabeth
Terra Australis cognita
Terra ——
Cape fortunate
port St Julian
The Bay of Birds C Scatted
our first acquaintance of Gyants
from ye River of Plate to the supposed Streights of Magilanus doth the Land of Gyants reach that is from 36 degrees to 52 beyond ye Equinoctiall ——
Terra Demonum
part Brasilia

110 Sketch map of Patagonia
and the 'supposed Streighte'
of Magellan, by Drake's
chaplain Francis Fletcher.
MS from a copy of Fletcher's
journal made by John
Conyers in 1680. South is at
the top. *British Museum,
Sloane MS 61.*

somtymes right against vs to driue vs further back in an houre then wee would
recouer againe in many but of all others this was the worst that sometyme two or 3
of these winds would com togeather & meet as it was in one body whose forces
being becom one. did so violently fall into the sea whirleing or as the Spanyard
sayth w:th a Tornado that they would peirse into the verry bowells of the sea &
make it swell vpwards one euery syde. the hollownes they made in the water &
the wind breakeing out againe did take the swelling bankes so raised into the ayer
& being dispersed abroad it rann downe againe a mighty raine besides this the sea
is so deep in all this passage that vpon life & death there is no coming to Anker.
Neither may I omitt the Grisly sight of the cold & frozen mountains, reaching their
heads yea the greatest part of their bodyes into the cold & frozen region, where
the power of the reflection of the Sonn never toucheth to dissolue the Ise & Snow:
so that the Ise, & Snow hang about the Spire of the Mountaine circulerwise as it
were regions by degrees one aboue another & one Exceeding another in breadth
in a wonderfull order as may apeare by the figure in the next Table: from those
hills distilled so sharpe a breath that it seemed to enter into the bowells of nature,
to the great discomfort of the liues of our men. The trees of the Ilands neere
adjoyneing to the rootes of these mountains feel the force of the freezing steames
w:^{ch} desend from them. for the Snow w:^{ch} falleth vpon them & the Raine w:^{ch}
cometh downe do both freez as they light vpon the trees & w:th their continuall
increase their is such a huge weight that the maine aremes & bowes are couched
downe so close together that no art or labour of man can make Closer & Sweeter

Arboures then they be: vnd^r the which the ground being defended from Colde is ingendered such temperate heat that the hearbes may seem all ways to be green & flourish as if it were in our sommer. Amongst other the simples we had in this place many being to me verry strange & vnknowne because I neither had seen them in other countryes in my trauailes nor found them mencōnes in anny aproued herballs were naturally growing without industry of man Thime, Marjerom Alexanders Scurvy grass as seamen call it (scirby grass) & dieuers others well known to vs all whereof were more Excell^t in their natures then wee find them in these partes in our Gardens And for other strange plants they were so gummy & full of ffattnes that toucheing them the ffatt & Gum would stick to our hands. being so pleasant that it yeilded a most comfortable Smell to our senses. whereby we receiued great help both in our diet, & phisick. to the great releife of the liues of our men The Ilands & plaine grounds further ofe were very farr sweet, & fruitfull, frequented by a comely & harmless Poeple but naked men & women & children. whom wee could not perceiue to haue either sett places or dwelling, or anny ordinary meanes of liueing as Tillage breeding of cattell or anny other profession but wanderers from place to place & from Iland to Iland stayeing in a place so long as it would naturally yeeld them provison to liue without labour saue onely to kill, gather, & eate, for the which purpose they builded little Cottages of Poles, & bowes like arbours in our gardens in England wherein they themselues for the tyme Lodg & keep their household stuff. The valew whereof would not Pay the chancelers curt for proof a Testam^t of vvj^d in our country for proof whereof I took an inventory of all the perticulers of one as it seemed of the cheifest Lords house among them as followeth

1 one water pale	
2 two drinking cupps	
3 2 boxes of stuff to paint	These are the substance & Riches of this poople all w:^ch they leaue behind them in the Place when they remooue till they returne againe at what tyme there is a new increase of Creatures for the supply of their nourishment
4 2 wooden spitts & one pare of Racks	
5 2 hatchetts one knife	

6 one fare floore of earth for a bedd to lay vpon without anny Cloathes

Their water pales drincking cupps & Boxes are made of Barkes of trees & sewed togeather w:^th threads of the guttes of som beastes like lute strings

Their Hatchetts & kniues are made of mussel shells being great & a foot in length the brickle part whereof being broken ofe. they Grind them by great Labour to a fine Edge & verry sharpe, & as it seemeth verry durable, they sett their Hatchetts in helues made of Writhen Rodds as Smiths do their wedges wherewith they cutt their barrs of Iron w:^th these & their knives they cutt their Poles & bowes whereof they frame their houses & barke their trees whereof they make their Pales, cupps, & Boxes & Boates with all other workes don with Edge tooles Touching their boates they being made of large Barke insted of other Timber. they are most artificiall & are of most fine proportion w:^th a starne & foreship standeing vp semicircler wise & wellbecometh the vessell w:^th these boates they trauel from Place to place among the Ilands carying euery man his family in all our trauells in anny nation we found not the like Boates at anny tyme for forme & fine proportion. in the sight & vse whereof princes might seeme to be delighted the forme whereof I haue sett forth as neere as I could take it the Poeple men & women are gentile. & familiar to strangers: & paint their bodyes with formes & diuers Collours. The men makeing Redd Circles about their Eyes & Redd strokes vpon their forheads for the most part & the women weare chaines of white shells vpon their armes & som about their Necks whereof they seeme to be verry

111 Magellan's Strait,
'Tijpus Freti Magellanici',
engraving, from Joris van
Spilbergen, *Oost ende West-
Indische Spiegel der 2 leste
Navigatien ghedaen in den
Jaeren 1614, 15, 16, 17 ende
18 . . .* (Leyden, 1619),
plate 3.

proud. They are well spedd for Bellyes. Brests & Buttocks. but nothing in Comparison w:^th the Giant women.

Now God in mercy at the last brought vs through this labrinth wee so long had intangled vs w:^th so many Extremityes & Iminent dangers to that w:^ch we so long desired that is to the Southerly cape of America entering into the South Sea . . .

. . . . .

which thing fell out most happily in his providence att the vttmost Iland of terra incognita. to the Southward of America whereat we arriueing made both the seas to be one & the self same sea & that there was no farther land beyond the heights of that Iland being to the Southward of the Æquinoctiall 55 & certaine minutes, to diuide them: but that the way lay open for shipping in that heigh without lett, or stay being the mane sea.

. . . . .

Wee departeing hence & taking our farewell from the Southern most part of the world knowne or as wee think to be knowne there. Wee alterd the name of those Southerly Ilands from terra incognita (for so it was before our comeing thither & so should haue remained still with our good wills) to terra nunc bene cognita/ That is broken Ilands, which in coasting it againe one that syde in returneing to the Northward wee prooued to be true, & were thoroughly confirmed in the same.[2]

The most serious and thorough exploration of Magellan's Strait in the sixteenth century—indeed the most thorough exploration ever made before the voyage of the *Beagle* in the nineteenth century—was undertaken as a direct result of Drake's incursion into the Pacific. The Spanish authorities had hitherto assumed the Pacific settlements to be immune from attack by sea, because of the difficulties and dangers of the Strait. The sudden appearance of a foreign raider off the coast caused great consternation in Lima, especially since Callao was one of the ports Drake raided. There were no adequate defences and he encountered little resistance. It took time, on that unwarlike coast, to collect and arm ships to send in pursuit; and by the time the pursuers reached Panamá Drake was away off California. The viceroy then—on the plausible (though mistaken) assumption that Drake would return to Europe by the way he had come—decided to call off the pursuit and instead to send his ships to the Strait. While awaiting Drake's return, they were to explore the southern coast of Chile and the Strait itself and to recommend sites which might be settled and fortified, in order to prevent further incursions into the Pacific by foreigners.

Pedro Sarmiento de Gamboa who commanded the expedition, was a seaman of wide experience—he had sailed previously with Mendaña—and of an experimental turn of mind. He was a more educated man, in the formal sense, than most seamen of his time; he understood Latin; and was the author of a serious *History of the Incas*. He was also—as the extracts which follow attest—a careful and skilful navigator, with a talent for precise description. He was given two ships, both small, each carrying two cast guns and a generous supply of small arms. What sort of showing he would have made against Drake's *Golden Hind*, which mounted eighteen carriage guns, can only be guessed. Of his distinction as an explorer there can be no doubt. He sailed from Callao in October 1579. Two months, from mid-November to mid-January, were spent in exploration—much more thorough than Ladrillero's, much of it in boats—of the inland waterways of southern Chile. Finally at the end of January, Sarmiento entered the Strait. The extract which follows is his account of the western half of the Strait.

Having left this port of Nuestra Señora de la Candelaria [at the north-east corner of Desolation Island, south-east of Cape Pillar], we followed the channel for about a league S.E. by E., and on this course the natives made signs that in a bay we were passing the bearded people had been, whom we took to be the English of the preceding year; and they were urgent that we should go there in the ship. We came near, and saw nothing but a bay to S.E., and three leagues further on there was the entrance to a clear port. Two leagues more S.E. and we saw a port to W., and further on a bay to S. Here the natives told us we should stop, for it was the place where the bearded men had taken in water. We entered this port at 3 o'clock in the afternoon. The tide flows here to the N.W. towards the South Sea, and more in the ebb than in the flood; so that with a fresh breeze we stemmed the tide with difficulty. This port was named 'Santa Monica' [53°2′S., 73°52′W.]. Its soundings are 20 and 22 fathoms, good sandy bottom; and it is sheltered from all winds. The strait here has a width of three leagues, the reach extending from this port N.E. to an island which was named 'Santa Ana'; which is the termination of the bay of San Geronimo.

On Sunday, the 6th of February, we left this port of Santa Monica in the name of the most Holy Trinity, and with an E.N.E. wind and smooth sea we navigated the strait, keeping more on the right hand, which trends E.S.E. for about three leagues to the point which we named 'San Ildefonso'. In the middle of this distance the coast forms a curving bay, and many creeks and inlets, where there appeared to be harbours. But we did not examine them, so as not to lose time. All this island is bare and rocky. The natives told us that the first bay was called Puchachailgua in their language, and the second was Cuaviguilgua. Here it was, the natives said, that the bearded men fought them, and they showed us the wounds they had received. The third bay, called Alguilgua by the natives [53°4′S., 73°44′W.], is large and turns to the south. On the opposite coast, on the left hand to the N.E. the native name is Xaultegua. To-day the day was fine and the sun clear. We observed the sun in 50°S. The bay called Xaultegua is in that latitude. From that bay of Xaultegua [still so named on modern charts] an entrance and arm of the sea goes inland to the roots of the snowy range of the mainland. Two leagues to S.E. of the position where we took the sun's altitude, we anchored in a port which we called 'Puerto Angosto' [53°13′S., 73°21′W.]: soundings in 22 fathoms, clean bottom, a cable from the shore. On the same afternoon the General went up a hill with Anton Pablos and two other men, to examine the strait. They discovered a long reach to the S.E. by E. The sun was clear and warm, with light winds from W.N.W., the current against us. We saw many other creeks and bays both to windward and to leeward. It was very hot at the top of the hill, where they set up a cross, and Pedro Sarmiento took possession for his Majesty, in token of which he and Anton Pablos made a great heap of stones, on which the cross was fixed.

Another cross was set up on the top of another mountain by a man named Francisco Hernandez, who had been sent to explore.

During this night, at one o'clock, to the S.S.E. we saw a circular, red, meteor-like flame, in the shape of a dagger, which rose and ascended in the heavens. Over a high mountain it became prolonged and appeared like a lance, turning to a crescent shape, between red and white.

On Monday, the 8th of February, at dawn, it was calm, and presently freshened from the W.N.W. with clear and fair weather, in which we made sail from Puerto Angosto in the name of the most holy Trinity, and sailed down the strait on a course S.E. by S. After three quarters of a league we discovered a bay on the right hand, with a large island at the entrance, called by the natives Capitloilgua, and the coast Caycayxixaisgua. There was much snow, and many snow-clad peaks. Here the strait is a league and a half wide.

Having sailed three leagues S.E. by E. along the right hand coast, we came to a great bay [53°22′S., 73°4′W.] which enters more than two leagues W.S.W., and has an island at the entrance. We called it 'Abra' because we could not see that it was closed in, and N.E. of it, on the left hand coast, there is another Port and Playa Prada, where there is also a sheltering island [53°18′S., 73°3′W.]. We named it 'Playa Prada.' Within the Abra the land was low, with rocks appearing above the water. Half a league further on there is a bay on the right hand, and to the E.N.E. of this bay, on the opposite side, there is a bay forming a port, called by the natives Pelepelgua, and the bay itself Exequil.

Beyond this bay, a league to S.E. by E., there is a great bay which runs inland for two leagues to the south to the base of some snowy mountains. We called it the bay of 'Mucha-Nieve' ['Snow Sound' on modern charts]. Here the coast turns to E.S.E. a league and a half. Both sides, to right and left, trend as far as a point which runs out from the east coast, and turns to south. Owing to this point it appeared, from a distance of a league, that the two sides joined [because the view is blocked by Carlos III Island, in the middle of the channel]. This was the cause of much sadness and distrust among many on board the ship, believing that there was no way out. In this distance of a league and a half the coast makes a great curve on the right hand, and from thence there is a large opening to the south. As we proceeded the point opened, and we found ourselves in a narrow port formed by it, being less than a league from land to land [the narrow channel between Carlos III Island and the south shore]. From this point another appears E. by N., and in front of it, on the opposite coast, there is another. Before reaching them it again appears that the two sides close in. Between these points, within this distance of one league, both coasts form two large bays; and in the one on the left hand there is an opening forming a channel which runs in towards the snowy range of the main land. At this opening the channel comes out, which commences in the bay of Xaultegua, by Puerto Angosto. The land between this channel running in towards the snowy mountains and that which we were navigating, is an island, called by the natives Cayrayxayiisgua. It is all rocky and bare, without vegetation. Having passed this opening, the current was with us. In these narrow places we met with several changes in the currents, and it was necessary to go with some care in watching them, so that we might not be turned round. Having passed this island, the main land begins to consist of plains near the sea, or valleys divided by low hills. From these points the strait trends S.E. by E. for a league and a half on the right, and two leagues on the left hand. On the left there are beaches and some beds of sea-weed which come out a long way. On the right it is the same for a league and a half, and then S.E. and S.S.E. for two leagues. At the S.E. by E. of this point there are four small islets in mid channel, in the space of three leagues, on the E.S.E. line ['Charles Islands' on modern charts. 53°45–46′S., 72°4′W.]. Between the first and second are four rocks, two on each side. This day we anchored to the east of the first island in 14 fathoms, good bottom, a cable's length from the shore.[4]

And so on through the Strait, describing its pilotage in precise and careful detail. One further extract may serve to illustrate Sarmiento's powers of observation. The plants and animals which he mentions can nearly all be identified from his descriptions.

The whole of this land, so far as we could judge, is rough and mountainous near the sea, and the heights bare, with craggy rocks, and in some places mud and spongy patches of grass. We recognised some trees like those of Spain, such as cypress, fir, holly, myrtle, evergreen oak, and among herbs, celery and water cress. All these trees are green and damp, yet they bear well, for they are resinous, especially the fir and cypress. The mass of the land that we saw, near the sea, did not appear good, for it had no earth mould. But, owing to the excessive humidity, there is such thick and close growing moss on the rocks, that it is sufficient for the trees to germinate in it, to enable them to grow and form forests. These masses of moss are spongy, so that in stepping on them, feet and legs sink down and in some places up to the waist. One man went in up to the armpits, and for this reason it is most laborious work to traverse these forests; as well as because they are excessively dense, so much so that, in some places, we were forced to make our way along the branches and tops of the trees. We were able to sustain ourselves there owing to the extreme thickness and interlacing of the vegetation, and we found this less laborious than making our way on the ground. But both these ways were exhausting, though we had to adopt them to avoid precipices.

The marine birds seen by us were black ducks, called by others sea crows; others grey, both large and small, gulls, and *rabios de juncos*. These birds are so called because they have a single, very long, and slender feather in the tail, which, when they fly, resembles a thin stick or wand. Hence the Spaniards gave them this name when they discovered the Indies. We also saw *rabi-horcados*, which are like kites, and have the tail parted. The grease of this bird has medicinal qualities. There were a kind of ducks, grey and black, without feathers, and which cannot fly, but they run on foot. In the water they cannot rise but by their feet, using their pinions as oars. They thus go through the water with great velocity, and they leave a track like that of a boat when propelled by oars. Their velocity is so great that a good boat under sail, with a fair wind, cannot overtake them. In the woods there are small black birds like thrushes, warblers, great owls, kestrel, and sparrow hawks. These we saw. No doubt there were other things to observe, but as our time was short we did not see them. There should be tapirs (*antas*) and deer; we did not see any, only the footprints and large bones. Of fish we saw red prawns—a good fish—cockle shells, and an immense quantity of other shells. In those which are on the rocks, out of the water, there are many very small pearls. Some of them are grey, but others white. In some places we found so many pearls in the shells that we regretted we could not eat the molluscs, for it would have been like eating gravel. For while we were on this service we cared much more for food than for riches. Very often we were in want of food, and in order to extend our discoveries from one point to another, we had to make four days' provisions last us for ten days. Then we had to eke them out by eating shell fish, and even the pearls did not stop us. Here we realised of what little value are riches not consisting of food, when one is hungry, and how useless. We reflected how much wiser the ancients were, who considered that riches consisted of tame flocks and cultivated fields, for which reason many strange people made their way to Spain.

In this season it rains very much, and the winds are very tempestuous from North, N.W., and West. When the storms begin to veer from north, there is hail, with intense cold, but the north wind is more temperate. When it rains all the woods are a perfect sea, and the beaches are rivers pouring into the sea.[4]

Sarmiento's expedition failed disastrously in its principal purpose, that of establishing a fortified settlement. A succinct account of the sequence of events is included in the narrative of the proceedings of the *Beagle*,[5] whose commanding officers, on her successive voyages, agreed in admiration of Sarmiento as an explorer. Captain Parker King concludes:

This was the first, and perhaps will be the last, attempt made to occupy a country, offering no encouragement for a human being; a region, where the soil is swampy, cold, and unfit for cultivation, and whose climate is thoroughly cheerless.

Sarmiento's expedition was not, in fact, the last attempt to occupy the shores of Magellan's Strait. Today, though the western stretch from Cape Froward to Cape Pillar remains as desolate as in Sarmiento's day, there are modestly flourishing settlements in the eastern portion and in the Beagle Channel, and there is considerable traffic, both of coasting freighters and of oil tankers, through the Strait. Nevertheless, on the evidence available in his own day, Parker King's forecast was reasonable enough. The modern growth of shipping and settlement in the Strait has been made possible by the development of powered ships. Punta Arenas, the only town of any size in the area, manufactures nothing, and nothing is produced in its hinterland; it owes its growth to its convenient situation as a fuelling station. As a commercial route for sailing ships, the Strait was too difficult, too unpredictable, for regular use; and where there are no ships there is no need of harbour towns. A few English and Dutch marauders, in the late sixteenth or early seventeenth centuries— Cavendish in 1587 and again in 1592, Sebald de Weerdt in 1598, van Noort in 1599–1600—sought to emulate Drake, passing through the Strait to raid Chile or Peru and to trade in the Spicery. Either John Davis, who sailed with Cavendish in 1592, or de Weerdt—each has his supporters— discovered the Falkland Islands. Otherwise these voyages added little to geographical knowledge. Some of them achieved limited and temporary successes, but they were too few to present a serious threat to viceregal Peru. There was no need, in fact, for fortification in Magellan's Strait, and for three hundred years after Sarmiento no further attempt was made to occupy its shores.

The navigation of the Strait was not only difficult; with its kelp-covered reefs and sudden vicious 'williwaws', it could be dangerous. Yet sixteenth-century seamen feared it less—to judge from the few surviving accounts—than they feared the ocean approaches to it. There were harbours within the Strait, where ships were more or less protected from the frequent violent gales and mountainous seas of the ocean outside. Navigators felt safer, once they got into the Strait; and this may explain, in part, why they showed so little interest in searching for an alternative passage. Such a passage, if it existed, would be further south, and its approaches would be even colder, stormier and more dangerous, than the approaches to the Strait itself. To this objection was added the discouragement of orthodox cartography. Most world maps in the later sixteenth century showed a great continental land mass on the south side of the Strait. Some explorers, it is true, had contradicted this theory from the first discovery. According to Maximilian of Transylvania, some of Magellan's people thought that Tierra del Fuego was an archipelago and not a continental head-land; but no one paid serious attention to them. Drake's people found open water south of Desolation Island; but Drake's discovery was made accidentally, at a time when he was trying to work to the north, to get away from the 'nipping cold', and it aroused no interest. Probably few people knew of it, for *The World Encompassed* was not published until fifty years later, and it left few cartographical traces. Even Ortelius, whose great *Theatrum Orbis Terrarum* set new standards of cartographical skill and accuracy, depicted the great southern continent. It was a Ptolemaic legacy; the revival of interest in Ptolemy in the second half of the sixteenth century lent added authority. The dead hand of Ptolemy lay heavy on the cartographers, at least until after 1616.

The expedition organised by Isaak Le Maire and commanded by Willem Corneliszoen Schouten, which in that year proved Drake's conjecture to be correct, had no direct concern with South America. Its object was to find a route to the Spice Islands which could be used by private Dutch shippers without contravening the monopoly of the Dutch East India Company. That monopoly covered both the Cape route and the route through the Strait. In the course of his search Schouten lost the smaller of his ships, which caught fire while her bottom was being breamed in a Patagonian harbour. In the larger ship, the *Unitie*, he passed through the Le Maire Strait which separates Staten Island from Tierra del Fuego; sighted the mountainous island which he called Cape Horn; established the existence of an open sea passage between Atlantic and Pacific; and came eventually to Bantam in Java. The following account of the most significant part of the voyage is from the narrative written by Willem Jansz, published in Dutch in 1618, and in English translation by William Philip in 1619. Philip's translation was reprinted by Purchas in 1625.

The thirteenth about noone, we sailed out of Porto Desire, but the sea beeing calme, wee anchored before the haven, and when the winde began to rise, hoysed anchor and put to Sea.

The eighteenth we saw Sebaldes Islands South-east from us about three leagues, they lie, as Sebald Dewert writes, distant from the Strait, East Northeast,

and West Southwest, about fiftie leagues, then we were under fiftie one degrees.

The twentieth, we saw Steencrosse drive, and perceived that we had a great streame that went Southwest, then we were under fiftie three degrees, and ghest that we were about twentie leagues Southward from the Straits of Magelan. The eleventh we were under three and fiftie degrees.

The three and twentieth in the morning, we had a South winde, and about noone it waxt calme, then the wind blew West, and we had ground at fiftie fathome blacke sandy, with small stones, after that the wind turned North, with smooth water and faire weather. The water shewed as white, as if we had beene within the land, we held our course South and by West, about three of the clocke afternoone we saw land West, and West Southwest from us, and not long after that we saw it also in the South, then having a Northe winde, we went East Southeast, to get above the land, it blew so hard in the hollow water, that we were forced to take in our Toppe-sayles.

The foure and twentieth in the morning, wee sawe land on starre-boord, not above a great league distant from us, there wee had ground at fortie fathome, and a West-winde, the land stretcht East and South, with very high hills, that were all

112 'Americae sive novi orbis nova descriptio', from Abraham Ortelius, *Theatrum Orbis Terrarum* (Antwerp, 1570); the earliest of a long series of distinguished world atlases published in the Netherlands.

291

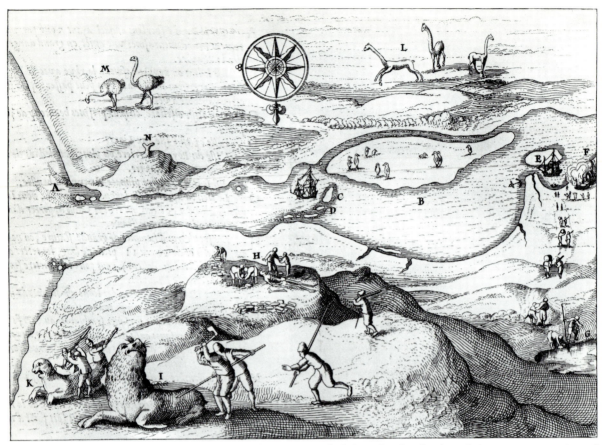

113 Patagonian curiosities; engraving from *Journal ou description de l'admirable voyage de Guillaume Schouten Hollandois . . .* (Amsterdam, 1619), p. 14; elephant seals, penguins, guanacos, rheas, and the exhumed skeleton of a Patagonian 'giant'. At F, extreme right, Schouten's smaller ship is on fire.

covered over with Ice. We sayled along by that land, and about noone past it, and saw other land East from it, which also was very high and ragged.

These lands as we ghest lay about eight leagues one from the other, and seemed as if there were a good passage betweene them, which we were the better perswaded unto, for that there ranne a hard streame Southward betweene both those lands.

Then about noone we were under fiftie foure degrees and fortie six minutes, and after noone wee had a North wind, and made towards this opening, but about evening it calmed, and that night wee drave forwards with a hard streame, and little wind. There we saw an innumerable number of Pengwins, and thousands of Whales, so that we were forced to looke well about us, and to winde and turne to shunne the Whales, least we should sayle upon them.

The five and twentieth in the morning, we were close by the East land, which was very high and craggie, which on the North side reacheth East South-east, as farre as we could see, that land we called Statesland, but the land that lay West from us, we named Maurice-land. We perceived that on both sides thereof, there were good roades, and sandy Bayes, for on either side it had sandy strands, and very faire sandie ground. There are Great store of fish, Pengwins and Porposses, as also birdes and water enough, but we could see no Trees; we had a North-wind in the entrie, and went South South-west, with a stiffe course, at noone we were under fiftie five degrees, thirty six minutes, and then held our course South-west, with a good sharpe wind and raine, and a stiffe gale: we saw the land on the South side of the passage upon the west ende of Maurice van Nassawes land,

reach West South-west and South-west, as farre as we could see it, all very high
and craggie-land. In the Evening the wind was South-west, and that night wee
went South with great waves or billowes out of the South-west, and very blew
water, whereby we judged and held for certaine that we had great deepe water to
loefward from us, nothing doubting but that it was the great South-sea, whereat
we were exceeding glad, to thinke that we had discovered a way, which untill
that time was unknowne to men, as afterward we found it to be true.

There we saw extreame great Sea-mewes, bigger of body than Swannes, their
wings beeing spread abroad, each of them above a fathome long. These birds
[Albatrosses] being unaccustomed to see men, came to our ship, and sat thereon,
and let our men take and kill them.

The sixe and twentieth, we were under seven and fiftie degrees, with a flying
storme out of the West and South-west, the whole quarter, with very high and
blew water, we held our course South-ward, and in the North-west we saw very
high land, in the night we turned North-Westward.

The seven and twentieth, we were under sixe and fiftie degrees, and one and
fiftie minutes, the weather very cold, with haile, and raine, the wind West and
West and by South, and we went South-ward, and then crost Northward with our
maine Sailes.

The eight and twentieth we hoysed our top-sayles, then we had great billowes
out of the West, with a West wind and then a North-east, and therewith held our
course South, and then West and West and by South, and were under fiftie sixe
degrees and fortie eight minutes.

The nine and twentieth, we had a Northeast wind, and held our course South-
west, and saw two Islands before us, lying West Southwest from us: about noone
we got to them, but could not saile above them, so that we held our course North:
about them they had dry gray Cliffes, and some low Cliffes about them, they lay
under fiftie seven degrees, South-ward of the Equinoctiall line, we named them
Barnevels Islands. From them we sayled West North-west: about Evening we saw
land againe, lying North West and North North-west from us, which was the land
that lay South from the straits of Magellan which reacheth South-ward, all high
hilly land covered over with snow, ending with a sharpe point, which we called
Cape Horne, it lieth under fiftie seven degrees and fortie eight minutes.

Then wee had faire weather, and a North wind, with great Billowes out of the
West, we held on course West, and found a strong streame that ranne West-ward.

The thirtieth, we still had great Billowes out of the West, with hollow water
and a strong streame that went West-ward, which assured us that we had an open
way into the South sea, then we were under fiftie seven degrees, thirty foure
minutes.

The one and thirtieth, wee had a North wind, and sayled West, and were under
fiftie eight degrees: then the wind turning West, and West South-west,
somewhat variable, wee passed by Cape Van Horne, and could see no more land,
and had great billowes out of the West, and verie blew water, which then fully
assured us that we had the broad South sea before us, and no land: the wind was
very variable, with great store of haile and raine, which forced us oftentimes to
winde to and fro.

The first of February, we had cold weather, with a storme out of the South-
west, and sayled with our maine sayles, lying North-west, and West North-west.
The second, the wind West, we sayled South-ward, and were under fiftie seven
degrees, fiftie eight minutes, and found twelve degrees North-ward variation of
the Compasse. That day we saw many great Sea-mewes and other Birds.

The third, we were under fiftie nine degrees twentie five minutes, with
indifferent weather, and a hard West wind and guessed that wee were that day

under fiftie nine degrees and a halfe, but saw no land, nor any signe thereof in the South. The fourth, we were under fiftie six degrees fortie three minutes, with variable windes, most Southwest, and wound to and fro as the wind blew, with eleven degrees Northeastward variation of Compasse.

The fift wee had a strong streame out of the West, with hollow water, whereby we could beare no sayle, but were forced to drive with the winde.

The twelfth, our men had each of them three cups of wine in signe of joy for our good hap, for then the Straits of Magellan lay East from us: the same day by advice of all our Counsell, at the request of our chiefe Marchant, the new passage (by us discovered betweene Mauritius land, and the Statesland) was named the Straights of le Maire, although by good right it should rather have beene called William Schoutens Straight, after our Masters Name, by whose wise conduction and skill in sayling, the same was found.

During the time that we passed through that New Strait, and sayling Southward about the New-found land, till we got to the West side of the Straits of Magellan, for the most part we had a very strong streame, hollow water, continuall raine, mists, moist and thicke weather, with much haile and snow: whereby wee endured much trouble, miserie and disease. But in regard that we had so luckily discovered that Passage, and hoping that the places which we were yet to discover, would likewise fall out well, we were encouraged; and not once thinking upon our former hard passage, with assured mindes determined to goe forward on our Voyage.[6]

Schouten's was a notable feat, not the least notable aspect of it being his success in keeping his people in good spirits and reasonable health through so long a voyage. He lost only three men, one of whom was Jacob Le Maire, the supercargo. For those days, this was a remarkable record. News of the discovery of Cape Horn soon spread about, and quickly affected cartography. As with many other important discoveries, however, its practical significance was not immediately apparent. Schouten himself gained little by it. When he arrived at Bantam, no one in authority would accept his story of a new route. His ship was seized by the East India Company's officials; her value was recovered only after protracted litigation in Amsterdam. The Spanish government, as soon as they received news of Schouten's discovery, promptly organised an expedition to investigate it. The voyage was jointly commanded by the brothers Bartolomé and Gonzalo García de Nodal, both experienced Galician pilots. The Nodals left Lisbon in September 1618 with two caravels; they watered and victualled in Rio de Janeiro in November; entered Le Maire's Strait in January 1619; rounded Cape Horn early in February; discovered the Diego Ramírez Islands, a major danger to navigation; entered Magellan's Strait at the Pacific end in late February; and emerged at the Atlantic end in the middle of March. This was the first circumnavigation of Tierra del Fuego, and altogether a brilliantly successful voyage. The caravels returned without loss of a single man.

Nothing much came of it all. There was no rush of traffic on the new route. Formidable though the Strait might be, many navigators, for a hundred and fifty years after Schouten, thought Cape Horn was worse. It was a choice of evils. The force, and often the screaming violence, of prevailing westerly winds might delay or wholly prevent a passage from east to west by either route. By either route, for the same reason, the

114 Magellan's Strait: map entitled 'Reconocimiento de los Estrechos de Magallanes y San Vicente', from *Relacion del viaje que por orden de su Magd . . . Hicieron los Capitanes Bartolome Garcia de Nodal y Gonçalo de Nodal . . . al descubrumiento del Estrecho nuebo de S. Vicente y reconosimjo del de Magallanes* (Madrid, 1621), between fos 34 and 35.

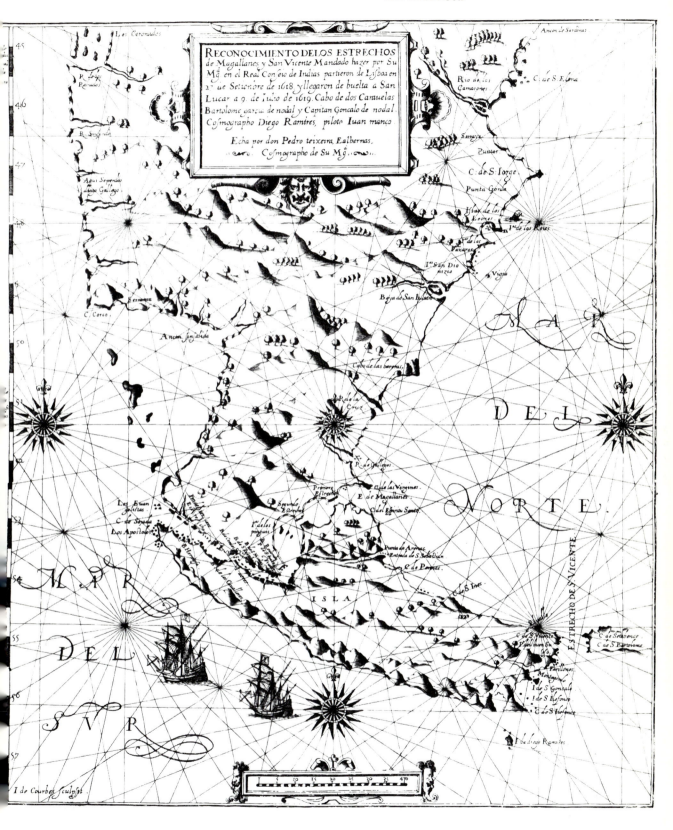

passage from west to east was usually easier; though one could not rely on it. To force a way through the narrow waters of the Strait in the teeth of a contrary gale was impossible; ships had to wait, in such anchorages as they could find, for a better wind, so that the westward passage of the Strait might take months. The Cape Horn route offered more sea room, enabling ships to beat on long boards, and to take advantage (as Schouten did) of shifts of the prevailing westerlies between north-west and south-west. Seventeenth-century ships, however, were ill-designed and ill-rigged for such wild work. Attempts to beat round Cape Horn might take many weeks, and on that savage coast there was no shelter, and no opportunity—such as existed in the Strait—to provision ship with salted seal or penguins.

In the early eighteenth century a number of technical improvements came in to improve ships' manoeuvrability and performance on a wind: fore-and-aft headsails replaced the old square spritsail and sprit-topsail; a gaff-rigged driver replaced the awkward lateen mizzen; and the wheel replaced the tiller and whipstaff as a means of control. Ships so fitted were better equipped for rounding Cape Horn against contrary winds. Even so, the argument over which of the two routes was preferable was not settled until after the middle of the eighteenth century. Cook wrote in 1769 that 'the doubling of Cape Horn is thought by some to be a mighty thing and

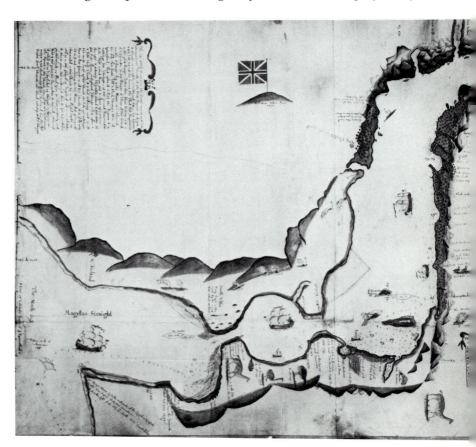

others to this Day prefer the Straits of Magellan'.[7] Cook did not agree with them. The century and a half from Cook's day until the obsolescence of deep-water sail in the early years of the present century, was the hey-day of the Cape Horn route. Today the waters about Cape Horn are almost as deserted as they were when Schouten first adventured them.

The Spaniards, after the Nodal voyage, lost interest in both routes. Trade and communication between Spain and the viceroyalty went either lawfully or officially via Panamá, or illicitly, but increasingly in the course of the seventeenth century, up the Río de la Plata and across Tucumán to Potosí. Spanish trans-Pacific trade, silver westbound, silk eastbound, was carried in one or two big ships each year, plying from Acapulco to Manila in the zone of the north-east trade winds, and back to Acapulco in the zone of the westerlies, by the route which Urdaneta had discovered in 1575. There was no further attempt at fortification in the far south; the authorities relied on the weather, the distance, and the reputed dangers of the southern navigation, to keep all but the hardiest and luckiest of interlopers away.

On the whole, Spanish confidence was justified. Few foreign ships visited Pacific South America in the seventeenth century; between van Noort in 1600 and Bartholomew Sharp in 1681, none of them did any serious damage. The most notable voyage between those dates was that of

115 John Narborough's chart of Magellan's Strait, MS 1670. South is at the top. *British Museum, K. Top. CXXIV 84.*

John (later Sir John) Narborough in the *Sweepstakes*. Narborough was no
raider, but a respectable naval officer conducting a commercial
reconnaissance in time of peace. His hope of initiating trade with Pacific
South America was defeated—he met Spanish opposition and got no
further north than Valdivia—but his voyage made its mark in other ways.
He passed through Magellan's Strait both outward and homeward,
apparently without difficulty, and—one might say—re-explored it. Like
Drake, Sarmiento, Cavendish and van Noort before him, he gave new

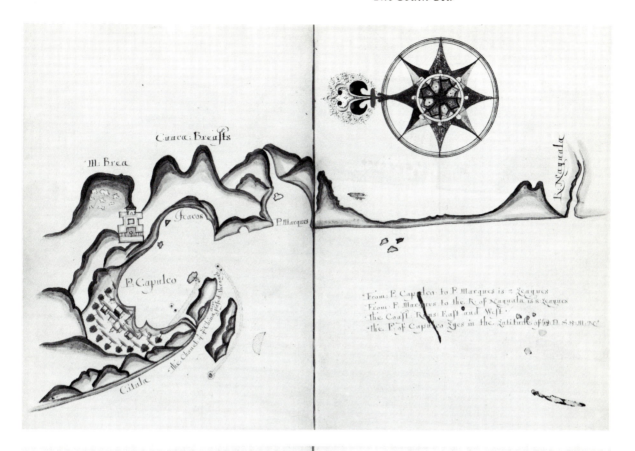

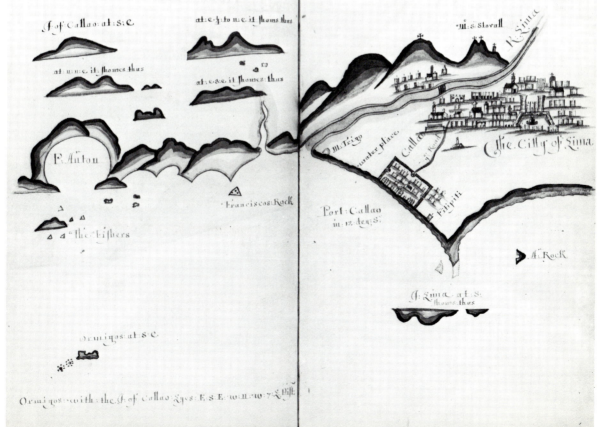

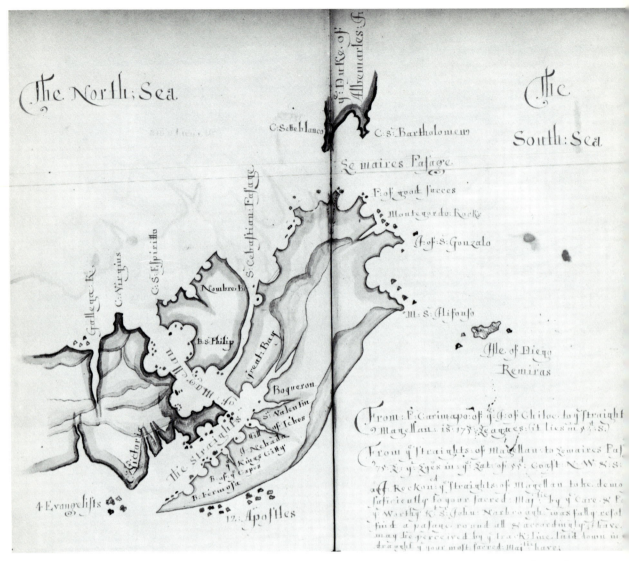

119 Magellan's Strait, from William Hack, 'Wagoner of the Great South Sea', fo 261–262

names to its salient features. Many of his names survive on modern charts. His own chart of the Strait was a marked improvement on its predecessors.

The difficulties confronting non-Spanish navigators in the eastern Pacific included not only the dangers of the route thither, but their own total ignorance of Pacific coast pilotage. Narborough brought back some information about southern Chile, but the coast further north, for English, French or Dutch pilots, was an almost total blank. Spanish security, in this matter, was always strict, and became steadily stricter in the seventeenth century. Sarmiento, while he was a prisoner in England, seems to have been fairly free with his information; not so his successors. Charts were issued to Spanish navigators shortly before they sailed, and collected immediately on their return; selling one to a foreigner might cost a man his head. The only way to get Spanish charts was by stealing them.

Stolen they eventually were, though not until towards the end of the

120 General Chart of the
Pacific Coast: 'Description of
the Coast and Islands in the
South Sea of America', by
William Hack, 1698. Hack
drew general charts of this
type to accompany copies of
the 'Wagoner of the Great
South Sea.' *British Museum,
K. Mar VIII 16 TAB 7 122
fo 1.*

century. In 1680 a buccaneer named Bartholomew Sharp led a party of
men across the Isthmus of Panamá, in emulation of Henry Morgan's
bloodthirsty exploit ten years earlier. Disappointed of loot on land, he
embarked on a Pacific cruise in stolen vessels, took a number of prizes,
and returned via Cape Horn to the West Indies. He was the first English
navigator to round Cape Horn, and clearly a navigator of considerable
skill. All this occurred at a time when the English government was
working hard for *rapprochement* with Spain; the Treaty of Windsor was
signed during Sharp's absence, and his conduct particularly infuriated Sir
Henry Morgan, the retired buccaneer, who as Lieutenant-Governor of
Jamaica was doing his loyal best to catch and hang his successors in the
trade. Sharp and his companions must have been in some danger; but
West Indian juries were always reluctant to convict successful
buccaneers, and Sharp had a valuable bargaining counter in his

possession. According to his own account, he had found in one of his Spanish prizes a *derrotero*, a set of charts and sailing directions for the Pacific coast of South America. He had seized the book before it could be destroyed, and had shrewdly kept it as part of his own share of the loot. Arrived in the West Indies, he promptly took passage from Antigua to London. There he took his *derrotero* to the Wapping establishment of Captain Hack, aptly named editor of narratives of voyages, and a cartographical draughtsman of skill and distinction.[8]

Little is known of William Hack, except through his work. Despite the nautical title he affected, there is no evidence that he commanded ships, or indeed that he ever went to sea; but he seems to have had an extensive acquaintance among sailors, including some retired Brethren of the Coast, from whom he collected the information which he subsequently sold in chart form. He was the man for Sharp's need. He made up a splendid fair copy of the *derrotero*, with an English translation of the Spanish text, which he called the 'Wagoner of the Great South Sea', and which Sharp, with matchless effrontery, presented to King Charles II. Thus Sharp and Hack between them, so to say, blew the Spanish gaff. Sharp was rewarded with a pardon for his crimes and a captain's commission in the Navy. Hack never published his 'Wagoner'—presumably considerations of security forbade it—but he made a dozen or more manuscript copies, which he sold to eminent clients for a handsome sum, and which grace great libraries today.

Many of the details of this picaresque story remain obscure. Most English editions of Exquemelin's celebrated *Bucaniers of America* contain an account of Sharp's adventures, written by Basil Ringrose, who took part in them. It is a well-written and circumstantial narrative, but it makes no reference to the *derrotero*. The only contemporary printed mention of this is in one of the several English editions of Exquemelin published in 1684. This version contains—presumably as the result of an oversight— an account of the *derrotero* episode by 'W.D.', believed to be William Dick, another participant in the cruise. What purports to be Sharp's own account of the matter is in a manuscript journal, in the Admiralty Library, and in several fair copies of the same, all in an elegant hand by the indefatigable Hack.

'W.D.' says:

In this ship the *Rosario* we took also a great Book full of Sea-Charts, containing a very accurate and exact description of all the Ports, Soundings, Creeks, Rivers, Capes, and Coasts belonging to the South Sea, and all the Navigations usually performed by the *Spaniards* in that Ocean. This book, it seemeth, serveth them for an entire and compleat Wagonaer, in those Parts, and for its novelty and curiosity, was presented unto his Majesty after our return into England. It hath since been translated into English, as I hear, by his Majesties Order and the Copy of the Translation, made by a Jew, I have seen at Wapping; but withal, the Printing thereof is severely prohibited, lest other Nations should get into those Seas, and make use thereof, which is wished may be reserved only for England against its due time. The Seaman, who at first laid hold on it, on board the *Rosario*, told us, the Spaniards was going to cast this Book over-board, but that he prevented them, which notwithstanding we scarce did give entire credit unto, as knowing in what confusion they all were. Had the Captain himself been alive at that time, this his story would have deserved more belief; yet, howsoever, if the Spaniards did not attempt to throw this book into the Sea, at least they ought to have done it for the reasons that are obvious to every mans understanding, and are hinted at before. We parted with the *Rosario*, and her Plate, the last day of July, 1681.[9]

Sharp's own account is shorter, and gleefully prophetic:

In this prize I took a Spanish manuscript of a prodigious value— it describes all the ports, roads, harbours, bayes, sands, rocks and riseing of the land and instruction how to work the ship into any port or harbour between the latt. of 17 d. 15′ N. to 57 S. Latt.—they are going to throw it overboard but by good luck I saved it—the Spaniards cryed out when I gott the book

FAREWELL SOUTH SEAS NOW[10]

List of Works Cited in Text and Endnotes

Acuña, Cristobal de. *Nuevo descubrimiento del gran rio de las Amazonas* (Madrid, 1641); trans. in *Voyages and Discoveries in South America* (London, 1698) as 'A relation of the great river of Amazons in South-America'.

Ailly, Pierre d'. *Tractatus de imagine mundi . . .* (Louvain, *c.* 1483); trans. E. F. Keever, *Imago Mundi* (Wilmington, N.C., 1948).

Altolaguirre y Duval, A. de. *Vasco Núñez de Balboa* (Madrid, 1914).

Andagoya, Pascual de. *Relación de los sucesos de Pedrarias Dávila . . .* (1541–42), in Navarrete, vol. III (1819), trans. C. R. Markham (Hakluyt Society, 1865).

Anghiera, Peter Martyr d'. *De Orbo Novo (Decades)*, trans. and ed. F. A. McNutt (2 vols.; New York, 1912).

Apianus, Petrus. *Cosmographiae Introductio* (Venice, 1533).

Bacon, Roger. *Opus Major*, trans. R. B. Burke (Philadelphia, 1928).

Barros, João de. *Da Asia* (Lisbon, 1552).

Beagle, The. Narrative of the Surveying Voyages of His Majesty's Ships Adventure and Beagle between the years 1826 and 1836 (3 vols.; London, 1839); vol. I: 'Proceedings of the First Expedition, 1826–1830, under the Command of Captain P. Parker King'.

Beaglehole, J. C., ed., *The Journals of Captain James Cook* (3 vols.; Hakluyt Society, 1955–67).

Cabeza de Vaca, *see* Domínguez.

Cabral, Pedro Alvarez. W. B. Greenlee, ed., *The Voyage of . . . Cabral to Brazil and India* (Hakluyt Society, 1938).

Carvajal, *see* Medina.

Castellanos, Juan de. *Obras* (4 vols.; Bogotá, 1955); vol. IV: 'History of New Granada'.

Chamberlain, R. S. *The Conquest and Colonization of Yucatán* (Washington, 1948).

Cieza de León, Pedro de. *Chrónica del Peru: Parte primera* (Seville, 1553), trans. C. R. Markham as *The Travels of Pedro Cieza de León* (Hakluyt Society, 1864). *Segunda parte* (1554), trans. C. R. Markham (Hakluyt Society, 1883). *Tercera parte* (*c.* 1554), ed. Raphael Loreda in *Mercurio Peruana*, nos. 27–39 (Lima, 1946–58). *Cuarta parte*, trans. C. R. Markham as *The Civil Wars in Peru* (Hakluyt Society, 1913, 1918, 1923).

Colección de documentos . . . de Indias, ed. Pacheco and Cardenas (Madrid, 1864–81).

Colección de libros y documentos referentes a la historia del Perú, ed. Romero and Urteaga (22 vols.; Lima, 1916–35): Molina de Santiago in vol. I.

Columbus, Christopher. *Journals and Other Documents on the Life and Voyages of Christopher Columbus*, trans. and ed. S. E. Morison (New York, 1963).

———. *Select Documents Illustrating the Four Voyages of Columbus*, trans. and ed. Cecil Jane (2 vols.; Hakluyt Society, 1930, 1933).

———. *The Journal of Christopher Columbus*, trans. Cecil Jane, rev. and ann. L. A. Vigneras (Hakluyt Society, 1960).

Columbus, Fernando. *The Life of Admiral Christopher Columbus by his Son Ferdinand*, trans. and ann. Benjamin Keen (New Brunswick, N.J., 1959).

Cook, *see* Beaglehole.

Cortés, Hernando. *Cartas de relación* . . . trans. and ed. A. R. Pagden as *Hernán Cortés, Letters from Mexico* (New York, 1971). *See also,* Gómara.

Cortesão, Armando. *The Nautical Chart of 1424* (Coimbra, 1954).

Davenport, F. G., ed., *European Treaties bearing on the History of the United States*, vol. I (Washington, 1917).

Díaz del Castillo, Bernal. *The True History of the Conquest of New Spain*, trans. A. P. Maudslay (5 vols.: Hakluyt Society, 1908–16).

Domínguez, L. L., trans. and ed., 'The Commentaries of Alvar Núñez Cabeza de Vacá, by Pero Hernándes (1555), 'The Voyage of Ulrich Schmidt to the rivers La Plata and Paraguai' (first published in a collection of voyages entitled *Warhafftige Beschreibunge* . . . ed. Sebastian Franck and Sigismund Feyerabend, Frankfurt, 1567), in *The Conquest of the River Plate* (Hakluyt Society, 1891).

Drake, Sir Francis. *The World Encompassed and analogous contemporary documents concerning Sir Francis Drake's circumnavigation of the world*, ed. N. M. Penzer (London, 1926).

Enciso, *see* Fernández de Enciso.

Ercilla y Zúñiga, Alonso de. *La Araucana* (Madrid, 1578–89).

Exquemelin, A. O. *Bucaniers of America* . . . (2d ed.; London, 1684).

Fernandes, Valentim. *Livro de Marco Paulo* (Lisbon, 1502).

Fernández de Enciso, Martín. *Suma de Geografia* (Seville, 1519).

Fernandez de Santaella, Rodrigo. *Libro del famoso Marco Paulo veneciano* (Seville, 1503); trans. John Frampton as *The most noble and famous travels of Marcus Paulus* . . . (London, 1579).

Fletcher, *see* Drake.

Frampton, *see* Fernandez de Santaella.

Friede, Juan. *Gonzalo Jiménez de Quesada a través de documentos históricos* (Bogotá, 1960).

García de Moguer, *see* Medina.

Garcilaso de la Vega, el Inca. *Commentarios reales de los Incas* (Lisbon, 1609); trans. and ed. H. V. Livermore as *Royal Commentaries of the Incas* (Austin, 1966).

Goldstein, T. 'Geography in fifteenth-century Florence', in John Parker, ed., *Merchants and Scholars* (Minneapolis, 1965).

Gómara, Francisco Lopez de. *Historia general de las Indias* (Saragossa, 1553).

———. *The Life of the Conqueror Cortes, by his Secretary, Francisco de Gomara*, trans. and ed. L. B. Simpson (Berkeley, 1964), from the *Istoria de la Conquista de Mexico* (Zaragoza, 1552).

Guerra, *see* Vigneras.

Hemming, John. *The Conquest of the Incas* (New York, 1970).

Hernándes, Pero, *see* Domínguez.

Hernández de Córdoba, *see* Wagner.

Herrera, Antonio de. *Historia general de los hechos de los castellanos en las islas y tierra firme del mar océano (Décadas)* (1601; Madrid, 1934–57).

Jérez de Salamanca, Francisco. *Verdadera relación de la conquista del Perú y provincia del Cuzco* (Seville, 1536); trans. C. R. Markham in *Reports on the Discovery of Peru* (Hakluyt Society, 1872). *See also, Los Cronistas del Perú.*

King, *see* Beagle.

Ladrillero, Juan Fernández. 'Relación,' in *Anuario Hidrográfico de la Marina*, Ano VI (Santiago, 1880).

Las Casas, Bartolomé de. *Historia de las Indias* (Mexico, 1951).

León-Portilla, M., ed., *The Broken Spears; the Aztec Account of the Conquest of Mexico*, trans. Náhuatl-Spanish A. M. Garibay, trans. Spanish-English Lysander Kemp (Boston, 1962).

Léry, Jean de. *Histoire d'un voyage fait en la Terre du Bresil, autrement dite Amérique* (1578), ed. J. C. Morisot (Geneva, 1975).

Lloyd, Christopher. 'Bartholomew Sharp, Buccaneer', *The Mariner's Mirror*, XLII (1957).

Los Cronistas del Perú, ed. R. Porras Barrenechea (Lima, 1962): Jérez de Salamanca; Pedro Sancho.

Magellan, Ferdinand. *The First Voyage round the World, by Magellan*, trans. and ed. Lord Stanley of Alderley (Hakluyt Society, 1874).

Mandeville, Sir John. Malcolm Letts, ed., *Mandeville's Travels, Texts and Translations* (2 vols.; Hakluyt Society, 1953).

Martyr, *see* Anghiera.

Medina, J. T. *Colección de documentos . . . para la historia de Chile . . .* (30 vols.; Santiago, 1888–1902).

————. *El Veneciano Sebastián Caboto al servicio de España* (2 vols.; Santiago, 1908): Ramirez.

————. *Juan Díaz de Solís* (2 vols.; Santiago, 1897).

————. *Los viajes de Diego García de Moguer* (Santiago, 1908).

————. *The Discovery of the Amazon according to the Account of Friar Gaspar de Carvajal and other Documents*, trans. B. T. Lee, ed. H. C. Heaton (New York, 1934).

Mena, Cristóbal de, [attributed to]. *La conquista del Perú . . .* (Seville, 1534), ed. A. Pogo, *Proceedings of the American Academy of Arts and Sciences*, 64, no. 8 (July 1930).

Molina de Santiago, Cristóbal de. *Relación de muchas cosas acaesidas en el Perú . . .* (c. 1553), *see Colección . . . del Perú*.

Molinari, D. L. *La Empresa Columbina* (Buenos Aires, 1938).

Montalboddo, Francanzano de. *Paesi novamente retrovati* (Vicenza, 1507).

Naval Historical Library (Ministry of Defence), MS F4: Sharp's account.

Navarrete, M. Fernández de, ed., *Colección de los Viages y Descrubrimientos que hicieron por mar los españoles desde fines del siglo XV . . .* (5 vols.; Madrid, 1825–37).

Núñez Cabeza de Vaca, *see* Domínguez.

Olschki, Leonardo. 'The Columbian nomenclature of the Lesser Antilles,' *Geographical Review*, XXXIII (July 1943).

Oviedo y Valdés, Gonzalo Fernández de. *Historia general y natural de las Indias* (Seville, 1547), ed. J. P. de Tudela Bueso (4 vols.; Madrid, 1959).

————. *Sumario de la natural historia de las Indias* (Seville, 1526).

Parsons, J. J., in *Geographical Review*, vol. L (1960).

Piedrahita, Lucas Fernández. *Historia general de las conquistas del Nuevo Reino de Granada* (1688; Bogotá, 1881).

Pigafetta, Antonio. *Magellan's Voyage around the World*, ed. and trans. J. A. Robertson (Cleveland, 1906).

Pizarro, Pedro. *Relación del descubrimiento y conquista de los Reinos del Peru* (1571); trans. P. A. Means as *Relation of the Discovery and Conquest of the Kingdom of Peru* (New York, 1921).

Polo, Marco, *see* Fernandes; Fernandez de Santaella.

Prescott, W. H. *History of the Conquest of Peru* (New York, 1847).

Puente y Olea, M. de la. *Los trabajos geográficos de la Casa de Contratación* (Seville, 1900).

Purchas, Samuel. *Hakluytus posthumus or Purchas his pilgrimes . . .* (1625; Hakluyt Society, 1905–07) containing William Philip's trans. (1619) of Willem Jansz' (1618) account of Schouten's voyage.

Quesada, *see* Friede.

Raleigh, Sir Walter. *Discovery of the Large, Rich and Bewtiful Empire of Guiana* (London, 1596).

Ramírez, *see* Medina, *Caboto.*

Ramos Coelho, J. *Alguns documentos do archivo nacional da Torre do Tombo* (Lisbon, 1892).

Sahagún, Bernardino de. *Florentine Codex, General History of the Things of New Spain,* trans. A. J. O. Anderson and C. E. Dibble (Santa Fe, 1950–   ).

Sancho, Pedro, *see Los Cronistas del Perú.*

Santaella, *see* Fernandez.

Sarmiento de Gamboa, Pedro. *Narratives of the Voyages of . . . Gamboa,* ed. and trans. C. R. Markham (Hakluyt Society, 1895).

Sauer, C. O. *The Early Spanish Main* (Berkeley, 1966).

Schmidt, *see* Domínguez.

Schouten, *see* Purchas.

Sharp, Bartholomew, *see* Naval Historical Library.

Simón, Pedro. *Noticias historiales de las conquistas de Tierra Firme en las Indias Occidentales* (1625), ed. M. J. Forero (2 vols.; Bogotá, 1953).

Solís, *see* Medina.

Staden, Hans. *Wahrhaftig Historia . . . in Neuen Welt . . .* (Marburg, 1557), trans. and ed. Malcolm Letts as *Hans Staden, the True History of his Captivity* (London, 1928).

Thevet, André. *Les singularitez de la France antarctique, autrement nommée Amerique* (Paris, 1558), ed. P. Gaffarel (Paris, 1878).

Tio, Aurelio. 'Historia del descubrimiento de la Florida o Beimini o Yucatán', Academía Puertorriqueña de la Historia, *Boletín,* II, no. 8 (1972).

Valdivia, Pedro de *Colección de historiadores de Chile* (Santiago, 1861).

Vélez, *see* Vigneras.

Verlinden, C., J. Martens, and G. Reichel Domatoff. 'Santa María la Antigua del Darién, première ville coloniale de la Terre Firme américaine', in *Revista de Historia de América,* no. 45 (1958).

Vespucci, Amerigo. *El Nuevo Mundo; Cartas relativas a sus viajes y descubrimientos, textos en Italiano, Español y Inglés,* Estudio preliminar de Roberto Levillier (Buenos Aires, 1951).

Vigneras, L. A. 'El viaje al Brasil de Alonso Vélez de Mendoza y Luis Guerra', in *Anuario de Estudios Americanos,* vol. XIV (1957).

———. *The Discovery of South America and the Andalusian Voyages* (Chicago, 1976).

Wagner, H. R., ed. and trans., *The Discovery of Yucatán by Francisco Hernández de Córdoba* (Berkeley, 1942).

Waldseemüller, Martin. *Cosmographiae Introductio . . .* (Mainz, 1507); ed. trans. E. Burke (Freeport, N.Y., 1969).

Williamson, J. A. *The Cabot Voyages* (Hakluyt Society, 1962).

Zárate, Agustín de. *Historia del Descubrimiento y Conquista del Perú* (Antwerp, 1555).

Notes

All translations, unless otherwise noted, are by the author

Chapter 1
1 Waldseemüller, cap. IX
2 Apianus, cap. XVII
3 Navarrete, vol. II, no. 5, pp. 7–8
4 Goldstein, p. 25
5 Cortesão
6 Mandeville, I, 129–31
7 Bacon, trans. Burke, I, 16–17
8 Toscanelli in *Columbus*, trans. Morison, p. 12. The MS. in Columbus' hand is in his copy of Aeneas Sylvius, *Historia rerum ubique gestarum*, in the Columbina Library in Seville. Facsimile and transcript of Latin text in Molinari
9 *Columbus*, trans. Morison
10 Barros (1552), I, iii, 2
11 Ramos Coelho, p. 40

Chapter 2
1 Columbus' *Journal*, trans. Jane, pp. 23ff
2 *Ibid.*, pp. 191ff; letter describing the results of his first voyage
3 Davenport trans., I, 82
4 *Columbus*, Morison, pp. 199–208
5 Olschki, pp. 397–414
6 *Columbus*, trans. Morison, p. 216
7 Columbus, *Select Documents*, trans. Jane, I, 73–113
8 *Columbus*, trans. Morison, p. 215
9 Navarrete, II, 143–49
10 Columbus, *Select Documents*, II, 1

Chapter 3
1 Anghiera, trans. McNutt, I, 64
2 Vespucci, trans. Levillier, p. 94
3 Las Casas, Bk. II, cap. 2
4 The earliest notice was by Rodrigo de Colmenares in 1510. Anghiera, *Decade* II, bk. 2
5 Fernando Columbus, trans. Keen, p. 231
6 Vigneras (1957), p. 333
7 *Cabral*, trans. Greenlee, p. 19
8 This is the opinion of Vigneras (1976), pp. 138–39
9 Vespucci, p. 126; from Cape Verde, 4 June 1501
10 *Ibid.*, trans. Levillier, p. 142; from Lisbon, undated (Oct. 1502?)
11 Fernandez de Santaella, trans. Frampton, **1 v. ff
12 Vespucci, trans. Levillier, p. 170
13 *Ibid.*, p. 252

Chapter 4
1 Navarrete, II, 285–92

2 *Ibid.*, II, 414–16

3 Puente y Olea, pp. 29–36

4 *Colección . . . de Indias*, XXII, 5–13

5 The exact site has long been a matter of controversy. See Verlinden, pp. 1–48; also Parsons, pp. 274–76. Recent investigation by M. Obregón and others seem to have settled the argument; they found Spanish colonial debris overlying an Indian site

6 Altolaguirre, p. 151

7 Fernández de Enciso, trans. from Sauer, p. 241

8 Oviedo, *Sumario*, cap. 4

9 *Colección . . . de Indias*, I, 315; Zuazo to Chièvres, 22 January 1518

10 Altolaguirre, trans. from Sauer, p. 225

11 Altolaguirre, p. 19

12 Oviedo, *Historia general*, Lib. IX, cap. 3

13 Medina, *Solís*, II, 134–40

14 Altolaguirre, p. 220

15 Pigafetta, trans. Robertson, vol. I

16 *Magellan*, trans. Stanley of Alderley, p. 194

Chapter 5

1 Tio

2 Herrera, Dec. II, lib. ii, cap. 17

3 Las Casas, trans. from Wagner, pp. 49–50

4 Díaz, trans. Maudslay, I, 31

5 Sahagún, Bk. X, cap. 29, trans. Anderson and Dibble

6 Of the five letters in the *Relación*, the first was from the town council of Vera Cruz, though inspired and perhaps drafted by Cortés

7 León-Portilla

8 *Cortés*, trans. Pagden, pp. 24–25

9 *Ibid.*, pp. 28–31

10 León-Portilla, trans. Kemp, p. 17

11 *Ibid.*, pp. 30–31

12 *Ibid.*, p. 33

13 *Cortés*, trans. Pagden, p. 75

14 León-Portilla, trans. Kemp, p. 41

15 Díaz, trans. Maudslay, II, 37–38

16 *Cortés*, trans. Pagden, pp. 102–06

17 *Ibid.*, p. 108

18 *Ibid.*, p. 106

19 León-Portilla, trans. Kemp, pp. 66–67

20 Chamberlain, trans., p. 165

Chapter 6

1 Trans. Markham

2 *Los Cronistas del Perú*, p. 56. The original is in the National Bibliothek, Vienna, Codex cxx

3 Mena, trans. Pogo, p. 254

4 Trans. Markham

5 *Los Cronistas del Perú*, p. 103

6 Trans. Markham, pp. 322ff

7 *Ibid.*, pp. 251ff

8 *Ibid.*, pp. 233ff

9 *Ibid.*, pp. 264ff

10 *Ibid.*, pp. 386ff
11 *Ibid.*, pp. 292ff
12 *Ibid.*, p. 211

Chapter 7

1 Trans. Markham, p. 144
2 *Ibid.*, p. 165
3 *Ibid.*, p. 167
4 *Ibid.*, pp. 141ff
5 Trans. Hemming, pp. 172–73. Two men named Molina wrote early histories of Peru. Our man was called, to distinguish him, de Santiago or el Almagrista, because he accompanied Almagro's expedition to Chile
6 Medina, *Colección . . . de Chile*, IV, 239–43
7 In *Colección . . . del Perú*, vol. I
8 Medina, *Colección . . . de Chile*, vol. VII
9 *Historia general*, Lib. IX, cap. 5
10 Medina, *Colección . . . de Chile*, V, 266. The horse was valued at 3,000 gold *pesos*
11 Lib. III, cap. 2
12 Valdivia, I, 55; to the King, 25 September 1551
13 *La Araucana*, Prólogo
14 Martín de Orduña. He and others subsequently tried to recover from Quesada. See Friede, I, 69–70 and Doc. 46
15 *Historia general*, Lib. XXVI, caps. 18–31
16 Castellanos, IV, 131–553
17 Simón and Piedrahita, published in 1625 and 1688 respectively
18 *Historia general*, ed. Tudela Bueso, III, 103ff
19 Castellanos, IV, 138ff
20 *Historia general*, ed. Tudela Bueso, III, 107
21 Friede, Doc. 102, p. 365
22 Ed. Forero, I, 141ff

Chapter 8

1 Medina, *Caboto*, I, 91. Medina prints all the known documents concerning the voyage
2 *Ibid.*, I, 442ff
3 *Historia general*, Lib. XXIII, cap. 4
4 Medina, *García*, p. 156
5 Domínguez trans., pp. 119ff
6 Medina, *Carvajal*, trans. Lee, pp. 171ff

Chapter 9

1 Ladrillero, pp. 515–19
2 Drake, pp. 128ff
3 Sarmiento, trans. Markham, pp. 113ff
4 *Ibid.*, pp. 52–54
5 *Beagle*, pp. 29ff
6 Purchas, II, 241ff
7 Beaglehole, I, 58
8 This is the generally accepted account of what occurred; see Lloyd. There are reasons for doubting some parts of this story
9 Equemelin, Pt. III, pp. 80–81
10 Naval Historical Library

Index